D1563984

Sarmiento

Sarmiento

Author of a Nation

TULIO HALPERÍN DONGHI
IVÁN JAKSIĆ
GWEN KIRKPATRICK
FRANCINE MASIELLO

University of California Press

BERKELEY   LOS ANGELES   LONDON

Contents

Preface

The centennial of Sarmiento's death in 1988 provided the occasion for a major international conference on the contributions and legacies of the Argentine writer and statesman. That conference took place at the University of California at Berkeley in October 1988 and was sponsored by the Center for Latin American Studies, the Department of Spanish and Portuguese, the Department of History, the Doreen B. Townsend Humanities Center, and the Chancellor's Office. The editors of this volume, who were also the organizers of the conference, believed that the papers presented at the meeting represented a significant reevaluation of Sarmiento and of Argentine and Latin American history. We also decided to supplement the presentations with some of the classic essays written on Sarmiento in order to provide a comprehensive collection that would combine new critical approaches with the best Sarmiento scholarship available to date.

Numerous debts have been incurred in the organization of the conference and the preparation of this collection. The Argentine Embassy in Washington generously supported the final translation of several essays originally written in Spanish. First drafts of those translations were prepared by Ann Gatschet, Lisa Bradford, and Janet Greenberg, whom we also acknowledge with gratitude. Virginia Bouvier also provided valuable editorial assistance. The editors of the University of California Press, in particular Eileen McWilliam, provided friendly and helpful guidance during the editing process. Last, but certainly not least, we wish to express our gratitude to the truly international and interdisciplinary team of contributors who have patiently worked with us on this project.

Contributors

CARLOS ALTAMIRANO is a sociologist and literary critic affiliated with CISEA in Buenos Aires.

ANA MARÍA BARRENECHEA is Professor of Literature and Director of the Instituto de Filología at the University of Buenos Aires.

NATALIO R. BOTANA is a researcher at the Instituto Torcuato Di Tella, Buenos Aires, and Professor of Law at the University of Buenos Aires.

JAIME CONCHA is Professor of Spanish at the University of California–San Diego.

ROBERTO CORTÉS CONDE is Professor of Economic History at the Universidad de San Andrés in Argentina.

ELIZABETH GARRELS is Associate Professor of Spanish at the Massachusetts Institute of Technology.

ROBERTO GONZÁLEZ ECHEVARRÍA is Bass Professor of Hispanic and Comparative Literatures at Yale University.

DIANA SORENSEN GOODRICH is Associate Professor of Spanish at Wesleyan University.

TULIO HALPERÍN DONGHI is Professor of History at the University of California–Berkeley.

IVÁN JAKSIĆ is Associate Professor of History and Director of the Center for Latin America at the University of Wisconsin–Milwaukee.

NOÉ JITRIK is Professor of Literature at the University of Buenos Aires.

MARINA KAPLAN is Assistant Professor of Spanish at Smith College.

WILLIAM H. KATRA is Assistant Professor of Spanish at the University of Wisconsin–Eau Claire.

GWEN KIRKPATRICK is Associate Professor of Spanish at the University of California–Berkeley.

FRANCINE MASIELLO is Professor of Spanish and Comparative Literature at the University of California–Berkeley.

MARTA MORELLO-FROSCH is Professor of Spanish at the University of California–Santa Cruz.

SYLVIA MOLLOY is Albert Schweitzer Professor of Humanities at New York University.

RICARDO PIGLIA is a novelist and cultural critic and has taught at Princeton University and the University of Buenos Aires.

ADOLFO PRIETO is Professor of Spanish at the University of Florida.

BEATRIZ SARLO is Professor of Literature at the University of Buenos Aires and the University of Maryland.

NICOLAS SHUMWAY is Tomás Rivera Professor of Spanish American Literature at the University of Texas, Austin.

DAVID VIÑAS, a writer and scholar, is Professor of Argentine Literature at the University of Buenos Aires.

Introduction:
Sarmiento between History
and Fiction

GWEN KIRKPATRICK
AND FRANCINE MASIELLO

The legacy of Domingo Faustino Sarmiento (1811–1888), more than one hundred years after his death, continues to evoke passionate commentary in Latin America. As the great nineteenth-century statesman and the dominant figure of a generation of nation builders, Sarmiento has earned a venerable yet polemical place in Latin American history. Architect of a nation, with a plan so far-reaching in design and scope that its consequences are still visible today, Sarmiento serves as a model of the triumphant romantic mind, linking projects of state with a radical feast of originality and selfhood traceable through his histories, biographies, and creative expressions. Today, Sarmiento is as controversial as ever, occupying the center of exuberant, conflicted, and often inflammatory discussions. Historians have debated the economic programs of this Argentine leader, his perceived strategies for democratization, the ways in which he planned a modern society through educational reform, his insistence on a professional army to attend state interests, and his conceptualization of formal state institutions to accommodate shifts in the political scenario—dramatic steps in the public sphere, even by today's standards. Inspiring the unhesitant admiration of some for his enlightened liberalism and visions of cosmopolitan change, Sarmiento has also engaged the attentions of adversaries determined to expose the contradictory nature of his designs for Argentina. The active core of debate concerning the programs of this illustrious figure takes form around the binarism of "civilization against barbarism," set forth in Sarmiento's *Facundo* (1845) to indicate the opposing tendencies of learned cultures set against the backwardness of a not yet consolidated society. A dichotomy that imposed a paradigmatic inflection upon Latin American thought for a century, Sarmiento's oppositional cluster invoked the conflicts of a newly formed society torn

1

between an insular parochialism and the circulation of new liberal ideals, set in motion by the impulses of boundless romantics determined to modernize the nation.

Sarmiento was a diplomat, statesman, president of his country, educator, and visionary, but it is as a writer that he exerted the most powerful influence. The great shapers of intellectual life in Latin America, among them Cuba's José Martí, Uruguay's José Enrique Rodó, and Peru's José Carlos Mariátegui, have entered, explicitly or implicitly, into debates with Sarmiento's vision of culture and progress in Latin America. Although the nature of his writings and actions varied widely, and was often contradictory, he has been seen as the standard-bearer for the ideals of European liberalism in Spanish America. With the intense self-examination occurring in Argentina and elsewhere in Latin America today, in the aftermath of military rules, the crush of the unresolved debt crisis, the fragility of democratic institutions, and the dominant role of the United States, many look beyond recent events to the postindependence period of the nineteenth century, searching for clues about current crises in the original blueprint cast by the founding fathers in the nineteenth century. And Sarmiento is clearly a necessary point of return for this reevaluation. Throughout the century, Sarmiento's models and visions for the modern state have been adopted, revised, and rejected many times. Many of the oppositions he saw in his own epoch are still central to Latin American culture today. Fiction writers as diverse as Alejo Carpentier, Gabriel García Márquez, and Augusto Roa Bastos, in their novelistic portrayals of political power and dictatorship in Latin America, have depended on Sarmiento's portraits of dictators and on Sarmiento's own political role in the definition of national and regional power building.

Sarmiento liked to remember that he was born at the same time as the Argentine republic, and to a great extent his lifework was to give shape to democratic ideals and European liberalism in his own country. The record of his life is as turbulent as the record of his century. A largely self-taught and insatiable learner, Sarmiento as a young man challenged the local military authorities, was imprisoned, went into exile, and established himself in Chile as a writer and educator. Sarmiento visited Chile numerous times during his life, but his stay there from 1840 to 1852 (with various absences in between) was not only the longest but clearly the most significant. It was in Chile during this period that Sarmiento's most important works were written and published. These include *Facundo* (1845), *De la educación popular* (1849), *Recuerdos de provincia* (1850), *Argirópolis* (1850), and *Campaña en el Ejército Grande* (1852).

If during the first part of his stay in Chile he became actively involved in Chilean politics and education, in the second part of his stay, dating from 1849, he primarily directed his attention to Argentine political projects and to denouncing the tyranny of Juan Manuel de Rosas. From his activity there, Rosas began to take Sarmiento seriously, which more flattered than intimidated the writer in exile, who referred, rather immodestly, to the exchanges between the two men as a "struggle between titans." Rosas sought his extradition, but the Chilean government refused, thereby increasing Sarmiento's stature as a major player in Argentine politics. His *Recuerdos de provincia*, drawn up as Sarmiento prepared for the imminent downfall of his adversary, was written in part to promote his own place in Argentine politics in the post-Rosas era.

During his stay in Chile, Sarmiento acquired the skills that turned him into a formidable polemicist, politician, and educator. His considerable experience with the enlightened authoritarian regime in Chile also led him to develop political views that supported a strong centralized government and the importation of European technology and labor. In particular, his reflections on dictatorship and his experience in exile would provide the basis for much subsequent writing on these themes. Although he was not the only prominent Argentine living in Chile, and he left as many enemies as friends there, it was thanks to him in great measure that Chileans engaged in a great deal of debate themselves, which led to the richness of intellectual activity of the time.

The acceptances and resistance to his plans, and his notable successes as well as failures, marked the course for other Latin American leaders. His famous dichotomy of "civilization and barbarism" included the struggles of urban and rural life, literate and oral culture, centralism and federalism, the modern secular nation versus a religious state of Spanish influence, admiration for the United States versus a rejection of the neighbor to the north, and the rights of conquest set against indigenous survival. These are not merely historical topics, but are critical issues even today. While Sarmiento was not the originator of all these debates, he became their most forceful and enduring symbol, largely through his voluminous writings. In *Facundo*, he sought to identify the peculiar nature of a land and a people emerging from the disarray of colonialism and the seemingly inevitable period of domination by local *caudillos* or tyrants. Part romance, part biography, travelogue, history, and fiction, *Facundo*'s myths and realities have become part of the cultural landscape of America.

A direct contemporary legacy of Sarmiento grows from his central role in the creation of a public school system in Argentina and, by extension, its influence on the other nations of Latin America. As a man born in poverty in the town of San Juan in western Argentina, he had definite and passionate ideas about creating routes of access to power for the many through the process of public education. Deeply influenced by the romantic belief in the strength of the individual to shape personal and public destinies, Sarmiento adapted European liberal and progressive ideas to Argentina in the postindependence years.

While he is seen as the great educator and self-made public man by some, by others he is regarded as the prototype of the betrayal of native values or, at best, a man whose vision for an expansion of prosperity and education for the many was based on an unworkable scheme. His views of progress have been anathema for some. Thus Borges, in his early *El tamaño de mi esperanza* (1926), caricatures the fervor of his conversion to liberalism, his unshakable faith in education, and his provincial upbringing: "Sarmiento (North Americanized–brave–Indian, great hater and poor interpreter of the *criollo spirit*) Europeanized us with his newcomer's faith in culture, and expected miracles from it." Even one of his most sympathetic biographers, Ezequiel Martínez Estrada, has expressed ambivalence about him, "Sarmiento has been among us the pioneer of great ideas and great works for the masses, but also the heresiarch who installed the cult of action as the tribal god, dislodging other sub-olympians. . . . Let us reject his adoration of the *homo faber* and *homo economicus* and exalt the *homo sapiens* and the *homo ludens*, and let us think before we decide if an Argentina of robots should replace an Argentina of shepherds." Martínez Estrada is one of many twentieth-century utopians who have questioned the legacy of Sarmiento and his insistence on progress as defined by nineteenth-century liberal ideals. According to this critic, Sarmiento did not accomplish some of his most pressing goals: to break the power of the landowning cattle barons and distribute resources more equitably, to break the power of the Church and eradicate Spanish colonial influence, to populate and democratize the interior of the country. He believed in progress and its inevitability, but the unruly realities of his time and place made his goals elusive dreams.

The major criticisms leveled against Sarmiento and his legacy are largely interwoven. Some of his adversaries condemn his support of centralized power in Buenos Aires and the resulting creation of an overwhelming city that extended its dominance into the provinces. The European immigration he so actively promoted, while it did move out in great numbers into the unpopulated provinces to develop the pampas, also created an enormous urban mass with social problems of its own. Sarmiento is also criticized for his unhesitant defense of the United States and his idealization of the Puritan work ethic as a model for Argentina. His stance on race, his anti-indigenist positions—urging extermination or suppression—and his belief in the superiority of North European types similarly left him vulnerable to criticism. One of Sarmiento's greatest contributions, popular access to public education and the promotion of literacy in Argentina, has also met with a mixed reception. Sarmiento considered his writings on education to be among his most important works, although he recognized with a certain irony that their main glory lay in never having been read.

More important, Sarmiento's dreams of promoting immigration to populate the rest of the country did not materialize. Large landowners remained, and by the late nineteenth century, the gaucho whom Sarmiento had identified as the barbarian became romanticized, especially by José Hernández in his *Martín Fierro*. This nostalgic evocation of the remnants of the premodern state will become a constant theme throughout the twentieth century, when Sarmiento becomes identified with the invading "outside" forces brought in by modernization.

A passionate admirer of the United States, his enthusiasm led him to promote not only American-style education, but to exalt other Yankee values and practices as part of a prized way of living. When he established the Normal School at Paraná, he brought in sixty-five female schoolteachers from the Midwest and upstate New York to show how it was to be done. He saw North American influence as a helpful guide, as a corrective to the Spanish model of colonialism he so opposed. In a letter to Mary Mann in 1866 he stated: "Societies so constituted need some external influence to correct their errors of judgment, in regard to the means of leaving the vicious circle in which they uselessly agitate; this influence must act on them, and it begins to act now from the United States."

Sarmiento thought it was possible to divide educational and political interests. He feared, however, the double-edged danger that this influence involved. In his *Life of Lincoln*, he criticized U.S. expansionist designs: "Slavery hunted a space to extend toward the South, toward Texas by annexation, toward Mexico by conquest, toward Central America by filibusterism. Happy with the golden captive of California, the spirit of invasion knew no limits . . . and when one has wanted to remember, with the generous purpose of Canning and Monroe . . . that 'America is for the Americans,' the irony of history has asked, because of the war with Mexico, if that principle does not include a double sense, like the replies of the Delphic oracle." Despite his harshly ironic view, Sarmiento found in the United States subjects for his profound admiration: Benjamin Franklin, Abraham Lincoln, and Horace Mann, the first two revered as self-made men and statesmen, and Mann as the great educator.

In *Conflictos y armonías de las razas* (1883), some of Sarmiento's earlier positions had hardened. His stance on race developed into an ideological racism. With the emerging force of the *indigenista* movements in the early twentieth century, his entire program has since become associated with the racial issue. In 1844, he responded to criticism against the Spaniards for exterminating native peoples by saying: "Let's be fair to the Spaniards; by exterminating a savage people whose territory they would occupy, they simply did what all civilized people do to savages, what the colony did deliberately or nondeliberately with the indigenous: it absorbed, destroyed, exterminated. . . . It may be very unjust to exterminate savages . . . but thanks to this injustice, America, instead of being abandoned to savages, incapable of progress, is today occupied by the Caucasian race, the most perfect, the most intelligent, the most beautiful, and the most progressive of those who people the earth." While his views on these matters anticipate the logic of social Darwinism, and were not exclusive to him, they have nonetheless marred the memory of Latin America's most energetic and brilliant thinker and actor.

Despite the enormous significance of his place in history, Sarmiento, today more than ever, is visible for his legacy to literature. Especially in light of recent critical theory and the focus on "mentalités" currently in vogue, Sarmiento offers the reader an entry into the discussion of historical and critical discourses in the Americas. The Argentine statesman who had one of the most forceful prose styles of the nineteenth century was especially concerned with organizing the images of his texts in a careful pattern of symmetries and repetitions, as if through narrative order, historical coherence might be achieved. In effect, Sarmiento developed his political texts from the strategies of artistic narration. From today's perspective, this instinctive mastery of the craft of writing and the exercise of the imagination brings Sarmiento's prose closer to literature than to the impartial recording associated with history. In itself, this is not problematic since, true to the belief of the romantics, he saw historical discourse as founded on intuitions close to those of the artist. Yet richer in suggestions for understanding his paradoxical projects is the possibility that the man so concerned with system was himself formed by ambiguity and conflict.

Sarmiento is the essence of contradiction. As a statesman in search of models, he refused to obey the structural laws that his own work proposes. North American readers clearly stand to gain from further clarification about the cross-cultural dissemination of ideas moving through the century of the great romantics. Yet their real discovery of Sarmiento's presence lies in locating his proposals and achievements in a radically innovative strategy with respect to the intersections of language, state, and institutions and with respect to the literary construction of the self.

In this sense, the essays in the present volume draw the attention of a critical audience to the vast heterogeneity of forms and ideas shaping not only Sarmiento but the members of his generation. Anxious to trace the circuits of power and resistance that flow through history and literature, the modern (or postmodern) reader will find in this formidable nine-teenth-century figure an example of the radical heterodoxy that destabil-izes any single proposal for altering a nation's course within history. Sar-miento's texts are infused with a multiplicity of meanings, while his literary persona unfolds in constantly changing forms.

Can we, in fact, read Sarmiento as an author of literature? The problem requires considerable revision of the status of prose fiction in Latin Amer-ica during Sarmiento's time and a rethinking of the categories of meaning used to isolate literature from history. While it may be true that the question of genre is more relevant to scholars only after the age of posi-tivism, and not to earlier writers, the instability of a text like *Facundo* nonetheless holds its attractions for modern readers. Moreover, a work like *Facundo* demands that we rethink the relation between literature and its social field.

Finally, Sarmiento's oeuvre invites many questions about the repre-sentation of self in writing. From the *Facundo,* for example, one cannot help but speculate on the creation of literary personae and their interac-tions; *Recuerdos de provincia* begs an inquiry about the efficiencies of the autobiographical pact, and obliges us to evaluate the positioning of per-sons and events as they emerge from public and private spheres of exis-tence. In *Campaña en el Ejército Grande,* Sarmiento claims to have made himself a myth within the historical imagination of the Argentine people. This forceful imposition of self upon popular historical memory is char-acteristic of all of Sarmiento's writing, and marks historical texts and es-says supposedly committed to objective inquiry.

Sarmiento, man of letters; Sarmiento, man of politics. This division is as arbitrary and fiercely contested as the paradigm of civilization and bar-barism that he used to define the nation. Separating action and contem-plation, description and narration, these bipolar opposites continue to en-gage critics. Consequently, we still ask if it is possible (or valid) to draw a boundary line separating political action and writing. At a time when the relationship between history and fiction is at the center of contemporary theoretical discussion, when the status of institutions is challenged, and the boundaries separating the disciplines are increasingly threatened with erasure, the figure of the nineteenth-century statesman issues a compelling plea for reassessment and interpretation. Historiography and literary theory have steadily moved toward this view of Sarmiento's heterodoxy, collapsing the boundaries that isolate intellectual practices while merging artistic pursuits with national political reform.

Sarmiento writes under the sign of romanticism, in an epoch when the blend of history and fiction is represented as an inseparable cluster. The major prose works in Argentina, written during the Rosas dictatorship, invariably fight against the government of tyranny and represent the otherness of subjects banished in exile. Esteban Echeverría, Juana Manuela Gorriti, José Mármol, and Bartolomé Mitre used the space of fiction to examine the travesties of justice enacted in the name of Rosas. Their works were conditioned by the experience of tyranny, exile, and displacement; and in each, the authors offered an alternative vision of Argentina.

In the case of Sarmiento, the basis for writing a fiction of the nation comes first from a study of the Argentine terrain. Sarmiento fosters analogies of landscape and national destiny, linking descriptions of the harsh geography of the pampa to the personalities produced upon it. Moreover, with his romantic vision, he sustained himself by analogies found in the imaginative field so that even the category of autobiography becomes inextricably bound to fiction. Literature and politics, individual and national destinies, man of letters and statesman: Sarmiento's writing entangles these categories of knowledge and action. It has been claimed that in the age prior to Argentine national consolidation (i.e., before 1880) all discourses are enmeshed. Literature clearly has a political role, intervening for juridic decisions, and functions in the capacity of official proclamations, while history is conceived as a process of recording and transforming the real. Aware of the dynamic possibilities of these empowering texts, Sarmiento takes full advantage of the conflation of fiction and history; indeed, he is nourished by it.

Sarmiento is situated at the center of national contradictions. A man propelled by a desire for national consolidation and personal power, he was at the same time decisively attracted to North American and European models. Under the rubric of "civilization and barbarism," he addressed the colonial past and Argentina's prospects for the future; he juxtaposed empirical and intuitive knowledge; he stressed the tensions of writing and political action. Throughout his career, Sarmiento gave attention to the forceful significance of metaphor and memory to turn the tide of history.

"On ne tue pas les idées," he cites at the beginning of the *Facundo*, introducing a system of (mis)quotation in his works that was to be the mark of his eloquent prose. As if in anticipation of Borges's ploys to (dis)arm his fictions with irreverent allusion to the texts of others, and to emphasize the reading experience as a play between a text and its sources, Sarmiento from the start unsettles the proposed stability of *Facundo* by underscoring its dependence on earlier works.

This deliberate ambiguity is seen throughout Sarmiento's career. In the exquisite prose style of his essays, in his feisty newspaper articles, in his memoirs of travel and self-celebratory letters, he multiplies avenues of meaning and purpose with a plethora of secondary projects, allowing his readers to question the formative principles of narrative itself. Latin Americanists often point to the *Facundo* as an example of the unstable generic forms emerging in the nineteenth century. Arguing that a bona fide novel was impossible because of the strong relationship between literature and political realities, critics take the hybrid form of the *Facundo* for its romantic typicality. Nevertheless, the *Facundo*, with its blend of fantasy and truth, does not exist as a failure of pure form but as a strident response to the limitations of genre. This project perhaps coincides with Sarmiento's romantic vision of language that defied strict boundaries of voice and form and challenged the authority of academic rule. Similarly, Sarmiento sought a freedom of expression in the structure of his books: challenging unity of meaning and generic identification, rebelling against the constraints of boundaries and the homogeneity of stable discourses. Sarmiento, who aspired to a totalizing system of knowledge in his writing—to know and say everything, to seize control of all living experience, to appropriate the languages of influence for his own prospectus on power—decenters the authority of canonical expression and exalts the presence of a mobile self. Each of his books is overpowered by a forceful "I," a great ego that often equates self-assertion and identity with the process of writing. The Argentine statesman masterfully imposed his voice upon his public, looming over events narrated, subordinating his adversaries, and transforming the destiny of Argentine politics and cultural life.

Sarmiento's curious relationship to literature—or, better, to the process of narration—evokes a certain irony, since it provides a metaphor for his inflated desires to absorb all human knowledge. In the *Recuerdos de provincia*, he even claims to have read all sixty of Walter Scott's novels and to have translated one a day. This great reader, who boasts an intimate relationship with his models, situates literature as a source for historical narration and autobiography. Accordingly, the biographies of Benjamin Franklin and the masters of classical antiquity inspire Sarmiento to construct his own life in the space of the text. Using the literary metaphor to represent projects of state, he also saw in literature the potential for one's rise to power. In *Recuerdos de provincia*, Sarmiento wrote: "I believe in the infusion of the spirit of one man into the spirit of the author by means of speech and example." The example here is writing; print tradition offers both a means of contact among individuals as well as a mode of leadership and social identity. Authorship, then, allows Sarmiento a way to write his way into history.

A well-known anecdote worth repeating tells of Sarmiento, after Rosas's defeat at Caseros, as he takes a seat before the tyrant's desk and practices writing with Rosas's pen. Rosas and Sarmiento, aggressive enemies over a lifetime, are here in this poignant setting merged as one in the scene of writing. Sarmiento dominates Rosas by assuming the position of writer. The dichotomies of self and other are thus resolved through the pen, suggesting the desperate necessity of Sarmiento to dominate his opponent in order to become fulfilled as an author. The fiction of the other serves to sustain the self.

Facundo elucidates this project. Time and again, Sarmiento denounces the tyrant Rosas for his authoritarian relationship to meaning. But as much as Rosas tries to control representation and meaning, Sarmiento counters with forceful rebuttals, showing the vacuity of his adversary's metaphors, the naming process, and the superficiality of his symbolic forms. One man's fiction set against the other's; system turned against system; two antithetical projects collide in Sarmiento's prose. In this way, history moves through the prism of literary art. In Sarmiento's time, this narrative strategy met with considerable opposition by his contemporaries. One of Sarmiento's unitarian colleagues, Valentín Alsina, offered an evaluation of the *Facundo*, objecting to its excessive literariness and its ponderous emphasis on systems, which he claimed distorted one's general understanding of historical process and weakened the objectivity of analysis. The statesman Alberdi said of Sarmiento that his work reflected "history forged from vanity, a kind of mythological politics." And Sarmiento himself, reflecting on the Italian translation of his book, likened his work to poetic discourse as a secondary means to approximate fact. Even in Sarmiento's time, *Facundo* offered abundant problems, confusing the simplicity of fact and clouding the truthfulness of history. As a foundational text, fundamental to all nineteenth-century discussion of nation building, *Facundo* is a composite of history and literature, and continues to inspire abundant commentary, as the essays in this volume will show. Highly ambiguous and problematic, Sarmiento's master achievement offers an expression of the writer's search for authority and power as it also builds the premises for ushering a nation into the theater of modernity.

*   *   *

The essays included in this volume reflect the importance of Sarmiento's place in both literature and history. They range from an analysis of Sarmiento's programs of state to Sarmiento's programs of writing. We have divided the essays into three major groups: first, "Sarmiento in Historical Context"; second, "The Writing Systems of Sarmiento"; and third, "Sarmiento: His Models and His Reception."

Part One, "Sarmiento in Historical Context," situates the Argentine statesman within the problematic of republican ideals of community. Common to the logic of the essays in this section is an emphasis on a community of citizens, functioning as subjects of the state or as members of a community of readers to be persuaded by the performances of the writer.

In "Sarmiento's Place in Postrevolutionary Argentina," Tulio Halperín Donghi emphasizes the discontinuities of historical vision and writing style that inform Sarmiento's autobiography. Halperín traces the unresolved tensions experienced by Sarmiento with respect to the colonial past, the divisiveness of civil wars, and the emerging institutions of postrevolutionary Argentine society. In view of these obvious conflicts, Sarmiento thus comes to emphasize, indeed to invent, his role as teacher and writer as the only way to assert his political authority. Through these roles, he transforms his relationship with his reading public and convinces his audience of the validity of his plans for remaking Argentine society.

In "Sarmiento and the Chilean Press, 1841–1851," Iván Jaksić focuses on Sarmiento's early experiences as a journalist and educator in Chile. There he developed the skills that turned him into a formidable reformer and social critic. More than anyone in nineteenth-century Latin America, Sarmiento realized the tremendous potential of the press as a medium for social and political reform. In Chile, he wrote profusely in the daily and periodical press to advance a reform agenda. As Jaksić argues, Sarmiento's experience with the Chilean press substantially added to his political conservatism, which was in line with the political experience of Chile, a country that was committed to gradual liberalization within a conservative social order. His engagements with the Chilean press, often less than favorable, made Sarmiento devise proposals for the conduct of public debate and invent mechanisms for restraining abuses of press freedoms. In general, Sarmiento made a substantial contribution to Latin American journalism, and in Chile he devoted considerable attention to the craft and to the role of the press in the advancement of what he considered to be enlightened social and political ends.

Ana María Barrenechea, in "Sarmiento and the 'Buenos Aires/Córdoba' Duality," draws attention to a recurring image in Sarmiento's writings, the depiction of the colonial capital of Córdoba as a conventlike space, representative of the closure and stagnation of colonial society. Barrenechea uses the duality Córdoba/Buenos Aires, the enclosed colonial world juxtaposed to the vital capital, as but one example of a fascinating dialectic in Sarmiento's writings throughout his entire career. Rejecting the idea of the *Facundo* as a secret defense of provincial culture, Barrenechea discovers a rich and complicated layering of concerns within Sarmiento's often contradictory writings. She asserts that Sarmiento as a writer is almost alone in his epoch in his attention to the existence of the dispossessed, and that the "X-ray of poverty" found throughout his writings belies the existence of simple formulaic dualities of "civilization and barbarism" and a single-minded push toward progress.

By focusing on the *Viajes*, William Katra addresses Sarmiento's understanding of the formation of the state within the terms of nineteenth-century republican ideals. For Katra, the *Viajes* is exemplary of the ambiguous representations of Sarmiento's ideas on race and national destiny, which depend for their articulation upon liberal values inherited from Europe and upon a careful rhetorical strategy designed to accentuate the performative aspects of writing. From his selective readings, Katra argues that Sarmiento, far from stabilizing a single vision of history, exposes instead a series of contradictions about writing and republican order.

Natalio Botana, in "Sarmiento and Political Order: Liberty, Power, and Virtue," describes the liberal faith in the nation communicated by Sarmiento from the time of the *Facundo* through his final works, tracing his visions of state order that draw upon philosophical ideals and the realities of nineteenth-century struggles for power. Sarmiento's liberal imaginings derive their historical and political coherence from principles of revolution and reaction to colonial rule and from ideals of civic virtue that circulated among European and Latin American intellectuals of the time.

Roberto Cortés Conde, in "Sarmiento and Economic Progress: From *Facundo* to the Presidency," explores the foundation of the modern state as seen in Sarmiento's times. Caught between the conflicting ideals of a colonial world in recession and a postindependence struggle for national identity and order, Sarmiento is described in his quest for progress in political society, drawing particularly on a need for community as a way to organize the modern state. Cortés Conde thus brings us in contact with Sarmiento's vision of the populace as a basis for economic development, exposing his strategies of market planning to finance a central authority in government and to facilitate coalitions.

Part Two, "The Writing Systems of Sarmiento," provides the North American reader with the essential statements on Sarmiento. As initiators of the current critical revision of Sarmiento that occupies our attention here, Piglia, Concha, Altamirano and Sarlo, Jitrik, Molloy, Viñas, and González Echevarría offer a general overview of Sarmiento's role in the Latin American historical and creative traditions.

One of Argentina's most successful contemporary novelists and deft social critics, Ricardo Piglia explores the systems of writing that interact with political history, claiming that in the defeat of political objectives the age of fiction announces its victory. Sarmiento provides the site of paradox as his works emerge from a field of defeat; in the failure of political strategies, the written text announces its triumph in history. Representing otherness, fiction narrates, paradoxically, the articulation of margination and silence. For Piglia, then, the age of fictional narrative finds its origins in the *Facundo*.

In "On the Threshold of *Facundo*," Jaime Concha locates the problematic of origins as drawn through the *Facundo* by examining names, rhythms, and the presence of the pen, metaphor supreme in Sarmiento's writing. He thus traces modes of inscription as they emerge from the *Facundo*, while exploring the lapidary presence of writing instruments to record the history of Sarmiento's exile, his anger and his silence. For Concha, then, writing is a way to reveal one's origins, to confer identity upon men in exile, and to expose the rhythms of self-constitution formed by the writer's pen.

In "The Autodidact and the Learning Machine," Carlos Altamirano and Beatriz Sarlo focus on Sarmiento's autobiographical reconstruction, in *Recuerdos de provincia*, of his defiance of and ambivalence toward his limited education, and how he creatively transformed the deficiencies of his formal training into a stunning literary virtuosity that changed the contours of lettered culture in his own epoch. Orphaned by an exclusive system dominated by the clergy and a university elite, he created a myth of self-generation, calling himself the "son of his own works." Sarmiento adopted the romantic tenets of sensibility and individuality, and in his *Recuerdos* reveals the ambitious path he chose through refusing the military path and glorifying the career of letters.

Noé Jitrik signals in the title of his essay, "*Facundo*: The Riches of Poverty," the paradoxes to which he will attend in his study of Sarmiento's principal work. Jitrik finds the source of Sarmiento's force, and even the very structure and rhythm of his writings, in his tempestuous eclecticism. For Sarmiento the realms of action and writing were indistinguishable; just as he proposes a future model for a possible national literature, he is proposing an ideological model for national institutions. Jitrik reveals the materiality of Sarmiento's text and, in signaling its rhythms as embryonic structures for a text that may be translated outside as well as within literature, probes the subconscious impulses of the often contradictory Sarmiento.

From a different perspective, Sylvia Molloy, in "The Unquiet Self: Mnemonic Strategies in Sarmiento's Autobiographies," identifies the origins of writing in Sarmiento's obsessions with the autobiographical subject. Drawing upon forms of self-constitution available through memory, Sarmiento constructs an image of his past consonant with the strategies of remembrance and transformation of that past. Here, Molloy insists on the importance of public and personal memory as two modes in conflict, which together constitute a life. As a man at odds with himself, Sarmiento places in question the evocative value of history projected by the workings of memory and imagination.

In "Sarmiento: Madness or Accumulation," David Viñas argues against a Manichaean vision of Sarmiento and rejects a type of personal dialectic for the writer that would place him outside history. While Viñas centers on the period of the publication of *Facundo* (1845), he also discusses the range of experience addressed in Sarmiento's journalism, linking these projects to the ascent of the "conquering bourgeois" in Europe as well as its beginnings in Argentina. He stresses Sarmiento's remedies for Argentina: the work ethic, monetary accumulation, and the expansion and conquest of "barbarous" territories. Viñas understands Sarmiento's program as manifested in his major books—the vast accumulative power of his writings and the obstinate moralism against his enemies' madness. Finally, Viñas situates Sarmiento as a forerunner of the Generation of 1880 in Argentina and describes his influence on twentieth-century writers, such as Roberto Arlt, who would unravel Sarmiento's dualisms and resist his moral imperative.

In "A Lost World Rediscovered: Sarmiento's *Facundo*," Roberto González Echevarría places Sarmiento's *Facundo* within the context of Latin America's "master fables," those narratives which arise in dialectical tension with the hegemonic discourses in circulation. In particular, González Echevarría traces *Facundo*'s dialectic with the literature of scientific voyages. Scientific discovery literature, as it is imitated and deformed in the hands of Sarmiento, attains its most dramatic manifestation. Part sociological study, part biography, part political pamphlet, part philological study of the origins of American literatures, the *Facundo* ostensibly adopts the model of scientific literature, but with the larger purpose of escaping the hegemony of the European vision. Sarmiento ceded his impartial gaze to that of his protagonist and, in doing so, established one of the most powerful variants of Latin America's master narratives.

In the third part of the present book, we turn to the dialogic relationship between Sarmiento and his models, and the ensuing conversation between Sarmiento and later writers. The matter of reception and interpretation, while it occupies the attention of all the authors in this volume, becomes the special focus of critical discussion in Part Three, where scholars discuss Sarmiento's work in terms of the models he borrowed and, subsequently, in terms of the paradigmatic writing forms he inspired.

Adolfo Prieto and Elizabeth Garrels focus on Sarmiento's periodical literature published in the years before *Facundo*. Prieto, in "Sarmiento: Casting the Reader, 1839–1845," reaches back into Sarmiento's early journalistic experiences, first in San Juan with *El Zonda* and later in exile in Chile, primarily with *El Progreso*. As Prieto traces Sarmiento's preoccupation with establishing a "map of readership" of these periodicals, he also outlines Sarmiento's concern with the delineation of his own public figure, and with his calculations of the direction and effect of the written word. Prieto defines a modus operandi in all of Sarmiento's work: his effort to insert himself within his public in order to best present his own image and gauge the force necessary to achieve his ideological aims. As Prieto notes, the measurement of readership finds its analogy in Sarmiento's larger projects of public education, where the role of persuasion is to be played out on a massive scale.

Elizabeth Garrels examines the sources and influences in circulation among Argentine intellectuals, especially in the periodical literature of the Generation of 1837. In "Sarmiento and the Woman Question: From 1839 to the *Facundo*," Garrels uses a rich array of periodical sources as an explanation for Sarmiento's views on women's education. She traces the influence of French intellectuals upon the Argentine writer and, from this, explores the shifts in ideology and rhetoric that inform his essays on women published in the years immediately prior to writing the *Facundo*. This discussion leads to a reconceptualization of community in terms of a gendered polemics.

Diana Sorensen Goodrich addresses the relationship between Sarmiento and Alberdi, and the reciprocal readings they offered of each other's work. Her essay, "The Wiles of Disputation: Alberdi Reads *Facundo*," examines the epistolary polemic between the two men and redefines the historicity of their texts. Each writer, probing the relationship between discourse and power, superimposes his own text upon the text of the other with an inevitable distorting effect. In this dialogic movement, Goodrich points out the real stakes of the battle, for the struggle for national organization was the political scene upon which the polemic was waged, and both resorted to writing as a way of representing acting-in-the-world. She notes that Alberdi's refutations of the *Facundo* have pre-figured almost all subsequent readings of the text. By exploring the context of this battle, she illuminates the continuing contemporary debates.

From a different perspective, Marina Kaplan addresses the hybrid formation of the *Facundo* in terms of the evolutionary patterns of the romance, describing in psychoanalytic terms the reception of models upon Sarmiento and his legacy to future generations of writers. In her essay, "The Latin American Romance in Sarmiento, Borges, Ribeyro, Cortázar, and Rulfo," she emphasizes the mixed generic form of Sarmiento's masterpiece not only in terms of its order of presentation, but in relation to its narrative structure and fabulation. Thus, Kaplan locates *Facundo* within the logic of romance, pushing the reader to rethink the relationship of literature and history by reading from the gaps in the text.

Also preoccupied with the legacy of Sarmiento, Marta Morello-Frosch traces the course of Sarmiento's reception by contemporary Argentine writers—among them Ricardo Piglia, whose essay forms part of this book—who have linked Sarmiento's models for history with the failures of Argentina today. She argues in "The Opulent *Facundo*: Sarmiento and Modern Argentine Fiction" that Sarmiento's paradigmatic text, *Facundo*, becomes a battleground for rereading history as well as a site for disputing meaning and testing the expansion of semiotic systems in conflict. Finally, Morello-Frosch claims that Sarmiento's writing offers modern authors a space to reconsider the role of the intellectual in Argentine national culture, insofar as Sarmiento traces a preoccupation for political action through the power of print traditions.

Nicolas Shumway traces the legacy of Sarmiento in the crucially important Peronist movement in twentieth-century Argentina. In "Domingo Faustino Sarmiento: The Unnamed Presence . . ." Shumway describes how Scalabrini Ortiz, a major proponent of Peronist populism, appropriated the archetypes inherited form Sarmiento and converted them into a mythic tradition of telluric force, undoing Sarmiento's program of liberalism. Shumway details Scalabrini's reversals of all Sarmiento's most treasured symbols, and he reminds us that Sarmiento's own forcefulness engendered rebellious sons, whose backlash against the liberal programs had effects reaching far outside literature.

1

SARMIENTO
IN HISTORICAL CONTEXT

1 Sarmiento's Place in Postrevolutionary Argentina

TULIO HALPERÍN DONGHI

Where did Sarmiento's social roots lie? Sarmiento himself gave several answers to this question. Although forced to do so by the savagely polemical tone of postrevolutionary Spanish American journalism, he gave himself gladly to the task. He enjoyed telling the story of his own life; moreover, he apparently felt a certain perplexity concerning the question so mischievously posed by his adversaries. Early in his career, Sarmiento offered two extreme versions of his social origins, both destined to reappear in attenuated form throughout his life.

The first of them we find in *Mi defensa,* written in 1843 during his second Chilean exile, in response to attacks that imputed to him a dubious past:

> I was born in an ignorant and backward province, not, as Mr. Domingo S. Godoy believes, in the barrio of San Pantaleón, but rather in the more obscure El Carrascal, equivalent to Huangalí [Santiago de Chile's shantytown]. I was born in a family that lived long years in mediocrity bordering on destitution, and which is to this day poor in every sense of the word. My father is a good man whose life has nothing remarkable except [for his] having served in subordinate positions in the War of Independence. . . . My mother is the true figure of Christianity in its purest sense; with her, trust in Providence was always the solution to all difficulties in life.
>
> From the early age of fifteen, I was the head of my family. Father, mother, sisters, servants, everything was subordinated to me, and this dislocation of natural relations has exerted a fatal influence on my character. I have never recognized any authority but my own; however, this subversiveness is founded upon justifiable reasons. Since that early age, care for the subsistence of all my relatives has weighed

upon my shoulders. It remains there still, and never has a burden been carried more gladly.[1]

Eight years later, in *Recuerdos de provincia*, the same elements reappear, organized in a profoundly different way. Again, Sarmiento claims as his justification the need to defend his good name, this time from a propaganda campaign orchestrated by Rosas in the River Plate and in Chile:

> I have evoked my reminiscences, I have revived, so to speak, the memory of my relatives who served their homeland well, rose high in the Church's hierarchy, and honored American letters with their works; I have wished to attach myself fondly to my province and to the humble home in which I was born. These are unsteady means of support to be sure, rather like floating planks that the victim of a shipwreck helplessly grasps, but which reveal to me that moral, noble, and delicate feelings exist within me because of the joy in finding them around me, in my ancestors, my mother, my teachers, and my friends. There is an undying democratic nobility that does not cast a shadow on anyone; it is that of patriotism and intelligence. I delight in counting among my family two historians, four congressional deputies of the Argentine republic, and three high dignitaries of the Church, as well as so many other servants of the homeland, who show me the noble path that they followed.[2]

The son of his own works has become the inheritor of a nobility, a nobility that, while "democratic," is nonetheless embodied in lineage. The change in approach reflects in part that of the author's life situation: between 1843 and 1850 he made a career in Chile as well as in his homeland, where *Facundo* brought him more than mere literary celebrity. The press campaign unleashed against him from Buenos Aires shows to what extent he had already emerged from the mob of famished emigrants. Nevertheless, that campaign, richer in insults than in precise imputations, could not really threaten him. Rather than being a self-defense, which was in great part unnecessary, *Recuerdos de provincia* is the self-presentation of a man who has already traveled the first lengths of his career and who is preparing for those which will follow. In 1843, obscure among the obscure, Sarmiento could only revindicate a background among the respectable poor to defend himself against vague but disquieting accusations; now he could exhibit without risk his pride in family tradition, proving that as journalist and educator he was no mere upstart.

While Sarmiento's situation was changing, the world around him was also changing, and with it his manner of seeing it. Between *Mi defensa* and *Recuerdos de provincia* is the trip to Europe and the United States—

on the one hand, the discovery of the secret failures of European civilization (the inability, Sarmiento would say, suddenly moralizing, to reach a certain level of civilization without corruption; the inability, above all, to overcome the contradictions of wealth and poverty within the new industrial civilization and the survival of an archaic yet unexpectedly vigorous peasant life-style); on the other hand, the discovery of that path to the future invented by the United States, a land that, in so many ways still marginal and provincial, had managed to avoid the conflicts in which an ever-brilliant Europe seemed more and more engulfed. That double discovery adds new hues to the old contrast between civilization and barbarism; it allows, above all, a new way to valorize a local tradition whose provincialism and extreme simplicity of life-style are no longer seen as unmitigated flaws. Thanks to this new perspective, the province, summarily described before as "poor and backward," becomes a noble refuge, to whose nobility—perhaps existing only in memory—the exiled writer would like fondly to attach himself.

Also between *Mi defensa* and *Recuerdos de provincia* comes something of perhaps greater importance: the Revolution of 1848 and its failure. From the predominantly French perspective with which Sarmiento followed it, the revolution seemed to reveal the abyss toward which Europe's progress to democracy was leading; the danger of social revolution (which in 1849 was presented in *Educación popular* as the equivalent to Spanish American triumphs of barbarism) awoke a new sense of prudence in Sarmiento. The prologue to *Educación popular* describes Huangalí (the shantytown in Santiago where human residues of urban and rural misery gather) as the training camp of the new, barbaric army threatening civilized order in Chile, just like the proletarian army that in June of 1848 defied that order in France.[3] In 1850 Sarmiento is understandably less ready to present himself—without additional qualifications—as the product of the transandean equivalent to Huangalí; poverty has become suspect. To describe his own origin, Sarmiento rejects the opposition between wealth and poverty as a criterion for separating social sectors, now favoring the distinction between civilization and barbarism. In *Recuerdos*, the urban culture that Sarmiento from the start identified with civilization has discovered an unexpectedly rich past; and loyalty to that past, very much alive among its prominent heirs, serves as the discriminating criterion.

That loyalty does not exclude readiness to engage in a radical reelaboration of the colonial legacy. Such readiness, however, is itself part of the tradition Sarmiento is proud to follow; it was reflected in the transitions that marked the history of his lineage, beginning with conquerors and clerics and continuing with servants of the revolutionary republic. Undoubtedly, this overly peaceful image of a process not unmarked by conflict and violence was related to one of the intentions that led Sarmiento to write *Recuerdos de provincia:* namely, to present himself not as a rootless revolutionary but as the heir to a long tradition of public service, as one who had learned to combine loyalty to the past with a prudent openness toward the future. Even if this stance was stressed for opportunistic reasons, however, the continuity was indeed very real, and therefore Sarmiento could never address the new options facing Argentine society during the decades of change following the fall of Rosas. That tradition to which Sarmiento was a proud heir was less fully renewed than he liked to imagine, and when it finally reemerged in the context of modern Argentina, Sarmiento refused to recognize in it the idealized portrait he had been perfecting for thirty years.

In mid-nineteenth-century Argentina, a new criterion for social differentiation was emerging: wealth. Only insofar as that criterion was universally accepted would the economic modernization of the country be possible. Acceptance of that ideal meant renunciation of very old aspirations by the intellectual leaders of the new nation. We have a particularly clear example of that renunciation in the writings of Alberdi, in which political liberalism and intellectual elitism are jointly repudiated. It was suggested instead that the solution to the national problem be given by a political power strong enough to impose a stable internal peace where economic forces could at last compete freely. These concepts, proposed by intellectuals who had shed their youthful illusions, were avidly appropriated by the political military leaders risen from the ranks of the landed classes in the littoral, whose new affluence was not endowed with the prestige of those less crude signs of superiority which usually accompany them.

Sarmiento was never to agree completely with that new system of solutions. Admittedly he had defined his struggle against Rosas as a battle on behalf of the rich and enlightened classes whom he believed oppressed by federal domination. But at the same time he would proclaim—amidst the universal exaltation of the individual struggle for prosperity—his disdain for "the path leading only to wealth" and his poor man's solidarity with the poor, straining against the solidarity of the wealthy in their defense of property. The story is told in *Recuerdos de provincia.* It falls upon Sarmiento to defend in court a "poor woman, whose drunken son had been killed by a landowner, one of whose sheep he had attempted to steal. . . . [A] worthy federal who happened to be my friend, wrote to me that I had defended a crime against property, and that he was henceforth a defender of the assassin. I answered him that it fit him well to defend property as a rich man, but it behooved me to defend the right to life for us poor people."[4] This is not an isolated reaction: one of his firmest objections to the order imposed in Entre Ríos by Justo José de Urquiza, victor over Rosas, was the ruthlessness with which property was defended; that objection gave motive to Alberdi—in the name of the new gospel uniting political authoritarianism and the intransigent defense of economic freedom—to accuse Sarmiento of communist tendencies, revealed in his finding it excessive punishment to execute a man for the theft of a pig.[5]

Despite such unfriendly correctives, Sarmiento would continue, with an anachronistic frankness, to set out his misgivings about the social order being imposed in Argentina. In 1856, concerning conflicts between landowners and farmers of Chivilcoy, a grain-growing district in the countryside of Buenos Aires, he was to evoke in a defiant tone the cruel fate of the children of the pampas, expelled from the land by the landowners' cattle.[6]

These outspoken doubts do not make Sarmiento a systematic critic of the social order whose weak points he perceived (with a lucidity exceptional for the time), let alone the communist tendencies discovered in him by his malevolent adversary. They confirm only that Sarmiento always refused to believe that the distinction between rich and poor established the most important internal boundary in Argentine society, or that such a distinction imposed an unambiguous choice of sides for him and his compatriots.

Already when he had proclaimed himself the defender of the rich and enlightened classes, the second term had modified the first. It would be tempting—but mistaken—to see in this invocation of enlightenment only a mask for the claim to political sovereignty for the rich (as had been the case with some European theoreticians of the sovereignty of reason). In Argentina in the 1840s, wealth and enlightenment did not necessarily go together; in the interior, the enlightened classes lost their economic predominance; in the littoral, a cattle-raising upper class grew rich faster than it grew enlightened. Sarmiento was well aware of this. He knew, of course, that Nazario Benavides was now the richest man in San Juan, and some years later he would not tire of evoking the great wealth of Urquiza. But while he knew all this, he did not take from it any conclusions at the individual level, except that the Argentine situation had grown entirely aberrant. For Sarmiento, wealth was simply one of the rightful privileges that the enlightened classes enjoy in a well-ordered society because they are enlightened; rule over the illiterate was also part of their birthright.

It would be equally tempting, equally mistaken, to see here only an individual revindication by Sarmiento the intellectual. There are without a doubt sections of *Recuerdos de provincia* which appear to justify this interpretation; perhaps the most significant is the one that opens the chapter "Los hijos de Jofré": "Whence do these men descend, whom we see shining in our times, in ministries, presidencies, chambers, courts, and the public press? From the mass of humanity. Where will their sons later be found? In the great womb of the people. For it is here that one has the first and the last pages of the life of each of our contemporaries. Those ancient privileged castes that crossed centuries recounting the number of their ancestors, those immortal names of Osuna, Joinville or Orleans, have fortunately, disappeared."[7] But the general drift of the argument works against this image of the aristocracy of talent: the aristocracy that Sarmiento proposes to his readers (in a book opened by a family tree) can only be hereditary.

But precisely what is that hereditary nobility "of patriotism and of talent"? In *Recuerdos de provincia*, by way of a sum of dispersed and unsystematic statements, Sarmiento comes to sketch a rather complex portrait. As already indicated, it is hereditary; and while Sarmiento likes to dwell on the continuity of familiar characters throughout three centuries of San Juan history, and to remind his readers that along with that psychological inheritance went a more precious cultural inheritance— namely, the tradition of enlightened public service with which Sarmiento identifies—he also acknowledges, albeit more discreetly, another continuity, that of a patrimony transmitted through inheritance. Precisely the crisis of San Juan society was opened by the impoverishment of the established families, in which Sarmiento recognized only one of the consequences that he ascribes to the federalist regime.

Colonial opulence is represented by Sarmiento's ancestor Doña Antonia Albarracín, whose magnificent gala dress—"enormous topaz drop-earrings, coral chokers . . . rosary of aventurines . . . divided into groups of ten by golden lemons twisted into spirals as big as eggs"—is evoked to shame the miserable San Juan of federalist times. Her leisurely life appears to her distant relative in equally magnificent colors: "Two young slaves slept in the gilded bedroom of Doña Antonia, to guard her sleep. At suppertime an orchestra of violins and harps, composed of six slaves, played sonatas to enliven the feasts of their masters; and at night, two slaves, having warmed the bed with silver heaters, and having perfumed the rooms, proceeded to undress the lady of the rich skirts of brocade, damask, or melanie that she wore at home."[8] Behind that wealth so unself-consciously displayed, was yet another, more substantial one. Sarmiento's mother witnessed the yearly airing of Doña Antonia's monetary treasure in her courtyard: "[the ground was] covered with cowhides upon which a thick mantle of heavily blackened coins was set out to dry in the sun while two old Negroes, who were the depositors of the treasure, walked among them stirring that noisy, moldy grain."[9]

These damp silver coins sustained the intellectual curiosity of the Albarracíns and enhanced the mercurial genius of the Oros. That wealth, whose lack of productivity Sarmiento indicates indulgently ("it was the mania of the colonials to hoard coin upon coin, and to take pride in it"), has faded forever. Why? Sarmiento is no doubt aware that the attitude toward wealth which he has so nostalgically evoked is past its prime. While he is ready to acknowledge that "the Spanish colonies had developed a way of living of their own, and were happy under the mild rule of the king," he is convinced that colonial times are irretrievably past and that the colonials sheltered for so long from the wind of the world must now survive a harsher climate. But why has San Juan failed in that transition? Because it has not found the nineteenth-century key to the acquisition and conservation of wealth in the new times: "railroads, steamers, and machines." All of these instruments of prosperity are products of a "cultivated intelligence." For Sarmiento it is that intelligence, rather than wealth, which grants the San Juan aristocracy its right to rule. Their loss of power has catastrophic consequences not because those who replace them are less wealthy but because they are more ignorant: "Have you heard resound in the world names other than those of Cobden, the wise English reformer, Lamartine, the poet, or those of Thiers and Guizot, the historians? And always everywhere, in the courts, in the Congress, in the government, educated men and not peasants or coarse shepherds, like those upon whom you have bestowed absolute power, much to your own damage."[10]

But what do the likes of Cobden have in common with Doña Antonia Albarracín or even with her eccentric relative, Fray Pascual Albarracín, whose merit was having come before Lacunza with prophecies based upon dubious interpretation of apocalyptic texts. While Sarmiento refuses to discuss the point, some passing allusions suggest that he is aware of the discontinuity between the San Juan tradition and the modern world. As an example, consider the version he offers of the political-social reform launched in 1825 by the young governor Salvador María del Carril.

Son of the richest man in San Juan, the young del Carril revealed "in his elegant and lofty manners, the culture of the period and the nobility of his family." These were also reflected in his political style. For Sarmiento, the son of the grandee of San Juan gives a rather unexpected twist to the actions of a disciple of the century's democratic ideas: "His words were brief and hasty, like those of the master who disdains explaining himself to his subalterns, and always accompanied with rapid movements and scornful, impatient gestures. Del Carril was the generous aristocrat who, while granting institutions to the masses, appeared convinced in advance that they would not know how to appreciate the gift and concerned himself but little with making it acceptable. 'Be free,' he told them in the May charter, 'for you are too inept for me to take you as my slaves.' " And his popularity was owing to his lineage rather than to his ideas: the masses had faith "in his talent and in his ideas, such that all of the reforms he adopted were supported and sustained in advance by public sentiment." Sarmiento thus continued in the attitude of "the Spanish colonists who, much like Negro slaves freed in old age, preferred slavery under the protection of their lord's roof to freedom that would have required them to think for themselves."[11]

This liberal experience marks the last flourishing of traditional San Juan. It is the last endeavor led by its colonial aristocracy, still marked by the conviction of its own superiority—at once social and intellectual—which accompanied the entire trajectory of this group (and which is still so much alive in the pages of the prodigal son who posthumously evokes it). Sarmiento clearly sees the causes of del Carril's failure; indeed, he sees them even more clearly because he had supported del Carril's political enemies. He refuses, however, to draw any conclusions about the emptiness of the tradition whose exhaustion was clearly reflected in the downfall of del Carril.

Even in defeat, that tradition remains alive as an exigency. Despite all their setbacks, enlightenment and intelligence have a right to govern; this obstinate faith is the permanent legacy of a dead past. This brings us back to our point of departure. Why is this aristocracy, in which talented men occasionally emerge, though more often rich than truly enlightened, described as one of "patriotism and talent"? Here, the succession of the terms is revealing: patriotism designates, strictly speaking, the tie between wealth and participation in the administrative—and, later, political—life of San Juan. It would be a mistake to see in this tie wealth as the cause and public power as the consequence. The version that Sarmiento prefers offers an embellished image of a sequence well known in colonies administered by local authorities, well versed in the art of procuring economic advantage with political power and controlled only laxly by a central administration itself vulnerable to corruption. Technically speaking, the "aristocracy of patriotism and talent" is an aristocracy of office; its preeminence is necessarily shaken by the collapse of an administrative apparatus in whose sheltered corners it had prospered before the federal order emerged. The aristocracy of San Juan had been a victim of the crisis of independence; an echo of its discreet nostalgia for the past, for "the mild rule of the king," reached into the pages of *Recuerdos de provincia*. But this group avoids systematizing that nostalgia into political adherence to a dead cause, and Sarmiento, for his part, refuses to linger in pure nostalgia: he wants to extract from such sentiment lessons for future use. Both the "aristocracy of patriotism and talent" and its literary heir conclude that, in the midst of such ruin, the group still has an impregnable cause for pride—as well as an instrument of survival—in its superior intelligence and enlightenment. Why should they have believed otherwise? When life's necessities forced some of them to offer their services to their rustic vanquishers, they soon discovered that the latter were willing to recognize that superiority: Benavides, the federalist governor of San Juan, very deliberately ran the risks implied in creating a legislature integrated with unitarians and disciplined only by fear. He preferred that risk to the alternative of a federalist legislature totally devoid of prestige.

What Benavides demanded from the ruined aristocracy of San Juan was not, however, what Sarmiento had hoped to find there. Benavides expected them to provide technical mastery of the labyrinths of an administrative apparatus inherited from three centuries of colonialism and of the political rituals forged in the crucible of revolution. Sarmiento expected far more: a rebirth that would change the heirs of the colony into the leaders of a modern polity. Alarmingly, he at times appeared to believe that this supremely difficult metamorphosis had already been accomplished. Sarmiento's project for a new Argentina fully reflects his reverence for the idealized San Juan, governed for three centuries by an aristocracy of knowledge.

As Alberdi was to denounce, Sarmiento's faith in education as the main instrument for change reflected his loyalty to an essentially archaic ideal. In Alberdi's view the dissemination of instruction could be dangerous in the absence of a clear understanding of the purpose of education; since economic progress was the objective, education should be entirely technical in orientation. Admittedly, Alberdi's views on the cultural requirements of economic progress were surprisingly narrow. (He believed it was possible, for example, that the illiterate could become skilled industrial workers through practical training alone.) However, his rejection of liberal education was not without foundation. Its unintended consequence would be to fatten the ranks—in his eyes, already overcrowded—of those who, unable to find employment in the productive economy, had to seek a living in politics or journalism.

The gospel of renewal by means of education is tied, then, to the desire to restore—in the context created by the revolutions of the nineteenth century—the sovereignty of intelligence in which Sarmiento recognized an enduring legacy of the colonial order. The reactions of the ruined aristocracy, in whom he had hoped to find heirs to the colonial tradition of public service, gradually revealed to him all the difficulties involved in this project. Hence the increasingly tense relations between Sarmiento and the aristocracy's survivors (who in San Juan and other Andean provinces, after the fall of Rosas, found a political home in the Liberal party, which inherited the unitarian tradition). Sarmiento returned to public life in San Juan in 1861, thanks to the victory of dissident Buenos Aires over the federalist Urquiza, himself the avenger of his friend Antonio Aberastain, the ephemeral Liberal governor of San Juan who had been executed by an agent of federalist President Santiago Derqui. In San Juan and La Rioja, Sarmiento was the most uncompromising practitioner of factional politics; in his view, not only Urquiza but the whole of the rural population addicted to barbarism had been defeated by Liberal-dominated Buenos Aires in 1861, and he demanded their extermination in words now memorable for their delirious bloodthirstiness.

While his deeds were much less ferocious than his calls to massacre, there is no doubt that Sarmiento still identified with an aristocracy oppressed for too long. He counted on their support not only to defeat the return of barbarism but also to introduce San Juan into the modern world. He was soon disappointed.

From then on, he appeared less certain of the place that the aristocracy and masses of the interior should have in the new order he sought to build in Argentina. His allusions to an aristocracy full of vain pride become more frequent. Recently it has been suggested that such harshness reflects the ambivalence of Sarmiento toward a group in which he himself occupied only a marginal place, while his hostility toward the masses reflects the fear of being engulfed by them. This interpretation does not seem entirely valid. Undoubtedly Sarmiento is a marginal figure in the San Juan aristocracy. This surprisingly large group included from its very beginnings a wide fringe of poor people, but in a society where the criteria of differentiation were partly those of caste and only partly those of class, it is not likely that "the decent poor" had to suffer—even in the first decade of the revolution—from the anxieties that were to characterize the aristocracy's existence once more strictly economic criteria were imposed. Admittedly, in the insistence with which Sarmiento characterizes the old upper class of San Juan as an aristocracy "of patriotism and talent," one sees a trace of his own roots in the segment of that aristocracy less endowed by that other sign of superiority, wealth. But it is not necessary to conclude that Sarmiento's nostalgia deceived him on this issue. Although he owed his position in San Juan society partly to family connections, he does not seem to remember with a feeling of humiliation the patronage that so decisively helped him in the early stages of his career. And it is not likely that the occasion upon which he returned to San Juan—as a representative of national power to rescue the *gente decente* after decades of oppression—would be used by the San Juan aristocrats to disabuse a savior whom, until then, they had treated as an equal. The resistance Sarmiento found in San Juan was directed against his politics rather than his social origin; the aristocracy that had inherited the tradition of talent and service grieviously disappointed him. On that point, the shock of reality was painful: not all aristocrats had fallen into poverty during the federalist reign; the "civilized" old wealth joined the "barbaric" new upstarts to oppose the high taxes introduced by Sarmiento to finance his ambitious projects as governor of San Juan. The decent poor had, for their part, a very traditional image of the proper tasks of the state. Rather than expanding schooling or investing in the infrastructure, the first duty of the state was to create for them positions appropriate to persons of social distinction. Thus, the tradition of public service, when seen up close, reflected a less lofty aspiration than was suggested in *Recuerdos de provincia*: it rationalized a claim to exclusive access to the spoils of power with arguments based upon a silly caste arrogance, ignoring the fact that talent and ability were not always reserved by Providence to members of the caste.

In his own party, Sarmiento rediscovered the traditionalism, the empty oligarchic pride that, beyond the Andes, characterized the most extreme Chilean Conservative faction. He was now ready to find in the federalist resistance a ferment of life: while the Chilean order, an order of the tomb, reflected the meekness of masses subjected to oligarchic domination, the rebellion directed by Felipe Varela showed that the people of Argentina's Andean provinces were made of stronger fiber and were ready to win a free future for themselves.

The future, however, would be less stormy and less renewing than Sarmiento was now ready to prophesy. It brought about the rise to power of General Julio Roca and of those who would benefit from the militarization imposed upon inland Argentina by the fight against the last traditional *caudillos* there. Roca was also heir to a federalist tradition that had learned after so many violent lessons to accommodate itself to, and finally to conquer, the structure of a national state founded by Bartolomé Mitre under the banner of liberalism. That triumph, which Sarmiento witnessed without optimism, found the survivors of the old provincial aristocracy among the most avid beneficiaries of the booty. Roca was ready to give them what Sarmiento had denied: aside from prosperity for a few made wealthy in national politics, others were offered a sufficient income under the shelter of the provincial and federal bureaucracy.

That new disappointment cast an even deeper shadow on the image Sarmiento now traced of the group to which he belonged. That group now appeared guilty of collective treason; or perhaps they were simply victims of a decadence even more radical than that of the masses, whose fall back into barbarism, if more visible, might be less irrevocable. Was this pessimistic conclusion unavoidable? A more sober vision of the aristocracy's past would perhaps have revealed that its history was not one of decadence but, rather, one of essential continuity. Sarmiento, however, was never to reach this more sober vision. If in the writings of his old age he gave a more negative image of colonial culture and society than in *Recuerdos de provincia*, he nonetheless continued to see the ruin of the colonial elite as an unmitigated calamity. By refusing to renew his ideals when the image of Spanish American society that had justified them fell to pieces, Sarmiento condemned himself to an ever more radical pessimism, well reflected in the desolate testimony of *Conflictos y armonías de las razas en América*, the book he called "the *Facundo* of his old age." In the depths of his despair, in the void left by his loss of faith in the enlightened classes that had guided Spanish America in colonial times and whose restoration was to offer a point of departure for the construction of a republican Spanish America, we can measure the depth of Sarmiento's loyalty to the political and cultural ideal of his youth.

Notes

1. *Mi defensa*, in *Obras completas de Domingo Faustino Sarmiento* (henceforth *OC*), vol. 3 (Buenos Aires: Editorial Luz del Día, 1948), pp. 6–7.

2. *Recuerdos de provincia*, in *OC*, vol. 3, p. 27.

3. *Educación popular*, in *OC*, vol. 11 (1950), p. 47.

4. *Recuerdos de provincia*, p. 184.

5. Juan Bautista Alberdi, *Cartas sobre la prensa y la política militante en la República Argentina*, new edition (Buenos Aires: Imprenta del Vapor, 1873).

6. Article in *El Nacional* (Buenos Aires), September 25, 1856, in *OC*, vol. 17 (1951), p. 318.

7. *Recuerdos de provincia*, pp. 39–40.

8. Ibid., p. 53.

9. Ibid., p. 54.

10. Ibid., p. 55.

11. Ibid., p. 82.

2 Sarmiento and the Chilean Press, 1841–1851

IVÁN JAKSIĆ

The basis of our governments being the opinion of the people, the
very first object should be to keep that right; and were it left to
me to decide whether we should have a government without
newspapers, or newspapers without a government, I should not
hesitate a moment to prefer the latter.
—Jefferson to Carrington, 1787

Without complete freedom of the press there can be neither
liberty nor progress. But with it one can barely maintain public
order.
—Sarmiento, *El Mercurio*, 1841

Domingo Faustino Sarmiento lived in an age when the fledgling Latin
American republics confronted fundamental questions concerning political organization and stability.[1] Most countries in the region sought, with
varying degrees of success, to strike a balance between social order and
the imported tendencies of liberalism, which included individual and press
freedoms. The press played a central role in this search because it could
claim to represent public opinion as well as the liberal principles that informed most postindependence government charters in the region. Yet in
fact the press became an instrument of various factions for attacking and,
it was hoped, supplanting or otherwise crippling governments in the name
of enlightened principles. Governments, in turn, claimed the need to preserve social order when they moved to limit or suppress freedom of the
press, the abuses of which often provided a suspiciously convenient device
to justify the suspension of constitutional guarantees. Unaccustomed to
the practice of democracy and the dynamics of opposition activities, government and the press led one another to extremes that threatened political stability and in some cases precipitated the demise of the established
order. The tension between the two became an important example of the
difficulties inherent in building durable institutions in nineteenth-century
Latin America.

Like many other liberals of his era, Sarmiento confronted these prob-

lems and offered solutions that made Latin American liberalism an ironically conservative response to the issue of establishing and preserving
social order. The fact that he confronted these questions in Chile, a conservative republic that promoted liberal reforms in a cautious and grad-
ualistic manner, influenced in important ways his approach not only to
the role of the press but to the larger problems of social and political
change. Sarmiento was neither a doctrinaire liberal nor an opportunistic
conservative. Rather, as a talented intellectual-in-exile who arrived in Chile
with little more than some experience in journalism and education, Sarmiento shaped his response to the fundamental problems of the age from
the perspective of his skills and in close dialogue with Chilean politics. It
would be precisely in the areas of journalism and education that he would
make a lasting contribution to Chilean society and culture, laying the
groundwork for his subsequent role in Argentine and Latin American
history.

Chilean Politics in the 1840s

Chile initiated its third decade of independent life under auspicious circumstances, having just won a war against the Peru-Bolivian Confederation (1837–1839), a victory that brought much prestige to the state and
muted, at least temporarily, many of the most divisive issues separating
Chileans. Political leaders could thus look forward to a peaceful transition
and could even relax the repressive measures that had kept liberal forces
in disarray during the Portalean period. Sarmiento made his appearance
in Santiago precisely at the time when the country was preparing for the
elections of 1841. His contributions to the press rapidly impressed key
political leaders of the incumbent administration of General Joaquín Prieto
Vial.

Although many prominent Chilean intellectuals, politicians, and publishers provided important insights into the evolution of the press, it was
Sarmiento who emerged as the most articulate observer of press developments and their links to politics. Unlike most writers during the period,
Sarmiento devoted a great deal of attention to journalism as a craft. His
understanding of the press as a medium, in addition to an eloquent prose,
turned Sarmiento into a powerful writer. Moreover, his journalistic skills,
combined with well-developed political instincts, made Sarmiento a force
to be reckoned with. The very strength of his position earned him both
popularity and hatred in almost equal doses.[2]

Sarmiento's central position in journalism and politics is closely associated with the rise of Manuel Montt as a key political figure during both
the twilight of the Prieto administration and the start of the first Manuel

Bulnes administration. Then-Minister Montt personally asked Sarmiento in 1841 to defend the candidacy of Bulnes in the press. Sarmiento hesitated at first but soon cast his lot with the forces represented by Montt, and he remained loyal to them through the end of his stay in Chile, when Montt replaced Bulnes as president in 1851. Sarmiento's main reasons for joining the incumbent government forces are clearly stated in his *Recuerdos de provincia* (1850) and can be summarized as 1) the lack of a credible liberal political alternative and 2) his wish to show that exiled Argentines were not permanent troublemakers, as the regime of Juan Manuel de Rosas would have it. One can add to this the strong impression Montt made on him when the minister, anticipating Sarmiento's fear of addressing Chilean political matters as a foreigner, stated: "las ideas, señor, no tienen patria."[3]

The political situation of Chile in 1840, which Sarmiento understood quickly, revealed a scattered, somewhat incoherent liberal opposition and a divided conservative force in power since the Revolution of 1830. The divisions within the conservative camp consisted of a traditional, oligarchic, proclerical wing, and a modernizing, secularizing wing composed of younger members of the conservative movement. The split between conservatives was serious enough that the former wing, known as the *pelucones*, advanced its own candidate, Joaquín Tocornal, and even sought alliances with the liberals in order to defeat General Manuel Bulnes. The modernizing wing did likewise and, riding on the popularity of Bulnes, hero of the war against the Peru-Bolivian Confederation, prevailed in the 1841 electoral contest. Because of a compromise with the liberals, in addition to an opportune marriage between Bulnes and the daughter of liberal candidate Francisco Antonio Pinto, the first Bulnes administration inaugurated an era of national reconciliation and implementation of liberal programs. The cabinet of Interior Minister Ramón Luis Irarrázaval presided over a period of peace and prosperity characterized by an important increase in public revenues and substantial investments in educational and infrastructural projects.

Manuel Montt replaced Irarrázaval as chief minister in 1845, when the country prepared for presidential elections the following year. Although traditionally an event surrounded by much expectation and tension, the elections of 1846 were marred by a militant press that had developed precisely as a result of the liberalism of the first Bulnes administration. Montt cracked down against the opposition press and sent many prominent publishers and political leaders into exile. Bulnes was reelected, but Montt resigned and the era of conciliation gave way to ever more militant hostilities against the government. At the outset of his second administration, Bulnes appointed Manuel Camilo Vial as his chief cabinet official, a man of tremendous political ambitions whose opportunistic liberal leanings upset conservatives, and who insisted—and succeeded—in occupying three of the four cabinet ministries at once (Interior, Foreign Relations, and Finance). Vial, who maneuvered to place his own followers in the growing machinery of government, generated significant opposition because of his methods. He was removed by Bulnes in 1849, but by that time the political damage was done. The disenchanted Vial joined liberal forces headed by José Victorino Lastarria in opposition to the government.[4] From then until the elections of 1851, the government found itself on the defensive, fighting against an increasingly antagonistic opposition, its own forces divided, and encountering a radical challenge from an emerging socialist movement that brought deep fears to Chilean society. Manuel Montt, in this context, emerged as the candidate of order supported by most conservatives and the Church. He won the 1851 elections, but at the price of civil war and continuing political conflict.[5]

Sarmiento, as indicated earlier, remained an unwavering supporter of Montt and the policies he represented. While the two men remained good friends for the rest of their lives, Sarmiento's loyalty to Montt stemmed from his own conviction that the only path for Chile—and Latin America—was one of gradual political liberalization in a climate of order. Until the populace became educated enough to understand the functioning of republican political institutions, public order had to be ensured, even at the price of restricting civil liberties. Sarmiento and Montt shared similar political views, but there was much else that brought them together. Both were of modest social background, had risen to prominence thanks to dedication, discipline, and ambition, and had spent significant time as educators. Sarmiento was the more prolific writer as well as a skilled journalist; however, their ideological convictions, particularly their distrust of political extremes, were quite similar.[6] During his stay in Chile, Sarmiento devoted his press efforts to advancing the political and ideological program that he shared with Montt, but he did so within the context of press traditions already firmly established in the nation.

The Chilean Press, 1828–1851

By the time of Sarmiento's arrival, the Chilean press had enjoyed a long, if tumultuous, history.[7] The 1840s witnessed the creation of many influential newspapers, but the press overall followed patterns of journalistic activity well established since the 1820s. Between 1828, the year of the first comprehensive law regulating the press, and 1851, the year when the press played a large role in the turmoil surrounding the presidential election, at least 152 new papers that published more than one issue appeared in Chile, roughly double the number of papers published between 1812 and 1827.[8] Of these, 30 percent appeared between 1828 and 1830, the year of the conservative revolution, with an average number of 11 issues. Another 30 percent of the papers appeared during the *decenio* of General Joaquín Prieto, with an average of 32 issues. The largest number of papers was published in the 1840s, during the two administrations of Manuel Bulnes (when Sarmiento made his contributions to the Chilean press). Between 1841 and 1851, 39 percent of the papers were published, with an impressive average of 140 issues per paper. Nearly a fifth of these papers, including some of the longest-lived, were published in the provinces, especially in the cities of Valparaíso, Copiapó, Talca, and Concepción. In addition, some of the main papers of Santiago and Valparaíso increasingly reached the far corners of the country during the period, and in fact became vehicles for introducing national political issues at the provincial level, thus contributing to national integration.[9]

Political events account for the growth and vigor of the press between 1828 and 1851. Chileans became accustomed to political journalism and had access to a wide range of political opinion, conveyed through the press during times of social and political turmoil. Political confrontation, in turn, brought more journalistic activity. However, as the titles listed in the Appendix suggest, most Chilean papers were little more than political pamphlets. Few even made the pretense of covering news or reporting on their subjects of interest with any objectivity. Large numbers of papers appeared at election time, particularly during presidential elections, of which there were five between 1831 and 1851. At other times, papers appeared in order to address specific issues such as federalism, to defend military groups, or even to discredit a minister or prominent figure, such as Sarmiento himself.[10] Ministries sponsored their own papers, known as *periódicos ministeriales*, often in competition with other ministries, to promote the policies of various cabinet officials. Yet despite the volatility of the press this is also the time when *El Mercurio, El Araucano,* and other long-lasting papers appeared. The tone of journalism overall during the period was one of belligerence, sectarianism, and slander. (See Table 1.)

Laws regulating the press during the first half of the nineteenth century evolved from relatively lenient to highly restrictive, but they could not contain the growing hunger with which Chileans consumed papers, and preferably those that castigated opponents. The two main laws promulgated during the period were those of December 11, 1828, and September 16, 1846. The 1828 law provided for freedom of the press with the exception of four violations: blasphemy, immorality, libel, and sedition.

Table 1. New Chilean Newspapers, by Year, 1828–1851

Year	No. of Papers
1828	15
1829	15
1830	16
1831	2
1832	4
1833	4
1834	2
1835	7
1836	9
1837	4
1838	2
1839	4
1840	8
1841	10
1842	6
1843	3
1844	4
1845	8
1846	1
1847	2
1848	2
1849	9
1850	5
1851	10
Total	152

Source: See Appendix.

Those found guilty of using the press in any of these categories could be fined or imprisoned. By far the most serious crime was sedition, punishable with up to four years of exile or imprisonment. Yet a sentence of sedition in the first or second degree could be commuted for a fine of 200 or 400 pesos, respectively.

In accordance with article 18 of the liberal 1828 Constitution, violators of press freedoms would be tried by a jury of their peers. Despite the hostility of the pelucón government toward liberalism in general, and toward the 1828 Constitution in particular, the law remained in effect throughout the period of conservative rule. Diego Portales, who was known to encourage the existence of an opposition press, introduced a minor modification requiring public employees to defend themselves from libel, but he retained the fundamentals of the law and enshrined trial by jury in article 12 of the 1833 Constitution. Freedom of the press without prior censorship was also enshrined in the 1833 Constitution.[11]

In contrast, the 1846 law provided for severe penalties in all categories. The crime of sedition was punishable by up to six years in prison or exile, plus a fine of up to 1,000 pesos. All crimes were punishable by both imprisonment and fines. In addition, although the law provided for trial by jury, it gave considerable powers to judges directly dependent on the executive branch (*jueces de derecho*). Moreover, it called for severe punishment of publishers, particularly in cases where the writer of an offending article could not, or would not, be identified.[12]

While the 1828 law was passed without much opposition, the 1846 law created a public outcry that heralded troubles to come during the second administration of Manuel Bulnes (1846–1851). One particularly articulate critique of the 1846 law came from an Uruguayan, Juan Carlos Gómez of *El Mercurio*. He argued that the country might be better off with prior censorship than with the harsh limitations contemplated in the law.[13] However belatedly, José Victorino Lastarria argued in Congress that the law was arbitrary, despotic, perhaps even unconstitutional, but failed to introduce his own version of a more enlightened press law.[14] In 1839 there had been a previous attempt by Justice Minister Mariano Egaña to introduce highly restrictive legislation concerning the press, but his proposal died in Congress. Still, the fact that legislation had been proposed indicates that by 1839 there were already serious concerns regarding the activities of the press.[15] By 1846, after various incidents and highly publicized trials concerning abuses of press freedom, the government was confident that public sentiment in favor of restricting the press ran high. As Justice Minister Antonio Varas, the government official introducing the legislation, put it, "The experience of more than sixteen years has shown the total failure of the current press law to stop even the most serious and blatant abuses. The most subversive principles have been expounded and disseminated; calls have been openly issued for sedition and the breakdown of public order; slander and libel have been thrown on the most respectable reputations."[16] Despite penalties imposed against some violators, the restrictions on press freedom did not deter journalists from testing and challenging the limits of the legislation.[17] Indeed, press attacks against government figures became even more virulent, culminating in the events of 1851, when papers ridiculed public officials and openly called for rebellion against the established order.[18] As nineteenth-century historian Isidoro Errázuriz put it in a famous quip, the law had as much effect on attempts to subvert public order as a bull of excommunication on the march of a comet.[19]

The issue of the meaning and limits of press freedom was highlighted in various incidents and trials involving the press and the government during the 1840s. In 1840, the government sued *El Diablo Político* for libel and succeeded in having the editor fined 600 pesos. In 1841, Minister Manuel Montt attempted to remove Colonel Pedro Godoy, publisher of the notorious *La Guerra a la Tiranía*, for slanderous attacks against both President Joaquín Prieto and his designated successor, Manuel Bulnes. When Godoy refused to move to a new post in Valdivia, the government backed down for fear of blowing the issue out of proportion. *El Buzón* was added to the list of papers found guilty of press abuses in 1840 and was fined 200 pesos. Yet this did not deter the paper from continued publication. In fact, highly publicized and heavily attended public trials against the papers, particularly that of *El Diablo Político*, brought great notoriety to the press and excited fears of popular upheaval. During the latter trial, a crowd celebrating the outcome turned unruly and had to be dispersed by force.[20]

Press trials proved to be extremely popular and cheap forms of entertainment. They guaranteed fiery rhetoric, embarrassing findings, and discredit for at least one of the parties involved, preferably the government. Careers were made or destroyed. Celebrations usually followed a highly publicized trial, and its results would become the subject of discussion from elegant salons to popular saloons.

Political and social rivals, and even diplomats, made their conflicts public in the press. One particularly famous press trial in 1843 involved Juan García del Río, a Colombian publisher of the *Museo de Ambas Américas* in Valparaíso. Del Río, who had been a supporter of Simón Bolívar, a member of the constituent assembly of 1830 in Colombia (known as the Congreso Admirable), and a prominent government official in Peru and Ecuador, turned an accusation by Bolivian Consul Casimiro Olañeta into a vindication of his colorful career as well as an indictment of irresponsible charges made through the press. A jury found articles written against him in *El Progreso* to be libelous in the highest degree and fined its editor 600 pesos.[21] It is an indication of the growing importance of the press as a forum for public discussion during the first Bulnes administration that Latin American diplomats and exiles continued their personal and political battles in the pages of the Chilean press. However, the vituperative character of political conflict in the press also brought calls for restraint and repression.

By far the most famous trial of the period was against Francisco Bilbao, a radical student who later became a prominent opposition firebrand. Although often described as a confrontation between liberal and conservative forces, where a romantic and heroic young student stood up against the backward and reactionary mores of his country, the trial was primarily the product of a government accusation of blasphemy, sedition, and immorality as specified in the 1828 law. In *El Crepúsculo* in 1844, Bilbao had published "Sociabilidad chilena," an article which government prosecutors considered an abuse of press freedom. The trial was in many respects typical of the period: heavy attendance and a great deal of hissing, cursing, and general unruliness in the courtroom. Bilbao undertook his own defense to the cheers of a crowd that considered his sentence for blasphemy and immorality (sedition charges were dropped) to be a victory. The audience quickly collected the 600-peso fine and proceeded to roam the streets in the sort of celebration that irked government officials eager to place limits on the press.[22]

Bilbao's trial cemented the determination of the government to introduce restrictive legislation, and it accounts for two of the most notorious articles of the 1846 law: 1) the prohibition against publicly raising funds to pay for fines imposed as a result of the judicial process (article 16) and 2) a hard-nosed statement to the effect that "he who attacks or ridicules the official religion of the state, or any of its dogmas," is subject to a maximum penalty of four years in prison and a fine of 1,000 pesos (article 5).

The government also grew weary of the court disruptions and crowd celebrations that degenerated into riots. In 1845, the Bulnes administration sued Pedro Godoy's *El Diario de Santiago* for libel, but lost. The resulting celebration by supporters of Godoy led to violent confrontations with police, who prevailed only after hours of battle and thanks to the intervention of heavy rain.[23] Various writers and publishers, including Pedro Godoy, Pedro Félix Vicuña, and Nicolás Alvarez, were sent into exile; but this did not deter the opposition press. The following year, *El Pueblo* called for rebellion against the government, which reacted with the imposition of a state of siege leading to more arrests and exile of publishers.[24] Much of the unrest was related to the 1846 presidential elections, but the press maintained a confrontational stance aggravated by government harassment and prosecution of journalists under the 1828 press law. Press trials continued, as did suspensions of government funding to selected papers. In the area of riot control the government proved somewhat more successful, but only due to authoritarian measures that alienated government supporters and opponents alike. To a great extent, these incidents provoked the harsher press law of 1846, adopted as Manuel Bulnes began his second term.[25]

Such tensions between government and the press were not confined to Chile. Between 1820 and 1850, a critical period in the establishment and consolidation of most Latin American nations, several countries faced a militant press that threatened the stability of the government. In Colombia in the 1820s, for instance, government and opposition indulged in all manner of personal attacks against opponents. The press law of 1821 proved unequal to the task of thwarting abuses of press freedom. Likewise, Venezuela in the 1830s and 1840s witnessed a flurry of journalistic activity, much of it aimed against the government of General Carlos Soublette. Ecuador under Juan José Flores was yet another example of the virulence of the press and the harshness of government repression against it. The press law of 1833, enacted by an outraged Flores after his failure to indict *El Quiteño Libre* for libel, provided for penalties as severe as ten years of exile.[26] At issue in all of these cases was the degree to which press freedoms could be reconciled with the imperatives of political stability. This task was made all the more difficult by the fact that the propounders of press freedom were by no means disinterested parties who had no stake in the overthrow of the established government. Governments, for their part, regarded the opposition press as a nuisance at best and often used its activities as a justification for the imposition of states of exception.[27] Latin American governments that had a constitutional mandate to ensure freedom of the press could not comfortably do without it; hence they resorted to coercion, legal or otherwise, to keep papers in line.

In Chile, despite strained relations with several papers, the administration of Manuel Bulnes was committed to supporting the press. A decree of November 23, 1825, guaranteed a government subscription of 200 issues for every paper published in the country. While this proved unfeasible in the 1840s, the government authorized expenditures in the amount of 16,468 pesos to support the press in 1843. For a national budget of 3 million pesos, this was a high figure, considering that the allocation to the national university was 14,000 pesos. As shown in Table 2, this figure had decreased somewhat by 1845, but it still represented a substantial commitment when seen in the context of an allocation of 1,127 pesos for the entire southern province of Valdivia.[28]

Few papers could survive on their own, and most did not. Santiago had a population of more than 60,000 inhabitants in the 1840s, but the largest

Table 2. Government Support for the Press, 1845

Paper Name	Pesos
El Tiempo	1,700
El Agricultor	270
El Araucano	2,272
El Progreso	3,770
El Alfa	300
El Mercurio	4,375
La Gaceta del Comercio	840
Total	13,527

Source: Diego Barros Arana, *Un decenio de la historia de Chile, 1841–1851*, 2 vols. (Santiago: Imprenta, Litografía y Encuadernación Barcelona, 1905), 1:485.

number of issues printed per paper fluctuated between 300 and 500 (the exception being the well-established *El Mercurio,* which published about 1,000 copies). More common were the 30 or so coarse copies of *El Valdiviano Federal,* published by José Miguel Infante in the basement of his home. Publication costs were not prohibitive, as the salary of a journalist—for those papers which had writers on the payroll—ranged from 60 to 100 pesos a month. Low readership was mainly owing to high illiteracy rates (less than 17 percent of the population was literate in the 1840s), low incomes, and the widespread practice of passing papers from hand to hand. Many read the papers at government offices, which supplied copies to employees. Additionally, the readership was more interested in political debates around election time than in cultural or news articles. Lieutenant J. M. Gilliss, the leader of the U.S. Naval Astronomical Expedition in Chile during the late 1840s and early 1850s observed with some surprise the absence of news in the existing papers as well as their limited circulation. "It may be inferred from this," he concluded, "that a taste for the reading of current events is not very general; and one may perhaps justly infer that there is a like indifference to more serious literature."[29] In this context, government support proved critical for sustaining the press during the period, even if government funding contributed to the politicization of journalism. Sarmiento's efforts would be geared to developing an interest in the press that, although politically motivated, attempted to transcend the vagaries of partisan political confrontation.

Sarmiento's Role in the Chilean Press

During his stay in Chile in the 1840s and early 1850s, Sarmiento wrote for numerous Chilean papers, including *El Nacional, El Mercurio, El Heraldo Argentino, El Progreso, La Crónica, La Tribuna, Sud-América,* and *El Consejero del Pueblo.* The great majority of his articles, however, were published in *El Mercurio* of Valparaíso and *El Progreso* of Santiago during the first Bulnes administration. It was at *El Progreso,* owned by the powerful Vial family, where Sarmiento contributed most of his important writings, including *Facundo,* published in the paper's *folletines.* Sarmiento had developed a successful career at *El Mercurio* but accepted the position of *redactor,* or principal writer, for *El Progreso* in 1842. Sarmiento shouldered the main responsibility for this first daily of Santiago until 1845, when he was commissioned by the Chilean government to study the educational systems of Europe and the United States. After his return in 1849, Sarmiento's journalistic activities were not as intense as in the earlier 1841–1845 period, but they continued to provide an important vehicle for his views.

Sarmiento conveyed his views on society and politics through the press almost as soon as he arrived in Chile. At the invitation of Montt, he joined Miguel de la Barra in the progovernment *El Nacional* to defend the candidacy of Bulnes. José Victorino Lastarria insisted that it was he who set Sarmiento off to a good start by introducing him first to Montt and then to his friends at *El Mercurio,* but it was clearly what Sarmiento had to offer that turned him into an avidly sought-after writer.[30] As mentioned above, it was his understanding of the press as a medium that gave him a significant edge. He had experience writing for the short-lived *El Zonda* in his native San Juan, and now the experience of exile had given him a certain distance that allowed him to address social and political issues with authority. Sarmiento took his political commitments seriously, but he could write about issues with a mix of humor and irony. This quality allowed him to be strongly critical of press activities and many social and political developments while writing in a detached, often hilarious, prose that aimed to amuse as much as inform a general audience.

Sarmiento's rise in the Chilean press was remarkably swift. He established numerous contacts quickly and soon even considered acquiring *El Mercurio* of Valparaíso. Within months of his arrival in Chile, he indicated in a personal letter to his friend Manuel Quiroga Rosas, who was then living in Copiapó, that he planned a career in journalism. As early as 1841, Sarmiento had surmised the nature of the journalistic career before him in Chile:

> I am sorry I have not written to you as often as I should, but I am always busy and never manage to meet post office deadlines. What can I tell you, I am so busy with writing for a daily and a periodical that I don't even have time to scratch my itching self. My career here is somewhat hazardous: I am the object of the hatred of some, the jealousy of others, the approval of many, and the friendship of still others. *El Mercurio* has given me a great reputation among knowledgeable people; the opposition press has both complimented me for the principles I espouse, and scolded me for taking their papers to task from time to time. In the middle of all this I build a reputation which I hope will bring me a little profit. After the elections, I plan to acquire *El Mercurio*, or associate myself with the enterprise in some fashion.[31]

Sarmiento viewed the role of the press as one of promoting freedom and progress. The press had to educate the public, particularly in countries where the educational system was weak. The press also had the obligation of calling the attention of both government and public to matters needing reform. From these general principles, Sarmiento set out to examine attitudes concerning the press as well as the actual performance of various papers. Not surprisingly, Sarmiento found that the Chilean press left much to be desired. During the early years of his journalistic work, Sarmiento concentrated on three major press-related themes in need of correction: 1) the alleged unfairness with which the liberal opposition used the press to castigate the established order for restricting civil liberties; 2) the proliferation of short-lived papers that concentrated on tendentious coverage of political issues, mainly elections; and 3) the lack of responsiveness on the part of the reading public toward the "serious" press—meaning papers covering broad cultural issues.

With regard to the first two themes, Sarmiento argued that the very existence of such belligerent papers as *La Guerra a la Tiranía* demonstrated that Chile enjoyed not too little, but perhaps too much, freedom of the press, as the slanderous attacks on political leaders indicated.[32] On a broader level, there is an important correspondence between Sarmiento's view that freedom requires certain limits, lest it turn into licentiousness, and his actual experience observing press developments in Chile. Sarmiento coincided philosophically with the views of Andrés Bello concerning the limits of freedom and politically with the Bulnes administration's aim to transform political institutions within a context of social order. His experience with the press helped cement his own beliefs as well as convey them in numerous articles. In an early statement on the press published in *El Nacional* in 1841, Sarmiento argued that journalism had proven to contribute to the common good where it had been free of sectarianism—mainly in European countries. In Latin America, however, papers were utilized to promote political causes that only poisoned the craft of journalism and reduced its civilizing potential. Sarmiento added that the very nature of political confrontation invited the opposition press to adopt a combative tone. The press, in his view, needed to rise above the political fray in order to play a constructive social role.[33]

With respect to the lack of public support for the press, Sarmiento was worried (following Tocqueville) that lack of appreciation for the press's role in society might play into the hands of demagogues who could use the press for the purpose of political destabilization. The public, Sarmiento thought, had to be educated to appreciate the serious press. But the public could be educated only if it subscribed to papers. As he put it in 1842, "these days, there can be neither liberty nor civilization without the aid of the press. But the press cannot survive without subscribers. There is a notorious lack of patriotism, civilization, liberalism, and love for the welfare of the people among those who can afford but fail to support the works of the press."[34] It is in this context that Sarmiento's folletines, articles on theater, and numerous pieces encouraging subscriptions are to be understood. If the public would not readily subscribe to papers out of commitment to civilization, perhaps they could be induced to do so by the promise of entertainment. The folletines, in particular, were for Sarmiento legitimate vehicles for capturing the interest of the public, or at least for creating the habit of reading papers. In 1842, he started a folletín consisting of an exchange of letters between two women, complete with references to fashion, spectacles, and gossip that would presumably capture the interest of the predominantly male readership. In one letter, a woman encouraged the other to continue writing so that *El Progreso* might get "algún suscritorcillo más."[35]

Ultimately, *El Progreso* survived thanks to significant government support (see Table 2). But Sarmiento's contribution should not be underestimated, for his articles spurred many controversies that in fact created significant interest in the press. Sarmiento advanced the cause of journalism overall, but the effort cost him personally. In effect, and in the process of advancing general principles and specific criticisms, Sarmiento elicited antagonisms that drove him to act in the same ways as the fellow journalists he criticized. Chileans had extended generous hospitality in the 1840s to numerous persecuted Latin Americans, especially Argentines, but many individual Chileans became jealous of their neighbors' talents and accomplishments in Chilean society. This was particularly the case of Sarmiento, whose friendship with Montt, but above all his hard-working habits and talent, made him a well-known and successful figure as well as the target of unusually vicious attacks. Sarmiento himself proved quick to move from lofty principles and aims to yellow press tactics and ad hominem arguments. He would rarely initiate a slanderous attack on opponents, either political or philosophical, but would spare no invective once under attack.

Even the most academic debates turned ugly on Sarmiento. When on April 27, 1842, he wrote about issues of language and culture, denouncing the emphasis on proper grammar as a threat to democratic development, he drew the measured and polite response of Andrés Bello. Soon, however, the discussion turned personal and Sarmiento became offended that opponents would disqualify his arguments on the grounds of his Argentine nationality. Yet the very polemic provided him with an opportunity to propose ground rules for debates in the press. In particular, he proposed that disagreements should focus on the ideas conveyed in the papers and not on the character or nationality of the individual authors. "It is wrong"— he argued—"to ask where a writer comes from or where he was born in order to determine whether he is right about issues."[36] Clearly, he was not very successful: a few months later, he and the writers of *El Semanario* became involved on opposite sides of a debate concerning the issue of romanticism and, although the subject was inoffensive enough, there were the usual, inevitable references to individual authorship. Sarmiento reacted angrily to *El Semanario*'s reference to the Argentine nationality of the writers who first brought up the issue, and he retorted that the entire paper served no useful purpose to society. It was he, however, who eventually called for moderation and took this new opportunity to advance a series of proposals for the conduct of polemics in the press. "It's about time that the periodical press follow its due course and that editors forget about themselves for the sake of the public, which is the true object of their work." Moreover, he made a compelling argument for tolerance, arguing that opposing views could coexist, thus obviating the need for excoriating individual authors. "Let us respect one another," he concluded, "and stop scandalizing the public. They need lessons in restraint from those who write, not the spectacle of uncontrolled passions."[37]

Although Sarmiento exited the polemic on a high note, calling for moderation and suggesting new rules for debate, he had become embittered and disillusioned about his efforts to promote sound journalistic practices. His "Diálogo entre el editor y el escritor," published toward the end of the second major debate, shows how hurt and dismayed he had become as a result of his experience with the press. Although the "Diálogo" mentions no names, the main characters are easily identifiable as Manuel Rivadeneyra, editor of *El Mercurio*, and Sarmiento himself. In the story, a weary Sarmiento refuses to write if he must avoid addressing polemical issues. The editor invites him to tackle those issues but in a less confrontational tone. Sarmiento shows such despair that he expresses no hope that the reading public will understand his motives or cease dismissing him as an outsider. Rivadeneyra, a foreigner himself, invites him again to do his job and be patient about the customs of Chilean society. Sarmiento obviously followed the editor's advice, as his prolific writings show, but the article shows the extent to which journalistic battles had taken a toll on the Argentine writer.[38]

But the worst was yet to come, as Sarmiento became embroiled in a bitter exchange of invectives with Domingo Santiago Godoy, a Chilean who claimed to have known Sarmiento in San Juan in the 1830s. Godoy accused Sarmiento of many unkind things, but the gravest was the assassination of defenseless victims in San Juan. That allegation sent Sarmiento into a rage, especially after he learned that Godoy had been repeating the accusations at the stock exchange building, which doubled as a social center for the elite. He wrote *Mi defensa* in several installments during 1843 to respond to Godoy's charges. But, as in his other autobiographies, Sarmiento omitted important information about the specifics of charges and countercharges leading to his arrest and about the legal process that followed.[39]

On January 25, 1843, Sarmiento filed suit against Godoy and demanded his arrest on the grounds that the Chilean was unfairly damaging his reputation. He also produced a list of names of individuals who had heard Godoy's statements, including Ramón Vial, José María Núñez, and Antonio Vidal. On the basis of the evidence provided by Sarmiento, Judge José Manuel Novoa ordered the arrest of Godoy on January 28, 1843, but by that time the accused had filed his own libel suit against Sarmiento. Apparently unsure of the outcome of a criminal suit, Sarmiento had decided to vent his anger by posting a pamphlet in the stock exchange calling Godoy "cowardly" and "wretched."[40] When he learned of Godoy's suit, Sarmiento posted bail on his own behalf but could not escape arrest. Sarmiento never mentioned having been arrested in Chile in any of his autobiographies, but on February 16, 1843, he declared in a legal document that "because it is unfair that I remain in prison owing to Mr. Godoy's contempt, especially since legally I could be released, I request that your honor accept the bail I have already posted and order my freedom so that justice might be served."

Sarmiento's suit had turned out badly. Judge Novoa, however, offered the parties in conflict the opportunity to settle the issue out of court and invited the mediation of Vicente Fidel López and Manuel Carvallo. Sarmiento and Godoy were given freedom to pursue their respective suits if mediation failed, as indeed happened in early March 1843. Carvallo made no retractions for Godoy and demanded that Sarmiento publicly apologize for the pamphlet he posted in the stock exchange, a proposition both López and Sarmiento found unacceptable. Mediator López, for his part, argued that while the accusation of "assassin" was far more serious than that of "cowardly" or "wretched," perhaps Sarmiento and Godoy could apologize to each other. Godoy and Carvallo refused and negotiations broke down. However, neither party decided to pursue the matter in the courts, and the case was dropped.[41]

Other incidents resulting from Sarmiento's role in the press included a fistfight with Juan Nepomuceno Espejo, a writer for the rival *El Siglo*, and a sharply written confrontation with his friend Lastarria, to whom he sent a letter making him responsible for the personal attacks he received from *El Siglo*.[42] The larger context for these disputes concerned the alienation between political forces supporting Irarrázaval and Montt, represented in the *periódicos ministeriales El Siglo* and *El Progreso*, respectively; but in the heat of battle, personal animosities prevailed.[43] By the end of the first Bulnes administration, Sarmiento felt tired and beleaguered, and he seriously considered leaving for Bolivia. Manuel Montt, however, was able to persuade him to accept instead a commission to travel to Europe, which Sarmiento accepted gladly.

Montt's invitation took place in the context of heavy pressure from Juan Manuel de Rosas against the press activities of Argentine émigrés in Chile. In April 1845, Rosas sent a special envoy to Santiago, Baldomero García, to persuade the Bulnes government to control Argentine exile agitation against his regime. Andrés Bello, who was an official in the Ministry of Foreign Relations at the time, indicated in *El Araucano* that the Chilean government had no authority to dictate what the press did. García grew frustrated as Argentines did not cease activities and Sarmiento began the publication of *Facundo*. Tensions mounted as an Argentine émigré, Elías Bedoya, attacked a consular employee in a Santiago street and stripped him of the notorious red ribbon that signified adherence to Rosas. Although the Chilean government arrested Bedoya, it did nothing to stop the press, which intensified its attacks against the Rosas regime. Despite pro-Rosas articles in *El Diario de Santiago*, which supported Rosas just to upset the Argentine émigrés, and Sarmiento in particular, nothing came out of García's mission, and he was eventually recalled in 1846.[44] Not only did Sarmiento succeed in issuing his *Facundo* despite diplomatic pressures, but he left Chile for Europe in charge of an important government commission.[45]

When Sarmiento returned to Santiago in 1849, he joined Antonio García Reyes and Manuel Antonio Tocornal at *La Tribuna,* a paper founded to oppose the ministry of Manuel Camilo Vial. Sarmiento and his Chilean colleagues, both of whom were distinguished members of the conservative establishment as well as members of Congress, waged war against the unpopular interior minister until Bulnes asked for his resignation in June of that year. Sarmiento had been the chief writer for *El Progreso,* but as politics pitted Vial against Montt the Argentine chose not to return to the paper, which moved closer to the liberals and eventually even supported the radical Sociedad de la Igualdad in their bid against the Bulnes administration.[46] As elections drew near, Sarmiento defended the candidacy of Montt, which became one of his main journalistic objectives during this period. A strong supporter of Montt, Sarmiento left the country only after his friend assumed office in September 1851.

The defense of Montt and Sarmiento's last writings concerning the press intersected in the articles he wrote against the derogation of the 1846 law, which Lastarria proposed in Congress in 1849. As noted above, Manuel Montt had presided over the Interior Ministry in 1846 when the law was passed. The timing of the 1846 law had to do both with the recent instances of press abuse and related trials in 1845 and with the desire to spare the new Bulnes administration any possible political damage resulting from a highly restrictive press law. In 1849, Sarmiento defended both Montt's action and the law. Although he stopped short of calling Lastarria a hypocrite, he did argue that while Manuel Camilo Vial was chief minister Lastarria had said nothing about the law he now so adamantly wanted abolished. Matters of the press, Sarmiento concluded, became easy prey to partisan political interests, in this case the discredit of Montt. Sarmiento went further in his expression of disillusionment when he argued that "the press law was issued to protect order, authority, and reputations. But the actual result has been the [opposition's] mobilization of the public after every press trial in order to take advantage of the passions of the moment and to test the subversive potential of the crowd."[47]

Sarmiento concluded that perhaps the press should not be judged by whether or how much it contributed to the advancement of civilization but, rather, by how effectively it manipulated public opinion in order to advance its various causes. Such a conclusion was particularly relevant on the eve of the presidential elections, when the press went into a frenzy of irresponsible charges and calls for rebellion against the conservative government and its handpicked successor. By the time a rebellion actually took place on April 20, 1851, Sarmiento was among the first to arrive at the government palace, on horseback and armed with a gun. Up to that point, he had produced a number of pamphlets in favor of Montt's candidacy, but the outburst of revolution convinced him that he would defend with force what he had defended in print. As an appropriate finale to his journalistic career, and Chilean exile, he ran back and forth from the battle scene to the printing house, issuing proclamations describing the course of events. This led José Victorino Lastarria to comment that Sarmiento proved he could defend with his life the government he had defended with his pen.[48]

Journalism and politics, which Sarmiento had sought to separate in the early years of his Chilean sojourn, became fused in the turmoil of 1851. As events in Argentina gained momentum during that year, Sarmiento focused his sights on other battles and brought his Chilean experience to bear when he once again traded the pen for the sword.

Appendix
CHILE: NEWSPAPERS AND PERIODICALS, 1828–1851

The sources for the following list are Ramón Briseño, *Estadística bibliográfica de la literatura chilena*, 2 vols. (Santiago: Imprenta Chilena, 1862–1879); José Victorino Lastarria, *Recuerdos literarios*, 2nd ed. (Santiago de Chile: Librería M. Servat, 1885); Jorge Huneeus Gana, *Cuadro histórico de la producción intelectual de Chile* (Santiago: Biblioteca de Escritores de Chile, 1910); Diego Barros Arana, *Un decenio de la historia de Chile, 1841–1851*, 2 vols. (Santiago: Imprenta, Litografía y Encuadernación Barcelona, 1905–1913); Raúl Silva Castro, *Prensa y periodismo en Chile, 1812–1956* (Santiago: Ediciones de la Universidad de Chile, 1958), and Guillermo Feliú Cruz, *Historia de las fuentes de la bibliografía chilena*, 2 vols. (Santiago: Editorial Universidad Católica, 1966).

These sources are sometimes in conflict concerning the exact dates of some periodicals and newspapers. The dates indicated below are confirmed by at least two sources, but dates of termination are in some cases unavailable. However, as is obvious from the number of issues, a large number of papers lasted less than one year. Excluded from the list are papers that published only one issue. Both *El Mercurio* and *El Valdiviano Federal* are included here because they started publication only one year prior to the promulgation of the 1828 press law, and remained important throughout the period.

Name	Date	No. of Issues
El Mercurio	1827–present	
El Valdiviano Federal	1827–1844	206
Cartas Chilenas de Theófilo a Christófilo	1828	5
El Canalla	1828	4
El Censor del Año de 28	1828	10
Registro Municipal	1828–1830	57
El Minero de Coquimbo	1828	25
El Mercurio Chileno	1828–1829	16
Sesiones del Congreso Constituyente	1828	7
El Almirez	1828	2
El Vigía	1828	7
El Constituyente	1828	5
El Pararrayo	1828	2
El Azote de los Logi-Unitarios	1828	2
El Sepulturero	1828–1840	27
Gaceta de Chile	1828–1829	16
El Centinela	1828–1829	22
El Tribuno del Pueblo Chileno	1829	2
El Avisador de Valparaíso	1829	81
El Observador Político de Aconcagua	1829	5
El Fanal	1829	10
El Penquisto	1829	5
El Cura Monardes	1829	23
La Lechuza	1829	2
El Sufragante	1829–1830	29
El Crisol	1829	6
El Espectador Chileno	1829	13
El Céfiro de Chile	1829	2
El Crepúsculo	1829	4
Documentos Oficiales	1829–1832	36
La Ley y la Justicia	1829–1830	3
El Correo del Pueblo	1829	4
La Antorcha de los Pueblos	1830	6
El Amigo de la Constitución	1830	4
El Avisador Imparcial	1830	2
El Periodiquito	1830	5

Name	Date	No. of Issues
El Coquimbano	1830	3
El Azote de la Mentira	1830	8
El Popular	1830	20
Boletín de Coquimbo	1830	8
La Opinión	1830–1832	33
El Observador Imparcial	1830	7
El Criticón Médico	1830	4
El Defensor de los Militares Denominados Constitucionales	1830	2
El Juicio	1830	5
El Araucano	1830–1877	4,842
El Escrutador	1830–1831	8
El Trompeta	1830–1831	14
La Bandera Tricolor	1831–1832	41
El O'Higginista	1831	3
El Correo Mercantil	1832–1833	390
El Hurón	1832	12
La Lucerna	1832–1833	32
El Celador	1832	9
Aduana de La Serena	1833–1835	29
El Cosmopolita	1833	22
El Constitucional	1833	14
El Faro del Bío-Bío	1833	60
El Filántropo	1834	2
El Minero del Año 34	1834–1840	115
El Cántaro contra la Piedra	1835	10
El Día y el Golpe	1835–1840	37
El Philopolita	1835	15
El Chileno	1835	3
El Farol	1835	12
El Defensor del Philopolita	1835	3
El Voto Público	1835	8
La Aurora	1836	8
Registro Municipal	1836–1843	170
El Barómetro de Chile	1836	41
El Republicano	1836	2
El Intérprete	1836–1837	30
El Nacional	1836	2

Name	Date	No. of Issues
El Eventual	1836	5
La Aurora	1836	7
Paz Perpetua a los Chilenos	1836	6
La Bandera Bicolor	1837	5
Boletín Oficial	1837	2
El Perrero	1837	5
El Nuncio de la Guerra	1837–1838	2
El Aguijón	1838	3
El Agricultor	1838–1849	78
El Diablo Político	1839–1840	31
El Clamor	1839	3
Cartas Patrióticas	1839	8
La Antorcha	1839	14
La Tribuna Nacional	1840	2
La Guerra a la Tiranía	1840	31
La Bolsa	1840	229
El Censor Imparcial	1840	5
El Buzón	1840	29
La Reforma	1840	40
El Conservador	1840	17
El Veterano	1840	17
El Artesano	1841	6
El Elector Chileno	1841	12
El Nacional	1841	9
El Voto Liberal	1841	3
El Porvenir	1841	7
La Estrella del Norte	1841	13
El Miliciano	1841	17
El Tribuno	1841	2
La Justicia	1841	3
La Gaceta de los Tribunales	1841–1854	912
El Progreso	1842–1853	2,739
La Gaceta de Comercio	1842–1847	1,572
El Telégrafo de Concepción	1842	287
Revista de Valparaíso	1842	6
El Semanario de Santiago	1842–1843	31
El Museo de Ambas Américas	1842	36
El Demócrata	1843	9
El Crepúsculo	1843–1844	16

Name	Date	No. of Issues
La Revista Católica	1843–1874	1,300
El Clarín	1844	24
El Vigía de Valparaíso	1844–1845	275
El Siglo	1844–1845	383
El Alfa	1844–1849	246
El Tiempo	1845	109
El Diario de Santiago	1845	208
El Republicano	1845	15
El Duende	1845	4
El Artesano del Orden	1845	20
El Artesano Opositor	1845	22
El Copiapino	1845–1879	9,355
El Orden	1845–1846	65
El Pueblo	1846	7
El Semanario de las Familias	1847	52
El Comercio	1847–1851	1,063
La Prensa	1848	180
La Revista de Santiago	1848–1851	7
La Serena	1849	110
La Crónica	1849–1854	61
La Tribuna	1849–1851	702
La República	1849	9
El Corsario	1849	116
El Timón	1849	37
El Aconcaguino	1849	30
El Ferrocarril	1849	91
El País	1849	89
El Amigo del Pueblo	1850	5
El Verdadero Chileno	1850	79
La Barra	1850–1851	175
La Reforma	1850	35
El Consejero del Pueblo	1850	8
La Tribuna de la Semana	1851	15
El Cazador	1851	24
El Voto Libre	1851	3
Diario de Avisos	1851	59
El Album	1851	4
La Situación	1851	39
El Pueblo	1851	1,145

Name	Date	No. of Issues
La Reforma	1851	40
Sud-América	1851	33
El Diario	1851–1858	3,034

Notes

1. I am extremely grateful to Jaime Concha, Tulio Halperín Donghi, Brian E. Loveman, William F. Sater, Sol Serrano, and Doris Sommer for comments on an earlier version of this chapter. I am, of course, entirely responsible for its shortcomings.

2. By far the most complete study of Sarmiento's exile in Chile is by Paul Verdevoye, *Sarmiento, éducateur et publiciste* (Paris: Centre de Recherches de l'Institut d'Etudes Hispaniques, 1964). There is a Spanish version of this book titled *Domingo Faustino Sarmiento: Educar y escribir opinando, 1839–1852* (Buenos Aires: Editorial Plus Ultra, 1988). I will use the more complete French edition for the purposes of citation. See also Armando Donoso, *Sarmiento en el destierro* (Buenos Aires: M. Gleizer Editor, 1927); Alamiro de Avila Martel, *Sarmiento en la Universidad de Chile* (Santiago: Ediciones de la Universidad de Chile, 1988); William H. Katra, *Domingo F. Sarmiento: Public Writer (between 1939 and 1852)* (Tempe: Center for Latin American Studies, Arizona State University, 1985); and Luis Alberto Romero, "Sarmiento, testigo y testimonio de la sociedad de Santiago," *Revista Iberoamericana* 54, no. 143 (April–June 1988): 461–475.

3. Domingo Faustino Sarmiento, *Obras completas* (henceforth *OC*), 53 vols. (Santiago and Buenos Aires, 1887–1903), 3:202–203. Another important motive, which Sarmiento confided to his friend Manuel Quiroga Rosas in a letter of March 15, 1841, was that "Bulnes nos conviene. Aborrece a Rosas de muerte." This and other important letters to Quiroga Rosas are in the Archivo Nacional (Santiago de Chile), Fondos Varios, vol. 253, pp. 337–357.

4. A somewhat predictably sympathetic view of the Vial ministry is by Benjamín Vicuña Mackenna, *Los jirondinos chilenos* (Santiago: Imprenta del Comercio, 1902), pp. 11–12. Vicuña Mackenna's political views brought him close to the most radical wing of the liberal movement. He eventually joined the Sociedad de la Igualdad and suffered government persecution after the events of April 20, 1851. An important interpretation of Vicuña Mackenna's source, and of Chilean liberalism in general, is by Alfredo Jocelyn-Holt Letelier. See his " 'Los Girondinos chilenos': Una reinterpretación," *Mapocho: Revista de Humanidades y Ciencias Sociales* 29, no. 1 (1991): 46–55, and "Liberalismo y modernidad. Ideología y simbolismo en el Chile decimonónico: Un marco teórico," in Ricardo Krebs and Cristián Gazmuri, eds., *La revolución francesa y Chile* (Santiago: Editorial Universitaria, 1990), pp. 303–333.

5. The most thorough account of Chilean politics during the period is by Diego Barros Arana, *Un decenio de la historia de Chile*, 2 vols. (Santiago: Imprenta, Litografía y Encuadernación Barcelona, 1905–1913). Concise but useful accounts include Simon Collier, "Chile from Independence to the War of the Pacific," in *The Cambridge History of Latin America*, ed. Leslie Bethell (Cambridge: Cambridge University Press, 1985), 3:583–613, and Brian Loveman, *Chile: The Legacy of Hispanic Capitalism*, 2nd ed. (New York: Oxford University Press, 1988), esp. chap. 5, "Modernization and Misery."

6. Sarmiento revealed the extent of his appreciation for, and indebtedness to, Manuel Montt in his *Recuerdos de provincia*, OC, 3:204–208. A series of articles by Sarmiento about Montt is included on pp. 349–380 of the same volume.

7. For overviews of press developments since Chile's independence, see Raúl Silva Castro, *Prensa y periodismo en Chile, 1812–1956* (Santiago: Ediciones de la Universidad de Chile, 1958); Alfonso Valdebenito, *Historia del periodismo chileno, 1812–1955*, 2nd ed. (Santiago: Imprenta Fantasía, 1956); and José Peláez y Tapia, *Un siglo de periodismo chileno: Historia de "El Mercurio"* (Santiago: Talleres de "El Mercurio," 1927). For a compilation of press articles during the independence period, see Pedro Godoy, *Espíritu de la prensa chilena*, 2 vols. (Santiago: Imprenta del Comercio, 1847). A bibliography of sources for an earlier period is José Toribio Medina's *Bibliografía de la imprenta en Santiago de Chile. Desde sus orígenes hasta febrero de 1817* (Santiago: Prensas de la Universidad de Chile, 1939).

8. According to José Peláez y Tapia, approximately 80 papers were published between 1812 and 1827; see his *Un siglo*, p. 30. The Chilean press was probably the most active in the continent, but it was not rare to find other countries in the region (notably Cuba) that published equally large numbers of papers.

9. The correspondence of Antonio Varas reveals how local officials, even Church officials, reacted with alarm to the arrival of opposition papers such as *La Barra* and requested the prompt dispatch of government papers. This was the case with Ancud during the candidacy of Manuel Montt. See *Correspondencia de don Antonio Varas* (Santiago: Imprenta Universitaria, 1921), pp. 108–109 and 161–162.

10. The paper *El Desmascarado*, which published only one issue in 1843, was written exclusively to discredit Sarmiento. He wrote about the publication of this paper in his *Recuerdos de provincia*, OC, 3:212–213.

11. For the relevant texts of the Constitution, as well as an examination of legislation concerning the press up to 1846, see Juan Bautista Alberdi, *Lejislación de la prensa en Chile, o sea, Manual del escritor, del impresor y del jurado* (Valparaíso: Imprenta del Mercurio, 1846). Alberdi's book represents a major attempt at shedding light on the institutional and juridical aspects of press activities in Chile.

12. For the text of both laws, see Ricardo Anguita, ed., *Leyes promulgadas*

en Chile desde 1810 hasta 1912, 5 vols. (Santiago: Litografía y Encuadernación Barcelona, 1912), 1:193–196 and 478–484. There had been an earlier law promulgated in 1813, but it was by far more concerned with establishing freedom of the press than with spelling out its limitations; see Anguita, ed., *Leyes promulgadas,* 1:37–39. U.S. Navy Lieutenant J. M. Gilliss, who visited Chile between 1849 and 1852, noted with surprise that the structure of Chilean government included "Censors of the Press" in each department of the republic, which had "no corresponding tribunals in the United States." He was referring to the special juries, their appointment and responsibilities as specified in the press law of 1846, articles 28, 29, and 39–41, among others. See Gilliss's *The U.S. Naval Astronomical Expedition to the Southern Hemisphere during the Years 1849, 50, 51, 52,* 2 vols. (Washington, D.C.: A.O.P. Nicholson, 1855), 1:138.

13. Peláez y Tapia, *Un siglo,* p. 275.

14. José Victorino Lastarria, *Proyectos de lei i discursos parlamentarios,* in *Obras completas de Don José Victorino Lastarria,* vol. 3 (Santiago: Imprenta, Litografía y Encuadernación Barcelona, 1907), pp. 93–139.

15. For congressional records, including press articles, see *Sesiones de los cuerpos lejislativos de la República de Chile, 1811 a 1845,* esp. vols. 26 and 28 (Santiago: Imprenta Cervantes, 1905–1906) for the years 1839 and 1840, respectively. See also Ricardo Donoso, *Las ideas políticas en Chile* (Mexico: Fondo de Cultura Económica, 1946), pp. 354–359.

16. Quoted in Donoso, *Las ideas,* pp. 360–361. This and all other translations in the present chapter are mine.

17. Santos Tornero, the owner of *El Mercurio* since 1842, had faced accusations of press abuse under the 1828 law. With the enactment of the 1846 law, he suffered additional accusations and even imprisonment, though in large part because he had fallen from government favor under the Vial ministry. Tornero claimed that part of the reason for the antagonism was that Manuel Rivadeneyra had refused to sell *El Mercurio* to the Vials, favoring him instead. He also maintained an independent line vis-à-vis the government, despite subsidies. At any rate, he did not think highly of the 1846 law. See his *Reminiscencias de un viejo editor* (Valparaíso: Imprenta de la Librería del Mercurio, 1889), p. 73.

18. Jack Ray Thomas, "The Role of the Press in the Chilean Rebellion of 1851," *The Americas* 36, no. 1 (July 1979): 59–78. Benjamín Vicuña Mackenna, *Historia de la jornada del 20 de abril de 1851* (Santiago: Imprenta del Centro Editorial, 1878).

19. Quoted in Donoso, *Las ideas,* p. 366.

20. José Victorino Lastarria, who had been one of the founders of *El Diablo Político,* described these events in his *Recuerdos literarios,* 2nd ed. (Santiago: Librería de M. Servat, 1885), pp. 56–64.

21. Barros Arana, *Un decenio,* 1:429–435. Sarmiento referred to the early stages of this incident in *El Progreso,* January 17, 1843, but mainly to

illustrate the degree of contentiousness characterizing the press (*OC*, 2:95).

22. Government prosecutor Máximo Mujica demanded the destruction of the *El Crepúsculo* issue containing Bilbao's article. There were no provisions for that in the 1828 law, and thus the prosecution appealed to the Supreme Court, which authorized the burning of the issue on the basis of an obscure law of 1609. This action brought even more notoriety to Bilbao. José Victorino Lastarria described Bilbao's article and trial in his *Recuerdos literarios*, pp. 277–293. Although he was one of Bilbao's mentors, Lastarria described "Sociabilidad chilena" as the work of a troubled young man. The piece had such an impact, according to Lastarria, fundamentally because of government overreaction; with a list of subscribers no larger than 200, he indicated, *El Crepúsculo* was simply not as influential as it had been made out to be.

23. Barros Arana, *Un decenio*, 2:67–77; Pedro Félix Vicuña, *Vindicación de los principios e ideas que han servido en Chile de apoyo a la oposición en las elecciones populares de 1846* (Lima: Imprenta del Comercio, 1846), p. 32. Vicuña, the father of Benjamín Vicuña Mackenna, was very active in the press since the 1820s and had a profound dislike for Presidents Prieto, Bulnes, and Montt; his opposition to the latter two brought about his Peruvian exile. See the *Memorias íntimas de don Pedro Félix Vicuña*, ed. Luis Valencia Avaria (Santiago: Imprenta El Esfuerzo, 1943).

24. The press, particularly the liberal press, was capable of major disruptions but did not represent a coherent opposition against the powerful and highly popular government of Manuel Bulnes. The administration reacted to press-related events not so much out of fear of losing the elections of 1846, which it was almost certain to win, but rather out of concern about the riots associated with press trials and the radical stances of some publishers. Government supporters such as Antonio García Reyes and Manuel Antonio Tocornal, both members of Congress, disagreed with actions against the press in general, and with the law of 1846 in particular, because they believed that restrictions only invited retaliation. Cabinet ministers Manuel Montt and Antonio Varas were strongly for restrictions. The tensions resulting from the press issue heralded the first cracks in the conservative government, which would burst apart in the 1850s.

25. The 1846 law became irrelevant sooner than expected, despite the severe penalties it prescribed. Diego Barros Arana attributes this to the fact that the jury of 1848 was totally supportive of the government, which shielded an important segment of the press from accusations. Opponents could likewise appeal to the Supreme Court in cases of unfavorable rulings, and successfully did so in 1849. Press trials became public exercises in oratory where matters of honor were more frequently discussed than judicial matters. One particularly assiduous visitor to the courts was Benjamín Vicuña Mackenna. See his *El castigo de la calumnia: Compilación de las principales piezas de los procesos de imprenta promovidos contra el diario "Ferrocarril" i los periódicos "La*

Linterna del Diablo" i "El Charivari" (Santiago: Imprenta de la República, 1868). See also Allen Woll, *A Functional Past: The Uses of History in Nineteenth-Century Chile* (Baton Rouge and London: Louisiana State University Press, 1982), esp. chap. 7. Eventually, the law fell into oblivion, but it remained on the books until its formal derogation in 1872.

26. See David Bushnell, "The Development of the Press in Great Colombia," *Hispanic American Historical Review* 30, no. 4 (November 1950): 432–452; Servando García Ponce, *La imprenta en la historia de Venezuela* (Caracas: Monte Avila Editores, 1975); Juan Bautista Querales, ed., *Soublette y la prensa de su época* (Caracas: Academia Nacional de la Historia, 1979); Julio Febres Cordero, *Historia del periodismo y de la imprenta en Venezuela* (Caracas: Academia Nacional de la Historia, 1983). For Ecuador, see Mark J. Van Aken, *King of the Night: Juan José Flores and Ecuador, 1824–1864* (Berkeley: University of California Press, 1989), esp. chap. 4. See also Frank MacDonald Spindler, *Nineteenth-Century Ecuador: A Historical Introduction* (Fairfax, Va.: George Mason University Press, 1987).

27. Brian E. Loveman, in his "The Constitution of Tyranny," provides multiple examples of how nineteenth-century Latin American governments devised government charters and laws that allowed them to pay lip service to liberal principles while repressing their manifestations in the name of public order. I am grateful to Professor Loveman for sharing his book manuscript, which is in progress, with me.

28. From 1853 to 1858, government funding for the press remained steady at 16,000 pesos. It increased to 40,000 pesos in 1859. Between 1861 and 1863 it decreased to 20,000 pesos. Funding went down again to 10,000 pesos between 1863 and 1876, the year when press support disappeared as an item in the national budget. See Peláez y Tapia, *Un siglo*, pp. 104–105.

29. Gilliss, *Astronomical Expedition*, 1:194.

30. Lastarria had a penchant for taking credit for most of the significant events that took place during his lifetime. He described his encounter with Sarmiento in *Recuerdos literarios*, pp. 81–84. There he called Sarmiento "embrión de grande hombre" and claimed the credits mentioned in the text. A view of Lastarria and the ideas of his time are in Bernardo Subercaseaux, *Cultura y sociedad liberal en el siglo XIX. Lastarria, ideología y literatura* (Santiago: Editorial Aconcagua, 1981). See also Norman P. Sacks, "Lastarria y Sarmiento: El chileno y el argentino achilenado," *Revista Iberoamericana* 54, no. 143 (April–June 1988): 491–512.

31. Letter to Manuel Quiroga Rosas, June 8, 1841, Archivo Nacional, Fondos Varios, vol. 253, pieza 12. In another letter, dated July 31, 1841, he tells Quiroga that *El Mercurio* is about to become his. Sarmiento's effort to acquire *El Mercurio* came to naught, and the paper and press were purchased by the Spaniard Santos Tornero in 1842.

32. See, for example, "Un jurado de imprenta," *El Mercurio*, March 16, 1841, and "Cosas de estudiantes," *El Mercurio*, April 3, 1841, included in *OC*,

1:17–19 and 23–25; and "Libertad de imprenta," *El Mercurio*, March 8, 1841, in *OC*, 9:55–59. This perspective was shared by another keen-eyed foreigner, Ignacio Domeyko, who was appalled by the tone and character of the press in the early 1840s, especially *La Guerra a la Tiranía*. See his *Mis viajes: Memorias de un exiliado*, 2 vols. (Santiago: Ediciones de la Universidad de Chile, 1978), 1:498 and 510–511.

33. "El diarismo," *El Mercurio*, May 15–29, 1841, in *OC*, 1:56–64.

34. "El Museo de Ambas Américas," *El Mercurio*, April 28, 1842, in *OC*, 1:202.

35. "Cartas de dos amigas," *El Progreso*, November 16, 1842–January 2, 1843, in *OC*, 2:24–44. On Sarmiento's strategies for building a readership, see Adolfo Prieto's chapter in this book.

36. See the various articles collected under the heading "Primera polémica literaria," in *OC*, 1:208–247.

37. The polemic on romanticism has frequently been cited as a hallmark of the intellectual renaissance of 1842. While it certainly represented a new level of intellectual debate, the issue was most significant in the context of press developments, as papers and writers calibrated the extent and limits of discussion. The series of articles by Sarmiento concerning the polemic on romanticism are in "Segunda polémica literaria," *OC*, 1:283–323. Another polemic involving Sarmiento concerned his proposals to reform the Spanish spelling system used in Chile; he presented those proposals to the University of Chile in October 1843, and they were approved in part in April 1844. Sarmiento's reforms were continuously attacked and, despite official sanction, fell into disuse. An example of Sarmiento's reaction to attacks from *El Siglo* is in *OC*, 4:210–218. The publisher of *El Mercurio*, Santos Tornero, refused to adopt the new system and was called by Sarmiento "El editor testarudo." See Tornero, *Reminiscencias*, pp. 54–56.

38. "Diálogo entre el editor y el escritor," *El Mercurio*, July 27, 1842, in *OC*, 1:323–329. Sarmiento candidly admitted that his personality brought him tremendous antagonisms. As he stated in *Mi defensa*, "I have always elicited either great antagonisms or profound sympathies. Mine is a world of friends and enemies where I am applauded and scolded at the same time." He added that "everyday I hurt sensitivities that create the desire for censoring my conduct. I must be more prudent . . ." (*OC*, 3:4–5 and 23). Still, much of the antagonism came from his association with Montt and the conservative government.

39. The following account is based on documents housed at Chile's Archivo Nacional, Fondos Varios, vol. 318, pieza 3, titled "Querella de Dn. Domingo Faustino Sarmiento contra D. Domingo Santiago Godoy," pp. 267–289, and on the pamphlet titled *Al público* by Domingo Santiago Godoy (Santiago: Imprenta Liberal, 1843). Surprisingly little has been written about this incident in the literature on Sarmiento. Verdevoye, in *Sarmiento*, pp. 461–462; Allison William Bunkley, *The Life of Sarmiento* (Princeton: Princeton

University Press, 1952), p. 165; and J. Guillermo Guerra, *Sarmiento: Su vida i sus obras* (Santiago: Imprenta Elzeviriana, 1901), pp. 88–90, refer briefly to the dispute but say nothing about the arrest. Of course, Sarmiento himself avoided the subject.

40. The text of the pamphlet is included in *Mi defensa, OC*, 3:36.

41. In case of mediation failure, the judge ordered that the case be forwarded to Manuel Rengifo and Diego José Benavente for another attempt at mediation. There is no archival evidence, however, that the litigation ever reached that stage.

42. The text of the letter, and Lastarria's response, are in María Luisa del Pino de Carbone, *Correspondencia entre Sarmiento y Lastarria, 1844–1888* (Buenos Aires: Bartolomé U. Chiesino, 1954), pp. 25–26. See also Armando Donoso, *Sarmiento en el destierro*, pp. 36–39, and Alejandro Fuenzalida Grandón, *Lastarria i su tiempo* (Santiago: Imprenta Cervantes, 1893), pp. 86–87. Sarmiento described his confrontation with Espejo in a letter to José Posse on January 29, 1845. See Verdevoye, *Sarmiento*, p. 325.

43. Sacks, "Lastarria y Sarmiento," p. 509.

44. Barros Arana, *Un decenio*, 2:130–137.

45. Sarmiento visited numerous countries between 1845 and 1849. Works that resulted from his observations abroad are *De la educación popular* and *Viajes en Europa, Africa y América*, published in vols. 5 and 11 of *OC*, respectively. A most interesting reaction to Sarmiento's *Viajes* is by Juan Martínez Villergas, *Sarmenticidio, o a mal Sarmiento buena podadera* (Paris: Agencia General de la Librería Española y Extranjera, 1853).

46. Gilliss, *Astronomical Expedition*, 1:194.

47. "Ley de imprenta," *La Crónica*, August 19, 1849, in *OC*, 9:73. Not long thereafter, Lastarria openly called for the press to act against conservative opponents "sin escepción de persona i sin reticencia" in his "Proyecto de reorganización del partido liberal redactado por el diputado don José Victorino Lastarria el 20 de marzo de 1850." See Vicuña Mackenna, *Historia de la jornada del 20 de abril de 1851*, app. p. vii.

48. Lastarria recalled these events in a letter to Sarmiento dated November 13, 1883, in Pino del Carbone, *Correspondencia*, pp. 141–142.

3 Sarmiento and the "Buenos Aires/Córdoba" Duality

ANA MARÍA BARRENECHEA

Sarmiento set forth a vision of the city of the future: a center of civilization that would serve as a model for the rest of Argentina. Although Sarmiento's ideal city is usually associated with the modernizing impulses of Buenos Aires, it was Córdoba, the traditional ecclesiastical and colonial center, that was the true focus of his dreams for progress. This is apparent not only in the *Facundo*[1] but in his later works. The play of oppositions in which he juxtaposes progress or backwardness, scientific advancement or ecclesiastical conservatism, is redefined continually throughout his writing career.

I am interested here in tracing the components of the Buenos Aires/ Córdoba pairing in Sarmiento's writing after *Facundo* in order to see their function in different historical and literary contexts. Perhaps one of the most significant of those contexts corresponds to Sarmiento's presidency in 1879, when he inaugurated the National Exposition of Córdoba.[2] On several occasions, in different periods of his life, he spoke of his motives for the exposition and of his plans for holding it in Córdoba rather than Buenos Aires. He expressed an eagerness to "civilize" and spoke of related projects he had accomplished (an astronomical observatory, a train to La Calera, budgets for schools).

Why did Sarmiento choose Córdoba and not Buenos Aires as the exposition headquarters? His grandson Augusto Belín recounts a long conversation in which Sarmiento explained his intentions.[3] He chose Córdoba, we learn, in order to show the possibilities of development to the inland provinces, governed largely by poverty, and to point out to those governing Buenos Aires—who knew little of the country's interior—the reality of their nation. Confronted with the argument that they would be embarrassed to reveal such backwardness to foreign countries, Sarmiento asserted the value of his decision for them as well. When some objected, claiming that Córdoba was resistant to the ideas of progress, he insisted on the need to bring the Industrial Revolution to Argentina's colonial and Catholic interior.

I will cite only a fragment of the dialogue transcribed by Belín:

N.: But here [in Buenos Aires] the foreigner would see a cultured city and would form a better idea of our people.

PRES.: [It is] for the foreigner, precisely. Start with the fact that he will see the great river leading up to Rosario—a spectacle more envied by the European than all the wares of an exposition, then Rosario, the only flourishing city to have developed since independence. After that, the pampa for countless leagues: silent, uninhabited, without culture; and he will contemplate it knowing that we have decreed its demise. And at last, Córdoba itself. *Do you believe Córdoba to be only a trifle?* It is the true jewel of the Republic. A colonial city, with the spirit of that time, with its university, its convents, its inheritance from the Inquisition. A traveler could cross all over Europe and the Americas, vainly seeking a piece of the Old World so innocent of all reform, of all innovation. [p. 201]

Belín's text suggests the image of a Sarmiento who looked not only at Córdoba but at the whole of his country, and even at Spanish America and Europe, in terms of progress and regression, factors that dominated the course of his political life. In order to defend his decision, Sarmiento appears to locate himself as observing from the viewpoint of the foreigner, a viewpoint nevertheless his own. To do that, not only does he place himself in the city of the exposition's headquarters, but (with a dynamic vision common in his writing) he unfolds the path that the foreigner would have to travel on his trip—the same one President Sarmiento had planned to follow with his retinue—from the port landing to the city of Córdoba: *the river* (Paraná), the communication route for commerce; *Rosario*, the new, progressive city in the greatest area of agrarian colonization initiatives; *the pampa,* plains either left uncultivated or turned over to the "barbarism" of cattle-raising (which was, is, and always will be Sarmiento's obsession); and on to the arrival at the Spanish and colonial city of *Córdoba.*

A sarcastic humor characteristic of Sarmiento is at work beneath the seemingly superficial but ponderous line of reasoning: "It is the true jewel of the Republic." He starts out in a positive direction but suddenly turns to the petrification of colonial life, left in a state impermeable to change. Shadow (pampa, Córdoba) and light (river, Rosario) share this dual description which presents the opposition "civilization/barbarism" only to unify the oppositions at the pole of progress. Here, in the space of that duality, he can exercise his own will so as to resolve the oppositions in a future of wealth: to be transformed, then, are the pampa for colonization and the archaic city for industrial development.

In his desire to hasten a utopian future, what Sarmiento really does is to imagine a time to come which, as president, he will soon see when he goes to inaugurate the exposition. En route to Córdoba, he unfolds his utopian vision, which he believes to be already close at hand:

> We have decreed the abolition of the pampa. We are at the starting point of a revolution that will make North Americans of us and will dethrone the farmer who fosters the rise of the gaucho and the *monta-nera*. A new society, a new nation is going to be constituted, leaving the dead to bury their dead. The pampa is an immense sheet of paper upon which a poem of prosperity and culture will be inscribed.
>
> We have land to provide homes for those who have nothing. We will improve the social conditions of the great majority and enter into the Republic's reality by way of education and well-being, so that those left unprotected by inheritance may come to see the government and fatherland as their own. [Belín, *Sarmiento anecdótico*, p. 203]

The redistribution of land back to those who labor on it was the plan Sarmiento had proposed at the outset of his presidency. Thus, upon arriving home from the United States, before he took office, he exalted land reform in a speech at Chivilcoy, where he promised to found "a hundred Chivilcoys." There, two years earlier (1857), he had accomplished his plan on a small scale, and even after he saw his colossal plans sharply reduced, that farming town locked within the cattle-raising flatlands was still an example and an emblem of glory.[4]

Years later, when Sarmiento witnessed the ascending figure of General Julio Roca, intent on dominating Argentine politics, and chose to oppose him, he resumed his hitherto failed efforts at "civilizing" Córdoba. This is the epoch of the articles gathered in vol. 48 of his works under the title "La escuela ultra pampeana" ("The Ultra-Pampean School"); various essays refer to Córdoba and its clericalism.

This brings us to Sarmiento's essay "Setenta años después. La Pompeya americana, por el autor de *Civilización y barbarie*" ("Seventy Years Later: The American Pompeii, by the Author of *Civilization and Barbarism*," *Obras*, 48:238–244). The title and byline already reveal the pitch Sarmiento has set for himself, corresponding to chapter 7 of *Facundo*. What is most interesting in this essay is its double system of enunciation. The first system takes its material from a text by Ernest Renan about his birthplace, Treguier, and is cited in extenso; the second is a three-tiered text ("paliers"), one included within the next like a game of Chinese boxes,

wherein the voice is passed from one narrator to another. Before discussing this second system, we should note the modes of textual transition
between Renan and Sarmiento. These mark out the passage from one
narrator to the other and are designed not to go unnoticed by the reader.
At the same time, the link between narrator and narratee (I–you) is
strengthened with an inclusive "we," which seeks to capture the reader's
complicity. Sarmiento begins by quoting Renan: "In a few years the city
came to be what it had been three centuries before, an *entirely ecclesiastical city*, foreign to commerce and to *industry*, a vast *monastery* where
not a single sound could penetrate from outside" (Renan, *Souvenirs
d'enfance et de jeunesse;* the emphasis is Sarmiento's). After identifying
the bibliographic source, he begins a new paragraph:

> It will be no secret to the reader that we come to a description of
> Córdoba, offered forty years ago via the memories of a young writer
> in Chile, whose visit left him stunned by such monastic greatness, so
> many towers, so many churches, monks and priests whom he saw
> gathered in the cathedral on May 25, 1820, listening to the famous
> preacher Fray Cayetano Rodríguez strike out from the pulpit against
> the tyrant [Juan Bautista] Bustos, who occupied the viceregal throne.
> Children and madmen speak truths. Let us hear the madman or child
> in 1843 [*sic*] tell his impressions of Córdoba in 1820. [*Obras*, 48:240–
> 241][5]

Each part of the text, each of the Chinese boxes, recalls a stage of Sarmiento's writing in different moments of his career. Henceforth an author-
narrator-character unfolds and is shown in different times and life
circumstances, but always in the space of the interior city. It is the
adolescent from San Juan who for the first time (1820 or 1821?) discovers
monastic Córdoba, succintly relived by the Buenos Aires publicist of 1883;
then the voice suddenly passes—recopied—to the writer formed in dramatic moments of Chilean exile, echoing the famous fragment in the *Facundo* (see note 1, below). Later in the text the voice will become that of
the President of the Republic, proposing in 1870 to transform the country
with an industrial exposition inaugurated in Córdoba, and will be accompanied by picturesque anecdotes. Yet this voice is given as it is remembered in 1883, by the ex-president, Sarmiento, now displaced from political power. This voice will belong to that same ex-president who lucidly
judges, from the plains, the slim scope of his reforms in Córdoba. But he
goes on fighting anyway, firing from above at the programs of President
Roca and at Miguel Juárez Celman, who now appears on the scene as a
future presidential candidate. He also continues to counter the clerics,
confronting them in his role as a partisan of lay education.

Both voices, those of Renan and Sarmiento, in themselves a combination of various Sarmientos, weave a fascinating textual dialogue. I use *fascinating* in its double sense of description and evaluation. Not only are they rich in literary terms, they are also consciously active. Under their apparent multiplicity of subjects, circumstances, places, epochs, and tones, these two voices send out the same image to one another like mirrors set face to face, so as to *hypnotize* the reader. This is a peculiar sort of hypnosis because, although it beguiles the reader with emotion and imagination, it also appeals through reason (albeit a reasoning that is constantly led along a path marked out by the speaker). It is not an attempt simply to dominate the reader by arbitrary means, but to dominate by forced conviction; Sarmiento undoubtedly has faith in the path he has chosen, and even when he takes human limitations into account, he holds to faith in man, so long as that man is prepared through education to strengthen his capacity for judgment. It is *fascinating* for the reader of that time, who becomes trapped by this play of voices; it is *fascinating* for the modern reader, at least for the author of these pages, who is allowed the privilege of critical distance and who, not without a certain awe, evaluates the spectacular discursive strategy that Sarmiento's work reveals.

After copying the fragment dedicated to Córdoba in *Facundo* ("ten crosses followed by cupulas and towers of the many temples decorating this Pompeii of medieval Spain"),[6] Sarmiento goes on to inquire about the effect produced by the juxtaposition of the quote by Renan—then a writer of universal prestige—with his own:

> Which seems to you, curious reader, the more exact and graphic of the two preceding descriptions of Córdoba? Let us keep to the first. Its philosophy is more profound. However, there is a single notable difference between the two, and it is that the first was confected by Ernest Renan from his homeland in Treguier, today a dark city of Brittany, and *previously a nest of convents*, while the other is genuinely from Córdoba, crafted and engraved some forty years ago. . . . Neither did Renan plagiarize Sarmiento, although he wrote forty years later, nor did Sarmiento plagiarize Renan. . . . I have given considerable thought to the comparison of these two descriptions of convent cities and the effects that their walls, cloisters, towers, and bells produce on successive generations. There is Córdoba. Nothing has changed materially except that now it has a *daily* paper, providing us *daily* with information about the life of the saint of the day, the nunship being celebrated, the holy novena in progress, and the indulgences earned from some practical prayer or image. [Emphasis Sarmiento's; *Obras*, 48:243–244]

Forty years have passed between 1843 and 1883. By now, Sarmiento has received Valentín Alsina's corrections to the *Facundo*, concerning the number of cupulas, churches, and crosses in Córdoba and regarding the university, along with commentary on Córdoba's participation in the campaigns for independence and in the life of the Republic. In his dedication and notes to the second edition, Sarmiento openly recognizes his own roguishly exaggerated strategic archaizing, but he refuses to correct such passages, not wanting to destroy the literary effect of the text.[7] Indeed, on this occasion, he repeats the same things and emphasizes even more the negative qualities of the city's backwardness and clericalism.

What situation so exasperated him? Sarmiento was agitated by the politics of Roca, as linked to the emerging candidacy of Juárez Celman; he bristled at the bitter fights between partisans of religious and lay education. These concerns are reflected throughout the "The Ultra-Pampean School" section.[8] The texts gathered there vary in tone. As an anticlimax to his grandiose project for renewal, Sarmiento collects the frustrating and comic anecdotes of his presidential visit to Córdoba during the time of the industrial exposition—for example, "requests for favors" (a small sum for a young woman, trained as a teacher, to help her enter a nunnery as a servant; another, from the Brotherhood of the Third Order of the Rosary, to replace their little statue of the Virgin with a bigger one, so as to outdo the larger Virgin belonging to the Second Order); streetfights between native Catholics and a Protestant foreigner.[9] At the other extreme, despite how severely the disheartening results depress him, he cannot help recalling, with a blend of nostalgia and fascination, moments when he dreamed of renewal through industry and culture:

> He went, instead, to visit the irrigation developments introduced in the mountains by the engineer Arguelles; he inaugurated, albeit in vain, a railroad to La Calera, for exporting raw materials; and he climbed Los Altos to welcome the astronomer [Benjamin A.] Gould, who already enriched the sciences with his *Uranometría*. . . . What beautiful things were said when those two workers shook hands, having met before when neither had a position corresponding to his intellect, and now found themselves capable of rendering some small good deed for the Republic! [*Obras*, 48:253]

(Note this new strategy of putting an internationally renowned scientist, who had been honored in London for his work, on the same level with the president of a "mere" South American republic.)

He is not, however, so deluded by grandeur, and he denounces the fact that the upper classes who govern the province will not spend for the primary education of the poor (p. 247); he even points to the fact that the ridiculous sacristy battle over big and little icons hid, as he later ascertained, an ethnic and social difference:

They were undoubtedly embarrassed to tell the president that the question of church statuary disguised issues of race, of nobles and peasants, of whites and blacks or *mulatos*. . . . In the end, color disappears; the *mulata* of Córdoba is eclipsed; and equality is established through civic customs. . . . In 1882 [*sic*], the craftsmen of Córdoba, the former civilians who allied with General [José María] Paz to spill their blood for freedom from the dominion that the powers of superstition and ignorance created at the dawn of the Confederation, thus blocking the formation of the Republic, now vainly invoke President Sarmiento's protection so that he might ensure their dignity as men and citizens; and in 1883 [*sic*] [10] they are still lamenting with Mr. [Andrés] Lamas about the impious monstrosity of certain communities of friars for keeping both a *mulata* and a noble Virgin, and for calling the craftsmen and townspeople to this very day members of the Brotherhood of Blacks, thus humiliating and debasing them by the same cult which they claim came to bring equality to all men on earth. . . . For the old Cordovan is still a true Brother of the Third Order of the Rosary, a true Catholic of the Middle Ages, isolated in his barracks and listening to the bells of the twenty churches and convents that he has heard since the cradle; nothing has changed except that he is offended because his Virgin is smaller than the Virgin of nobles and, as he himself proclaims, because the former, the *mulata* Virgin, is the Virgin of tradition, although *mulatos* as a race have disappeared. If the Virgin were the same size as the other one, well then alright. But if his people were ever to get public attention, they would demand that she be made larger than the other! What glory! What vengeance! And we would say: that is Córdoba, the fossil of old Christianity which has remained like a thing forgotten in the middle of the pampa, like the old Frenchman in *Low Canada* [Sarmiento's emphasis], who still receives no new impressions from outside despite railroads, expositions, telegraphs. . . . They will sink or they will extinguish their clamoring voices in the grave! [*Obras*, 48:254, 256–257]

Much has been said about the inconsistencies and contradictions of Sarmiento during his lifetime. For my part, I have discussed in another essay the changes that develop within a single book (*Facundo*, between chapters 7 and 9). However, by comparing the various texts written from 1845 until 1883 (and I could even extend my reading to 1886), what draws one's attention are certain central points: the reappearance of such a consistent image of Córdoba, for example. Sarmiento always votes for progress, for industrial and commercial development. This is tied to his promotion of an immigrant work force, an educational system that reaches the most underprivileged classes, and an agrarian policy opposed to cattle-raising, which he considers a force of barbarism. Undoubtedly all of this takes place in accordance with the belief of the times—that one must provide education and encourage agrarian and industrial development in order to get people to raise themselves up by their work and by their personal inclination to pursue ownership of property and happiness.

Another side to this plan is that Sarmiento's faith in education and progress would mislead him, that the distribution of land at modest prices to the farmers who had cultivated it would yield hardly any results. His land distribution plan foundered when confronted with the cattle-raising elite (who controlled the land) and with the land speculation and distribution organized by the Roca government after the "Conquest of the Desert."

Noël Salomon and Noé Jitrik have read *Facundo* as the secret defense of rural areas against Buenos Aires; for them, the text must be deciphered as a palimpsest.[11] I am not so convinced. For Sarmiento, there is always a good and a bad interior, just as there is always a good and a bad Buenos Aires. There are inland cities and provinces that are good when they support progress according to the plans of the liberal bourgeoisie. Sarmiento identifies these in San Juan del Carril, or with Tucumán or Mendoza, when they introduce the cultivation of sugar, mulberries, indigo, grapes, and so on, and also in Córdoba de Paz, supported by craftsmen and civil servants. There is also the provincial backland that is bad when it is dominated by *caudillos* who betray the masses and by federalist elites who want to utilize caudillos to secure their power, or when the interior stagnates in its backward colonial inheritance.

There is also the Buenos Aires that is good so long as it embraces those ideals of progress, fostering them in the provinces, like the Buenos Aires of President Bernardino Rivadavia, who proposed to nationalize the income of the port. But there is also the Buenos Aires that is bad when it gives in to Rosas and to the cattle-raising elites, when it is concerned only with its own gain and monopolizes the income of foreign commerce, denying the provinces the same benefits it obtains from them. Somewhat later, it is also bad when it resists President Sarmiento's innovations, calling them utopian or insane. But for Sarmiento, who believes in possibilities of development modeled on Europe—and, even more so, modeled on North America—who has faith in the liberal bourgeoisie of the city, Buenos Aires is the port opening onto the exchange of merchandise and ideas, the center of greatest cultural destiny in the country, and of the greatest power to produce what he calls a "revolution" destined to change traditional mentalities. Whether the city always fulfills its role or misrepresents it is, again, another matter.

I will not speak now of the accomplishments and failures of Sarmiento's projects, for this is not a historical study; but I will suggest some lines that should be followed in order to understand the phenomenon of Sarmiento as well as the persistence of his image as a subject of scandal or as a magnet of devotion. His is never an indifferent text, always a text of forceful presence for the Argentine reader, and it is one that ought to live in the memories of Americans and Spaniards for what he says and how he says it.

One reason for this is his prose, in which we Argentines speak for the first time with our own authentic voice, as Juan María Gutiérrez pointed out in his review of *Facundo*: "it is written as they speak in America" (*Facundo*, Palcos ed., p. 324). It is written with the widest, most inclusive register of the many voices of our people. His discourse unfolds a fan of possibilities, whose wealth is inexhaustible—humor and indignation; a rhetorical skill of the highest quality; a strategy used to argue and convince, to register the terse language of statistics, to narrate vividly and with compassion, or to synthesize in a phrase an idea or a world of cultural allusions; at times, intimate in his public writing and passionate in his private correspondence.

Another reason is that his discourse creates men who are symbols, yet who seem to be of flesh and blood, enlarging them to mythic proportions while denuding them in their trivialities. Furthermore, no Argentine writer of his time—except José Hernández—has stood like Sarmiento alongside the underprivileged (and here I am not referring to the famous portraits of the gaucho trailblazer and tracker). It has been said of Sarmiento (and he himself said it in special circumstances) that it did not matter to him if Indians and gauchos died in bringing an end to what he called "barbarism" and in gaining "civilization" for his country. But when as president he received an Indian who was to be his servant, according to the rules of property distribution in those times—something done by all politicians, military officers, and civil servants—he taught that Indian to read and write along with an illiterate, immigrant employee, something done by none of the politicians of that era. And he would tell the story of Juan Chipaco, the Indian who shamed José Posse with his sense of personal dignity,[12] or the story of the Indian who denounced the Third Order of the Rosary of Córdoba for its humiliation of mulattoes, thus revealing the social and cultural reasons that kept them from recognizing their own subjugation and finding their liberation.

We know that this same writer did not understand or expose with clarity in *Facundo* the economic reasons for the endurance of the colonial structure that privileged the port of Buenos Aires, encouraged provincial alliance with the coast, and led to the development of caudillo leaders (and that previously had privileged the position of Francia in Paraguay and Artigas in Uruguay). Still, Sarmiento was able to perceive in statistical evidence (albeit very primitive) the history of the decline of cities named in the *Facundo;* and, later, in the case of Córdoba, he employed numerical argumentation drawn from the census to prove its underdevelopment. Such historical research allows him to recall data from the census of 1869: Córdoba, with a total population of more than 26,000 families, has only 2,738 who live in houses with solid roofs; the rest have straw roofs and "represent life in the jungle," since "the form and material of the building indicate either the poverty of its inhabitants or the underdevelopment of culture." Worse yet, he stresses in his commentary, are the 6,000 families who have no house of any kind, "which proves that they are attached to other families, as servants, relatives, or maids" (*Obras,* 48:260). This X-ray picture of poverty was hardly common among politicians and writers of his day, and it is fitting to conclude here with Sarmiento's 1883 text on the Argentine reality, which still holds bitterly true.

Notes

1. In another essay, I have discussed the transformations throughout *Facundo* that are revealed by the Buenos Aires/Córdoba duality. There I tried to explain the system that the major duality constitutes in conjunction with other sets of oppositions as well as the play of its constants at each stage of Sarmiento's work. See "En torno al *Facundo* de Sarmiento: Buenos Aires vs. Córdoba," in *Homenaje a Alonso Vicente* (Madrid: forthcoming).

2. The exposition was convoked by the Executive Assembly. It was given legal sanction on July 28, 1869, and was inaugurated in October 1879.

3. See Augusto Belín Sarmiento, *Sarmiento anecdótico (Ensayo biográfico),* the definitive edition corrected and expanded (Saint-Cloud: Imprenta P. Belín, 1929), pp. 200–208. Belín does not clarify who Sarmiento's interlocutor is, nor how he transcribed the dialogue. In the prologue "Al lector" (To the Reader), pp. xiii–xvii, Belín explains that in general he relied on authentic anecdotes, either having been witness to the events or keeping in line with his grandfather's temperament. Some commentators have assumed that Córdoba was chosen as the exposition's headquarters in order to promote the candidacy of Andrés Avellaneda as president, to which end Sarmiento gathered a group of provincial governors. (J. Guillermo Guerra, *Sarmiento, su vida y sus obras,* 2nd ed. [Santiago de Chile: Imprenta Universitaria, 1938], p. 238, suggests the idea.) Perhaps one must look for motives in Sarmiento's own position as president (at a time when he was checked by the "mitristas," a typical group from Buenos Aires, favorable to a politics that would give more weight to the inland provinces without causing any harm to the interests of the capital). Furthermore, it is not certain that Sarmiento was a de-

clared partisan of Avellaneda or that he tipped his hat in Avellaneda's behalf during the election.

4. In *El Nacional* Sarmiento defended the project of occupying public lands and thus obtained the sanction of a law that authorized the sale of 100 leagues on August 6, 1857, and, on October 16 of the same year, the "separation of public lands from the party of Chivilcoy" in the legislature of Buenos Aires (see Guerra, *Sarmiento*, p. 162). His true program included the possession of the land, housing, and school: "they have not been duped by electing me president, and I promise to make *one hundred Chivilcoys* in the six years of my presidency and with land for every head of household, with schools for the children" ("Discurso pronunciado en Chivilcoy en una fiesta dedicada al presidente electo el 3 de octubre de 1868," *Obras*, 21:258–267, esp. 266). See also pp. 60–76 of the same volume and, in vol. 22, "Rosario de Santa Fe. Discurso pronunciado en la inauguración del Hospital de la Caridad, 25 de noviembre de 1883," where he returns to his colonizing projects (pp. 201–209). There Sarmiento recalls having said that he "will make one hundred Chilvilcoy [*sic*]," and he continues: "the province of Santa Fe has made seventy colonies for me, and another thirty are [located] throughout all the other territories" (p. 203). Except for the *Facundo* (see note 6, below), all my citations of Sarmiento's texts are from *Obras de D. F. Sarmiento*, published under the auspices of the Argentine government, vols. 1–53, 1885–1903, with varied place and publisher, initiated in Santiago de Chile, Imprenta Gutenberg, under the direction of Luis Montt and continued by Sarmiento's grandson Belín. Spellings are modernized. On immigration, see Ezequiel Gallo, *La pampa gringa. La colonización agrícola en Santa Fe (1870–1895)* (Buenos Aires: Sudamericana, 1983) and Natalio R. Botana, *La tradición republicana* (Buenos Aires: Sudamericana, 1984).

5. Sarmiento frequently makes factual errors when writing at length. *Facundo* was written and published in 1845; as for the first childhood trip to Córdoba, it is uncertain whether he made it in 1820 or in 1821.

6. In reality, in chapter 7 of the *Facundo*, Sarmiento had written and underscored an audacious inversion: "de la media edad" ["edad media" is the standard Spanish word order for Middle Ages, while "media edad" would mean "middle-aged"—TR.]. I am using the critically documented edition with a prologue by Alberto Palcos (La Plata: Universidad Nacional de La Plata, 1938), p. 126. In the article commented on, nevertheless, Sarmiento reintroduces the surprising wordplay at the end: "sigue labrando las entrañas de aquella Iglesia de la media edad" ("it continues to stir the entrails of that middle-aged Church" [*Obras*, 48:255]).

7. In the Palcos edition (note 6, above) see "Notas de Valentín Alsina al libro *Civilización y barbarie*," pp. 364–426; the dedication "A Valentín Alsina" from the second edition, pp. 23–27; and the few corrections that Sarmiento accepted in the description of the city, in "Córdoba," pp. 122–128.

8. On the occasion of his resignation as minister of the interior for Presi-

dent Nicolás Avellaneda, announced before the legislature on October 6, 1879, Sarmiento read a telegram from Córdoba's Governor Antonio del Viso to Miguel Juárez Celman, about the need to denounce Sarmiento for his stand against *roquismo*. In September 1883, he left the editorial board of *El Nacional* because its editor disapproved of his hostile allusion to Juárez Celman, who already had surfaced as a possible successor to Roca (Guerra, *Sarmiento*, pp. 267–278).

9. For these incidents, see the following articles in *El Nacional*: "Córdoba intelectual," February 28, 1883 (*Obras*, 48:205–208); "Córdoba con clérigos, tres siglos de ignorancia; por Sarmiento, diez años de mejoras, 1873–1883," March 6, 1883 (48:219–221); "Setenta años después. La Pompeya americana, por el autor de *Civilización y barbarie*," n.d. (48:238–244); and "Importación de jesuitas," April 17, 1883 (48:273–276).

10. There are errors in the author's memory here: the craftsmen of Córdoba visited him in 1870 (the year of the exposition), not in 1882, and they wrote a letter to Lamas dated September 30, 1882, not 1883 (published in *Obras*, 48:255–256).

11. See Noé Jitrik, *Muerte y resurrección de "Facundo"* (Buenos Aires: CEAL, 1968) and Noël Salomon, *Realidad, ideología y literatura en el "Facundo" de D. F. Sarmiento* (Amsterdam: Rodopi, 1984).

12. See "El indio Juan Chipaco. Escenas en Tucumán" (*Obras*, 42:346–354), published in *El Censor*, August 10, 1886. For Sarmiento's position regarding the popular classes and cities, see Luis Alberto Romero's "Sarmiento, testigo y testimonio de la sociedad de Santiago," *Revista Iberoamericana* 54, no. 143 (April–June 1988): 461–475.

4 Rereading *Viajes:* Race, Identity, and National Destiny

WILLIAM H. KATRA

Perhaps the most engaging reading of the last section of *Viajes por Europa, Africa y América* (1849), which treats Sarmiento's short 1847 trip to the United States, is that which focuses on the writer's values and perspectives, especially those applicable to the South American society of his time. This type of reading exercises the powers of extrapolation, because one has to go beyond the text's surface content, which consists of a delightful but nevertheless impressionistic, idealized, subjective, and highly plagiarized view of life and society in the United States.[1] Indeed, given his poor command of the English language (in spite of the brief months he had been tutored in that language as a young man) and the brevity of the trip itself, Sarmiento was simply not in a position to offer an authoritative account of the subject he had set out to write about: in the short span of six weeks he raced through twenty-one states and most of the major cities of the East, even finding time for a brief excursion to Montreal. Borrowing from the formula articulated by Julio Cortázar, the contemporary reader therefore finds more interest in Sarmiento's process of seeing, rather than in what he actually saw or attempted to see. Yet this requires more than armchair speculation or the vision of the psychiatrist's couch. It also requires a familiarity with the total scope of Sarmiento's views and actions, for many passages of this text exemplify the expression "His silences speak more loudly than his words."

If the act of writing was a rhetorical exercise for Sarmiento, the composition of the last part of *Viajes* was especially so. I use the word "rhetorical" in reference to the intention of causing a calculated effect in the reader by means of stylistic artifices and the calculated presentation of certain themes. The theorist J. L. Austin used the term "performative" to describe this type of composition which has for its goal the alteration of reality rather than the description of it. This contrasts with a writing practice that is "constative," that is, one for which there is an attempt to make all its parts faithful to an internal logic and, consequently, to achieve a general coherence in the textual weave of arguments presented.[2]

In the course of this essay I will explore several aspects of Sarmiento's "performative" writing. The first focus has to do with the importance Sarmiento held for these writings as political propaganda. Even more than the epistolary "pretense" of the text (he undoubtedly had from the beginning an intention to publish these long, descriptive letters written about his two-year excursion),[3] I am referring to his wish to promote a desirable image of himself before the liberal intelligentsia who, within a few years, were destined to occupy the positions of public authority in Buenos Aires. Sarmiento already realized his own tremendous capacity for public service. In an article published within a month of the publication of *Viajes*, he criticized what he considered to be the great failures of the Rosas regime and delineated in detail the program of action that he would promote if he were president of Argentina. The struggle between Sarmiento and Rosas, he wrote, was "una lucha de titanes."[4] That is to say, this article, just like his travel commentaries—and, to an even greater extent, like *Recuerdos de provincia* (1850) a few months hence—invites readings that interpret content in the light of the political options then available. In *Viajes* Sarmiento had a clear objective—to present a humanized image of himself—for he probably wanted to avoid the controversies that inevitably would have erupted had he explained in detail the more radical side of his thinking.

However valid the image of a crafty writer ever calculating the impact of his words, it must be paired with a different, but not incompatible, image of a writer truly enraptured over what he has seen, one who bubbles forth a vision of rarefied optimism. In truth, the trip to the United States constituted for Sarmiento a quasi-religious experience. His previous illusions about an exalted "civilization" had been thoroughly shaken after viewing close-up the abject misery of Europe's general population, who nevertheless lived within a stone's throw of salons whose artistic and intellectual brilliance had no rival. But men such as Sarmiento, men who thrive on action oriented toward the future, cannot long exist with their *sistema magna* in crisis. Even had he not found in the United States the grand hotels, buildings, and canals worthy of his exuberant hyperboles, he would have invented them. In short, his abstract idea of civilization fortuitously found a new, more deserving model, and its prophet was able to take out a new lease on life. From start to finish Sarmiento was predisposed to embellish what he saw, for this New World vision provided a

new justification for his class, and revitalized directions for his own energies. This intellectual intoxication was still in force at the trip's end when,
on a steamer bound for the Caribbean and then South America, he finally
found the time to write about his experiences and observations. Almost
every passage of these commentaries implicitly points to his approaching
return to South American society. For these—and surely other—reasons,
Sarmiento's travel commentaries about the United States could not, and
do not, represent faithfully some of his strongest convictions.[5]

An example of Sarmiento's contradictory representation of his own
ideas occurs in the passages treating the different races in the United States.
In the text of *Viajes* we read Sarmiento's attempt to include himself with
that distinguished group of world citizens who were situated at the highest stage of moral consciousness because they considered no human being,
however different his skin color, as a "foreigner by race" or an "enemy"
(*OC*, 5:385). In expressing this view, it is probable that Sarmiento was
attempting to demonstrate his moral "superiority" to Alexis de Tocqueville, the famous French visitor to the United States a decade and a half
earlier, whose opinions about the North American black population were
quite negative.[6] Despite the supposedly "liberal" values that Sarmiento
professed, the opinions in *Viajes* about blacks and slavery are quite vague.
Historian Michael Rockland correctly observed that Sarmiento did not
criticize the North Americans for having tolerated the practice of slavery
within their frontiers; Sarmiento only believed—and in this he followed
Tocqueville—that that peculiar institution constituted an ulcer which would
grow to disturbing dimensions.[7]

In other texts written in more or less the same period, however, Sarmiento demonstrated greater generosity toward the black race. In the biography, *El General Fray Félix Aldao* (1845), he praised the Negro Bar-
cala for having been one of the most distinguished leaders in the struggle
for independence from Spain a generation before. In an earlier chapter of
Viajes, he called attention to the positive moral characteristics of the blacks
and mulattoes he had observed in Rio de Janeiro, and stressed their "ed-
ucability" (*OC*, 5:60). But despite this favorable judgment, there is much
to suggest that Sarmiento, beneath the veneer of his liberalism, still remained vaguely faithful to some of the values of colonial society. In *Recuerdos de provincia* he states: "¡Costumbres patriarcales de aquellos
tiempos, en que la esclavitud no envilecía las buenas cualidades del fiel
negro!"[8] It is true that Sarmiento rationally accepted many ideas of the
Enlightenment, and he surely believed that any form of slavery degraded
man and society. Still—as Adolfo Prieto explains—"El Sarmiento evoca-
dor se ha arrojado a la infancia como a un estanque, y trae a la superficie

profundas aguas de extraño, alquitarado sabor."[9] That is to say, vague attitudes and values learned during one's most formative years sometimes make themselves present despite a person's sincerely held intellectual baggage.

And what are Sarmiento's opinions with regard to the other races inhabiting the American continent? In *Viajes* Sarmiento is respectfully silent about the American Indians. During his trip, his scarcity of funds did not allow him to visit any region with a significant population of indigenous people. Regardless, his opinions about them generally followed the lead and the tone of Tocqueville's studied comments. For example, Sarmiento wrote the following passage about South American Indian people some four years before his trip to the United States. It copies almost word for word the opinionated view of his French mentor:[10]

> We must be just with the Spaniards; by exterminating a savage people whose territory they were going to occupy, they simply did what all civilized peoples do to savages, which the colony deliberately or not did with the indigenous peoples it absorbed, destroyed, exterminated. If this terrible procedure of civilization is barbaric and cruel to the eyes of justice and reason, it is, like war itself, like conquest, one of the ways Providence has armed diverse human races, and among these the most powerful and advanced, to replace those who, by their organic weakness or backwardness in civilization's path, cannot achieve the great destinies of man on earth. [*OC*, 2:217–218]

This passage reveals the opinions held by Sarmiento since his childhood concerning the biological inferiority of the American Indians. Furthermore, these words would require little if any alteration if we wished to use them for describing his views about the Indian's *mestizo* descendants.[11] For example, in *De la educación popular* (1849), his work most noted for its enlightened promise of instruction (and therefore progress) for the masses of his continent, Sarmiento excludes the Indian on account of his "ineducability" (*OC*, 11:212), just as he excludes people of mixed blood, who are "incapable or inadequate for civilization" (11:38). Toward the end of his life he published *Conflictos y armonías de las razas en América* (1883), an unfortunate attempt to document, through the doubtful application of scientific ideas, that the backwardness of his continent was in large part owing to the inferior genetic composition of that continent's majority population of Indians and mestizos.

As such, Sarmiento's opinions in *Viajes* about people of African descent in the United States are ambiguous, and the absence of any discussion about the Indian (or the mestizo) masks his strong racial prejudices.

Whereas some commentators (Manuel Gálvez and Carlos Octavio Bunge, for example) have proposed that this is an indication of Sarmiento's "antiliberal" attitude, I believe it is more correct to see the conservative position of Sarmiento as, paradoxically, an outgrowth of one aspect of his liberal persuasion when it is followed to an extreme. This can be convincingly seen in the long quote above, in which Sarmiento explains that the predominantly white population in western United States was a historical result of people exercising the right of *free movement;* he argues that the modern culture of this new population made impossible the survival of indigenous groups and their traditional cultures. Therefore, Sarmiento's liberalism combined handily with aspects of social Darwinism. According to this hybrid theory, the world could be compared to a gigantic free market of people, in which those groups with less-developed cultural values would disappear when confronted by a new society of men who could efficiently exploit the resources of the land, build factories, and busy themselves in the commerce of material possessions.

A similar argument then colored his opinions about nationality and territorial rights. Since his youth Sarmiento had been witness to a social conflict in his country between two groups: on the one hand, there was the *criollo* element, owners of immense extensions of land and heirs to the feudal traditions and now archaic values that had thrived during the colony; on the other hand, there was the European or Europeanized element, educated and progressive, that strove to develop the industrial and commercial potential of the region. According to Sarmiento's schematic generalizations, the first group came to be defined as the defenders of retrograde "Americanism," or barbarism; the second group came to be associated with progress, internationalism, and civilization. This conceptual opposition, which from the distance of a century and a half seems to us simplistic and even harmful, constituted the foundation upon which Sarmiento based his social projects and actions. One can now understand Sarmiento's support, before 1852, for the petition by the constitutional Chilean government (despite its authoritarian character) to rule the southernmost regions of Patagonia, in opposition to a similar petition by the "barbarian" Juan Manuel de Rosas in Argentina. His distorted world vision also explains in large part the dogmatic support that he almost always demonstrated for "foreign," European, international, and liberal interests. On this basis one can also explain his blindness to many local demands or needs. In that period, had Sarmiento declared his "homeland" to be the community of international and liberal interests, he would have denied his obligation to any given extension of land simply because it was the nation-state of his birth. Of course, these views would be modified in later years, when he and his generation of militants occupied the positions of leadership in Argentine society.

This attitude explains in great part the support shown by Sarmiento for the intrusions of the European powers in American lands. A similar case was the Mexican-American War, which was quickly approaching its end at the time of Sarmiento's travels. Rockland calls attention to the fact that Sarmiento did not criticize the U.S. government, whose territorial ambitions were the obvious cause of that war; Rockland correctly states that Sarmiento implicitly "supported" the thesis of the United States' "manifest destiny" in waging its war against weaker neighbors to the south.[12] Sarmiento would have believed the same things about U.S. pretensions in Mexico as he had expressed a few months earlier about French rights in North Africa (OC, 5:208). Providence, he believed, was a liberal goddess who supported the actions of those Anglo-European powers which hoped to dominate the world and instruct local populations everywhere about the possible benefits of progress. It was through his radically liberal convictions that Sarmiento came to affirm implicitly an imperialist doctrine; he was convinced that the historical advance of Argentina would be promoted best by uniting its destiny to Europe's capitalist expansion.

Sarmiento's Contradictory Liberal Values

It is appropriate to signal here that Sarmiento's distinction between European and Latin or Hispanic American priorities was characteristic of the period.[13] It was product of a century when the commercial and military influence of the European countries had spread to every continent. A similar situation existed in relation to ideas: thinkers of almost all ideological tendencies shared a similar vision of European societies as the culmination of a universal historical process. Inherent in this Eurocentric perspective was the notion that non-European beings and societies were inferior. One can see this system of differentiations in the thought of John Stuart Mill; it is present even in the ideas of Karl Marx when it came to applying his conceptions of liberty or revolution to Asiatic societies or to India.

It is not surprising, then, that Sarmiento, as a faithful disciple of the most advanced tendencies of European thought, internalized a similar perspective of discriminations that accepted European or Anglo-Saxon culture as the privileged norm. This is particularly evident in relation to his ideas about liberty. In his travel commentaries, Sarmiento offers a hymn to the liberty enjoyed by people in the United States, as demonstrated in the patterns of individual behavior that he had observed. For him, the primary accomplishment of that society was the individual having become "dueño de sí mismo" (*OC*, 5:363) in all spheres of life. This was especially evident in the totally unrestricted choice of U.S. citizens in relation to association, travel, work, and religious practice. On this issue Sarmiento's enthusiasm knew no bounds; the theme of universally enjoyed liberty becomes elevated to the status of a leitmotiv that reappears throughout these commentaries.

The informed reader will know about the ambiguous attitude of Sarmiento in regard to liberty, as he manifested throughout his life in both acts and writings. In other works, this takes the form of a profound contradiction in his advocacy, as I demonstrate elsewhere.[14] On the one hand, when Sarmiento presented himself as a utopian liberal and heir to the values and persuasions of the Enlightenment, liberty is praised. On the other hand, when Sarmiento wrote or talked as a positivist (or prepositivist), he criticized the excess of liberty in the aftermath of the French Revolution and in what for him was the corresponding period of Argentine history, the May Revolution. According to this latter perspective, the *bateau-ivre* of liberty became transformed into anarchy, a state of affairs that later invited civil war in both countries, France and Argentina. His ideals for the organization of any future society were therefore tempered by the overriding need for social stability. The word "liberal" in this context did not refer to the promotion of democracy or equality—in the short run, at least. Instead, it referred more to the constitutional principles upon which the state and the economy were to be organized. Specifically, these pointed to the need for 1) a progressive authoritarian regime guided by a small, educated elite; 2) laissez-faire economic activities with an international orientation; and 3) full religious liberty.

This understood, the political program prescribed by Sarmiento and the other activists of the Generation of 1837 for the next period of the nation's history would revolve around two key concepts: less political liberty and more authority. For this reason Sarmiento, shortly after the fall of Rosas, became identified with groups or individuals that advocated a strong central government capable of directing the institutional transformation of the country according to the new ideas emanating from Europe and the United States. But such a transformation did not involve a broadening of democratic practices according to the free inclination of each citizen—not yet, at any rate. According to Sarmiento's way of thinking, the Argentine masses had already demonstrated their preference for the barbarism of Rosas. The Argentine people, unlike their counterparts in the United States, refused to follow the dictates of reason in carrying out their daily tasks and in organizing their community. In such a situation, the transformation that Sarmiento envisioned for Argentina had to be imposed from above, and at times against the public will. During the three decades following the fall of Rosas, when Sarmiento exercised public authority as governor of San Juan, auditor of war, minister and adviser under Bartolomé Mitre, and then president, he remained faithful to the type of "democracy" he had described in the pages of *Facundo*. In that work, when he addressed the issue of how to progress beyond the "barbarous" life of the *caudillo* and the institutions associated with the cattle industry, he advocated: "Customs of this type require vigorous means of repression, and to repress the soulless still more soulless judges are needed" (*OC*, 7:52). Harsh measures from an authoritarian state would be in order in the first moment. Only when peace and stability were achieved—according to this theory—could society gradually move toward democratization and political decentralization.

A similar confusion of ideas awaits the reader who, on the basis of the content of *Viajes*, tries to define the attitude of Sarmiento with regard to equality. The text at times exalts the mystified equality of U.S. society, as reflected in its "uniformity" and conformism. Most contemporary readers would be repelled by the multiple images given by Sarmiento of a people who resembled a beehive in their invariable way of dressing, laughing, and traveling, or who as hotel guests obediently pattern their activities according to "the unbearable vibration of Chinese hong-hong" (*OC*, 5:357). However, Sarmiento undoubtedly experienced authentic joy upon observing "this uniform decency . . . the monotonous uniformity" (5:351) of an entire country enjoying the advantages of material well-being and unencumbered association.

The ideas that Sarmiento expressed in other texts about the desirability of social equality are well known. Noël Salomon and Tulio Halperín Donghi have indicated that Sarmiento was never an enthusiastic defender of equality for South American societies.[15] To repeat here what has been stated earlier, Sarmiento and the other members of his generation of exiled publicists realized that the renovation they prescribed would be possible only if an educated elite were able to supplant the popular caudillos in the positions of authority at all social levels. They distrusted the masses. They were convinced that it was the attempt of the old unitarians of the previous generation to establish a kind of equality within a radically democratic political order that led to the dissolution of authority and, later, to civil war.

Armies and Schools

In Sarmiento's travel commentaries the wary reader finds in the idealization of Yankee society an implicit criticism, and at times denigration, of

South America's own institutions and social practices. Stated another way, his optimistic, utopian images are profiled against the shadowy presence of what has been termed a "demonic discourse."[16] This dialectic between the United States and Argentina is at play throughout these pages. The first of these countries was the target for all his idealizations and dreams, and the other was the object of what at times assumes the dimensions of a severe, critical realism. We have already given attention to how passages from *Viajes* badly represent Sarmiento's ambiguous ideas about liberty and equality for South American society. Or perhaps what is at issue here are the distinct reading publics to which Sarmiento addressed his different works: for a reading public with humanistic values, he wrote euphoric and idealistic words like those found in the last chapter of *Viajes;* but when he directed his words to men of property, in whose charge was entrusted the future of the nation, what became emphasized was his serious and pragmatic tone.

These two tones, discourses, or perspectives are evident in the passages Sarmiento wrote about the role of military forces in civil society. In *Viajes* he celebrates U.S. society, whose cities and towns rarely, if ever, saw the like of soldiers or a permanent army. But the situation was very different in South American countries, whose people did not enjoy such a high level of cultural development. In these less orderly societies, armed soldiers or militia many times protected the people of "society" from disorder and anarchy. He writes in *De la educación popular:* "The existence of armies is a great necessity for peoples habituated to coercion as the only stimulus of order; the infancy of governments also requires perhaps the ostentation of force" (*OC,* 11:39). The comparison between the behavior of South American societies and that of a baby is not an accident: Sarmiento was convinced that lack of civilization was a direct result of some deficiency in the educational level of a people. On account of their immaturity, the "demonic" underdeveloped societies required a type of authoritarian government that would have been offensive for more-developed ones. But the pace at which an underdeveloped society, like a baby, went about acquiring experience in the use and application of reason paralleled the progressive loss of warlike instincts and the attainment of those values conducive to greater peaceful linkages and community endeavors.

A logical extension of these arguments explains the presence of utopian and demonic discourses in the pages written by Sarmiento about the role of education in society. In a significant passage from *De la educación popular,* Sarmiento compares the role of public education to the function of the military: "the army satisfies the state's necessity of foresight; as public education satisfies another more imperative, less dispensable need" (*OC*, 11:39). According to this perspective, arms and letters both played a part in guaranteeing social stability.

What was the role of education in the advanced society? In *Viajes*, Sarmiento's words have a utopian flavor. He proposes that in the United States peace and harmony owed their existence to the high level of instruction received by the whole population. Long years of schooling guaranteed the prevalence of social practices governed by reason. In his words: "a man achieves the plenitude of his moral and intellectual development only through education" (*OC*, 5:385). With a humanist tone, Sarmiento explains the necessity of each citizen receiving instruction about "precepts, obligations, rights, and duties that can serve as rules for individuals in relation to the masses, to society" (5:383). This leads to his idealization concerning the people of the United States: "twenty million inhabitants, all educated, reading, writing, enjoying political rights . . . [I]n this sense no other country on earth has a greater number of rational beings" (5:383). Education in the North American society, then, fulfilled the humanist mission of developing the highest faculties of the intelligence. Thanks to public-school instruction, the behavior of the whole population was governed by a rational criterion. The results of each new educational conquest were considerable: the increasing liberation of the population from material scarcity and an ever-higher level of participation in society.

To Sarmiento's mind the countries of Latin America offered a clear contrast to North America with regard to the predominance of reason and, as a consequence, the role of public education in society. According to Sarmiento, every society first and foremost needed to undergo a type of moral education that would then make possible "the intelligent and active life that republicans and members of the Christian family should carry out" (*OC*, 11:39). But because the South American nations lacked this high level of education, they were plagued by disorder and social conflict. As such, it fell upon the joint efforts of the army and the school to perform the necessary task of *civilizing* the population. This word, in the context of Sarmiento's world vision, almost always carried a positivist connotation of the need for imposing *order* before a society could hope to progress. For the students of his mythicized public school, mere attendance taught them indirect lessons that were, perhaps, even more important than those they would learn from books. Sarmiento writes that a child, upon merely becoming accustomed to the daily routines of school, becomes able to "accustom the spirit to the idea of regular, continuous duty, providing him with regular habits in his actions; to add another authority to the paternal one [and] . . . to mold the spirit to the idea of an authority outside the family circle" (11:48). "Popular" education, then, added the voice of the teacher and, more indirectly, that of the state to the authority already exercised by the father of the family. Schooling, in this light, anticipated the forces of the future by combating retrograde interests and fortifying the authority of society's leaders.

The case of New York City a few decades earlier provided Sarmiento with a good example of the indispensable role of public education in a society tormented by disorder and chaos: in the midst of popular uprisings and frequent incidents of violence, "the best and cheapest police system that could be adopted" was none other than the public school (*OC*, 11:68). The lesson of the well-to-do families of New York had to be disseminated throughout South America. It is understood that they would be in favor of a school system that could help educate their own children. But Sarmiento argues that their support for a public school system was also in their interest on account of its role in inculcating in the poorer classes a respect for order and in teaching them to exercise control over their baser passions. In this way, education, for the richer classes, served as a "safety valve for their properties and lives in difficult times" (11:68). In this context one can understand the observation of Ezequiel Martínez Estrada with regard to Sarmiento's ideas on education: "Teaching was always for Sarmiento one of the ways of leading."[17]

The Adventurous Conservative

The diligent reader who attempts to compare Sarmiento's commentary about democratic institutions in the United States with that of Tocqueville has to take into account the silences of the first-mentioned text and those passages in it which distort or only partially represent the living thought of the writer. If such care is not taken, one could easily mistake the naive enthusiasm of the Argentine as an indication of his fervent defense of North American institutions; a similar error would be to interpret the criticisms of the Frenchman as an indication of serious reservations. Here, I register my disagreement with the opinion of Alberto Girri that Tocqueville and Sarmiento represent diametrically opposed opinions.[18] While it is difficult to accept Allison Williams Bunkley's claim that the French aristocrat's most memorable impression of the practice of democracy in the United States was its negative and even "threatening" nature, what seems more solid is Bunkley's observation that Sarmiento's text expresses "inspiration" and "optimism on the surface."[19] Bunkley correctly detected an interesting phenomenon in Sarmiento's text—that there was some aspect to the writer's thought that had to be covered over with an inspirational tone that was not entirely genuine. According to my own reading, the principal difference separating the travel commentaries of Sarmiento from those of Tocqueville is one of style and not substance. Tocqueville, a realist observer with social-scientific criteria, had the foremost objective of calling attention to obvious or potential dangers; this contrasts with the euphoric and calculating Sarmiento, who wanted to surprise and entertain the reader with an impressionistic text. In actual substance, there is little distance separating the two: both writers felt a deep admiration for what they saw and learned in the United States; but both, for similar reasons, hesitated to embrace the practices they observed as panaceas for their own countries. Sarmiento's reactions to life and institutions in the United States, like those of his French mentor, were those of an "adventurous conservative."[20]

It is important to situate the voyages of discovery by both these observers of democracy within a historical context. Tocqueville (1805–1859) and Sarmiento (1811–1888) were children of the revolutionary experience in their respective countries: the French Revolution beginning in 1789 and the May Revolution of 1811. The period of turbulence and social instability that followed initial euphoria coincided with the childhood and early youth of both men; the arrival of both to intellectual maturity occurred in a period of full "restoration." Both were men divided between two sets of persuasions and imperatives. On the one hand, they were fundamentally liberal and republican in their deepest convictions, but they criticized the first revolutionary generation in their respective countries for being excessively romantic and deficiently realistic. With regard to social origins, on the other hand, both Sarmiento and Tocqueville hailed from the relatively privileged strata, a fact that helps to explain their trepidation regarding the participation of the uneducated masses in society, their fear of anarchy and social instability, and their attraction to authoritarian means for organizing society. Both of them, then, were representatives of a generation whose mission was to achieve a synthesis of two tendencies: rapid institutional change according to liberal principles, and restoration. In the case of Sarmiento, whose fundamental social perspectives reveal the influence of Esteban Echeverría, Juan Bautista Alberdi, and the other militants of the Asociación de Mayo, this hybrid ideology was evident in Sarmiento's adhesion to the Saint-Simonian theories of "eclectism" and the "socialist," or prepositivist, program of social transformation. The objective of all these programs was to promote material progress and the moral elevation of the people, but without endangering the stability of an already traumatized social order.

Accordingly, Sarmiento, like Tocqueville, placed little priority on equality as a social goal, and at times even opposed it. He was convinced that in many societies the status of liberty would be endangered by too much equality among the people. This would occur if the lower classes, who were guided more by base instincts than by reason, were to challenge society's elites or overturn the social structures so laboriously constructed by those elites. This being said, Sarmiento's travel commentaries still seem to offer a defense of the vulgarization of culture in the United States and its movement toward greater conformity. The contradiction is explained by taking into account how strong social pressures there operated for the well-being of the system as a whole. In one passage Sarmiento calls attention to how public opinion expressed through the press could exercise a corrective influence on the behavior of a political dissident or a disgruntled debtor (*OC*, 5:394). He also expresses his admiration for how the Yankees peacefully resolved almost all their doctrinal or political differences: "Americans, in politics and religion, profess the admirable and conciliatory principle that one should argue only with those of one's own sect or opinion" (5:360). He appreciated the double edge of the strong social pressures that led people to conform to group norms: although detestable on account of the coercion involved, they nonetheless had the positive effect of civilizing the masses. Thus, "In the United States, civilization exerts itself over a mass so large that its refinement comes slowly, with the masses exerting influence over the individual and forcing him to adopt the habits of the majority, creating finally a kind of national taste that becomes pride and preoccupation" (5:360). There was cause for worry about the prevalence of crass social values and "hábitos de rudeza" throughout Yankee society, but there was also cause to celebrate: such uniformity, though hardly enlightened, nevertheless was the source of a social stability unknown in any other country of the West. In brief, both Tocqueville and Sarmiento derived inspiration from the North Americans, a people enamored with change but detesting revolution.

How could society's leaders guarantee that the impetus for change would not be converted into a destabilizing revolution? Sarmiento's simplistic cure is a society's exercise of periodic elections for all public officials. In his hurried itinerary he had only been able to observe firsthand a municipal election in Baltimore. But a desire to treat the topic more authoritatively than what personal observation would warrant leads him to quote extensively from a text written by the phrenologist George Combe, whose praise for the electoral system in the United States serves to reinforce the optimistic perspective of Sarmiento. The exuberance of the quoted material contrasts with the more circumspect approach of Tocqueville a decade and a half before. Tocqueville, for example, saw that elections in the United States guaranteed a tyranny of the depersonalized majority: the political system, in spite (or because) of the right to vote, perpetuated a "soft totalitarianism" in which the price for a candidate's arriving at the top was the sacrifice of individual character. Tocqueville, then, understood that the nominal exercise of democratic rights through periodic elections did not deter the progressive movement toward oppression.

Sarmiento reinforces this same conservative opinion when he describes the typical, and in great part idealized, character of the North American. The consumption-oriented Yankee was "born irrevocably proprietary," he affirms (OC, 5:371); the one-dimensional drive of the Yankee to improve his own situation left neither time nor energy for anything else. He was an "uncivil husband, though *good-natured*, sweating by day and snoring by night" (5:350), and his greatest life commitment was periodically enlarging the family dwelling so that there would be ample space for the newest members of "the wasp nest of little blond, jumpy children" (5:350). Sarmiento, like Tocqueville and Cooper, celebrated the mild-mannered Yankee, with humble aspirations and common sense, who set an example for other national groups. In short, the Yankee exemplified for Sarmiento almost all the characteristics of the ideal citizen in the democracy of his dreams: he was a sober, serious worker, whose energies were nearly consumed in the activities of working, saving, and producing; through his labor and his vote, he supported and stabilized the system that benefited him. But Sarmiento, in contrast to Tocqueville, passed over the more alarming aspects of the North American psychology: the Yankee's excessive hunger for acquisition; traumas that arose from the fear of possible failure in society or the workplace; an incessant striving to improve his lot; and the high frequency of mental problems.

In another work I explain in detail the *bricoleur* character of Sarmiento's thought,[21] for which there is no better example than his surprising opinion about the negative impact of European immigration upon U.S. society. I say surprising because, both before and after his visit to the United States, there were few people more persistent than Sarmiento in defending the role that European immigration would play in the process of colonizing and civilizing South American societies. However, when treating this issue in his travel commentaries about the United States, his arguments resemble those of the ideological bricoleur, with an underlying value or sentiment providing the only point of contact for otherwise incongruent ideas. The underlying value here seems to be—again—the necessity for order and stability in society. But in the process of affirming these values, Sarmiento apparently contradicts another idea at the heart of his lifelong program for Argentina's social and material amelioration. He states (OC, 5:397) that "European immigration is [in the United States] a barbarous element—Who could have believed it!" Immigration, instead of being the panacea for progress, becomes in the United States just one more element of barbarism. This was because those abject immigrants fleeing from European poverty were completely unschooled in the democratic practices that prevailed in municipality after municipality of that new land. Sarmiento states that the Welsh, Irish, and Germans were "undisciplined democrats . . . ignorant of North American laws and institutions, and persons without any education" (5:490). He laments the corruption that resulted from these groups being permitted to participate in and even dominate local elections: "Thus, foreigners in the U.S. are the basis of scandal and the yeast of corruption that is introduced annually into the mass of blood of that nation so anciently educated in the practices of liberty" (5:397).

Sarmiento demonstrates consistently that he supported a social system in which the material and social needs of the people would be satisfied, but not at the expense of order and decorum. He was a man of transition: democratic and elitist values alike exercised strong influence over his social and political ideas.

In this light, one should not be surprised to discover Sarmiento's fascination with the image of ancient Rome, a society that also enjoyed extensive democratic practices and an estimable level of material comfort, but under the firm control of an aristocracy. With Tocqueville he shared the tendency to offer ancient Rome as the prototype of a desirable regime for the new republics of the Americas (both men omitted from their exemplary portraits the Roman practice of slavery). He compares the magnificent public buildings of New York City with the Roman Senate (*OC*, 5:430). In reference to the wide avenues, magnificent hotels, and ambitious public works programs in the United States, he writes: "The North Americans can only be compared today to the ancient Romans. . . . The same virile superiority, the same persistence, the same strategy, the same preoccupations with a future of power and greatness" (5:386). Sarmiento also demonstrated his admiration for the highly evolved system of law and the broad participation of people on all levels of society, as he had been able to read about in Tocqueville and Cooper, and as he must have superficially observed in Boston, New York, and other cities of the East. In the comparison he makes between Rome and the United States with regard to the people's daily activities, one finds clear evidence of that fusing of democratic and authoritarian tendencies which typified Sarmiento's ideas at the time. The United States, constantly striving to improve the life of its citizens through new technological discoveries and a more just application of the law, deserved an art that was worthy of its noble aspirations. With contradictory democratic faith adulterated by an aristocratic tradition, he urged North American leaders to emulate the Romans by constructing monuments of the most durable materials available, marble and granite. It was necessary that the United States leave for posterity a permanent record of its greatness, in order to "imprint on forgetful earth the eternal path of its footprints" (5:335).

Cities and "Civilization"

In addition to the implicit aristocratic base for the democratic experience, there is another curious aspect to the comparison that Sarmiento makes between U.S. society and classical Rome. This involves the incongruence in his proposing the Roman capital as prototype for the development of the city and civilization in Argentina. What was the relevance of the classical model of urbanization for the demographic concentrations in North or South America midway into the past century? Here it is necessary to investigate the possible reasons for this dubious comparison and to hypothesize about its functions within the totality of Sarmiento's thought.

The image of the urban experience appears to undergo a significant transition in Sarmiento's thought as a result of his trip to Europe and the United States. In *Facundo* Sarmiento presents as one of his principal theses the association of the Argentine city with society's valued civil institutions. There is nothing original in this idea, since it was prevalent in the thought of several of the principal writers of the European Enlightenment, receiving perhaps its most eloquent defense in the writings of Voltaire. The idea maintained its force well into the middle decades of the nineteenth century, as witnessed by the writings of J. G. Fichte and Adam Smith.[22] The relationship existing between the city and the growth of culture seems obvious at first glance, even tautological: without a certain concentration of population, a functional community is impossible. In *Facundo* Sarmiento argues the same when he refers to Rome as the metropolitan model that enjoyed a high level of material development as well as a population educated in the practice of the arts. He proposes as a universal law that the institutions associated with "civilization" were concentrated in the city, and that this center provided the impetus for modernizing the countryside. Sarmiento somewhat simplistically contrasts the European cities of the Renaissance and the feudal period: "There was no public being during the Middle Ages, and there could not have been, because landowners lived in relative isolation" (*OC*, 7:30). Renaissance society, he argues, was able to achieve a respectable level of culture only when the center of political and military power shifted from the country-

side to the cities. It was obvious: the city was the place where one encountered workshops, stores, schools, and those institutions which had to
do with the interpretation and implementation of the law (7:27).

After his trip to the United States, this image of the urban experience
suffers a change of emphasis in his writings. In France and Prussia, Sarmiento had observed the thousands upon thousands of workers who sub-
sisted on the miserable salaries earned from arduous toil in factories and
sweatshops, and who now constituted a militant force that threatened the
very fabric of society as it then existed. This perspective was prophetic,
because the revolutionary outbreak of 1848 was only months away. It is
difficult to say which caused the more negative impact on Sarmiento: the
sight of this human misery or his intuition of its revolutionary threat.
Engraved in his mind was a contradictory image of Europe's urban centers; they were the site of both greatness and abjection, where humanity's
most sublime and miserable attributes existed side by side (*OC*, 5:92).
Upon arriving in Switzerland, toward the end of his European stay, he
was no longer in search of great monuments or dazzling artistic or intellectual products; no longer was he impressed by the glow of scientific
discoveries and the expression of new philosophical truths. Perhaps only
upon arriving at this stage of his travels was he able to understand the
changed advocacy of Guizot, France's foremost historian and at the time
its foreign minister, whom he had heard months earlier argue before the
French parliament against "progress." Sarmiento now understood that
Guizot was not opposing the forward march of civilization but only the
type of urban modernization that results in the spread of ugly industrial
plants and the subservience of the worker to the machine.

In Switzerland, however, he saw another, and this time superior, type
of development. In that country there was no abundance of great cities
and grand monuments, but only small villages with humble and poor
populations, which nevertheless enjoyed a communitarian existence that
ennobled the name of democracy (*OC*, 5:316). Consequently, the urban
experience in and by itself had already lost any claim to special status.
Sarmiento realized his previous error; he saw that the mere existence of
industries did not guarantee either a high level of culture or greater material comfort for the people in general. He realized, too, that the opposition he had so eloquently described in his previous writings—that of the
supposed civilization of the European city versus the barbarism of the
American countryside—was hardly clear and unambiguous, and that it
had perhaps little relevance for the societies in which he had lived. But
typical of Sarmiento is that instead of questioning the utility or validity

of any such schematic duality, he merely altered its content. From now on, he would defend the town or the village, and not the city, as the source and center of progress.

It is worth emphasizing that this theoretical change had occurred in Sarmiento's mind even before he arrived at the docks of New York City; similarly, the very hurried circumstances of his six-week trip in the United States could not have allowed sufficient time for him to verify whether this new conception of civilization, as centered in the small village of the United States did, in fact, conform to the existing evidence.

However, Sarmiento was hardly alone in reassessing the source and focus of human progress. His enthusiasm for the rural township or frontier village was in full accordance with the myth that thinkers from all parts of the Western world were in that moment hurrying to embrace. Sarmiento gives absolutely no indication of his being aware of the turbulent social and political transformations then occurring in U.S. public life, changes that then, as today, were associated with the Age of Jackson. He still accepted, at least implicitly, some of the mythic components of that movement. Relevant here is the importance of the image of the American West, with its emphasis on the self-made man of the frontier village, surrounded by nature. In the context of the United States at mid-century, this myth was the revitalization of an older myth, that of the Golden Age of the founding fathers. Washington and Jefferson were paragons of self-sacrifice and morality; they were worthy models of the public man who, before and after his period of public service, was an agricultural producer. But this mythic aspect of the Age of Jackson swam against the current, since the promise of a society peopled by yeoman farmers, as idealized by Jefferson, had died with the mortgage of Jefferson's own land upon his death and with the bankruptcy of thousands of other small agricultural producers in the face of the new forces of progress. It was no coincidence that this aspect of the Jacksonian myth enjoyed nostalgic popularity during a period when the large capitalist interests, headquartered in the metropolitan centers of the East, were extending their definitive hegemony over the civil institutions of the entire country.

During the period of Sarmiento's trip to the United States, the myth linking the old urban centers and the expansion of prestigious cultural institutions was also in crisis in intellectual centers across Europe. Undoubtedly Sarmiento's imagination concerning the role of the village in a country's march toward progress had been fueled by his familiarity with the thought of the utopian socialists, whose influence on Echeverría, Alberdi, and consequently on Sarmiento himself, is well known. These thinkers, for example Fourier and Saint-Simon, also doubted the value of the social and material changes that in recent decades had occurred in the great industrial centers of Europe. In their writings prevailed a new image of the city, one that contrasted with the image of a mythical civilization; for them, the city now appeared as "symbol and stigma of . . . societal vices."[23] Before, enlightened thinkers had portrayed the industrialized city as the realization of a future utopia. It is apparent, however, that the prophets of "socialist" modernization had already concluded that Europe's recent industrial development had created gaping wounds in society: there now existed extensive neighborhoods, disease-ridden and crime-infested, in which masses of poor and potentially rebellious workers were concentrated.

One can imagine that the new rural image for Roman civilization was particularly attractive for thinkers like Sarmiento, in that it offered a potentially useful model for South American, but especially Argentine, development. In those days, the mainstay of the Argentine economy was the class of large landowning cattle producers who employed a considerable number of rural workers. Out of this system characterized by gross social differences arose the caudillo, who exercised nearly absolute authority over rural society. Sarmiento understood correctly that the overturning of this system would not come about merely by replacing the caudillo in power with a more enlightened leader. He knew that the political power of the caudillo was only the most visible aspect of another type of domination which was even more profound: the interminable extensions of pampa without human presence, the cattle-based economy, and the majority population of poor gauchos—all these together constituted a network of impediments to the advancement of the nation. Sarmiento's plan for civilizing the countryside involved the elimination of overly large landholdings and the establishment of numerous agricultural colonies of European immigrants. These changes, in their moment, would stimulate the formation of new sources of wealth and labor and would hasten the demise of a system that linked the powerful caudillo to a rural majority population living in servitude and misery.

All these ideas are clearly echoed in Sarmiento's writings following his trip to the United States. What is implicit in *Viajes* receives explicit treatment later: the prototypes of a "civilized" society would be consistently portrayed as the residents of those towns or villages which are surrounded by thriving agricultural zones. In *Comentarios de la Constitución*, making use of what he had briefly observed on the Western frontier and in the small townships of New England, Sarmiento would again discuss the North American municipality. Now, however, he would also employ extensive written documentation—the information he had gathered during his trip but that he did not have an opportunity to examine thoroughly until later. In this later work, idealizations about the municipality would abound: "The base of all liberties in the United States is in the municipality; each village possesses a complete government, its own system of institutions or independent authorities" (*OC*, 8:222). He would quote extensively from the constitutions of the frontier states of Iowa and Oregon, and from that of sparsely populated Maine (8:192–195 et pass.). The only examples from a Spanish-speaking country that Sarmiento was to propose as worthy models of community association were the villages and rural communities of his native province of San Juan. There, he would explain, the citizens working in agriculture became experienced in the practice of community government through their deliberations about the maintenance of irrigation canals and the distribution of water resources (8:196, 223–224). He would, in short, provide seasoned arguments for what he had argued implicitly in *Viajes*: the successful resolution of agricultural problems led to coordinated community action with regard to other social and cultural necessities; thus there emerged the beginnings of a municipality, and all that meant for the region.

On the theoretical level, it would be difficult to find fault with Sarmiento's inspiring analysis of the benefits of self-government in the towns of both Americas. But a perverse question arises in the mind of this reader: How is the idealized Rome of Romulus and Remus, the small town of the Americas, or even the fortunate (and exceptional) agricultural experience of San Juan relevant to the future development of a modern urban center? In other words, what aspect of the idealized practices of the democratic town might serve as a guide for the development of republican institutions in and around Buenos Aires? In all this it is apparent that Sarmiento's ideas had fallen under the spell of a myth with enormous persuasive power. That myth, however, had dubious relevance for the most urgent problems of his own society, whose institutions and practices had been inherited from a decrepit colonialism—a society that was now on the verge of being thrust into a preponderant international economy.

The detailed analysis of the city as a theme in Sarmiento's thought has yet to be written. Or perhaps it would be more correct to talk about the absence of such a theme in his ideas. In a brilliant essay, Noël Salomon has documented the overdetermination of a provincial perspective in the thought of the young Sarmiento.[24] Before writing *Facundo*, Sarmiento had never seen Buenos Aires, and his perception of the role of the nation's capital in developing Argentina's rural resources for the future was understandably influenced by his own experiences in the far-off region of Cuyo. One cannot deny the prophetic powers of Sarmiento's vision. But, at the same time, many aspects of his thought reveal that he was first and foremost a provincial townsman who did not understand the metropolis of his country. One must question whether the ideas Sarmiento proposes in his writings, beginning with *Viajes*, concerning the municipal township of the United States and the sort of democracy that arose from the rural community, had relevance for his own country aside from its future frontier communities.

This is not the place to debate the polemical assertion, made by Tulio Halperín Donghi in 1959, that the impossible dream promoted by the activists of the Generation of 1837 was successful in impeding the occurrence of a true revolution in Argentina.[25] In all probability such a Machiavellian, conservative idea never would have occurred to Sarmiento on the conscious level. It is worth considering, however, whether the proposal of the North American township as a model for Argentina may have had the effect of stifling other real possibilities. Perhaps one should also ask whether Sarmiento's propensity for utopian projects bears any relation to a similar tendency—that of exaggerating the importance of superficial details at the expense of other, more significant factors. Some clear examples: the emphasis Sarmiento placed on the manner of dress, as if that were a faithful indication of a person's or a group's level of cultural attainment; or his tendency to take refuge behind moral denunciations upon confronting unexpected results, instead of reevaluating his original plan of attack. In this context, one can understand the stern condemnation of Sarmiento that Martínez Estrada makes at the conclusion of *Radiografía de la pampa*: in his acts and his ideas, "utopia devoured reality."[26] Sarmiento, with his tendency to seek inspiration for his actions in mental constructs at the expense of actual observations, serves as a prototype and personification for both the promise and the tragedy of the Argentine nation.

The Utopian Text

The text that Sarmiento wrote about his trip to the United States in 1847 occupies a special place within the totality of his writings: no other work projects a more consistent and sustained expression of his "utopian" message. I use the word "utopian" in reference to the baggage of ideas defended by the young Sarmiento and other members of the Asociación de Mayo in the period of their tenacious resistance to the Rosas dictatorship and at the beginning of their careers as writers and social activists.[27] In these early writings *socialista* thought predominated, having been learned from readings of Saint-Simon, Fourier, Pierre Leroux, and Félicité Robert de Lamennais. This eclectic body of ideas spoke to the necessity of improving social institutions by raising the moral and educational level of the population. It also spoke to the need of returning to many of the ideas formerly associated with the Enlightenment: republicanism, organic democracy, and promotion of the municipality as the building block of the liberal society. The "utopian" quality of this program was in part a result of the great diversity, and at times inconsistency, of its ideas; the passionate tone of its exiled defenders in articulating it; its moralist, idealist, and even mystical focus; and the distance separating desired transformations from the actual possibilities for realizing them.[28] Elsewhere I demonstrate that this utopian focus predominates primarily in the early writings of Sarmiento, those written during his long Chilean exile and before the fall of Rosas in 1852.[29] (In his writings after 1852 a more realist or positivist tendency would predominate, in agreement with the ideology of dependent liberalism favored in official circles.) Among all the works of this early period—*Facundo, Campaña en el Ejército Grande, Educación común,* and *Recuerdos de provincia*—only the last-mentioned rivals his travel commentary on the United States with regard to the expressive force of a utopian vision.

In the above paragraphs, I have attempted to situate the exuberant comments of the Argentine traveler within a sociohistorical context, and to evaluate the ideas he expresses in relation to the totality of his thought and the ideological context of the period. It is not surprising, therefore, that the utopian nature of the *Viajes* text has been the object of a negative hermeneutics emphasizing the lack of agreement between written words and corresponding realities. At other moments I have suggested that the utopian flavor of this text and, consequently, the gap existing between text and context, derived from a form of bad faith on the part of the writer: that is to say, Sarmiento entertained contradictory orientations and an ambiguous worldview, corresponding to the clash he continually experienced on both a conscious and a semiconscious level between liberal and authoritarian values. He was a political man who manipulated written images with the primary goal of legitimizing himself as leader and spokesman for his readership.

However, the negative hermeneutics that I have exercised until now does not deny the possibility of viewing Sarmiento's utopian focus from a different, this time positive, perspective. In fact, there is no doubt that posterity has preferred this second—idealistic and optimistic—reading, not only of *Viajes* but of nearly all Sarmiento's important works. For this reason, professors and students of literature have canonized the rare fragments of *Facundo* that express the author's admiration for the "social types" of the pampas—the pathfinder, the gaucho singer, the bad gaucho—while for the most part they have chosen to ignore the scorn and even hatred that Sarmiento expresses in other passages for the traditional rural society that, he believed, perpetuated material backwardness and constituted an obstacle to progress. For this reason, generations of school-children across South America have learned to pay homage to the man who promoted public education for the common people, while largely forgetting how that same man, when he was president of the country, would send national troops to the interior provinces in order to put down bands of common people who organized in defense of their right to assembly. Consequently, most critics treating the last part of *Viajes*—in particular those hailing from the United States—have ignored fundamental aspects of Sarmiento's ideological and political program, perhaps out of their own need for identifying, at least in word, with such lofty ideals.

This persistence of the positive perspective has obeyed clear political principles, according to Fernando Operé. In the Argentina of the post-Rosas period, which was governed by men such as Mitre and Sarmiento, "[t]he economic and political monopoly of the ruling class was paired with a cultural monopoly. The oligarchy that governed uninterrupted since [the Battle of] Pavón possessed everything, intelligence, fortune, and so-cial prestige, feeling proud of its absolute supremacy. Some condemned and some privileged, the ruling class imposed a culture and a history, desiring that it might reflect on the present." [30] Regardless of the fact that the history of this project of cultural manipulation has yet to be written, its results are beyond dispute. On the one hand, little survives today of what must have been an extensive oral tradition treating the *montoneras* and traditional creole culture; in large part, the positive heritage of the country's popular caudillos of the interior—Artigas, Güemes, López, He-redia, and Facundo Quiroga—has been all but effaced from the public record; almost any mention of the federalist contributions during the first half of the past century has been purged from the country's collective memory. On the other hand, the texts of literature and history written by and for the Europeanized population of Buenos Aires are encountered everywhere; still supreme is an official culture and history that has been propagated throughout the world as the only true history of the Argen-tine nation. The survival of a near-monolithic, positive image of Sar-miento obeys the same principles: it is the text privileged by and preferred by the social and political interests that, after the fall of Rosas, succeeded in imposing their will over the country. Those interests fostered the proj-ect of rewriting history and propagating a new version of the national past that would justify both their supremacy in society and the monopoly of political-economic power that they came to exercise.

A text, however, can never be appropriated by a sole owner; a written work can never be reduced to a single, exclusive reading. It is in this light that the utopian content of Sarmiento's texts ought to be considered. During a period in time, Sarmiento had allowed his energies as statesman as well as his written works to be placed at the service of interests, concentrated in and around Buenos Aires, who sought unification of the country under the positivist banner. In his old age, though, he realized that the modernization of his country, regardless of its enviable successes, still evidenced great areas of concern. He realized that the survivors of the old aristocracy of the province of Buenos Aires, now allied to foreign commercial interests, and not a new capitalist class of small producers, were the avaricious beneficiaries of the new society—a society that had emerged largely as a result of his generation's dedication and service.[31] The elder statesman, then, had become thoroughly disillusioned with the political and commercial leaders whom he had once seen as the foundation of a republican Argentina.

Searching for a way to protest this unacceptable situation in his later years, Sarmiento came around once again to affirm a utopian perspective. Anderson Imbert explains the paradox of this man who, despite his eminently conservative views, would once again in his old age embrace an idealistic program for social change: his conservatism was a form of dissent; his opposition to the system of privileges that he himself had helped form in the post-Rosas period was manifested in his defense of a "Golden Age" in the history of Argentina, the principles for which had been clearly articulated in the revolutionary program of 1810 and then again in the program of the Asociación de Mayo during the Rosas tyranny.[32] After a hiatus of nearly forty years, Sarmiento would again highlight a utopian message similar to the one that had flavored his youthful thought. Dreamy projects, like those he had mentally lived during the period of his long exile in Chile and during the six weeks he had spent traveling across the United States in 1847, once again came to exert a strong influence over his thought and his actions.

This is precisely the most redeemable aspect for present-day readers of the commentaries Sarmiento wrote on the occasion of his first trip to the United States. The different Latin American societies, today as before, attract more for their promise in the future than for their realizations in the present. What has not changed is the image of those societies as the setting for revolutionary aspirations. If one talks of the Mexico of 1911, Bolivia in the 1950s, Cuba in the 1960s, Peru under Juan Velasco Alvarado, Chile under Salvador Allende, or Sandinista Nicaragua, one talks or has talked in terms of the "todavía posible"—exactly as Sarmiento wrote about the United States a century and a half ago (*OC,* 5:334). In the past few decades, the imagination of progressive people across the world has become focused—once again—on the states of Latin America as the scene for realizing old dreams and for fulfilling displaced or postponed promises. But what Sarmiento once saw as the great society of the future, emerging in the form of villages surrounded by enormous forests, no longer exists in either America. Such a description no longer applies to contemporary reality, with its tremendous—and alarming—modifications over the past few decades with regard to urbanization, technological dependence, and industrialization. But what does still hold is the metaphorical description of Latin America as a New World: in many circles today, the region is still seen as a collection of young societies proceeding along "the path of development." These societies, it is supposed, can still offer radically new alternatives for realizing their own civilizing project. This would be accomplished under the gaze of a supposedly "developed" world whose populations are accosted by the perturbing problems of urban crime and overcrowding, environmental pollution, and dehumanizing technology. One still hears of a possible "new society," but it would have to be one that could arise in a land that is no longer considered "new." Many thinkers of the tired Western world resemble Sarmiento in a former day: they have become intoxicated with images that emanate from a possible "estado larva" (5:337), the revolutionary society that could exist in their own historical moment. The utopias inherent in such a vision are instrumental in the task of criticizing the defects of the existing order and for projecting a program of action in order to overcome those defects.

The contemporary reader would perhaps consider Sarmiento's unreal description of U.S. society in *Viajes* to be a pardonable defect, given his far more important accomplishment: the presentation of a fascinating image of social perfection; the dissemination of a myth with indestructible power for any people who yearn for liberty. In this sense, Sarmiento's text can be read as an exercise in *desiring* to see instead of a representation of what was actually seen. Sarmiento dreamed of a social experience that would result from human logic, rather than from violence or exploitation (*OC,* 5:362). Such an idealized society would offer a level of material satisfaction that could spare humanity from great suffering (5:340); it offered the possibility for all men to be "owners" of their own energies, and not simply objects manipulated by strong commercial and material interests (5:363). In Sarmiento's dream, liberty would thrive without legal impediment or economic want, and a people could take advantage of any technological innovation or institutional improvement that might derive from the infinite powers of human intelligence. All citizens would enjoy equal access to jobs or land and, at the same time, could develop their talents through the civilizing institutions of the city. His dream was that each collectivity of citizens could write their laws and form their patterns of association in accord with their own interpretation of need and inclination. It is necessary to remember here that Sarmiento was projecting an ideal vision that went far beyond the accomplishments of the society he was supposedly describing. In Latin America today, it must also be noted, there exists no society in which any of these ambitious projects has even come close to being realized. The utopian promise of the young Sarmiento remains unfulfilled. The descriptions he has presented to us in *Viajes* remain images of what is possible; or, better yet, they constitute a program of action that a new generation of revolutionaries will attempt to fulfill.

Notes

1. I provide documentation for these assertions in the first half of my "Sarmiento en los Estados Unidos," *Todo es historia*, no. 255 (1988): 6–45. For other points of view, see Michael A. Rockland, "Introduction" to Domingo F. Sarmiento, *Sarmiento's "Travels in the United States in 1847,"* trans. Michael A. Rockland (Princeton: Princeton University Press, 1970) and Elda Clayton Patton, *Sarmiento in the United States* (Evansville, Ind.: University of Evansville Press, 1976).

2. J. L. Austin, *How to Do Things with Words* (Cambridge: Harvard University Press, 1962).

3. Rockland, "Introduction," p. 78, is wrong in doubting the letter status of these travel commentaries about the United States: he forgets that Sarmiento, who returned directly to Chile via Panama, had to send them in letter form to Montevideo, where Valentín Alsina, the letters' designated recipient, resided.

4. Domingo F. Sarmiento, *Obras completas* (henceforth *OC*), 52 vols. (Buenos Aires: Luz del Día, 1948–1956), 6:227.

5. For example, *Viajes* hardly touches upon the topics of public education, the division of public lands, and the legal and institutional foundation for the municipality, topics Sarmiento would treat in detail in later works such as *De la educación popular* (1849), *Argirópolis* (1850), and *Comentarios de la Constitución* (1853).

6. Alexis de Tocqueville, *Democracy in America* (New York: Alfred A. Knopf, 1945), vol. 1. The two parts to the original French edition were published, respectively, in 1835 and 1840.

7. Rockland, "Introduction," p. 96.

8. Quoted in Adolfo Prieto, *La literatura autobiográfica argentina* (Rosario: Editorial Biblioteca, 1968), pp. 65–66.

9. Ibid., p. 66.

10. See Tocqueville, *Democracy in America*, 1:355.

11. Although the early writings of Sarmiento reveal what seems at times to be a romantic appreciation for the South American Indian, this perspective takes second place to his conviction, which was nourished by the socioscientific theories then in vogue, that the Indian constituted an impediment to his continent's march toward progress. To date, the most authoritative studies published about the opinions of Sarmiento with regard to racial issues are Jaime Alazraki, "El indigenismo de Martí y el anti-indigenismo de Sarmiento," *Cuadernos Americanos* 140, no. 3 (1965): 135–157, and Antonio Sacoto, "El indio en la obra literaria de Sarmiento y Martí," *Cuadernos Americanos* 156, no. 1 (1968): 137–163.

12. Rockland, "Introduction," p. 97.

13. Edward W. Said, "Crítica secular," in *Punto de Vista* 9, no. 10 (1987): xiii–xiv (translated from the prologue to *The World, the Text, and the Critic*, 1984).

14. William H. Katra, *Domingo F. Sarmiento: Public Writer (between 1839 and 1852)* (Tempe: Center for Latin American Studies, Arizona State University, 1985).

15. Noël Salomon, "El *Facundo* de Domingo Faustino Sarmiento: Manifiesto de la preburguesía argentina de las ciudades del interior," *Cuadernos Americanos* 39, no. 5 (1980): 121–176; Tulio Halperín Donghi, "Prólogo," in Domingo F. Sarmiento, *Campaña en el Ejército Grande Aliado de Sud América* (Mexico: Fondo de Cultura Económica, 1958), pp. xx–xxvi.

16. Hernán Vidal, *Literatura hispanoamericana e ideología liberal: Surgimiento y crisis (Una problemática sobre la dependencia en torno a la narrativa del boom)* (Buenos Aires: Hispamérica, 1976), discusses three discourses frequently found in the romantic writing of the Southern Cone: the utopian, the demonic, and the Adamic.

17. Ezequiel Martínez Estrada, *Sarmiento* (Buenos Aires: Argos, 1956), p. 7.

18. See Rockland, "Introduction," pp. 102–103, quoting Girri.

19. Allison Williams Bunkley, *The Life of Sarmiento* (Princeton: Princeton University Press, 1952), p. 303.

20. Marvin Meyers, "The Great Descent: On Cooper and the Age of Dodge and Bragg," in *The Jackson Persuasion: Politics and Belief* (New York: Vintage Books, 1960), calls Tocqueville the "venturous conservative" (p. 34).

21. Katra, *Sarmiento: Public Writer*, chap. 3, "Sarmiento: Bricoleur."

22. Carl E. Schorske, "La idea de la ciudad en el pensamiento europeo: De Voltaire a Spengler," *Punto de Vista* 30 (1987): iii.

23. Ibid., p. x.

24. Salomon, "El *Facundo*."

25. Tulio Halperín Donghi, "El espejo de la historia," *Contorno* nos. 9–10 (1959): 76–81.

26. Ezequiel Martínez Estrada, *Radiografía de la pampa* (Buenos Aires: Losada, 1968), p. 341.

27. I do not follow the definition of "utopia" used by Sarmiento himself—according to Carlos M. Rama, ed., *Utopismo socialista (1830–1893)* (Caracas: Ayacucho, 1977), p. 132—when, out of supposedly "utopian" principles, he criticized Fourier's opposition to science, commerce, social progress, and the central role of the state as means of achieving "civilization." Nor do I follow the meaning offered by Juan Guillermo Durán, "Literatura y utopía en Hispanoamérica" (Ph.D. diss., Cornell University, 1972), who uses the term in relation to the racist ideas expressed by Sarmiento in *Conflictos y armonías de las razas en América* (1883).

28. Karl Mannheim, in *Ideology and Utopia: An Introduction to the Sociology of Knowledge*, trans. Louis Wirth and Edward Shils (New York: Harcourt, Brace & World, 1936), pp. 219–229, discusses the "liberal-humanitarian ideal" in relation to the thought of the Enlightenment. The period of utopian liberalism in Argentina can be said to extend from the first administration of Bernardino Rivadavia until the fall of Rosas; during this period, according to Domingo Millani, "Utopian Socialism: Transitional Thread from Romanticism to Positivism in Latin America," *Journal of the History of Ideas* 24 (1963): 515–522, there predominated in liberal discourse the utopian social objective of steering the development of political and historical events. José Ingenieros, *Las direcciones filosóficas de la cultura argentina* (Buenos Aires: Editorial Universitaria de Buenos Aires, 1963), pp. 71–72, refers to the ideas of Echeverría as "el socialismo utópico." According to R. Picard (quoted by Millani, "Utopian Socialism," p. 328n), the ideas of Echeverría and the other activists of 1837 were "idealistic and sentimental like the poetry of the time." Their programs for action were forged under the pressures of exile and the inspiration of romanticism; for this reason, they had no need to concretize or actualize their "mystical virtuoso ideas."

29. Katra, *Sarmiento: Public Writer*, pp. 198–206. Toward the end of the present chapter, I discuss how in his last years Sarmiento would reaffirm a utopian vision similar to the one he had defended earlier during his years in Chilean exile.

30. Fernando Operé, *Civilización y barbarie en la literatura argentina del siglo XIX: El tirano Rosas* (Madrid: Conorg, 1987), p. 193.

31. Tulio Halperín Donghi, "Sarmiento: Su lugar en la sociedad argentina post-revolucionaria," *Sur* 341 (1977): 121–134.

32. Enrique Anderson Imbert, *Genio y figura de Sarmiento* (Buenos Aires: Editorial Universitaria de Buenos Aires, 1967), pp. 142–149.

5   Sarmiento and Political Order: Liberty, Power, and Virtue

NATALIO R. BOTANA

In *Recuerdos de provincia*, Sarmiento established the point of departure for a long journey: he described how "the day after the revolution . . . we had to look around in all directions . . . searching for something to fill the void"; then he asked, "How are ideas formed?" and answered "in the spirit of those who study. [Ideas] come like river floods, when the passing waters deposit little by little the solid particles that fertilize the soil."[1]

The images of void and torrent are very significant in Sarmiento. In order to understand his fate and his view of political order, one must understand the suffering caused by Argentina's civil wars. It is in this context that Sarmiento probed various ideas and projects, consuming them voraciously in order to inform his writing and his actions as a political leader.

The notion of political order first came up in Sarmiento as an intellectual representation of civilization. Later, it became an instrument of legislation and government. Sarmiento's idea of political order resulted from an interior battle between a philosopher's dream and the reality of power. Such conflicting tendencies residing in the same consciousness rarely produce effective results. Bartolomé Mitre accompanied him in this journey, but not Juan Bautista Alberdi or Alexis de Tocqueville, political thinkers who did not know how to deal with power.

This confrontation between theory and practice contributed to a conception of republic in which three tendencies coexisted: a forward-looking liberal tradition; a strong republic capable of concentrating power in the state (and combating the still-existing characters portrayed in *Facundo*); and the old idea of a republic inspired by the civic virtue of the citizen dedicated to the public good. Sarmiento entered headlong into the debates on the nature of the republic in the 1800s, and he applied his views to the

Argentine situation. The debate had begun in France and the United States, and was carried on in the first decades of postindependence Argentina.

Beginning in the eighteenth century, the discussion concerning the meaning of the republic divided those who promoted notions of individual liberty, protected by strong guarantees, from those who believed in the ancient ideal of a community of citizens founded on equality, sacrifice for the public good, and education directed by public authority. This debate took place not only in France but also in the United States.

As Benjamin Constant noted in a lecture in 1819, in both revolutionary and restoration France, two antagonistic views of liberty competed and were oftentimes at war: that of the nostalgia for the ancient idea of liberty which, supported by Rousseau, sought to re-create an active citizen in the classical sense; and that of the modern supporters of liberty whose main tenets were individualism, limitations of power and, therefore, a constitutional regime.[2]

This dichotomy runs across a great part of the history of ideas in the nineteenth century, up to and including Renan, Fustel de Coulanges, and Taine, three of Sarmiento's favorite authors of the 1870s and 1880s. This tension between individual rights, which generate a spontaneous order, and the will to create an enlightened citizen through public education had left marks and effects on the republican ideology of the Third Republic. On the one hand was the notion of republic as guarantor of liberty; on the other, the notion of a programmatic republic that places limitations on the exercise of power. As Claude Nicolet has written, "the originality of French republicans . . . lies in that . . . they have always cherished in their cartesian and universalist spirit, the unavowed dream of becoming a fourth Rome."[3]

Although French discourse provided the archetype for this debate, it is no less true that the U.S. rhetoric of the first half-century of independent existence reflected similar alternatives. It is instructive to follow the controversy between, on the one hand, authors such as Louis Hartz and John P. Diggins, who observed in the birth of the republic (1776–1787) the persistence of a liberal paradigm inspired by the traditions of Locke and Puritanism; and, on the other, historians such as Bernard Bailyn and J. G. A. Pocock, who have sought in the discourse of the independence and constituent periods a civic paradigm rooted in Machiavelli and Aristotle.[4]

Later, in the 1830s and 1850s, two individuals admired by Sarmiento, Hubert Howe Bancroft and Horace Mann, took up these topics again. The history of liberty, which Bancroft imagined as an epic written by a new chosen people, and the redeeming vision of education which Horace Mann untiringly preached until the end of his days, contributed to enriching the dialogue between the republics of liberalism and civic humanism.

These major strands of the republican tradition reached rocky terrain in Argentina. The metaphor of the desert, used frequently at the time, transcended the mere geographic image in order to underscore the weakness of the first republican experiments which paved the way to anarchy and despotism. Numerous testimonies appeared to illustrate this. They told of an initially constructive period, led by independence leaders and unitarian legislators, which was soon replaced by disillusionment and failure. The republic certainly lacked legitimacy, but even more basically it lacked power and authority. Just like the land devastated by the *caudillos*, the far-off republic of the River Plate envisioned by this type of historical imagination was also an empty space. It was a mere potential republic recorded in written projects and ephemeral governments. The search for that necessary conjunction between the republic and legitimate power was an obsession that accompanied Sarmiento from his adolescence to his grave.

The Liberal Republic

Sarmiento fought against dictatorship in the name of a liberty that had many faces. Freedom, in his view, did not emerge from outside forces but rather from the "convulsions that rip out the entrails of a noble people." Such freedoms as civil safety and progress, which are presented in the conclusion of *Facundo*, were expected to result from the end of Rosas's tyranny.

Sarmiento's first intellectual representation of political order appeared in *Facundo*. This "essay and revelation" of his own ideas is, without a doubt, a portrait of local customs. However, it is also an original attempt at applying various political theories to the understanding of historical reality. *Facundo* has a theory of civil war; a theory of the classical polis which resonates with echoes of the Enlightenment from Montesquieu to Rousseau; a theory of modern republicanism inspired by Tocqueville; and, finally, a theory of the "other society," the land ignored by colonial society which the wars of independence brought to the fore.

Sarmiento took the romantic myth of "barbarism" from Gibbon, Michelet, Guizot, and Thierry and turned it into his main line of argument. In a passage written in old age, Sarmiento described how this world of barbarism affected his sensitivity as a fifteen-year-old inhabitant of a village that still carried the strong imprint of its long colonial existence:

> I was a merchant in 1826 when I first went to Chile. I was standing in the doorway of my store across the street from what today is, as if by Providence, the Sarmiento School of San Juan (formerly San Cle-

mente) watching six hundred men arrive at the neighboring barracks
. . . with the triumphant air that dust and intoxication can give. What
a sight! They were riding spirited steeds, taken from artificial mead-
ows. In order to shelter themselves on the plains from the rough
brush, they used the enormous chaps of the region consisting of two
tough protectors of rawhide for keeping legs and even the head safe
from the two-headed, dartlike thorns. The noise produced by this apparatus is impressive, and much of the contact and collision evoke the
sound of shields and weapons in combat. The spirited horses, perhaps
more domesticated than their riders, were frightened by these noises
and strange encounters. On the unpaved streets, we spectators
watched a dense cloud of dust advance, pregnant with muttering, yell-
ing, cursing, and laughing; here and there dusty faces appeared between tangles of hair and rags, looking almost bodiless because of the
wide chaps, as if cherubs or half-centaur devils. This is my version of
the road to Damascus, of liberty and civilization. All the ills of my
country suddenly became evident: Barbarism![5]

One can easily identify the protagonists of the drama from this description: a city under siege and the outsiders that conquer it.

In contrast to the reality of rich and poor, of the learned gentlemen
and *montonera* fighters described by José María Paz in his *Memorias,* in
Facundo Sarmiento subsumed these actors into two elements of struggle—city and countryside—that throb, feel, and suffer as human archetypes that assume the names of Bernardino Rivadavia and Salvador María
del Carril, Facundo Quiroga, and Juan Manuel de Rosas. Each of these
characters manifests his strength or lets his utopian views conform with
a scenario in which various cities appear in succession: the aristocratic city
of colonial times; the independence city which becomes the unitarian city;
the city of Rosas, seat of urban tyranny; and, on the horizon, the possible
city of the consolidated republic that will emerge from the rubble of despotism.

Eventually, the sheer force of the "other society" will undermine the
legitimacy of the cities of the independence and unitarian periods. An
independence process, which had occurred without major trauma and
without affecting the distribution of urban power, turned into civil war.
In the end, barbarism prevailed in those cities and, by means of urban
tyranny, brought about a social system that for the first time incorporated
the rural world.

Curiously, this urban tyranny completed the cycle and unlocked the
doors leading to the new civilization. As Sarmiento wrote:

[D]o not think that Rosas has failed to develop the Republic that he
tears apart. No: he is a great and powerful instrument of Providence,

who does everything the future of the nation needs. Let us observe how. There existed before him and before Quiroga the federal spirit in the provinces, in the cities, in the federals and the unitarians themselves; he extinguishes them and organizes for his own benefit the unitarian spirit that Rivadavia wanted for the benefit of all. Today all those little caudillos in the provinces, demoted, degraded, stand fearful of displeasing him; they dare not breathe without his consent. The idea of the unitarians has materialized; only the tyrant is unnecessary. The day a good government is established, it will find the local resistance defeated and everything at the disposition of the UNION.[6]

This conversion from a primitive order to a political regime that enhances human dignity is similar to that of James Madison and the liberal tradition: however redundant it may seem, in order to limit power it is necessary for power to exist. This is the distance that separates Thomas Hobbes and John Locke, and also the distance, as Sarmiento saw it, that separated the utopia of Rivadavia from the much more realistic project advanced by himself and the men of 1837.

In the first instance, the rationalism of the Buenos Aires legislator ignored this secret society (the world of caudillos and montoneras) which subjugated the colonial cities where the *criollo* elite had forged the process of independence. In the second, the new generation recognized the combination of city and countryside as not only positive but as the necessary condition for building a national constitution. Power, in effect, became entirely revealed.

The imaginary traveler of *Facundo* had come to these conclusions. An actual trip to the United States was now necessary for that conception of liberty to arouse fervor and enthusiasm in Sarmiento. In *Viajes*, he confessed his disillusionment with Europe and confirmed his unyielding faith in a republican, federal, and therefore decentralized political model—also in an open society into which immigrants and capital could flow and where civil guarantees would naturally open the way to progress. Toward the end of 1845, Sarmiento left aside for a moment the shadow of Quiroga and the power of Rosas in order to travel "with the object of seeing with my own eyes, and of palpating, if I may use the expression, the state of elementary education in nations where it is a branch of public administration."[7]

There is a close relationship between Sarmiento's trip to the United States and Tocqueville's fifteen years earlier. In the River Plate region and in Chile, publicists tended to interpret the republican experience in the United States through the French prose of Tocqueville as well as that of Michel Chevalier, the author of *Lettres sur l'Amérique du Nord* (1836). The image of U.S. democracy was thus shaped in Sarmiento's mind by those intellectuals who, in the spirit of Montesquieu and Saint-Simon, explored the nature of equality and the destiny of industrial society in that land.

Furthermore, both Sarmiento and Tocqueville traveled under government commissions from Chile and France, respectively (Tocqueville went to study the penitentiary system in the United States). Each fulfilled his commission and, as a result of their reports, they wrote two enduring works. If *Democracy in America* acquired the dignity of a classic work, Sarmiento's *Viajes,* though not reaching the same heights, shared the same ambition. In their effort to understand the present, Sarmiento and Tocqueville did not question history but, rather, the future. Their horizons were not the introspection of *Facundo,* nor Tocqueville's subsequent *The Old Regime and the Revolution,* but the promise offered by human liberty when it encounters the novel experience of democracy.

Sarmiento's admiration for democracy in the United States came from his disillusionment with Europe. Before landing in the country of Horace Mann, Sarmiento, who viewed Europe as a "terrain deeply mined with elements of one of the most terrible convulsions that has agitated the minds of people,"[8] determined that European society was condemned to oscillate between revolution and reaction.

The battered legitimacy of these governments, still hurting from the open conflict of 1789, was compounded by a heterogeneous and divided social state. From the moment he arrived and found himself surrounded by indigents and beggars, Europe became a stage of strong contrasts for Sarmiento. This was, in many respects, a model culture violently undermined by inequality. "Ah, Europe," he wrote at that time, "sad mixture of grandeur and abjection, of knowledge and at the same time depravation, sublime and dirty receptacle of everything man upholds or degrades, kings and lackeys, monuments and lazarettos, opulence and savage living!"[9]

His disdain toward Europe's aristocratic liberty was as complete as his instinctive distrust toward revolutionary and reactionary extremes. Sarmiento's reading of Michelet, Blanc, and Lamartine inspired him to use models, words, and metaphors to represent the historical world. But these authors never captivated his literary passion sufficiently to enable him to see the Jacobin period as the culmination of equality.

At some point during his travels, Sarmiento became attracted to Fourier's socialist humanitariansim, but what he wrote about this utopia was closer to Tocqueville's view of the inevitability of democracy than it was to any sympathy for the austere distribution of property in a phalanstery. On the opposite side of the revolutionary universe, Chateaubriand and

Sir Walter Scott influenced Sarmiento's romantic comprehension of the past.

Sarmiento was disappointed, and to a certain extent alone, because he could not find an effective political model in the reality of Europe. Spain seemed to him a curse; the Italian cities, a mosaic where time seemed to have stopped; Prussia, nothing more than a timely lesson on the administration of public education; and Switzerland, a republic disfigured by its particularism and feudal tradition.

France, and Paris, remained as the places where Sarmiento expected to find literary fame. The article that introduced *Facundo* to the judgment of the *hommes de lettres* was not long in coming, despite the anguish of the young writer. In contrast, French politics, dominated by the doctrinaire party, was much more indifferent. At the time, Guizot was in charge of the cabinet while Thiers was in the opposition. Neither of them satisfied Sarmiento, but, as could be expected, he was mollified by Thiers's cordial reception. At any rate, the centralist solution offered by doctrinaire liberalism since the Revolution of 1830 was, for Sarmiento, a slope leading to failure.

The eclecticism in which this political position was based suggested a historical pact between the opposing principles of revolution and reaction. Although the program was theoretically attractive, in practice it undermined the traditional legitimacy of the monarchy as well as the authority derived from popular sovereignty.

A political model based on a weak monarch and an electorate deformed by the *censitaire* suffrage seemed scandalous to Sarmiento. Moreover, after an unfortunate interview with the minister of foreign affairs, Sarmiento came to the conclusion that to be doctrinaire in Europe was the same as being a Rosist in Buenos Aires. Even the parliamentary rhetoric in the *Chambre,* that "half of a cockfighting ring with colossal dimensions," left him with a bitter aftertaste.

He departed from Europe by way of England, a country he barely had time to visit, and crossed the North Atlantic on a ship where he could see the faces of famished Irish emigrants on deck. This spectacle predisposed him favorably to the United States, because he viewed Europe as casting its own ruins to the New World. Sarmiento's arrival in the United States represented, therefore, the beginning of a commitment with the republicanism of the future.

Before their arrival in the United States, Sarmiento and Tocqueville viewed the republic as little more than fiction from the prehistory of modernity. The tiny cities of Thucydides and Machiavelli did not represent a relevant model. The republican revolution had succumbed in France; in

Buenos Aires, the unitarian republic, with its "clumsy cultivators," was compromised by "its mistakes and its fantastic illusions." Finally, Portalean Chile, enhanced by the progressive impetus of Manuel Montt, had given birth to an aristocratic republic. But it was a small republic just awakening in the central valley between the Andes and the sea.

The United States was another matter (even if an unlikely one, at least from the standpoint of Sarmiento's political theory), for it embodied radically incompatible principles and realities: unlimited space, large population, social equality and economic freedom, a huge market, a vast number of public centers of initiative and control and, as crowning features, federal decentralization, political freedom, and education. It is true that the blemish of slavery persisted; nonetheless, the "American liberties" watered a tree more luxuriant than the "parasitic vegetation" of other political experiences.

The revelation of this new democracy gave Sarmiento a strong argument for erasing the past from his political project, a past that in *Facundo* was still presented as a token of eclectic compromise. A few years later, the reminiscent nature of *Recuerdos de provincia* turned the past into a distant object that inspired an admirable reconstruction of a colonial life which was so paradoxically recent.

After *Viajes*, the Battle of Caseros took place. When Sarmiento initiated his public career in the state of Buenos Aires, we find his views of the United States reflected in the *Comentarios de la Constitución* (inspired by Joseph Story and the nationalist constitutionalism of the United States), a volume in which Sarmiento intended to respond to the eclectic proposals of Alberdi in *Bases* and *Estudios sobre la constitución argentina*.

Sarmiento's proposals in *Argirópolis* and in *Comentarios de la Constitución* advanced a constitution, autonomy as opposed to the centralizing pretensions of his 1853 text, limited power, and drastic legislative changes in order to do away with colonial protectionism. They represent Sarmiento's first liberal hour in the constitutional debates of 1860.

A Strong Republic in Civil War

The emergence of liberalism in Argentina occurred at a time of continued civil war. The contradiction between a theory based on peaceful citizen participation in the establishment of local governments, associations, schools, and enterprises and the Argentine reality of incessant combat, regional fragmentation, and the resistance of the caudillos, was never completely solved during Sarmiento's lifetime.

Had the republican pact changed its meaning? Sarmiento intuited that behind the notable metaphor of the social contract, which had the legitimacy he desired, there was still the need for a powerful government. Authority, as he had already written in *Facundo,* implied public consent; but this voluntary acquiescence was long in coming.

Civil war continued, and no single battle managed to definitively break the circle of discord. From Caseros to the bellicose division between Buenos Aires and Paraná; from the expeditions to squelch rebellions in the northern provinces to the War of the Triple Alliance; from the revolutions in Entre Ríos to the federalization of Buenos Aires—there was little peace in Argentina between conflicts.

Sarmiento had no choice but to remain on stage and play his part. He believed that this discord was a constant factor in Argentine history (as the pessimistic conclusions of *Conflictos y armonías* attest), and he sought to eradicate that discord. He resorted to states of exception and to federal intervention, and he instituted a professional military that was subordinated to the constitution and the president. Inevitably, at the end of his presidency in 1874, the state that he had molded and led became much more centralized and departed significantly from the model he had designed twenty years earlier under the influence of Tocqueville and Story. Furthermore, new foreign examples seemed to support his views: the federal government of the United States had won the Civil War, and the Third Republic laid its foundations in France upon the rubble of the 1870 Commune.

"We need to establish governments, and up to this point, we have given no example of such," Sarmiento wrote to Nicolás Avellaneda in 1865. "Half a century ago we marched with blood on our ankles in order to be free and to leave our children security and tranquillity."[10] What does this sentence mean to a man who five years earlier, while participating in the Reform Congress of 1860, had successfully completed a liberal constitution?

The concentration of popular sovereignty in a limited government was a problem left unsolved by republican theory until the representative regime was implemented. However, to define political representation according to currents generated from below, from the people to the magistrates, is not the same thing as resorting to the principle of representation as a necessary artifice for the establishment of authority, even if this means justifying unloyal habits and practices. In the first instance, representation is a reflection of popular sovereignty, and its emblem is the congressman chosen in free elections; in the second, representation is a reflection of the state in the process of imposing obedience through a civilian or military bureaucracy.

In this context, Sarmiento sometimes presents a benign and wise demeanor; at other times, he seems arbitrary and domineering. Argentine institutional history shows how he sought to reform the system of prepared lists in order to implement a uninominal system by circumscription and thereby eradicate electoral fraud and corruption. During the time of Julio Roca in the mid-1870s, the aging Sarmiento joined a new generation of democrats, including Aristóbulo del Valle and Leandro N. Alem, in order to push for new political reforms.

These efforts to establish a representative regime that would reconcile policymaking with procedural fairness stood in contrast with Sarmiento's own reactions to provincial rebellion. A government that defeated sedition and conducted a devastating conquest of Indian territory turned the principle of representation around so long as representation emanated from the presidency. General Sarmiento, as he liked to call himself, exercised government representation in the form of national power in those areas where its absence had encouraged an energetic sense of autonomy.

Sarmiento made use of power, but there were limits to his actions. Sarmiento's administration can be seen in the context of those founding governments which consolidated individual freedoms and the rule of law in a climate of civil violence. Power was not built so as to escape anarchy at any cost but to guarantee individual autonomy. The republic may have seemed strong in the face of challenges to constituted authority, yet there was a strong restriction on the passions of the ruling leaders: the legitimacy of constitutional order.

The Republic of Civic Humanism

This constitutional legitimacy seemed to have been the goal of that "slow and painful transition from one way of being to another," as Sarmiento wrote in *Recuerdos de provincia*. One may wonder whether the dichotomy "republic of liberties versus republic of constitutional power" suffices to explain Sarmiento's politics. The answer is, of course, no. What individual, what Argentine citizen of flesh and blood, did Sarmiento envision as occupying the center of his emerging civilization? The question sounds much the same as it did two centuries ago: What is the nature of the individual in a republic? Is it the ancient liberty of the *zoon politikon*, or the modern liberty that seeks legal guarantees to protect the essential rights of the citizen?

Sarmiento did not decidedly lean toward either of the two poles, but he always did embrace the old dream of a more egalitarian republic of citizens. The dream consisted of a republic capable of instilling virtue in its members by means of public education, the exercise of political freedom, and the distribution of small agricultural plots.

Two texts of his *informes*, presented to the Ministry of Public Instruction and the University Council in Chile (1848 and 1856, respectively), show the close relationship that existed for Sarmiento among education, citizenship, and virtue. In the first he stated:

> [T]he equality of rights for all individuals, even in those countries
> ruled by tutelary systems, serves, in the republics, as the basis for so-
> cial organization, whatever may be the modifications introduced by
> national circumstances or other causes. On the basis of this principle,
> every government has the obligation of providing education for future
> generations, since it cannot compel members [of the current genera-
> tion] to receive the intellectual preparation required for the exercise of
> their rights. The social condition of the individual oftentimes depends
> on circumstances beyond his will. A poverty-stricken father cannot be
> held responsible for the education of his children; however, society as
> a whole has a vital interest in ensuring that every individual who in
> time will contribute to shaping the nation has been sufficiently pre-
> pared through his childhood education to carry out the social functions
> he will be called on to perform.[11]

In the second informe, Sarmiento reproduced the following paragraph from an 1812 public education project in New York State:

> In a government such as ours, where the people are the sovereign
> power, where the law of the land is the will of the people, whose will
> is openly and directly expressed, and where each act of government
> can properly be called an act of the people, it is essential that all indi-
> viduals be educated. They must possess intelligence and virtue; intelli-
> gence to perceive what is right; virtue to do what is right. Our repub-
> lic, one could then say, is founded on intelligence and virtue. This is
> why the enlightened Montesquieu said quite appropriately that in a
> republic all the power of education is needed.[12]

Sarmiento's meditation on citizenship went through different stages, beginning with the influence of Benjamin Franklin and Thomas Paine and extending to the polemics of the Julio Roca and Miguel Juárez Celman administrations, when he demanded that all immigrants become naturalized and take part in national politics. As a child of his century, Sarmiento also received the influence of Horace Mann, Jules Ferry, the romantic historians, Darwin, and Herbert Spencer.

However, Sarmiento's inquiry into the conditions of life in a republic concentrated on other topics as well: the meaning of the city and the municipality as centers of political liberty; the organization and equality of education; the role of agricultural property in the development of habits of autonomy and association; the threat hovering over a nation of immigrants when the newly arrived population, ignorant of the duties of citizenship, takes part only in civil life; and history as an epic where heroes play a central role in war and in peace. The Argentine citizen that Sarmiento intended to shape, almost in the same way that a master molds his disciple, was an active citizen who could discern the public good, take up arms when the nation required, and—in time—participate, deliberate, and decide on behalf of the people. Political freedom was not, for Sarmiento, a spontaneous, slow, and gradual process, as Alberdi would have it, but rather a deliberate act of legislators or leaders. In his view, the republic was an institution for the creation of citizens. It was also a guarantee for freedom and for programmatic endeavors; a peaceful organization at the service of the citizenry and nation; and a custodian of the fatherland, which required lifetime service.

Sarmiento explored these issues because he wanted to rescue Argentina from a fatal loneliness. This was the loneliness of the criollo who sorrowfully observed how the bonds of traditional society fell apart (the same bonds that the modernizing passions of Sarmiento contributed to destroying); the loneliness of the illiterate who could not read that which was in the collective interest; and the loneliness of an immigrant bereft of politics and civic models.

Sarmiento attempted to settle this debt with history and with the future by omitting some critical questions, by euphorically embracing the latest discoveries in the field of education (which explains the character of Sarmiento's second liberal phase, inspired in the French centralism of the 1880s), and by devoting considerable energy to public affairs. As a distant relative of the Renaissance humanists, Sarmiento believed that civic virtue redeemed and purified. Was this not the relationship linking his admirable prose with politics? He took leave of the private sphere, which he considered unimportant and opaque, in order to address matters of public concern in the press. The republic of civic humanism, which involves literacy as well as the establishment of the civilization of the written word, represents Sarmiento's long-lasting effort to turn civil society into a political community.

Sarmiento bid farewell in Asunción about a century ago, invoking this promise: "education for everyone. This represents liberty, republic, democracy."[13] Liberty, power, and virtue combined? Clearly, in this sentence he emphasized the civic dimension of the republic. In the final analysis, the elderly Sarmiento might have realized that with his actions he had attempted to bring together the creative act of the individual, the coercive power of the state, and the craft of citizenship.

Notes

1. Domingo Faustino Sarmiento, *Recuerdos de provincia*, in *Obras completas* (henceforth *OC*), 52 vols. (Buenos Aires: Luz del Día, 1948–1956), 3:117, 172.

2. See N. R. Botana, *La tradición republicana. Alberdi, Sarmiento y las ideas políticas de su tiempo* (Buenos Aires: Editorial Sudamericana, 1984), chap. 3.

3. Claude Nicolet, "Civis and Citoyen," *Government and Opposition* 21, no. 2 (Spring 1986): 197.

4. Bernard Bailyn, *The Ideological Origins of the American Revolution* (Cambridge: Belknap, 1967); J. G. A. Pocock, *The Machiavellian Moment: Florentine Political Thought and the Atlantic Republican Tradition* (Princeton: Princeton University Press, 1975); Louis Hartz, *The Liberal Tradition in America: An Interpretation of American Political Thought since the Revolution* (New York: Harcourt, Brace, 1955); John Patrick Diggins, *The Lost Soul of American Politics: Virtue, Self-Interest, and the Foundations of Liberalism* (New York: Basic Books, 1984). See also Richard K. Matthews, "Liberalism, Civic Humanism and the American Political Tradition: Understanding Genesis," *The Journal of Politics* 49, no. 4 (1987): 1127–1143. The concept of "civic humanism" belongs to Pocock, who states that it is the most convenient term for describing this tradition of political thought.

5. Sarmiento, "En los Andes (Chile)," speech of April 8, 1884, in *OC*, 22:238.

6. Sarmiento, *Facundo*, critically documented edition, prologue by Alberto Palcos (La Plata: Universidad Nacional de La Plata, 1938), p. 292. See also Natalio R. Botana, "José Luis Romero y la historiografía argentina: Mitre y Sarmiento," a paper prepared for the seminar José Luis Romero y Su Epoca, as part of the symposium Jornadas de Homenaje al Profesor José Luis Romero (Buenos Aires, April 4–8, 1988).

7. Sarmiento, *Viajes por Europa, Africa y América, 1845–1847*, in *OC*:5:x.

8. Ibid., 5:xi.

9. Ibid., 5:92.

10. Sarmiento to Avellaneda, November 16, 1865, in "Cartas a Avellaneda," *La Biblioteca* 6 (1897): 12.

11. Sarmiento, *Educación popular. Informe presentado al Ministro de Instrucción Pública* (Santiago de Chile, March 8, 1848), in *OC*, 12:34.

12. Sarmiento, *Educación común. Memoria presentada al Consejo Universitario de Chile sobre estas cuestiones* (1856), in *OC*, 12:272.

13. Sarmiento, "El último discurso. En una manifestación de las escuelas en la Asunción" (June 3, 1887), in *OC*, 22:355.

6   Sarmiento and Economic Progress: From *Facundo* to the Presidency

ROBERTO CORTÉS CONDE

The idea of economic progress was neither original nor exclusive to Sarmiento. A great many of Argentina's national founders adhered to this concept. Furthermore, as Alejandro Korn has pointed out,[1] it was one of the main tenets of European and American positivism. The Argentine idea of progress, however, was not a simple repetition of European thought. Alberdi and Sarmiento, in particular, were keenly aware of Latin American reality. They learned about this reality during the years of struggle and frustration, and it occupied long hours of meditation during their years in exile.

Sarmiento offered an explanation of the social and economic roots of the Argentine crisis in his *Facundo*. In the first chapters of that book, he masterfully described how a reality (backwardness, barbarism) had to be changed not only because of the benefits of progress but because backwardness and isolation had brought about social habits that caused Argentina's political troubles. Like Montesquieu and Adam Smith, Sarmiento believed that political society required norms and roles for the interaction of individuals. That is to say, there had to exist a *community* so that the bases for government could be established.

The colonial political system was based on cities where a community and a political society certainly existed. However, the Wars of Independence destroyed that system, along with the community that served as its basis, without replacing it with another. A community, which is required for the existence of government, could no longer be found. This is why we find a political theory in *Facundo*. I will describe the reality analyzed by Sarmiento.

Sarmiento's World

Sarmiento was born at the height of a clash between two worlds: the world that, after three centuries of orderly colonial life, was ending and the revolutionary world that was beginning to confront questions of independent life. The revolutions for independence broke the legitimacy of the old monarchical order and brought about profound changes that later would be difficult to control. The replacement of monarchical legitimacy with popular sovereignty (considering how imprecise that concept was at the time) was a much more difficult task than the leaders of independence had anticipated. The authority succeeding the viceroyalty was opposed by competing forces that had survived because of enormous distances and a lack of central government resources. Years of anarchy and civil war became the unwanted result found by those who had hoped for a brilliant period of peace and prosperity after the collapse of absolutism. Not only did political changes unleash uncontrollable forces, but serious conflicts caused by economic and social changes also emerged.

Colonial Life, Mining, and a Network of Cities

The oldest Argentine urban network was formed along the silver route to Alto Perú. The stretches uniting Buenos Aires, Jujuy, Salta, Tucumán, Santiago, and Córdoba had significant urban activity involving commerce and transportation to and from Potosí. In contrast to European cities, which depended on their local markets, these South American cities depended on far-off centers of production. This is what prompted Sarmiento to comment that these cities were surrounded by the desert and had no way out.[2] They did not live on the production of their own hinterland but, rather, on distant markets.[3]

For three centuries, the colonial political regime was based on this network of cities. In the largely unpopulated area of Alto Perú only territorial outposts were established along the lengthy journey from mine to port. Administrative and commercial cities dominated the space, a domination made possible by the mining wealth that financed urban life. This gave a sparkle to life that other colonies in the Americas did not possess. Generally, what distinguished Spanish colonization from English or Portuguese endeavors was its dependence on mining and its complex network of cities and regional markets.

With independence Alto Perú became a separate entity, and mining ceased to be the focus of economic activity in the River Plate region. Ranching along the littoral took its place. These circumstances changed regional arrangements: the northeast, linked to Alto Perú, entered into a crisis; the littoral of the Paraná (Buenos Aires, Entre Ríos, Santa Fe, Corrientes) thrived. However, it was not just the northeast but all of urban life that entered into a prolonged crisis. The cities became highly dependent on commerce from poorer neighboring areas, and thus began the enduring conflict between city and countryside, between unitarians and federalists.

The decline of the cities and the ruralization (barbarianization) of social life brought an end to association and thus an end to the political system; both events were much more significant than even the crisis of government. Sarmiento pointed out that although the *criollo* elite won the war against Spain, it was the desert that won the war against the cities. In the desert there is no political society, so no government is possible. As he put it in *Facundo:* "On the Argentine plains, there is no nomadic tribe; the herdsman is established on the land as if he owned it with title deed. However, in order to occupy it, it has been necessary to dissolve all association and spread families over an immense area. Imagine an extension of two thousand square leagues populated with each inhabitant at a distance of four leagues from the other, eight at times, two at best. . . . Society has completely disappeared; the municipality does not exist, the police cannot function, and civil justice does not possess the means to reach criminals."[4]

Political society depends on a social fact: community. A community did exist in the cities during the colonial period, in the manner of Republican Rome. Citizens had emerged in the Greek polis, but the fall of Rome signified the end of a world of cities and the triumph of a rural formation. In Argentina, the rural world that emerged with independence was not a world of farmers; it was a world of herders, composed of associations of ranches "at a distance of four leagues" of each other, where the only place for social interaction was the general store and tavern, the *pulpería*.[5]

Economic Resources, the State, and Public Finances

The political instability and chronic weakness of postindependence governments can also be traced to a lack of resources for the maintenance of the political system, the payment of salaries to the armed forces, and debt service. The state, in other words, did not have the resources to ensure its sovereignty over the area. This was because the new nations appropriated the administrative units of the Spanish Empire, which depended on different resources (silver mines) and pursued different objectives.[6] Spain had created an imperial system based on the domination of cities extending from Mexico to Chile and Argentina, and within these cities there existed a complex bureaucratic structure through which the empire could ensure control of the mining resources of New Spain and Alto Perú. The new states, however, were forced to find other resources to replace silver, and income fell accordingly. Involved in a war against Spain that lasted much longer than the war between England and the United States (in the case of Brazil, there was no war with the mother country) and plagued by internecine conflicts, the new Spanish American states confronted enormous problems as well as tremendous economic and financial hardship.

One of the attributes of the modern state is its exclusive right to exercise the power of coercion over territory where sovereignty is claimed. To make sovereignty effective, the state must possess an organization and coercive force that can prevent the emergence of competing powers. Thus, the state is able to offer essential public services (defense, security, justice) and can require support from those who reside within the state's jurisdiction. Without the backing of silver wealth, though, the governments of postindependence Latin America had only nominal authority over the enormous and far-flung territories of the former colonial regime. Professional armies that could be dispatched to distant areas were unthinkably costly for these modest criollo governments. The winners in this situation were those who did not have to rely on the voluntary payment of taxes to finance bureaucratic structures, but who could instead (at least locally) count on men and horses to impose their will. The *caudillos* could exercise authority based on the effective, albeit extralegal, monopoly of violence within their territories. They could offer defense and security and receive tribute from those who lived in areas under their domination.

National authority, then, was exercised in an intermittent fashion and only when a national armed force could be convened. As distance from the central government increased, moreover, the loyalty of the army decreased.

The main problem for these fledgling states went beyond the achievement of a consensus among the different regions regarding the political formation of the nation-state.[7] Rather, debate centered on the resources the regions had to contribute in order to finance central authority. In the lengthy discussion between the province of Buenos Aires and the interior provinces, no one questioned that customs duties collected in the port should be allocated to the nation. The interior provinces simply demanded a different distribution—one that would include them. Without such resources, though, the very existence of the central government was in jeopardy, regardless of how fervent the declarations in favor of national unity may have been.

As a result, war costs represented an enormous burden for the young nation.[8] For decades, war represented the largest item in the budget. This was true not only in the administration of Buenos Aires but in practically every Argentine province.[9] The situation did not improve even after the fall of Rosas and the proclamation of the new constitutional regime. Those administrations which preceded Sarmiento's—not to mention his own—faced financial difficulties owing to the burdens of war upon their limited budgets.

After a conflict of nearly ten years between the national government in Paraná and the province of Buenos Aires, the now-unified nation assumed a great part of the debt accrued by the warring factions. The national government accepted the obligation to amortize the debts of Buenos Aires for 1859 and 1861, and it contributed monies to the province until 1865 (amounting to 5,000 pesos fuertes in public funds). It also took over the Peru-Bolivian Confederation's debt by paying creditors 7,000 pesos fuertes in public funds. In order to understand the impact of this delinquent debt on the national government's budget, one should keep in mind that in 1864 the tributary income was just above 6,000 fuertes. The ability to pay came with the cession of customs duties from the port of Buenos Aires to the national government, and this quid pro quo represented a way to end the long political conflict between the interior and Buenos Aires.

War expenditures during the presidency of Bartolomé Mitre reached 42 percent of the national budget, and in Sarmiento's government they amounted to 30 percent. This level is even higher when war expenditures are seen in relation to tributary income: 51 percent and 42 percent, respectively. The magnitude of the difficulties faced by the central government is underscored by the fact that half its tributary income was committed to activities upon which its very existence depended.[10]

Progress, in this context, represented something more than the mere idealization of foreign models. More than an economic recipe, it was the basis for a political arrangement that would permit the consolidation of the central government and ensure peace and national unity. It was also a response to the crisis unleashed by independence. Populating the pampa and developing agriculture would permit the creation of new communities of people who would interact and decide the rules of government. The establishment of conditions for economic progress would, furthermore, make resources available to ensure the functioning of national government.

The Revolution in Agriculture and Transportation

Since it was impossible to return to the old world of cities, new social conglomerations had to be established by populating the countryside. This was to be accomplished with families of settlers who were committed to working the land, and these communities of settlers and farmers—the basis of economic progress and democratic life—would elaborate the rules of governance. But this Argentina of wide-open spaces faced nearly insurmountable difficulties. The Paraná was the only navigable river in the region; in the pampa, the only communication was overland. To put an end to this isolation required an undertaking of unthinkable proportions: the construction of an extended railway network. This was indeed an enormous undertaking, for the railroad business demanded huge amounts of capital even in countries enjoying a high degree of development.

Economic progress, then, given the conditions of Argentina, meant transforming the country, converting a ranching society—thanks to a railroad and an imported population—into an agricultural society. With agriculture as a starting point, markets and industry would soon follow. The results were to be somewhat different, at least in regard to the sequence just sketched, but economic growth was nonetheless quite impressive.

The Market

A society of free individuals depends upon the existence of conditions that permit communication, interaction, and exchange based on equality of opportunity and access to information. This, in other words, is a market in the modern sense. The establishment of such a market, however, requires the elimination of distance as an obstacle. Remote markets are imperfect markets and permit such inequalities as monopoly discrimination. Modern, competitive markets emerge only when the legal and physical barriers that keep societies in isolation are removed. A competitive market requires access to information. This, in turn, requires a literate population.

Tulio Halperín Donghi has pointed out the significance of Sarmiento's fascination with the use of advertising in the United States. Advertising can contribute to better markets by bringing together producers and consumers and thus saving the costs of commercial exchange. But for this to occur, consumers must know how to read in order to have access to information. As Halperín Donghi puts it: "The importance of the written word in a society organized around a national market—instead of semi-isolated local markets—seemed decisive to Sarmiento: this market could become structured only by means of a truly vast and widespread potential public. The omnipresent commercial advertisement appeared to be an indispensable instrument for this new form of social articulation, and at the same time an additional justification for Sarmiento's interest in public education."[11]

As noted above, political society can only exist in a community. Only a hardworking, industrious people could make self-government prevail. This is what Sarmiento finally discovered in 1868 in Chivilcoy, "I am discovering something that had not been part of my program: the republican spirit; the feeling of the government itself; the sewing machine that makes its sweet trick-track sound in every village of the civilized world and says: 'I state to all the towns of the Republic that Chivilcoy is a program of President Don Domingo Faustino Sarmiento,' and adds with a trace of humor 'Doctor of Law from the University of Michigan,' as I have been jokingly called." [12]

The Achievement

More than one hundred years later it is difficult to perceive the depth of the transformations that took place during Sarmiento's administration. In his last message to the National Congress, Sarmiento offered a comparison between what he had proposed as part of his mandate and what had actually been accomplished:

National income jumped from twelve million fuertes in 1868 to twenty million last year. . . .

Immigration accounted for thirty-nine thousand individuals then, eighty thousand last year, and promises to reach one hundred thousand at present. . . .

The mail handled four million printed or handwritten items in 1868, and seven million in 1873. The pony express has delivered a million letters. . . .

In 1870 six thousand telegrams were sent through a 129-mile wire; in 1873, one hundred seventy thousand through the 2,618 miles that function today. . . .

In 1868, 1,006 children received an education in the national schools; in 1873 this figure increased to 4,000. . . .

At the time of Rosas's fall in 1852, there were twenty schools maintained by the state of Buenos Aires, and not even that number in the rest of the provinces; today there are 1,117 public schools. . . .

In 1868 there was one public library in San Juan. Today there are 140, distributed in every town, even the most obscure and remote. . . .

In 1868, communication with Europe was carried out by four monthly steamers. Today there are nineteen, which means that we have a steamer every other day. . . .

Until 1868, fewer than twelve thousand reams of paper were utilized for printing. In 1872 and 1873 consumption increased to two hundred thousand per year. Until 1868, only 51,000 pesos were spent on books. The amount spent in the past two years reached 348,000 pesos fuertes, or 174,000 pesos per year. . . .

Auxiliary machines were calculated at 5,360 in 1868; in the past two years they increased to 70,000. The factories' central smokestacks, the one hundred periodical publications, and the libraries are all indications of the demand for and the requirements of intellectual activity. Since the population has not doubled in the last quinquennium, it is evident that each inhabitant has doubled his well-being, doubled his wealth, doubled his intelligence and activity.[13]

Here we have the summary of a transformational plan. The accomplishments mentioned in Sarmiento's report were intended to end Argentina's main problem: isolation. Railways crisscrossed the territory in three main directions: 1) the Central, initiated during Mitre's administration, reached Córdoba in 1870 and began to open Argentina's spacious territory, another stretch from Córdoba to Tucumán having been completed in 1876; 2) from Villa María, a new branch through Río Cuarto extended toward Mendoza and the Andes; and 3) in the littoral the plan was to reach Mercedes, in Corrientes. While the province of Buenos Aires continued the extension of lines toward the west and south over the vast space of the pampas, the national government—in a common effort uniting such different parties as those of Justo José de Urquiza, Mitre, and Sarmiento—undertook this enormous project in order to integrate the interior into the national market.

Seen from the perspective of more than a century, such an achievement seems to have been dictated only by geography. However, this was not the case in a country with such immense land area, scarce population and stubborn economic patterns, traversed only by warring Indians and *montoneras*. At the time, it took months to travel the difficult routes in uncomfortable and costly wagons. There were no navigable rivers, except for the Paraná, that might have served as communication, transportation, and commercial routes. The railways may have represented an obvious solution, but they demanded capital outlays of unprecedented magnitude even in the most advanced countries of Europe. It was very difficult to mobilize this capital in a place where savings and markets were lacking, and where social life still resided in the pulpería, in brawling, and in the montoneras. In order to create this capital, the country needed to change its physiognomy. It had to establish a system of justice and law enforcement that did not depend on the caudillos. This meant, at least with regard to constitutional guarantees, that the system had to be federal. Clear norms of social interaction had to be dictated. As stated in Sarmiento's report, the national court system (which began in 1862 with the establishment of the Supreme Court) and the civil and commercial codes had been implemented in response to such needs.

However, habits and customs had to be changed on the basis of a social life of exchange and communication resulting from sedentary work. In order to bring people together they also had to be placed in contact with one another. For this purpose, thousands of kilometers of telegraph lines were installed to establish instant contact with previously inaccessible places. The postal service was organized. Sarmiento recalled with pride the distribution of thousands of pieces of mail because they signified a true revolution in human communication, breaching the intellectual isolation of the population. The national budget shows significant allocations for the creation of innumerable post offices across the country. These post offices bore witness to the presence of the federal government and, in this respect, were more significant than army posts. National schools in every provincial capital, normal schools to train new teachers, and 10,000 public primary schools attest to this notable transformation. These fundamental changes permitted the formation of markets, the basis of the country's progress.

Backwardness seemed very distant from the world of farmers, engineers, and scientists desired, and to a large extent accomplished, by Sarmiento. Immigration, settlements, the Astronomic Observatory and the Academy of Sciences in Córdoba, the Department of Agriculture and the Office of Statistics were all creations of an administration anxious for progress. In 1869, the first national census was completed; at the time of his farewell, Sarmiento inaugurated the transatlantic telegraph lines. Indeed, the man who fought for progress and order as conditions for advancement had inaugurated, on October 12, 1868, six decades in which constitutional governments succeeded each other without interruption, and in which economic growth placed Argentina among those nations having the highest per capita income in the world.

Notes

1. Alejandro Korn, *Influencias filosóficas en la evolución nacional* (Buenos Aires: Claridad, 1936), p. 175.

2. Domingo Faustino Sarmiento, *Facundo* (Buenos Aires: La Cultura Argentina, 1915), p. 54.

3. Roberto Cortés Conde, "Aspectos económicos en la formación de las ciudades," in *De historia e historiadores. Homenaje a José Luis Romero* (Mexico: Siglo XXI, 1979), p. 345.

4. Sarmiento, *Facundo*, pp. 56–57.

5. Ibid., pp. 83 and 91. Daniel J. Boorstin, in his discussion of nineteenth-century westward expansion in the United States, notes the appearance of the

wagon train as a nucleus of social interaction where roles and norms were decided by the group. He refers to this phenomenon, which is very different from Argentina's experience, as that of community before government. Boorstin, *The Americans: The National Experience* (New York: Vintage Books, 1965), p. 122.

6. Roberto Cortés Conde, "Las finanzas y la formación de los estados nacionales en Hispanoamérica," *Revista de Occidente*, 2nd ser., 13, nos. 62–63 (July–August 1986): 152–159.

7. See Juan Alvarez, *Las guerras civiles argentinas y el problema de Buenos Aires en la república* (Buenos Aires: La Facultad, 1936).

8. With governments almost always on the verge of collapse, war spending was often grossly enlarged because of favoritism to certain suppliers, producers, or merchants. Enrique M. Barba points out that during the "Conquest of the Desert" carried out by Juan Manuel de Rosas, each soldier received some twenty-one pounds of meat. Barba, "La financiación de la Conquista del Desierto," *Todo Es Historia*, 4, no. 48 (April 1971): 50.

9. See Tulio Halperín Donghi, *Guerra y finanzas en los orígenes del estado argentino, 1771–1850* (Buenos Aires: Editorial de Belgrano, 1982).

10. Miron Burgin, *Aspectos económicos del federalismo argentino* (Buenos Aires: Hachette, 1960), p. 76.

11. Tulio Halperín Donghi, *Proyecto y construcción de una nación, 1846–1880* (Caracas: Biblioteca Ayacucho, 1980), p. xxxvii.

12. Ibid., p. 413, citing Sarmiento, *Obras completas*, vol. 21.

13. H. Mabragaña, *Los mensajes (1810–1910)* (Buenos Aires: Compañía General de Fósforos, for the Comisión Nacional del Centenario, 1910).

2

THE WRITING SYSTEMS OF SARMIENTO

7 Sarmiento the Writer

RICARDO PIGLIA

To speak of Sarmiento the writer is to speak of the impossibility of being a writer in nineteenth-century Argentina. The first problem: one must visualize within this impossibility the state of a literature with no autonomy; politics invades everything, there is no space, functions are intermingled, one cannot be only an author. The second concern: that same impossibility has been the condition for writing an incomparable work. Sarmiento was able to write some of the best texts in Argentine literature because to be a writer was impossible. His greatest works (particularly *Facundo*) express within their forms this central paradox.

The euphoria felt by Sarmiento regarding the power of his written word is part of the same contradiction. His linguistic megalomania seems to be an example of the arrogant ideology of the failed artist, as analyzed by Philip Rieff in various contemporary politicians. If it is true that the politician triumphs where the artist fails (the case of Mario Vargas Llosa comes to mind), we might say that in nineteenth-century Argentina, literature can exist only where politics fails. Indeed, political eclipse and defeat are at the origin of the founding works of this nation's literature. *Facundo, Martín Fierro, Una excursión a los indios ranqueles,* and the novels of Eugenio Cambaceres were all written under the conditions of a forced autonomy or trial.

In the case of Sarmiento, his literary writing can be dated (1838–1852), and it is not able to survive his triumph. After the fall of Rosas, Sarmiento can no longer write. He turns to other fields, as his fifty-two volumes of *Obras completas* cannot fail to show. (There is a particular scene in which Sarmiento narrates this termination: "That night I went to Palermo and, taking pen and paper from the desk of Rosas, I wrote four words to my friends in Chile with this date, *Palermo de San Benito, February 4, 1852.*"

A decisive moment, a symbolic gesture: his writing has reached the plateau of power, and from this moment on there will be almost no room, separation, or place for literature.[1])

José Hernández, half fugitive, half hidden in a room at the Hotel Argentino after the defeat of Ricardo López Jordán, writes *Martín Fierro* in order to kill "the tedium of hotel life." Lucio V. Mansilla, relieved of active duty while being tried for the execution of a deserter, awaits the verdict and during this empty time writes *Una excursión a los indios ranqueles.* The clearest and most deliberate example of the construction of such distancing is that of Eugenio Cambaceres, who in 1876 resigns his seat in the House of Representatives and abandons his political future so as to dedicate himself to literature. (And the Argentine novel owes a great debt to that resignation.)

During the nineteenth century, Argentine writers seem to live a dual reality. There is a secret interior to their public lives: they are ministers, ambassadors, representatives, but they cannot be writers. ("I am well, relatively well, but I shall be happy only when I begin writing novels," Eduardo Wilde says to Miguel Cané.) Argentine literature of the nineteenth century might have been the metaphor of Hell for a writer like Flaubert.

Indeed, there is a close contemporaneity between Flaubert's well-known letter to Louise Colet, written in January of 1852, in which he expresses his desire to write a book about nothing, and Sarmiento's writing of *Campaña en el Ejército Grande.* Flaubert's desire synthesizes the highest point in the independence of literature: to write a book about nothing, a book that searches for absolute autonomy and pure form. And it is within that private letter from Flaubert to his lover that we find contemporary literature's manifesto. A historical process is condensed: Marx and Flaubert are the first writers to speak of the opposition between art and capitalism. The unproductive character of literature is antagonistic toward bourgeois reasoning, and Flaubert's artistic conscience is an extreme case of this opposition. He creates a book about nothing, a book that would be good for nothing, that would be beyond the register of bourgeois utility: the maximum autonomy in art is at the same time the most acute moment in its rejection of society. Quite the contrary, in January of 1852 Sarmiento searches within the effectiveness and utility of the written word. In *Campaña en el Ejército Grande* he argues with Justo José de Urquiza (who neither listens, nor recognizes him, nor answers much, and who finally intimidates him with his dog, Purvis) and futilely attempts to convince him of the importance and social power of the written word. *Campaña* narrates this conflict and in truth represents an explicit debate (a campaign) about the function and utility of writing.

The asymmetry between Sarmiento and Flaubert (each representing the best writing in his respective language at the time) summarizes the problems of that incongruence in contemporary culture which has defined Argentine literature ever since its beginnings. The fringe and *desert* positions of this literature[2] (distanced from both colonial heritage and pre-Hispanic tradition, and Europeanized from the margins) are made manifest in shapes of scission and dual temporality. Things appear concurrently contemporaneous and outdated. The first readings of the Salón Literario (1837) seek to define a strategy to permit both the desintegration of this distance and the materialization of present culture. The dominant cultural tradition in Argentina up to the time of Jorge Luis Borges is characterized by the tension between anachronism and utopia. (Obviously, Borges understood how to explore the combination of anachronism and utopia to the utmost, and he built on it both his fictions and his theory of reading. This combination represents the fundamental material of "Pierre Menard.") So we find the basic question always to be, Where is the present? Or, better yet, How can one be in the present? And this question is a central theme in the works of Sarmiento.

In the origins of Argentine literature, this nonsynchrony is evident above all in problems having to do with the autonomy and function of literature. While European literature has achieved an institutionalized separateness in literary practices and categories, in Argentine literature these issues exist only in the conscience of writers and in their will to establish a national literature. We might say that in Argentina there exists a dual history of the place of literature.

On the one hand, Argentine literature responds to general logic and defines its function in relation to other social practices. In the nineteenth century, the practice that determines the place of literature is politics. (There exists a close relationship between the history of the autonomy of literature and the history of the constitution of the state.) Argentine literature is a selfautonomizing force; it tends to dissociate political power from another power that transcends it ("the intelligentsia"). It is here that the specific function of writing is defined. On the other hand, we discover the attempt to create an emancipated literature whose autonomy is defined in relation to foreign literature. Argentine literature is autonomous because it seeks to sever links with the Spanish tradition and to

carry out in literature the same revolution undertaken in politics and economics. However, this emancipated literature is constructed in alliance
with one foreign literature (already autonomous): French literature taken
as world literature.

This dual relationship—with political practices and foreign literature—
represents a unique method of autonomization of literature and its function. The definition of what it means to be an author is developed in this
double bond. "One must keep one eye on the French intelligentsia and
the other fixed on the entrails of the nation": Esteban Echeverría's motto
synthesizes this dual process. *Strabismic vision* represents the true national tradition: Argentine literature is constituted within a double vision,
a relationship of difference and alliance with other practices and other
languages and other traditions. One eye is on the Aleph, the very universe; the other eye sees the shadow of barbarians, the fate of South
America. The strabismus is asynchronic: one eye sees the past, the other
is on the future.

The history of Argentine literature is marked by separation, double
temporality, two autonomies, by strabismus.

I would now like to analyze this pattern in the figure of Sarmiento the
writer. For a certain indecisiveness of place determines an uncertain aspect
within his works: the displaced use of fiction. Sarmiento himself, in *Recuerdos de provincia,* so defines his entrance into the world of writing:
"With 'La pirámide' the fantastic fictions of the imagination helped me
for the first time to mask the indignation of my heart." The question, of
course, is, On which subsequent occasions was this also true?

In the use of fiction in nineteenth-century Argentina, the tension between politics and literature becomes coded, and one could say that the
difficulty of autonomy in this literature is made manifest in the form of
resistance to fiction. During the birth of Argentine literature, fiction is
antagonistic toward the political use of language. For the effectiveness of
words is bound to truth in all its forms: responsibility, necessity, serious-
ness, the morality of deeds, the weight of reality. Fiction becomes associated with idleness, gratuitousness, a squandering of the senses, that which
cannot be shown. "It would have been simple for me," says Marcos Sastre
during the inauguration of the Salón Literario, "to have gathered together
a great number of those books which so praise youth. That multitude of
useless novels piling up daily in the European presses. Books that should
be viewed as a truly barbaric invasion in the midst of civilization. Vandalism that seizes from the light of progress an immense number of vir-

ginal intellects and perverts a thousand pure hearts." Sarmiento uses similar terms, and in *Viajes* he refers to the "mob" of novelists "who possess those agitated spirits which make a childish society out of Paris, as they listen with gaping mouths to those tellers of tales who entertain children, Dumas, Balzac, Sue."

The keenest example of this reading of the period can be found in the fate of *El matadero* by Esteban Echeverría. Argentine literature's first fictional text remained unpublished for more than thirty years. It should also be stated that this text failed to be published precisely because it was fiction, and fiction had no place save as a private, secret writing. Within the pages of *El matadero*, written in 1838 and lost among Echeverría's papers until its publication in 1871, one finds hidden a metaphor of the displacement of fiction in Argentine literature.

To attempt to create a history of this place of fiction is to trace the history of Argentine fiction's double autonomy: on the one hand, its relation to political discourse; on the other, its relation to foreign forms and genres of an already autonomous fiction (in particular, the novel). Sarmiento's writing is defined within this dual bond.

1

It should be said that the history of Argentine fiction begins twice. Or perhaps it is better to say that the history of Argentine fiction begins with the same twice-told scene of terror and violence. Initially, on the first page of *Facundo*, which is to say the first page of Argentine literature, and at the same time (but in a displaced fashion) in *El matadero* by Echeverría.

Recall the anecdote that opens *Facundo*. Sarmiento chooses a decisive moment in his life:

> Toward the end of 1840, I left my native land, banished because of shame, crippled, full of bruises, jabs and blows received the day before in one of those bloody bacchanalias staged by soldier-types and political gangs. Upon passing by the baths of Zonda, under the nation's coat of arms which on happier days I had painted in a salon, I wrote with coal these words: *On ne tue point les idées*. The officials who received word of the deed sent a commission assigned to decipher the hieroglyphics, which were said to contain ignoble outbursts, insults, and threats. Once the translation was heard, they said, "Well, what does that mean?"

A story both comic and pathetic, this is the tale of a persecuted man who flees into exile and writes in another language. He takes his body, marked by the violence of barbarism, but also leaves his mark: he inscribes a hieroglyphic in which culture is coded, thus creating a microscopic counterpart to the great enigma that he endeavors to translate by deciphering the life of Facundo Quiroga. The opposition between civilization and barbarism is crystalized in this scene where readability comes into play.

Sarmiento seeks to create a clear distance between himself and the barbarism from which he becomes an exile by resorting to culture. We must not forget that his motto is a quotation: a sentence from Diderot which Sarmiento misquotes and attributes to Fortoul, thus opening up a line of equivocal references, false quotations, and apocryphal erudition which is a sign of Argentine culture at least up to the time of Borges. Within this anecdote we find condensed a situation that Argentine literature will repeat with certain variations throughout its history: the head-on collision between the man of letters and the world of the barbarians.

El matadero represents the horrible counterpart to the same situation. In Echeverría's story the cultivated man is inserted into the world of the other, in the working-class neighborhood of the slaughterhouses and the borders of the riverbank. Rather than beginning with exile and flight, this fiction begins with the hero's entry into enemy territory; the violence that Sarmiento escapes appears as the nucleus of the tale. The hero is trapped by the barbarians and dies harassed and tortured.

Facundo could be viewed as beginning where *El matadero* left off, and this continuity of violence, torture, and exile found at the start has been maintained throughout Argentine history, taking shape in various signs. However, if for Sarmiento the violence has been left behind and the power of the written word affirmed in the form of another language used to mark the difference ("What does that mean?" the barbarians asked themselves), in Echeverría the violence is up front, and the story's language remains trapped, like the body, by the confrontation. The text reproduces the conflict on a lexical plane creating a disjunction between the cultivated, presumptuous language (almost unreadable for us today, a language of translation we might say) of the learned unitarian and the oral, popular language of the marginal riverbank federals. And it is paradoxical that the lasting value of *El matadero* lies in the vitality of this popular tongue which has betrayed Echeverría's presumptions and explicit ideology. The author sought to duplicate within its style a value judgment presupposed by the collision between a refined man and uncultivated barbarians. The story's texture has inverted this opposition, and the most vital aspect of *El matadero* is the oral register where popular language appears for the first time in Argentine literature (apart from the *gau-*

chesca). On the very first pages of *Facundo* and *El matadero*, we discover a confrontation of translation—the foreign tongue, the literary tongue (lacking footnotes, a more-or-less savage erudition), bilingualism—with the signs of violence and voice: the popular phrasing, the primitive tones of the national tongue. Moreover, the tension of the dual register is marked in works as different as those produced by Roberto Arlt, Borges, Leopoldo Marechal, Julio Cortázar, Cambaceres, and Arturo Cancela, and it is when the fracture is welded that the greatest texts of Argentine literature are produced.

Thus we find two versions of the origin of Argentine fiction: one, the triumphant and parodic; the other, the hallucinative and paranoid re-creation of an oft-told confrontation. Furthermore, it could be said that paranoia and parody are the two great modes of representation of the popular classes in Argentine literature.

Between those initial texts, however, there exists a key difference that I am particularly interested in delineating, for it is this difference which synthesizes the topic of the present essay. While the beginning of *Facundo* is set forth as a true story and has an autobiographical form, *El matadero* is a fiction—and because it is a fiction, it can enter into the world of the barbarians and give them a place and make them speak. In Argentina fiction is developed in an attempt to represent the world of the other, whether he be called barbarian, gaucho, Indian, or immigrant. This is because, during the entire nineteenth century, in order to speak of one-self, to tell about one's group or one's class, autobiography is used. Learned men account for themselves in the form of true tales; they account for others with fiction.

Literature does not exclude the barbarian, it fictionalizes him, which is to say that it constructs him precisely as the author subjectively imagines him. The enemy is an object that has the privilege of being represented. One must enter the enemy's world, imagine his interior dimensions, his true secrets, his ways of being. The other must be made known in order for him to become civilized. The strategy of fiction implies the ability to represent the hidden interests of the enemy.

The barbarian is a synecdoche for that which is real: in his physical traits one can read, as with a map, the dimensions and characteristics of the reality that determines him. Phrenology is cartography. The other is not just a subject or object, but rather the expression of an alternative world. Barbarism is a metaphor for the spatial conception of a culture: they are on the other side of the border; in order to get to know them, it is necessary to enter (like the unitarian) into their world, to move within one's mind to that enigmatic territory which begins beyond the confines of civilization.

The invention of this split reality is the nucleus of *Facundo*. The opposition between civilization and barbarism[3] describes this dual, conflictual universe politically; at the same time, though, it constructs it. The complexity of the book derives from the attempt to keep the two realms united. One could comment that Sarmiento invents a form so as not to fracture this connection. The pure difference is what the text unites: it is not simply a question of theme; the writing reproduces the split reality (and constructs the unity). The form of civilization and the form of barbarism are represented in different ways. The system of quotations, cultural references, translations, epigraphs, and marks of foreign reading that support civilization's word stand in opposition to the oral roots, the testimonies and tales, the traces of lived experience that duplicate and give voice to the barbarian world. ("I have heard it during an Indian celebration . . ." "An illiterate man has provided me with many of the deeds to which I have been referring." "I myself have heard the terrible details." "Later I obtained the circumstantial narration from a witness to the deed.") There are two forms of truth, two systems of proof that reproduce the structure of the book and duplicate the topic. The tension between the written word and reality, between culture and experience, between reading and hearing, generates a basic difference. Civilization and barbarism are cited in distinct ways, and the man who writes *Facundo* has access to both versions and is able to translate them. This double movement is represented in the very first page of the book: the writer stands on the border, between two tongues, between European quotation and the marks on his body, and this is the place of enunciation.

Facundo establishes an imaginary relationship between two juxtaposed and antagonistic worlds. The book's problems with literary form are concentrated within the title's *and*. (No one possesses a more personal sense of the conjunction than Sarmiento. His writing unites heterogeneity. Polysyndeton is the mark of his style.) Politics tends to make this *and* be read as *or*. Fiction establishes itself within this conjunction. The book is written on the border: to situate oneself at the limit is to be able to represent one world from the vantage point of another, to be able to narrate the passage and the crossing.

For this reason, Sarmiento is interested in the way James Fenimore

Cooper was able to fictionalize the intersection between two realms. "The only North American romance writer who has been able to acquire European celebrity is Cooper, because he has taken the theater for his descriptions to the border between the barbarian and the civilized ways of life."

In reality, Sarmiento attributes to Cooper the virtues that belong to the genre. In *Theory of the Novel*, Georg Lukács defined the novel as the form imposed upon an alienated world.[4] Beyond normalized existence and trivial experience the horizon of another enigmatic reality appears (simultaneously demonic and poetic) which seems to be past logic and reason. The novel form can be constituted (as *Don Quijote* illustrates) when it is possible to conceive of a more intense existence in another world, juxtaposed against everyday life. The nostalgia for an experience that would transcend immediacies is transformed into an imaginary construction of an alternative reality with its own truth and its own laws: the novel narrates the relationship between the two worlds, and the hero is the one who goes from one side to the other.

The opposition between civilization and savagery is the ideological name for the novelistic scission. The dual reality that constitutes the genre's form appears inverted and politicized in Sarmiento. This is why Raúl Orgaz is right when he insists that Sarmiento constructed the opposition between civilization and barbarism with Cooper's novels in mind.[5] The struggle between two opposite forces that define this reality forms a constant in historical thought during this period, and it appears in Sarmiento from the very beginning. However, *Facundo* is written as it is (and it is a unique book) because Sarmiento discovers within the genre a method to represent the experience of a divided world. As Lukács has pointed out, the genre transforms the single discursive dimension of the metaphysical order and shows that the dual reality can also be grasped as figure and anecdote. What Sarmiento reads into the genre is this figurative and not only discursive representation of meaning: to produce the experience of signification; to foreclose interpretation in an image before it becomes an idea. The novelistic experience of this divided reality is the kernel of the literary form in *Facundo*.

We do not read *Facundo* as a novel (which it is not) but rather as a political use of the genre. (*Facundo* is a proto-novel, a novel machine, a museum of the future novel. In this sense it establishes a tradition.) The argument with the genre stands implicit in the book. *Facundo* is written prior to the consolidation of the novel in Argentina and prior to the constitution of a state. The book is situated in relation to these two future forms. It both discusses the conditions that the government should possess (chap. 15) and the possibilities of a New World novel in the future (chap. 2). On the one hand, *Facundo* is the kernel of the state (in the sense used by Claude Lévi-Strauss in discussing totemism as the kernel of the state); on the other, it is the kernel of the Argentine novel. Possessing something of the prophetic and the utopic, it produces a *mirage* effect: within the vacuum of the desert, whatever one hopes to see shines as if real. The book is constructed between the novel and the state: anticipating and announcing them both, it stands between these two antagonistic forms. *Facundo* is neither José Mármol's *Amalia* nor Juan Bautista Alberdi's *Bases:* it is composed of the same but transformed material, like a crossbreed or a double form.

The key to this form (the invention of a genre) resides in the fact that the novelistic representation does not gain autonomy by itself but is, instead, controlled by the political word. This is where the effectiveness of the text and of its strategic function is defined: the fictional dimension acts as an instrument of truth. Therefore, the book presents a dispute regarding its own norms of interpretation that move throughout the story. *Facundo* proposes a type of truth different from what it practices. The discussion concerning the distortions, errors, exaggerations, and novelization of reality delineated by Sarmiento's contemporaries is directly bound to this issue. From the detailed revisions made by Valentín Alsina up to the opinions of Alberdi, Gutiérrez, and Echeverría,[6] all criticism tends to agree that the book fails to obey the norms of truth that it posits. At the same time, everyone recognizes that this incongruity is the basis of its literary effectiveness. (Only when the book becomes canonized through its ideological triumph does this debate find its resolution.)

Facundo is constructed within the tension between the discursive and the figurative character of meaning: according to where the emphasis is placed, one reads one thing or another. On one level, the book is neither true nor false; it simply proposes an experience of reality, and this is founded on belief. At the same time, however, truth itself is posited as the most faithful reconstruction of the struggle between civilization and barbarism ever to have been achieved. The problem of norms of interpretation resides within the structure: at times, Sarmiento perceives the freedom of reading which stands as implicit in the book. "[About the] *Facundo* to which you refer with such interest, an Argentine friend of mine said that the many errors it contains are the cause of its popularity," he writes in a letter to Miguel Luis Amuchastegui (December 26, 1853), adding: "Among us there exists a divorce between the reader and the book."

The reader takes his turn as author to be able to correct a faulty narration or an effect attributed to a cause different from the real one. The fascination of the text and its possible uses and transformations are related to its errors, that is, its veering away from the truth and its figurative and fictional construction of signification.

The first page of *Facundo* centers on this issue. First there is a warning about the inexactitudes and errors concerning the relationship between truth and falsehood; then Sarmiento narrates an anecdote. We encounter an immediate link between the discussion of tergiversation concerning reality and the story that opens the text. The initial anecdote defines the conditions of the true enunciation: the first page constructs the frame, perhaps, between subject and truth. Lived experience inaugurates the text; he who calls himself "I" affirms his right to the word, and the autobiographical form is the guarantee of truth. In *Facundo,* Sarmiento presents the terms that define his entry into writing "for the first time" in an *inverted fashion:* now it is the indignation of his heart which serves to hide the fantastic fiction of his imagination. (This inversion is the discovery of a form and the invention of a genre.)

Fiction is subordinated to the political use of language, but fiction constructs the stage where the political word can enter. The initial scene of *Facundo* is there in order to write the quotation. It does not matter whether it is true or false (it is written *as if* true); it is told so that the sense may remain fixed in an image, so that the signification may be the result of an experience.

However, the place where the discursive truth is concentrated is also sculpted by the tergiversation, the distortions, the fictional use. Sarmiento finds a phrase from Diderot in an article from the *Revue encyclopédique* ("On ne tue pas les idées"), he reproduces it in an article in 1842,[7] uses it at the beginning of *Facundo,* misquotes it, and translates it in his fashion ("Men are beheaded, ideas are not"); he transforms, displaces, and appropriates it. After this metamorphosis, the French quotation ends up as a sentence from Sarmiento: Barbarians, ideas cannot be killed.

In this microscopic example, the procedure that Sarmiento is going to expand and reproduce throughout the entire book (and in his literary writing) is synthesized. This writing process is characterized by a manipulation of truth, bound at once to error, to translation, to plagiarism, to falsification, to urgency, to appropriation, to fictional liberty, to political necessity. Yet, the foundation of the form that we see here in miniature resides also in the figurative use of truth: Sarmiento synthesizes an abstract network of meaning in an experience represented by an indelible image. In this way, he constructs an imaginary scenario for writing the truth. What I mean by this is that Sarmiento is able to create a dramatic scene that condenses the abstract lines of an interpretation. It does not matter whether this construction is true or false, since fiction is at the same time true and false, since fiction seeks to produce an experience of truth.

2

Sarmiento is the founder of Argentine literature because he finds a solution that attends both to the freedom of writing and the necessities of political efficacy. The backwardness and lack of autonomy of nineteenth-century Argentine literature hinder the institutionalized constitution of genres, making their boundaries uncertain. Sarmiento exploits the possibilities of this formal immaturity like no one else. Constructed of all his readings and all his books, *Facundo* is a book unlike any other. Its basic traits are those of juxtaposition and the mixture of fragmented genres: we find simultaneously the essay, journalism, private correspondence, historical chronicles, and autobiography. (Indeed, the practical effectiveness of the book depends on this use of genres.) Sarmiento uses genres as distinct modes to enunciate truth: each genre has its system of evidence, its legitimacy, its method of making credible. The genres are stances of enunciation that guarantee the criteria of truth. In this sense, there exists a direct relationship between the fragmentary use of genre and the effect of truth (key to political efficacy).[8]

The need to mask and conceal the fictional use of language is what explains the movement of writing among the different genres. Yet, the fictional construction is the knot (the internal form) that unifies and maintains this constellation intact. The use of fiction is what keeps any particular genre from predominating and makes possible the expansion and proliferation of Sarmiento's writing. The basic formal situation that unifies the multiple registers in *Facundo* is fictional.

Sarmiento constructs the nucleus of this internal form for the first time in "La pirámide" (*El Zonda*, no. 6, August 25, 1839). This writing process marks the beginning of his literary works; by this I mean that it is found at the chronological origin of his literature, and it repeats itself every time he writes. The underlying scene is simple: the fictionalized other is convoked as a spectre (at once monster and enigma, the synthesis of the enemy culture); the agent of truth broaches a dialogue and a personal struggle with him. The writing is the stage for this confrontation.

In "La pirámide" we find the Spanish cultural tradition personified in the ghost of a dead father. "The desembodied shadow" defends the negative tradition: Spanish heritage is that monstrous figure which insults "the damned patriot, the parricidal son."

The invention of a genre consists in constructing an imaginary form directly and personally related to both history and politics. The writing reproduces the movement of this dialogue with an interlocutor who is both the object and receiver of the discourse. The complex pronominal mechanism typical of Sarmiento's writing is the expansion of this basic situation: the writing represents an oral scene of polemics and insults possessing forms of interrogation, sermon, political oratory, slander, self-defense, and a denial of charges. The interrogations, interjections, negations, suppositions, and implicit questions all work on the imaginary construction of the enemy (and his allies) as a basis for the situation of enunciation. The other man is the *you* of the discourse, but he is also the object. When *you* is converted into *he*, and he forms his group and alliances (*them*), we are transported into the area of intrigue and paranoia.

Undergoing a metamorphosis, the spectre changes places, and its content becomes modified. In *Mi defensa* it is the nation that "sinks below my feet, it evaporates, it turns into a horrible spectre." In *Facundo*, "the terrible shadow" is the ghost of a dead man who contains all the enigmas of barbarism. In *Campaña en el Ejército Grande* the place of the monster and the enigma is occupied by General Urquiza (and his dog!). *Campaña* is truly one of Sarmiento's greatest books because this dramatic form of direct confrontation with the other enigmatic figure—who in all his monologues does not hear and whose deep reasoning one must imagine—functions as a mold for representing a concrete historical situation. (Urquiza attends to this figuration with certain ironic indifference, but he undoubtedly grasps the excesses of Sarmiento's overacting and paranoid burden. "I owe to Urquiza the coining of 'crazy' as a label," Sarmiento writes to Mary Mann in 1868.) In *Campaña* the figurative character of meaning dominates the purely discursive signification once again.

The secret drive behind this personal and imaginary struggle with the figure of the quintessential other is, of course, Juan Manuel de Rosas. The image of the spectre and its metamorphosis is Sarmiento's way of representing his impossible dialogue with Rosas. Sarmiento is a great writer because this dialogue with Rosas, in his texts, is always displaced and fictionalized as well as indirect and mediated. The writer of *Facundo* never writes a book about Rosas, yet he does nothing but write about him: Sarmiento's great literary (and political) decision lay in choosing Quiroga as the subject of a book (about Rosas). This displacement allows the writer total liberty because he constructs a disputed figure between Sarmiento and Rosas. Just as Rosas politicizes language and uses it to construct a rigid symbolism for the federalists, which condenses the lines of interpretation, on the other side of the battlelines we find Sarmiento, constructing a scenario to use Quiroga's ghost for his own creation of a symbolism designed to condense within a series of images and mottoes the other sense of history. "A noisy controversy has erupted between Rosas, hero of the desert, and Sarmiento, member of the University of Chile. It is a battle of titans by the look of things," writes Sarmiento (as always using indirect discourse as a subtle mark of fictionalization). Sarmiento's writing constructs the illusion of a struggle between equals (an equality that Urquiza refuses to recognize).

In Sarmiento, literature lasts as long as the illusion of this dialogue lasts, a dialogue that is nothing more than the fictional representation of a political confrontation. Or perhaps it is better to say that literature has its place as long as Sarmiento can re-create Argentine history as a personal struggle. What one should actually say is that Argentine history is a struggle whose privileged stage is Sarmiento's writing. There must exist a counterpositioned "other" to fight against so that the confrontation can lighten the megalomania and autonomy of the agent, thus justifying all the excesses and tergiversation and uses of language: this is why the political struggle against the enemy tradition overlaps with Sarmiento the writer.

For the confrontation and dialogue to be possible, it is necessary not only to find the "other" present in writing in the form of an ideal adversary, but also to construct the author as the personification of civilization and truth. He who marches in *Campaña en el Ejército Grande* is a perfect example of this work of the figuration: Sarmiento presents himself in the forms of emblem and allegory. This complex construction of a subject able to engage in a personal dialogue with Argentine history runs throughout Sarmiento's works. "Everything in the world can be personified," he writes in *Recuerdos de provincia*. ("Rosas is the personification of barbarism.") The personification of himself as an example of civilization is the other great moment in Sarmiento's writing (together with the construction of the spectre).

The writer must become a dual personage, speak of himself in the third person, introduce himself. Sarmiento utilizes the classical means of changed identities to allegorize himself: he narrates a story with an enigmatic (and admirable) protagonist and finally discovers, "that was I!" At times he dramatizes himself: Sarmiento is present at a scene where everyone is speaking of him, but no one knows him; or, even better, where everyone is praising him, but no one realizes that the young man standing to one side of the room is the selfsame Sarmiento.

In Sarmiento, the unexpected figuration of his identity is a form of literary construction. Just as important is the figuration of the enemy tradition embodied in the "other" as spectre. Here we perceive the traits of his novelistic writing: as in serial fiction, we find dead traditions and scenographic twists, the play of false identities, of changed names, of appearances that represent the basic modes of representation of the story's truth. In Sarmiento, however, the hero is the one who writes: like those great protagonists of the genre, he is the only one who can pass from one world to another, the only one who really knows the laws that allow passage into this enigmatic reality.

The story of the exile and the quotation are placed at the beginning of *Facundo* so that the hero can make his appearance. In this border scene his place is defined: during the entire book we will see him move and march, enter and exit the story, pursue the figure of the monster that is lost in the desert, struggle to decipher the meaning of the enigma. Megalomaniacal, paranoid, omnipotent, this agent will speak both as prophet and geographer, as hunter and traveler, as historian and poet; he will tell everything about himself and speak for everyone (as if he were everyone); he will say that he knows all the secrets and all the stories, that he has read all the books and studied all the languages: in reality, the only thing the hero does is write. He does nothing else; he writes as no one else, all the time. *Facundo* is at once the story of the spectre that contains the native land's enigma and the history of the author as well.

It is worth noting that the man who writes the quotation at the opening of *Facundo* has been writing for some time and is working to make himself a name as a writer. His beginnings are marked by anonymity and invented names: at first Sarmiento calls himself "incognito" (the unknown), and he writes to Alberdi under the pseudonym of García Román in order to send him some poems. We are now in 1838: "Although I have not had the honor of meeting you, the brilliance of your literary name . . . encourages the shyness of a young man who wishes to hide his own name in order to subject the enclosed composition to your indulgent and illustrious criticism." This is how the history of his relationship with literature begins, and the end is found in *Las ciento y una*. Now in 1852, Sarmiento has made a name for himself and deliberates with Alberdi as an equal. And the epic road he takes from being a nobody to becoming a writer is one of the great bildungsromans of Argentine literature. "I was a writer," he says in *Recuerdos de provincia*. "How many mistaken vocations did I attempt before finding the one that had a chemical affinity, I might say, with my essence?"[9]

Prior to everything else, Alberdi and Sarmiento debate the autonomy and function of learned men. This is the area where Alberdi makes his objections. Moreover, the central point is his criticism of Sarmiento's use of language: he accuses Sarmiento of making fiction ("He invents an apparent Rosas") and of placing politics at the personal service of his writing. In one sense, Alberdi is right: Sarmiento conceals his personal exploitation of the Argentine tongue beneath the form of a political use of language.

This writing brings him into power. Sarmiento reminds one of the serial writers of the nineteenth century who, as Walter Benjamin said, had made a political career out of their ability to illuminate the collective imaginary. But Sarmiento goes further than the rest: the best Argentine writer of the nineteenth century becomes President of the Republic. And then something extraordinary occurs: Manuel Gálvez tells the story of Sarmiento writing a speech for his inauguration that is rejected by his ministers. Sarmiento's inaugural speech is written by Nicolás Avellaneda.

We might say that it is here, in an emblematic figure, that all the tensions between politics and literature running throughout Sarmiento's literature are resolved. From this point on, Sarmiento will have to adapt himself to the necessities of practical politics. Furthermore, he will first have to adapt his use of language.

We can envision this speech as the great text of Sarmiento the writer: the last text, his farewell to language. At times I think that we Argentine writers also write in an attempt to save and reconstruct that lost text.

Notes

1. Sarmiento's literary writing is interiorized. It could be said that it is confined to private circulation. Correspondence is the place where the history of Sarmiento's literature from 1852 on should be reconstructed. The letter as a personal form of relating with a known and absent interlocutor is a central form in his writing, and Sarmiento's masterly use of this form can be observed in *Campaña en el Ejército Grande* and in *Viajes*.

2. "Concerning your books, I have had no word," Andrés Bello writes to Friar Servando Teresa de Mier in a letter dated November 15, 1821. "Only the Devil could have given you the idea to send 750 copies of your work (whichever) to Buenos Aires, which of all the countries of the Americas is without a doubt the most ignorant and where the least is read" (Andrés Bello, *Epistolario* [Caracas: La Casa de Bello, 1984], 1:116). This cultural poverty and debility are, contrary to what one might think, related to the so-called condition of Europeanism in Argentine literature.

3. In order to reconstruct the historical line and the implicit interpretative threads in this opposition, see Tulio Halperín Donghi, *Revolución y guerra* (Mexico: Siglo XXI, 1972). His analysis of the process of ruralization in the

power bases, of the relationships among the masses, discipline and the army, and of the relationship between Rosas and the May Revolution represents an extraordinary development of the central content of *Facundo*. In this sense, *Revolución y guerra* is the best book written on *Facundo*: one of the few cases in which the commentary (though displaced) about a classic reaches the heights of that classic.

4. This hypothesis, formulated by Lukács in 1920, is implicit and has been brought into discussions and enlarged in nearly all the subsequent theories on genre. See Walter Benjamin, "The Storyteller," in *Illuminations* (New York: Schocken Books, 1978); Claude Lévi-Strauss, on myth and novel, in *Mythologiques. III: L'Origine des manières de table* (Paris: Plon, 1978); and René Girard, *Mensonge romantique et vérité romanesque* (Paris: Grasset, 1961). For a synthesis of the relationship among the philosophical traditions, the double realities, and the beginnings of the novel, see Ian Watt, *The Rise of the Novel* (London: Chatto & Windus, 1957), chap. 1.

5. See Raúl Orgaz, "Sarmiento y el naturalismo histórico," in *Sociología argentina* (Córdoba: Assandri, 1950).

6. See "Notas de Valentín Alsina al libro *Civilización y barbarie*," in Domingo F. Sarmiento, *Facundo*, ed. Alberto Palcos (La Plata: Universidad Nacional de La Plata, 1938), pp. 364–426; and Juan Bautista Alberdi, "Facundo y su biógrafo," in *Escritos póstumos* (Buenos Aires: Imprenta Europea, 1897), 5:273–383. Juan María Gutiérrez writes to Alberdi in a letter of August 6, 1845: "What I said regarding *Facundo* in *El Mercurio* I do not regret; I wrote before having read the book; I am convinced that it will have a negative effect on the Argentine republic, and that every sensible man will see it as caricature: this book is like the portrayals made of our society by those travelers who report strange things: *the slaughterhouse*, the *mulata* fondling the little girl, the cigar in the mouth of an older woman, etc., etc. Argentina is not a pool of blood." At a later date (July 1850), also in a letter to Alberdi, Echeverría refers to the errors and exaggerations committed by Sarmiento in his war against Rosas ("Sarmiento wanders about like crazy").

7. See Paul Verdevoye, *Domingo Faustino Sarmiento, éducateur et publiciste* (Paris: Institut des Hautes Etudes de l'Amérique Latine, 1963).

8. The two problems are actually only one. The issue could be synthesized in the expression "There is no book like this one." On the one hand, the natural question—What kind of book is this?—is implicitly answered ("poem, pamphlet, history"). On the other hand, it is presupposed that no similar work exists ("It is worth more than a battalion of cuirassiers sent by a valiant leader"). The key, of course, is the relationship between these two issues: in the intersection we find the play between the problematics of dual autonomy and the place of Sarmiento as writer. As late as 1876 (*Obras completas*, vol. 22), in a speech about the railroads, Sarmiento states that in the midst of the silence and the Rosist terror, "one could hear from beyond the Andes a voice, and from Chile there arose something like a light, a flier, a romance, a book,

call it whatever you like, which appeared in the Chilean press." The book's generic uncertainty is the direct result of its efficacy. However, the lack of autonomy and the urgencies of practicality represent the circumstances of that generic uncertainty and of *Facundo*'s ambiguous uses of truth and fiction.

9. The problematic regarding merit, fame, success, and recognition run throughout the entire history of Sarmiento's relationship with writing. "I neither practice nor accept the axiom of Rosas of sacrificing fortune, life, and reputation for the nation. The first two I have won because of keeping the last intact, according to my understanding of things," he writes in *Campaña en el Ejército Grande*. This concept of holding personal fame before the nation as well as before the requirements of practical politics is at the center of consciousness in Sarmiento the writer.

8 On the Threshold of *Facundo*

JAIME CONCHA

In Memoriam
Noël Salomon

> Born in the foothills of the Andes, all the noteworthy events of
> my life have begun going back and forth from one side to the
> other.
>
> —Sarmiento, *Campaña en el Ejército Grande*

At the end of March 1988, I had the opportunity to travel to Buenos
Aires after a fifteen-year hiatus. What I saw was not just curious, but
frankly pathetic. The economic crisis lashed out mercilessly, and the reactions to it were, in general, confused and contradictory. The collective
ego of the nation—more often a superego—was rapidly crumbling away,
definitively shattering the identity of that once-flourishing *argentinidad*.
Inflation finished off everything the dictatorship and the Falklands/Mal-
vinas war had started. The press, whose decline in quality of information
was evident, was covering the current candidates on the eve of an election
period that enlivened, somewhat, the population's mood. The outstanding
figures of the day, whose public personae wisely mixed smiles with shadows of melancholy and concern, were the governor of La Rioja, always
smiling; the governor of the province of Buenos Aires, smiling and worried; and, as a possible candidate of succession (who did become a candidate later on), the governor of Córdoba, more worried than smiling, with
the additional melancholy of the gens accustomed to the onerous art
of ruling. The polarization between Peronism and Radicalism became
"overdetermined," as an Althusserian would say, by the weight of the
provinces and the interregional struggle.

One hundred and fifty years after the writing of *Facundo*, history seemed
to be repeating itself, though with the inevitable differences observed long
ago in a famous passage. Was this an indication of the relevance of Sarmiento's essay? Or perhaps proof of the anachronism of a republic that
its author, later president of the nation, had contributed to create and
organize?[1] The answers are not merely rhetorical, nor incompatible, but

are complementary. Paradoxically, it may be that the very relevance of the essay demonstrates the intellectual defeat of its author.

It may be appropriate, before undertaking the principal topic of these pages, to justify why a Chilean would want to add to a bibliography, already dense and daunting, on Sarmiento and his *Facundo*. This is not a "Chilean perspective"—first of all, because that is an oxymoron (there is no country more blind than the one trying not to be involved) and, second, because the *Facundo* is a work that reaches all of Latin America. The issue, rather, is this: Are the internal Chilean elements in *Facundo* merely accidental, or do they possess a significant textual projection that would be, to a certain extent, structural? Surely the fact that *Facundo* was written in Chile at the suggestion of a Chilean minister is circumstantial. Unfortunately, there are ministers everywhere, so Sarmiento could have written his denunciation during an exile in Montevideo, for example. All the same, because *Facundo* is addressed principally to a Chilean audience (though not exclusively, since there were many exiled Argentines living there at the time), there are interpolations such as "because my Chilean reader must know . . ." (p. 126), ad hoc comparisons such as to "the ravine in Santiago" in the chapter on Córdoba (p. 107), and references of different sorts, such as to the mines of Chilecito in the description of La Rioja (p. 91). It is more interesting to note that toward the middle of the "Introduction" (i.e., the introduction to the 1845 edition which will reappear in the fourth edition of 1872), he gives eloquent credit to the Chilean press: "From here in Chile, we can give nothing to those who persevere in the struggle! . . . Nothing, except ideas, except consolation, except encouragement; no arms can we take to the combatant, save what the free press of Chile supplies to all free men. The press! The press!" (p. 14).[2]

These lines prompted me to reread the foreword ("Advertencia del autor"), which opens the *Facundo* and which rarely receives proper attention.[3] At first glance, it appears to be a singularly complex part of the work, since the second part, beginning below the inscription *On ne tue point les idées*, represents a montage of experiences at once synthetic and perturbing, demanding an almost microscopic study of its contents.[4] Indeed, it is possible to discern three parts in the foreword: first, the beginning of Sarmiento's trip into exile, "crippled" by a beating from the Rosist henchmen; second, the phrase in French he inscribes "with charcoal" below the nation's coat of arms; and third, separated by a blank space with various dotted lines, Sarmiento's personal translation, representing his promise to continue the fight from Chile. The typographic artifice clearly points toward a road, a physical and temporal itinerary whose exact terms are "I was leaving my homeland" and "it simply meant that I was coming to Chile" and, where the decisive stretch seems to have been, "Upon traveling by the Baths of Zonda. . . ." A text en route, without a doubt; a road into exile that becomes both potential action as well as the actions of his return. Let us focus on this fragment.

Judged in terms of its propositional statement (in the sense of the logical positivists), the French quotation simply says that ideas are immortal. Here, however, the form of the articulation is as important as its meaning. In its negative structure, in the faith Sarmiento proclaims and the energy with which he does so, in its polemic tension, the phrase reveals *in nuce* the mentality of Sarmiento and the peculiar slant of his ideology.[5] It is an apothegm, one of those maxims which the liberals of the nineteenth century chose to summarize an ideal life: "Improve yourself"; "Honor your commitments"; and the like. Here, however, the inscription represents opposition, struggle, resistance. Though negative as a judgment, the phrase becomes thoroughly affirmative; idealistic in spirit, it demands to be extended into a practical exteriorization. Therefore, it is an act of affirmation. It is, as the author himself states at the end of his note, a "protest," that is to say, both a rejection and a vow that must be turned into public "conduct."[6]

There is also a biographical aspect to be considered. "Ideas cannot be killed" is a sentence that Sarmiento writes after having been near death in a jail in San Juan. He has been harassed, humiliated, speared, and wounded. That event, which the victim relates in a letter to his friend Manuel J. Quiroga Rosas and which will become the vivid memory of *Recuerdos de provincia* ("La vida pública"), is omitted here, just barely touched upon, in an ellipsis full of meaning. Thus, the sentence represents a testimony to his salvation; it is an anti-epitaph, a statement of resurrection. And, as one might readily suspect, the sentence becomes a hyperbolic translation of his own circumstances. "Ideas cannot be killed" really means "They have not killed my ideas," which is to say "They have not killed me."[7] The famous French sentence is an ellipsis and a hyperbole at the same time: ellipsis of his own lived experience and a European hyperbole of the self. Ellipsis, hyperbole; soon we will see the parabola in this conic elemental geometry. It will become part of the rhetorical repertory of the exile and will be printed on the cover of his major work.[8]

Moreover, the sentence is written by Sarmiento ("I wrote") below a symbol of his country. In effect, these words represent hieroglyphs that government agents are to translate literally, yet not understand because of their lack of awareness of the value of ideas. The journey sketched in this passage is no longer the personal trip from San Juan to Chile but, rather, the long historical and cultural distance between the remote, deceased writing of an empire representative of oriental despotism[9] and the modern, emancipating writing he sees in the Chilean press.

It is also interesting to examine the material that the traveler uses to etch his inscription. The "charcoal" that permits Sarmiento to record his ire and hope stands light-years away—literally speaking—from the "luminous rays" of the free press. The distance no longer represents the transandean route; nor the historical, multisecular line that runs from Egypt to Chile: it is now a cosmic distance between the order of matter and geology, on the one hand, and the superior order of the spirit, on the other. Abyss-distance, we could call it, since it coincides with the metaphysical and axiological hierarchies that are at the basis of Sarmiento's thought.

There is, however, another side to the coin. Being a precarious and deficient material in one respect (subliterary in its gross and antispiritual facets), the charcoal acquires another value when connected to the French text. The European knowledge contained in that phrase is "geologized" in the charcoal; the philosophy of the ideas encapsulated in the sentence is materialized by the charcoal.[10] In short, through this incidental writing element, Sarmiento appropriates the original French phrase, at once Americanizing and creolizing it.[11] The ideas become concrete and local by means of the charcoal. This deed is a typical example of what, at the end of his "Introduction," Sarmiento will see as a desideratum of future historiography. There, in his sketches on Simón Bolívar, it is clear that Sarmiento sought to promote an authentic New World portrait of the independence hero. Bolívar was there awaiting the moment "when he is translated into his native tongue" (p. 18). In this paradoxical expression, admirable in its depth, Sarmiento offers us yet another key to his literary purpose and the actions of his mountain crossing. The "ideas painted with charcoal," we might call them, are not just the incident that precedes the conception of *Facundo;* they constitute its very center and they characterize a crucial aspect of his cultural project: namely, the appropriation of that which is foreign, the contemplation of its possibly becoming alienating, and the resulting will to shed that alienation.

That we are truly addressing the core of *Facundo* can be proven by other events. The first poem written by Sarmiento, unfortunately lost to us, was called "Mis memorias del Zonda." His first newspaper, when he was director of the press for the province of San Juan, was named *El Zonda,* surely alluding to the winds of the pampa. The place and the name lie, then, at the bottom of Sarmiento's activities as a writer and publicist. In the letter that accompanies the poem sent to Juan Bautista Alberdi, Sarmiento says that it portrays "a country scene in my native land and the recreation at the Baths, which are enclosed by the valley it describes."[12] The idea of "native land" is crucial here. The concentric circles of his native land (Cuyo, the province, San Juan) stretch out from this valley or gorge, place of rest and summer vacation situated at the foot of the Andes. This land is from that moment forever bound to his writing project, "Upon traveling by the Baths of Zonda. . . ." In 1840 Sarmiento resumes the impulses that had emerged in 1837. And in 1845, the year of *Facundo*'s publication, the reference to his native land will bloom again in a greater and more definitive form. The passage ends with this final paragraph: "This simply meant that I was coming to Chile, where freedom was still shining, and that I intended to project the rays of her enlightened press across to the other side of the Andes" (p. 5).[13] From these lines one can make some observations, as follow.

Optical dynamism. The optical metaphors that appear constantly in the Enlightenment and in the progressive ideology of the eighteenth century acquire a dynamic character, closer to a mechanical process than to the transmission of light as such. These "rays" are discharges that Sarmiento catapults against the Rosas dictatorship: missile rays, coal now lighted by the candle of reason. Sarmiento's syntax, which links a double infinitive and a pair of noun constructions, produces a strong and active tension in the statement, communicating the impression of consecutive collisions that, in parabolic curves, are propagated above the Andes. The parabola of *Facundo* begins from this point, with the explosion of ideas that crosses to "the other side of the Andes."[14]

Strategic distance. The place from which Sarmiento shoots his darts defines the struggle as well as the form of his tactics and objectives. Away from the battleground of the pampa, his contest will be neither man-to-man nor a cavalry charge, which would inevitably smack of gaucho. No; he takes a position in the rear guard with the artillery, which he regards as a civilized and rational form of combat.[15] In this fashion, he can hold a dual aim represented by two distinct and asymmetric objectives: Facundo and Rosas; one dead, the other alive and dominating; the provincial *caudillo* and the national *caudillo*; the instinctive representative of barbarism and the figure who has made the city an example of savagery. Looking into the future, the author sketches out in the final chapter ("Present and Future") a curious philosophy of history that permits him both to see Rosas's crimes as a horror story of the past and to appreciate the positive side of the experience and suffering of his people.[16]

Rhythm and passage. We have already seen that the text provides a bridge across the Andes. It is a "passage" in the proper sense: it provides a rhythm, a latitudinal movement that was quite present in the author's mood and that acquired a chimerical character already recognized as such in the article announcing the appearance of *Facundo*. Thus, "Impertinent writers suggest that we want to involve this country in a war with Rosas. For much better reasons we understand that a war is impossible: there will never be interests between Chile and Argentina of sufficient magnitude to merit sending twelve thousand men across America from ocean to ocean."[17] In the almost physical force underlining this impossibility ("America from ocean to ocean"), one can easily sense the nostalgia and secret ideals that motivated Sarmiento.

Echoes of the independence campaign.   The Cuyo of Sarmiento's childhood was the cradle of José de San Martín's independence strategy, which the Argentine revolution would make continental. In *Facundo*, Sarmiento travels around many of these places, which become holy places in his imagination. His first journalistic article in Chile concerned the anniversary of the Chacabuco battle for independence.[18] In the distance between the actual battle and the subsequent official and popular festivities, Sarmiento observes and complains about how the glories of the past have been forgotten, about the injustices endured by the combatants. "What is left after all that glory?" he asks. To a certain extent, the firing of arms in that historic battle is transformed by Sarmiento into arms of light, those "luminous rays" with which he wants to forge the defeat of the heir to the old colonial order.[19] In *Facundo* he writes: "A fixed idea . . . dominates [Rosas] . . . the reconstruction of the former viceroyalty of La Plata" (p. 218). A new freedom expedition is justified. This time, though, it is not the collective act of the independence period, but the act of an intellectual hero who works with the weapons of the press and reason.[20] It is interesting to note, at the beginning of the chapter entitled "Chile," in *Recuerdos de provincia* (1850), that Sarmiento should link the Zonda episode with his subsequent article on Chacabuco, presenting himself almost as a war casualty: "with my hand and arm full of bruises from the day before, I wrote. . . ."[21] It is a wounded man who is writing; Sarmiento writes with those very wounds. Therefore, the lights of the press that he will send forth from Chile are like the sun of the May Revolution, a bit paler perhaps, but moving in the opposite direction so as to reverse the historical route of independence. The series of articles from May and June 1845, which compose *Facundo* and which Sarmiento launches from *El Progreso* against Rosist barbarism, is his Andean campaign, the artillery of his idea-weapons.

The establishment of perspective.   The notion of "projecting" is a mechanical and dynamic concept that can also be interpreted in terms of Arguesian geometry, two of whose basic notions are the correlative operations of projection and perspective.[22] In the "Anuncio de la vida de Quiroga," the Rosas dictatorship is viewed from the perspective of the Chilean institutional order. This perspective allows for a systematic comparison of these two countries, a comparison that contains *en raccourci* a government plan elaborated in the conclusion of the 1845 edition.[23] It constitutes a perspective for criticizing the present and, at the same time, for aiming at the construction of the future after the elimination of tyranny.

Again, one must not try to "Chileanize" *Facundo*. Its being Argentine suffices. Furthermore, to make it Chilean would be to add to the humiliation of both Southern Cone countries. This has only been an attempt to broaden the Cuyo horizons of the author of *Facundo*, to elevate the sights to see beyond the Andean wall, so full of memorable historic roads, and to show not only that the transandean background provides strategic depth to Sarmiento's struggles ("still left to him are the rear guards of Chile and Bolivia": *Facundo*, p. 233) but also that Chile provides him with a fundamental perspective for understanding the state of affairs in his own country. If, in 1988, on horseback at the top of the Andes, our hero could have glanced toward the Pacific and then at the "planetary pampas," the spectacle would surely have irritated him. In fact, our visionary would have found himself rather disoriented. To the west, he would have seen Rosas in power, though not in gaucho style. Instead, he would have seen him ruling with all the trappings of civilization: with French parentage, with a German-style army, with bank credits from the great democracy of the North, and with henchmen that possessed the latest in the technology of terror. In his own country, toward the Atlantic, he would have seen the caudillos amusing themselves in parliament, taming and dominating the administration, keeping justice from casting light on a vast panorama of blood and tears.[24] Whereas Rosas had his French blockade, which gave him a fleeting Americanist aureole, the caudillos of 1982 undertook their anti-British adventure with sympathetic and, of course, impotent Third World support. In one of the most glaring such episodes of the late twentieth century, the combination of an extemporaneous colonialism and an uncouth militarism seems to have surpassed even the most extreme version of the *Batrachomyomachia*. Indeed, writes Sarmiento (*Facundo*, p. 110), "what else was to happen to a country that in only fourteen years has punished England, harassed half a continent, equipped ten armies, fought a hundred pitched battles, conquered everywhere, become involved in every event, violated every tradition, tried every theory, gambled everything and come out well in everything: a country that has lived, become rich, and become civilized?"

Notes

1. Does the change from barbarian *caudillismo* to learned *caudillismo*, which Juan Bautista Alberdi so strongly criticized, really begin with the founders of modern Argentina? One could surmise, for example, that the War of the Triple Alliance against Paraguay, one of the least laudable events of Sarmiento's presidency, is only an international extension of the previous Argentine civil war; also to be remembered is that Julio Roca, patriarch of oligarchic and agro-exporting Argentina, was the head of the desert campaign, the "pacifier" par excellence. The former projects externally an internal problem; t' ᴉ latter exterminates in the interior in order to commercialize *ad extra*.

2. Throughout the present chapter I am quoting from the Biblioteca Ayacucho edition (Caracas, 1977). The best edition of *Facundo* is still Alberto Palcos's critical edition, dated 1938; a recent printing is that of Ediciones Culturales Argentinas (Buenos Aires, 1962).

3. In a monographic study of *Facundo*, C. A. Jones does not even mention the "Advertencia"; see Jones's *Facundo* (London: Tamesis Books, 1974), p. 36. José Campobassi, in an extremely detailed study amounting to more than 1,000 pages, also fails to refer to the foreword; see his *Sarmiento y su época*, 2 vols. (Buenos Aires: Losada, 1975), 1:216.

4. Regarding this "Advertencia del autor," there are certain problems of denomination. It would seem to contain two parts: the first, dated 1845—thus before the composition of the book—is by its very content the "foreword" (*advertencia*) as such; the second part, as noted, begins with an epigraph (*On ne tue point les idées*) and was labeled as "Prólogo" in 1851. Because most editions do not make the distinction and because the second part tends to disappear for typographic reasons (see pp. 3–5), I prefer to refer to the entire two-part section as "Advertencia del autor." Palcos, who is usually conscious of details, calls it an "introducción" (see p. 6n.), which leads to a confusion with the more extended "Introducción" that follows.

5. It is quite common, even among the best critics, to call Sarmiento an "idealist." Obviously, when explaining American independence in terms of "the movement of European ideas" (*Facundo*, p. 65), he was; but the assertion is modified when, in his vision of revolutionary Buenos Aires, Sarmiento recognizes that "commercial activity had brought Europe's spirit and general ideas" (p. 109). It is easy to show that such paired ideas and concerns appear constantly in *Facundo* (p. 138 et pass.); and there is no criticism of idealism so emphatic as Sarmiento's criticism of Bernardino Rivadavia and the old unitarians. Idealism as theory of knowledge, as morality, and as philosophy is systematically condemned because of its inadequacy when confronted by the conditions of Argentina (p. 113). Leopoldo Lugones's characterization seems more to the point: "His essentially positive spirit, his absolute tendency toward action, his materialist concept of utility . . ." (*Historia de Sarmiento*, 2nd ed. [Buenos Aires: La Comisión Argentina de Fomento Interamericano, 1945], p.

17). Lastly, a statement in *Facundo* as famous as that "contradictions terminate by contradicting themselves" (p. 14) does not appear to be very idealistic.

6. The fragment concludes: "Those who know of my conduct in Chile know whether I have fulfilled that protest" (*Facundo*, p. 5).

7. Manuel Gálvez, who writes with resentment toward Sarmiento, ironically points out that, in the episode analyzed, those ideas are absent; see Gálvez's *Vida de Sarmiento* (Buenos Aires: Editorial Tor, 1952), p. 68.

8. On the cover of the *El Progreso* edition, the title is placed at the top; below it, toward the center, the name of the author. Toward the right, one finds the epigraph in French with its corresponding gaucho translation, so that Rosas might understand it.

9. The "asiatic" (Egypt as well as North Africa are part of this suprageographic notion) is much more than a picturesque reference in the conception of *Facundo*. Certainly it is more than a simple "taste for oriental comparisons," as Ana María Barrenechea would have it. See her "Función estética y significación histórica de las campañas pastoras en el *Facundo*," NRFH ("Homenaje a Alfonso Reyes"), 15, nos. 1–2 (1961): 321n. Straddling both the Enlightenment and exotic romanticism, this element stands as a central component in the ideological landscape of the work: together with the European Middle Ages it supplies a basic paradigm for the representation of barbarism. Both factors unite in a Spain which is Arabian in part and medieval in nearly all the rest of its social body. Sarmiento's readings? Montesquieu, of course. Also, among much else, the works of Volney—*Les Ruines de Palmyre* (1791) without a doubt, since Sarmiento quotes it; and, probably, *Voyage en Syrie et en Egypte, pendant les années 1783, 1784, et 1785* (Paris, 1787, 1792, and the definitive 1799 edition)—not to mention the numerous miscellaneous articles he must have explored as an assiduous reader of *Revue des Deux Mondes*. The topic is quite an important one because it covers the entire artistic map of *Facundo*: the iconographic, the metaphoric, and the lexical registers among others. It therefore deserves a separate treatment.

10. It is curious that the official commission in charge of verifying the precise location where Sarmiento wrote the sentence would have determined—contrary to actual fact, it seems—that it was a rock in the Andean foothills. See Allison W. Bunkley, *The Life of Sarmiento* (New York: Greenwood Press, 1952), p. 136n. There are commissions *pa' to'o*, as the Andalusian of the tale would say; surprisingly, however, the error represents a good guess in that it reveals the author's deep motivation. Cf. the inscription from *Argirópolis* in Sarmiento's *Campaña en el Ejército Grande* (Mexico: Fondo de Cultura Económica, "Biblioteca Americana," 1958), pp. 119–120, which links the epigraph to *Recuerdos de provincia* with words carved into "the crag . . . near the beach" of his utopian island, Martín García.

11. The sentence appears two times in the brief text: above, toward the outer edge; and then in the center, as if with the intention of internalizing it.

The graphic arrangement reproduces, then, the latent movement of incorporation that dominates the fragment.

12. Letter of January 1, 1838, signed in San Juan with the pseudonym García Román. Its transcription can be found in Paul Verdevoye, *Domingo Faustino Sarmiento, éducateur et publiciste (entre 1839 et 1852)* (Paris: Institut des Hautes Etudes de l'Amérique Latine, 1963), p. 16n.

13. There are many changes to the text in the different editions, and the variants are significant. At times, for example, "project the rays" becomes "make the rays . . . project"; "the rays of her enlightened press" is abbreviated to "the enlightened press" or is extended with "the luminous lights of . . .". Sarmiento works and reworks this particular passage. [TRANSLATOR'S NOTE: The Spanish in the Biblioteca Ayacucho edition reads: "Significaba, simplemente, que venía a Chile, donde la libertad brillaba aun, y que me proponía hacer proyectar los rayos de las luces de su prensa hasta el otro lado de los Andes."]

14. If one should doubt this interpretation, consider the following text: "I speak to you of the press and of war because the words that are hurled in the press become rounded upon passing through the air and are received on the battlefields by persons other than those who have spoken them" ("Dedicatoria" to Alberdi, in *Campaña*, p. 75). Ideas are seen as physical particles or bullets subjected to natural forces. In the sphere of imagination, at least, Sarmiento should be described as a materialist of ideas.

15. Sarmiento's preference for the artillery branch is worth mentioning; it is at once psychological and ideological. His article on the Battle of Chacabuco (see note 18, below) was signed, "a Lieutenant from the Artillery at Chacabuco." His military portrait of General José María Paz, in *Facundo*, is also unforgettable: "He is the war spirit of Europe, even in the arms he enlisted: he is a gunner and, therefore, a mathematician, scientist, thinker" (p. 141). Years later in France, when Sarmiento refers to *Facundo* he will revealingly call it "my Parrot cannon," adding "Nothing can resist it" (letter to Aurelia Vélez, October 15, 1865; see Emilio Carilla, "Dos ediciones del *Facundo*," in *Estudios de literatura argentina (Siglo XIX)* [Tucumán: Universidad Nacional de Tucumán, 1965], pp. 133–145).

16. The "dialectics" of *Facundo* (i.e., the structure and nuances of its historical discourse) are quite difficult to describe. Noël Salomon, who came very close to capturing its spirit, falls into error at times: for example, when he speaks of the "preoccupation with deductive demonstrations," in *Realidad, ideología y literatura en el "Facundo" de D. F. Sarmiento* (Amsterdam: Rodopi, 1984), p. 5. Good pages on this matter can be found in Tulio Halperín Donghi, "Prólogo" to the Mexican edition of *Campaña en el Ejército Grande* (see note 10, above), pp. vii–lvi, esp. pp. xvii and xix.

17. "Anuncio de la vida de Quiroga," in Palcos ed., p. 2.

18. The article is entitled "12 de febrero de 1817," and it was published in

El Mercurio, February 11, 1841. See Alberto Palcos, *Sarmiento* (Buenos Aires: Emecé Editores, 1962), pp. 53–55.

19. The "arms of light" (*arma lucis*), a New Testament image from Paul, appeared as a motto for the 1837 Salón Literario. The apostolic character of the image changes by 1840 in the face of Rosist persecution. For Sarmiento, it will become a metaphor linked mainly to the press and to journalism.

20. "Arms and ideas" is a recurring pair in Sarmiento. At the beginning of *Facundo*, one can find it in the "Advertencia del autor" (the "hieroglyphs" in question) as well as in the passage from the "Introducción" cited above. The duality likewise appears in the first page of *Mi defensa* (1843): "without knowing . . . where I have tempered those arms used in my sudden initiation into the press" ([Buenos Aires: El Ateneo, "Clásicos Inolvidables," 1952], p. 540). Also see the quotation in note 14, above, where "press and war" are seen as two complementary and related activities.

21. *Recuerdos de provincia*, 10th ed. (Buenos Aires: Editorial Sopena, 1966), p. 168. The passage is worth reading in its entirety.

22. See Carl Boyer, *A History of Mathematics* (Princeton: Princeton University Press, 1985), pp. 392–396; A. Flocon and R. Taton, *La Perspective* (Paris: PUF, 1970); and, in English translation, the remarkable treatise by Luigi Cremona, *Projective Geometry*, 3rd ed. (London: Oxford University Press, 1913).

23. See "Anuncio de la vida de Quiroga," p. 3; cf. *Facundo*, p. 235.

24. In a document repudiating the military amnesty, the Asociación de Madres de la Plaza de Mayo (*Fin de Siglo*, no. 7 [July 1988]: 9) stated: "The Armed Forces and the Security Forces are smeared with blood." That statement, with its popular roots, is charge. with Sarmientine resonances and, in particular, with those of *Facundo* (see chap. 5, esp. p. 79).

9 The Autodidact and the Learning Machine

CARLOS ALTAMIRANO AND BEATRIZ SARLO

In *Mi defensa*, Sarmiento describes his childhood experience as a learning process. He learns to read and, while practicing, discovers the origins of his lifelong intellectual interests. There is no other Argentine in the nineteenth century for whom the nexus between reading and culture is so compelling and personal. For Sarmiento, the ability to read represents not just an instrument but the very basis of an intellectual education. This is a model of solitary learning in which reading is always "instructive." Utilitarian and moral, Sarmiento's childhood and adolescent reading leaves an imprint that will last throughout his life: a distrust of poetry, which in his view does not help to advance knowledge.

Sarmiento states that he "has learned to read very well,"[1] and it is valid to wonder about the special value of this aptitude. Learning to read is normally remembered only as a childhood episode, especially for someone who, writing at age thirty, is already a journalist in Chile and a spokesman for or in the protection of prominent politicians. Nevertheless, in *Mi defensa*, this declaration holds a special meaning. The ability to "read well" is not yet a given, even in a man like Sarmiento, who has already won his first intellectual victories. To be able to read was the condition for intellectual independence: surrounded by priests, and a student of many of them, Sarmiento not only acquired the ability to "read very well" but also achieved access to culture without the mediation of the typical learned men of that traditional society, the priests. The ability to read and the acquisition of cultural tools and intellectual emancipation are fused in Sarmiento's personal experience. In the provinces of his childhood and adolescence, reading is the means to acquire a symbolic patrimony and a set of attitudes that, combined with those inherited from the family lineage evoked in *Recuerdos de provincia*, will allow him to erase the distance that separates him from the poverty of the Albarracín family.[2]

Sarmiento values reading as the ability that placed him above an illiterate society and as the skill that exempted him from the need to become a priest. To "read well" (an ability that his mother had mastered, he tells us, but that she lost at age seventy; his father was not a "well-read" man) is to separate himself from the world of manual labor and to become a part of the society of cultivated souls. Moreover, in Sarmiento's memoirs, his father's voice expresses the same conviction: his son should know how to read and not take up a manual occupation.

In Sarmiento's experience, "to read very well" gives birth to the love for learning, thus charting the path of the self-taught man. In *Recuerdos*, Sarmiento talks about two types of cultural relationship, joining his learning of reading and his educated genealogy in one *constructed family*. As an autodidact, he fills his childhood and adolescent years with mentor figures, many of them priests: the bishop Quiroga Sarmiento taught him to read at four years of age, and for many years Father José de Oro imparted lessons, more a set of practical moral rules than a body of knowledge resulting from systematic instruction. These mentors, along with those who encouraged a democratic environment at the Escuela de la Patria, founded in postindependence San Juan, did not go beyond the primary level. It is for this reason that Sarmiento was left forever marked with the conviction of being a self-taught man.

In effect, the entire history of his education is also a history of the material and social difficulties of his training: "destiny intervened so as to block my path."[3] Chance and politics are the two manifestations of destiny, and it is precisely in opposition to both that Sarmiento acquired his culture, in order to use it as a weapon against barbarism and arbitrariness.

The history of the Argentine civil wars provides *Recuerdos* with an account of the obstacles that fate or barbarism put in the way of Sarmiento's education. The text utilizes these obstacles as themes, but it only obliquely refers to another obstacle rooted in provincial society itself: the traditionalist weight of religious and clerical predominance on the intellectual life of San Juan. While Sarmiento praises the priests who were his first teachers, in the text of *Recuerdos* he is virtually silent about the series of dangers that the self-taught adolescent confronted before reaching his first lay models: Cicero and Franklin. Only in one section does the narration show the depth of such dangers, and that is when he relates his experience with Father Castro Barros. In the portrayal of this religious and political fanatic, one finds summarized in one man an entire situation:

the fanaticism of the Inquisition and the colony (which is also the cultural climate of the Rosas period) in contrast to the philanthropic and liberal religiosity of the Oros.

At sixteen years of age, however, that opposition was not clear to the adolescent who went to Castro Barros's confessional to "consult with him about my doubts, to draw closer and closer to that source of light which my sixteen-year-old mind found empty, dark, ignorant and deceptive."[4] An oxymoron organizes the construction of this sentence, with its classical procedure of condensation. Yet, this oxymoron becomes manifest not only in a formal manner; this opposition is not merely semantic. The figure uncovers and synthesizes the contradiction that permeates religiosity, both in ideology (liberal versus fanatical priests) and in politics (the debates on the relationship between church and state are important in the history of Oro as narrated in *Recuerdos*). Within this sphere dominated by religion—the intervention of the Church in politics and the dominance of priests in the intellectual world of the province—the adolescent had to build his new culture. This is the other obstacle of social fate that obstructs the autodidact's path. As in the oxymoron, however, the obstruction also represents the first stage in his education: religion provided him with his first letters.[5]

There is a basic ambivalence in *Recuerdos* regarding the career of this self-taught man. On the one hand, the romantic and gigantic dimensions of his undertaking are exalted, and the difficulties he overcomes along the trajectory are judged as valuable. This effort, centered on the frantic activity of reading, leads him to culture with the nearly exclusive mediation of books. But, on the other hand, a constant competitive tension is experienced regarding academic culture. The existence of an academic space with its hierarchy and systems of promotion becomes visible proof of his difference, which he cannot endure except as mortification. Sarmiento lacks all the titles that can be acquired through formal procedures: he has neither material wealth nor a distinguished surname; he has no military career, and he does not belong to the Church as did his most illustrious relatives; he is not even a scholar. These shortcomings provide the narration of *Recuerdos* with a constant tension between the autodidact and the academic. The text possesses a tone of disproportionate indignation when he recalls some of the labels used to attack him in Chile. For Sarmiento, these attacks were always deadly because he believed they were placing his career, name, and identity in jeopardy. The following example is illustrative:

> Not at the beginning of my career as a writer, but later, in Santiago, a certain disdain toward my inferiority began to develop, in which even the schoolboys began to participate. Today I would ask to those young

men of the *Seminario*, if it were necessary, if they have truly studied with more dedication than I. Did they also intend to fool me with their six years at the National Institute? So what! Do I, today university examiner, not know what is taught in the schools?[6]

In effect, Sarmiento has moved from examinee to examiner, but the wounds from his struggle to acquire knowledge remained open all his life. South America was not like the United States he had already visited, where one could change from miner's gear to morning coat and rise from laborer to legislator. This is why he would always seek a doctorate, a military rank that would signal an academic recognition of his knowledge in the field. He was, as he would repeat in many of his autobiographical references, a child of his works. However, if the text of *Recuerdos* states "I succeed my progeny," and this formula dominates the tale of the career of the poor, young man, it also reflects the contradictions that the autodidact suffers when faced with traditional hierarchies. This contradiction appears often in Sarmiento's life, and the irritation shown in his answer to the young Chileans of the seminary seems also to anticipate the disdainful judgment of Juan Bautista Alberdi in *Cartas quillotanas:* Sarmiento is a journalist who has not written a single "dogmatic book"; that is, he is unable, owing to his lack of education, to construct a system.

Nevertheless, his obsession with the disadvantages of being self-taught is tempered by the gratification provided by knowledge. In fact, his improved social position is directly related to his acquisition of culture. In the text of *Recuerdos*, solitary instruction is also presented as a model: one might triumph over the difficulties of an unsystematic education, even to the point of realizing that self-instruction is better and more independent than academic training. The catechistic form of instruction used by his uncle Oro, with its questions and answers, examples, and easy rules, is presented as the solution to solitary education. This catechism provides Sarmiento with a dialogue between teacher and pupil which allows him to pose questions and find answers to them. "I have found them!" he writes in *Recuerdos*. "I could say these words like Archimedes, because I had foreseen, invented, and sought out those questions of catechism."[7] Moreover, his experience with the catechism of Rudolph Ackermann on history influenced his model for the transmission of knowledge. Sarmiento's democratizing impulses as an adult are rooted in the experiences of the adolescent of *Recuerdos*, as shown by his efforts to simplify both writing and methods of teaching in order to advance popular education.

The Chain of Books

For the autodidact, the only means for the production of knowledge is through what we might call "the chain of books." This chain excludes the teacher, and it interlaces text to text in such a way that books refer to one another in a constant movement. This is a learning machine that Sarmiento conceived as a fundamental vehicle for the transmission of ideas.

The book chain becomes an autobiographical motif from *Mi defensa* to *Recuerdos de provincia*. As Sarmiento states in *Mi defensa*, "My readings continued, and as some books made me aware of the existence of others, I searched throughout San Juan for those authors I knew by name."[8] The situation contains a certain intellectual drama if one considers how he first had to discover the existence of the author and then search for the book. The creation of the chain (with books that, as we have seen, Sarmiento at times intuited before actually ascertaining their existence) illustrates the intellectual climate of his formative years and also explains the symbolic value that the written word acquired for Sarmiento from then on.

The book becomes a metaphor for various forms of learning and cultural acquisition. The examples for this fusion of the oral and the written or printed appear throughout his works. For instance, in reference to the oral instruction he received from Father Oro, he states: "The reminiscences of that oral rain that fell upon my soul each day appeared as the plates of a book whose meaning we comprehend through the attitudes depicted in the drawings. Peoples, history, geography, religion, ethics, politics, all were listed as in an index."[9]

Sarmiento portrays a significant learning situation as one of "books without teachers." Other than his attendance at the Escuela de la Patria, his only teacher was Oro, whom he followed to his exile in San Luis. There the situation was the opposite: the teacher was without books. A book came to be written in the form of a catechism; that is, it consisted of the exchange between teacher and pupil. Once separated from Oro, and deprived by fate of a systematic education, the protagonist of *Recuerdos* hypothesizes on the existence of books ("but there must be books, I told myself").[10] The most significant part of the narration is when he concludes that the solitary act of reading can replace the social relationship of learning ("provided that one can understand what one reads, it is possible to learn—all systematic subjects—without teachers").[11] Sarmiento thus compensates for the deprivations of his personal history with the typically willful gesture of the autodidact.

The chain of books has the arbitrariness of catalogues and library bookshelves. Its disorder is like the disorder of the autodidact's culture: both are connected by random references or by the accidents of the alphabet. Sarmiento will always suffer from the consequences of this disorder, which he sometimes presents, characteristically, as an advantage.

The book chain, constructed by Sarmiento during his adolescence from books that the colonial and postrevolutionary culture had deposited in the libraries of San Juan, lacked key links that would prove decisive in Sarmiento's subsequent intellectual growth. It was not until 1838, when Manuel J. Quiroga Rosas returned to the province with his "modern authors library," that Sarmiento learned about some of the key names of his intellectual maturity: Villemain, Guizot, Tocqueville, Leroux, and the *Revue Encyclopédique*. In the figurative system of *Recuerdos*, these names came to represent a "university training" and, once the reading was concluded, Sarmiento felt ready to chart the course of his future activity. From first conceiving of the intellect as simple reflection during the first years of reading, to the interlude represented by the typical library of the Generation of 1837, he moved on to the application of his knowledge. Significantly, this activity is again conceived in bookish fashion as translation and adaptation: "Translating the European spirit into the American spirit, with the changes that the diverse stage requires."[12] Translation in the figurative sense, but also in the proper sense: Sarmiento gives special mention, toward the end of *Recuerdos*, to the books he had either translated or arranged to be translated, because it is precisely this other machine—the translating machine—that, together with the book chain, produces the learning model described in *Recuerdos*.

Polyglotism in the River Plate Region

Sarmiento defended not just the legitimacy but the necessity of polyglotism and, concurrently, the right to contaminate American Spanish. The Rosas period was, at the ideological, religious, and cultural levels, strongly xenophobic; xenophobia and xenophilia marked the extremes of an opposition that would be repeated in the political history of Argentina. While Rosas had employed an Italian scholar to write his gazettes in Spanish, Sarmiento and the romantics of 1837 wrote their texts in imitation of European languages, especially French.

In *Recuerdos*, Sarmiento compared the cultural climate of the Rosas era with that of the colony on the basis of the issue of foreignness. For their part, the *caudillos* labeled Sarmiento a heretic and a Jew, words that in the period's system of political insults functioned as slanderous equivalents of "foreigner." There is a streak in Argentine culture that links linguistic purity and "racial" purity, and the variants of this linkage define the diverse positions regarding books and foreign languages. The Generation of 1837 claimed (and on this point Sarmiento adopted the same perspective), for the first time in the history of Argentine culture, the right to contaminate peninsular Spanish in order to make it Argentine through the use of other European languages. The movement away from the Spanish norm was practically the declared program of the Salón Literario, the intent being the projection of such changes onto Argentine politics, ideology, and culture.

This linguistic contamination (essentially gallicisms) is not regarded as a perversion of polyglotism, but rather as a necessary stylistic manifestation, even an aesthetically beautiful one. If polyglotism signals an assimilation of European modernity, linguistic contamination shows the "depth" of that assimilation: the deeper the assimilation, the greater the impact on the Spanish norm; the "naturalness" of the relation between the cultures is greater when the written language becomes modified by mirroring the foreign language. Juan María Gutiérrez's statement, to the effect that Spanish must be gallicized so as to gallicize ideas, becomes the program of romantic polyglotism. In fact, it is a bilingualism rooted principally in the act of reading.

"In the Spanish-speaking countries," Sarmiento writes in *Recuerdos*, "to learn a living language involves only reading; at least one such should be taught in the primary schools."[13] Once reading is identified with the reading of foreign books, the acquisition of knowledge again becomes for Sarmiento the adventure of learning by means of a machine: "a simple language-learning machine that I have successfully applied to the few languages I know." The model again becomes one of bookish learning, without teachers, in which the autodidact is alone in a room with a grammar, a dictionary, and a text. To learn how to read, for Sarmiento, means simply to put a lexicon and a syntax to work.

The function of this written polyglotism has been described by Sarmiento in *Recuerdos:* the reading machine is the mastering of a technique that has no value beyond that of the text it makes available. Sarmiento does not speak English; he probably speaks French with serious difficulty. And yet, he speaks of learning these languages as if he had reached all his objectives. This was in fact true: a foreign language, understood as merely a manifestation of written culture and a reading instrument, was an eminently practical tool that distinguished its user from those who could not read it. In Sarmiento's view, there was nothing worth reading in Spanish anyway.

A hyperbole from the text of *Recuerdos* reveals the completely instrumental character of Sarmiento's relationship with a foreign language: Sarmiento states that after six weeks of English lessons, he read "at the rate of one volume per day the sixty volumes of the complete collection of novels by Sir Walter Scott."[14] In order to read with such speed, the language certainly had to be transparent, if not a mere system of lexical equivalents that, once set in motion, allowed the reader to grasp the text's contents or "essence." That is to say, this is a type of reading which feeds the knowledge machine with the urgency demanded by the social and cultural condition of the autodidact. Sarmiento's skill with this "simple machine" is what he transmits to his young friends when he teaches them not French but, rather, a way in which the language can be learned.

To overcome the barrier of Spanish, rather than to master a foreign language in order to achieve social distinction, is the objective of the romantic polyglotism program. Sarmiento, who always exaggerates, goes beyond this objective when he stubbornly seeks to be translated into French so that civilized Europeans might read his *Facundo*. In his attempt to overcome the barrier of Spanish, Sarmiento establishes a nexus between language and knowledge, and opposes the purism of grammatical conventions with a gallicism that results from the content of his readings.

The Career Based on Talent

Sarmiento is convinced that a book can make a man's fortune. Such a conviction, which is not uncommon during the period, gives talent the responsibility for success or failure in a meritocratic society. There is even the conviction that it is possible to achieve success despite one's social origin; this is why ambition can change from private vice to public virtue. Sarmiento thus proclaims his ambition without eliciting the alarm of society. Criticism is generally directed to the careerist rather than to the ambitious man. At the same time, ambition and careerism are separated by a subtle line that, according to the judgment of his contemporaries, Sarmiento crossed too often.

Merit, of course, needs such impulses and allows certain transgressions: merit rests upon talent (as opposed to social origin), upon acquisition (as opposed to inheritance), and upon personal peculiarities. Merit provides the space for the unfolding not only of one's vocation but also of extravagance, which simply exaggerates what that vocation is about. Merit presupposes the tension of the will as it becomes tested in competition. Finally, merit sees humiliation as a terrible offense. The career based on talent involves comparison, choice, rejection, appreciation, or condescension according to one's determination of worth. Since nothing is guaranteed by social origin (although social origin can be a powerful lever or a stumbling block), those who rely on talent are under tremendous pressure: failure can lead to suicide or to rejection by friends and family.

Ambition, failure, and death are thus combined in the career based on talent. They find expression, for the first time in Argentine literature, in an episode from *Recuerdos:*

> One day my exasperation reached delirium; I was frantic, deranged, and I thought up the sublimely erroneous idea of punishing Chile itself, of declaring it ungrateful, vile, infamous. I wrote some sort of diatribe; put my name at the bottom, and took it to the presses of *El Progreso,* placing it directly in the hands of the printers, upon which I retired to my house in silence, loaded my pistols, and waited for the explosion of the mine that would blow me up.[15]

The description is ambiguous; Sarmiento appears ready to kill himself or die fighting as a vengeance against a society that allegedly dismisses him as a foreigner. This romantic desperation in the face of failure, a sentiment more of a social than a psychological nature, comes from the idea that the future of a man is always gambled on a card. The episodes of initiation and the anecdotes of recognition are therefore decisive. The desperation in the face of failure, the gesture of loading two pistols and awaiting death, mirrors in important ways the exaltation that dominates Sarmiento after his first literary triumph.

A book can in fact make a man's fortune. Literature is one of the roads open to the career based on talent. Yet, how to construct a society where the respect for talent awards a meritorious man "a name, a rank, a character in the World to which I should not otherwise have been entitled"?[16] Sarmiento wrote in *Recuerdos* that, in America, great personalities have to build not only their own destiny but the appropriate theater for their actions. That is why for Sarmiento a literary career must also be a career in politics, with journalism providing a synthesis of both. This role was played by enlightened leaders of the fledgling Spanish American states, but their achievements were destroyed by the caudillos. In *Recuerdos* there is an unresolved tension between the careers of letters and military action. All the models on which Sarmiento constructs his heritage are intellectual, as shown by Dean Funes and the Oro family. While in Europe, according to Sarmiento's perception, politicians are always learned men, and no abyss separates Victor Hugo or Lamartine from Louis-Adolphe Thiers; in the Americas, the intellectual finds his path obstructed. Military and rural barbarism plot every type of intrigue and violence against intellectuals.

The European model suggests that the intellectual's career should not be governed by chance but by merit. In Latin America, however, barbarism disturbed this *cursus honorum;* therefore, the military represented an alternative. A military career provided another means of upward mobility for destitute youth, and as a child Sarmiento had considered that option: "My mother brought me up in the persuasion of my becoming a cleric and a priest of San Juan, in imitation of my uncle, but my father impressed me with his military coats, chevrons, sabres, and other military paraphernalia."[17] However, to undertake a military career would have meant enrolling not in the independence army of his father but in the militias of the caudillos who, by recruiting their members from the "abject classes of society," made possible the rise of obscure young men. Sarmiento did not choose this path, for he wanted to rise "without sinning against morality and without attacking liberty and civilization."[18]

It is significant that in the genealogy of *Recuerdos* Sarmiento neither includes military men among his ancestors, nor does he register any military victories. Nevertheless, the military plays a role in the text. On the one hand, we find the parody of war in Sarmiento's stone-throwing childhood battles on the outskirts of San Juan. On the other hand, there is the detailed account of the minor skirmishes of the "Jáchal Campaign" against Facundo, when Sarmiento was not quite twenty years old.

Even in the childhood stone-throwing episode, Sarmiento cannot avoid shifting from the parody of ancient battles (Leonidas, Thermopylae, and descriptions of heroism in the fashion of Homer) to the serious comparison between his own fight and that of General Mariano Acha at Angaco. Nor does parodic irony exhaust the meaning of the references to the qualities of the ringleader, Sarmiento himself. "I would have been a hero," he declares, and although he did not follow a military career, he is convinced that his portrait would not be complete without a reference to the physical courage of the soldier.

The accumulation of merit and the tests passed in various fields of activity punctuate a trajectory full of honors. The text of *Recuerdos* includes episodes that dwell on the recognition of merit, the passage from obscurity to light, the achievement of excellence, and the elevation from poverty and obscure social origins. These episodes have the form of a short novel and are obviously linked to the literary conventions of romanticism. As a reader of Balzac, Dumas, and dozens of other writers who share the same rhetorical arsenal, Sarmiento finds that several social impulses have already been formalized: ambition, usurpation, envy, talent as a civilian, courage as a soldier. The romantic sensitivity and psychology are condensed into the literary-moral space that the hero of *Recuerdos* crosses in the episodes concerning the recognition of hidden or obscured merit. In these adventures, Sarmiento vindicates the right to rebel against the place assigned by birth or fortune. This right legitimizes the ambition, the daring, the glory, or the tragedy of Lucien de Rubempré, Mark Antony, or Julien Sorel.

In the episodes of *Recuerdos* where a change of fortune symbolizes and anticipates the entire biography of Sarmiento, there is one that is particularly telling. In fact, the fiction of this Rousseauesque anecdote[19] can serve as a key to the reading of the entire history of the protagonist, because there he bridges the social distance that separates manual labor (in this case, that of a miner) from intellectual work.[20] It is the history of a change of fortune that for two reasons is limited to the symbolic plane. The first reason: the change from miner to scholar is only figurative. The second: the figurative change is produced by means of knowledge.

In this episode, Sarmiento dresses as a miner in part because of his extravagant taste for costume, and in part for comfort's sake. A visitor, in fact, takes him for a miner. During a twist in the conversation, Sarmiento reveals a level of culture and language inappropriate to his (apparent) social condition. The stranger cannot get over his amazement, until someone explains the reason for his deception: namely, the lack of correspondence between the working clothes and the true condition of the man wearing them. Leaving aside the roots of this literary anecdote in reality, it can be judged as a formal and ideological organization of experience. As a construct, the anecdote is built on two axes: 1) origin—Who is the young man who looks like a miner but turns out to talk like a scholar? Where is he from? Does he really belong to that corner of the room where he was hiding and from which he radiates such knowledge?—and 2) merit, in this case moral merit, acquired through effort rather than inheritance.

The tale is both ingenuous and artificial. No transformation actually takes place: in truth, what occurs is the unmasking of a quid pro quo. The trick of presenting someone for what he is not is used by Sarmiento for the exaltation of the young protagonist. In order to postpone and consequently increase the pleasure of the eventual recognition, the man does not intervene in a conversation that had already covered several topics. The risk is minimal, and the gratification from the recognition of merit is maximal. Therefore, the outcome of the episode is ensured from the very beginning. There is *suspense*, but not dramatics, because the protagonist is not a true laborer but, rather, someone who has adopted a laborer's outfit. At the same time, however, Sarmiento is someone who needs, as a foreigner, to prove his worth (symbolic worth, the worth of knowledge) and mend a family history of decadence: "I have found the Albarracines," he writes in *Recuerdos*, referring to his mother's brothers, "on the verge of the charnel house of the obscure and impoverished mass."[21] The vertigo of social decline, which is illustrated as an abyss that opens like the hole of the charnel house, sickened Sarmiento during his youth. Thus, the anecdote that Sarmiento recalled, altered, or invented in 1850 offers a moral satisfaction in the form of symbolic compensation: Sarmiento moves from a kitchen corner to the respectful consideration of a stranger. The moral of the anecdote is that the recognition of knowledge places each person in his place. This is not the place that in traditional society is tied to origin; it is the place that a society open to merit assigns to talent.

Notes

1. *Mi defensa*, in Armando Donoso, ed., *Sarmiento en el destierro* (Buenos Aires: Gliezer, 1927), p. 160.
2. As will be seen, both the maternal and the paternal family had gradually fallen into economic decline, although in the case of the Albarracín family the deterioration was more dramatic. This is recalled in *Recuerdos*, where a description is made of the family fortune.
3. *Recuerdos de provincia* (Buenos Aires: Centro Editor de América Latina, 1979), p. 157.
4. Ibid., p. 159.
5. Tulio Halperín Donghi points out that "Sarmiento was not so much shaped by Moratín or Jovellanos as by an archaic ecclesiastical culture based on the Scriptures." See his prologue to Sarmiento's *Campaña en el Ejército Grande Aliado de Sud-América* (Mexico: Fondo de Cultura Económica, 1958), p. xxxvii.
6. *Recuerdos*, p. 169.
7. Ibid., p. 158.
8. *Mi defensa*, p. 162.
9. *Recuerdos*, pp. 157–158.
10. Ibid., p. 158.
11. Ibid.
12. Ibid., p. 168.
13. Ibid., p. 164.
14. Ibid.
15. Ibid., p. 205.
16. Edward Gibbon, *Memoirs of My Life*, ed. Georges A. Bonnard (London: Thomas Nelson & Sons, 1966), p. 188.
17. *Recuerdos*, p. 152.
18. Ibid., p. 189.
19. We have analyzed this episode in "Identidad, linaje y mérito de Sarmiento," *Punto de Vista* 3, no. 10 (November 1980).
20. The twenty-four-year-old Sarmiento was exiled in Chile, where he worked as a supervisor in the mines of Copiapó. The passage in *Recuerdos*

reads as follows: "One night a Mr. Codecido joined us at Mardones's kitchen. He was a neat and well-off man who complained about the inconveniences and deprivations of the day's journey. Everyone greeted him with respect. I gestured with my cap, and retreated to a corner to escape the stares that my outfit would surely cause. . . . The conversation touched on various topics, until a disagreement developed over a fact of modern European history as well as some geographic names. Instinctively, Carril, Chenaut, and the others turned toward me to establish the truth about the matter. Thus provoked to take part in this gentleman's conversation, I stated what I knew of the case, but in such dogmatic terms, and with such minute detail, that Codecido stood in disbelief with his mouth wide open, seeing a book's pages come from the lips of one whom he had taken for a miner" (*Recuerdos*, p. 166).

21. Ibid., p. 30.

10 *Facundo:* The Riches of Poverty

NOÉ JITRIK

Facundo offers the modern reader two kinds of surprises. First of all, telling expressions emerge, in the form of images that are at once strange and profound ("And while he lets himself fall into a dangerous indolence, each day the boa comes closer to suffocating him with twisting knots"). Second, certain of Sarmiento's ideas anticipate their appearance within systems (influence of the environment upon character, the force of education, the traditions of great men, etc.) while revealing an uncanny astuteness of psychological observation ("Argentines of every class, civilized or ignorant, have a high sense of their worth as a nation; all other countries of the continent reproach them for this vanity and seem offended by their presumptuousness and arrogance"). At first, we might be tempted to seek a unity between images and ideas—a temptation I do not reject—but if we follow such a course, we find ourselves in a position where "truth" must emerge from either the perfection of image or the validity of observation. We should perhaps note that it is the sensitivity of these images which gave and still gives authority to *Facundo*'s power as "literature," while the text's revelation of ideas has allowed the reader to perceive the embryo of a national sociology born of extraordinary intuition, well ahead of its time.

1

Facundo's images appear disseminated throughout the text, but each one of them obeys a different constitutive schema. Some emerge through antithesis, others are shaped by accumulation, and the majority reveal a marked metaphorical reach. If something unites them, it is the general rhythm of elocution, which we might call "impulse." Never as in this text has rhythm become so tangible: the rhythm appears to us as a pure state precisely because of the breathing, with hesitations and pauses that mark the pace of life itself. Too, it is like a tapestry or, seen from another angle, a structure within which the images are placed, perhaps unpredictably. The rhythm gives an idea of totality; the images, of fragmentation. Is there a coherence between totality and fragmentation? We need not search for one, though, because as these two aspects appear in the text, we find we can manage both. On the one hand, the text is fragmentary; the images are sudden materializations, almost fleeting, forming no system in the sense of a constructive beginning. But they all tend toward an identical finality, bound to literature in the end.

On another level, however, rhythm—a sustained creation of peaks and caesuras—does not represent pure movement. Theoretically, its function would consist in preparing the production of a meaning, not in the sense of a mere frame but as a necessary "condition" for the emergence of signification. In this sense, rhythm possesses instances, plans, materializations that appear on two levels as "thematizations" and as "structures" that give it form. This is the point I wish to emphasize. I believe that in *Facundo* the structure emerging from rhythm is that of "knowing how to tell" in the most primary sense of the concept: to possess a corporal relationship with "the known" (he who tells, according to Jean-Pierre Faye, is a *gnarus*, i.e., a narrator[1]) and to attempt to transmit, having as a consequence a liberation from "formal" agreements of theme and logic.

This topic can be explored further in *Facundo*. What is "known" lies in the past, considered as a sum of experiences, traditions, readings, and transmissions of data, but it also lies in a linguistic horizon, the knowledge of a tongue that presupposes, concretely in Sarmiento, a conflict between ideas of heritage, colonies, and provinces[2] and a world of models—something achievable—whose presence modifies all reference points and confers upon the author, in this conjuncture, a vibration, at once unique, dramatic, and irrepressible. This conjuncture is made evident in the coexistence of archaisms and gallicisms—consequently revealing the author's complicated mental pattern—and also shows many other equations that still occupy our attention and are related to the arduous task of defining a national literature as well as forming a national policy in relationship to the past.

Of course, this "knowing how to tell" rests upon the past and is projected toward the future, representing a distribution of roles that may appear now as a decisive separation; nevertheless, it does not signify a schism but, rather, a necessary methodological limitation. From this perspective, the past of the "telling" is an unconscious cauldron: that which one affirms in spite of oneself and which guides a relationship not apparent in the exposition. The future implies an ideological dimension that has been followed, chosen in order to reduce and channel the demands that constantly seethe within that secret alliance linking what is told with what tells.

2

In focusing in on these aspects, a broad range of issues emerges that permits us to rethink *Facundo.* First of all, the conflicts between past and future (terms sufficiently cited and defined) become apparent in the sentences of *Facundo* as a convulsive and confused ebb and flow in which the movement toward "finality" seems to dominate that of "construction." For this reason, perhaps, one could subscribe to Borges's judgment declaring that each sentence could be corrected and even modified but never suppressed, because if this should happen, it would undermine the general impulse of Sarmiento's writing.[3] We might raise an ideological doubt: Borges is thinking, perhaps, from a certain notion of "style," whose components are well inscribed within a broader conception of literature; for the same reason, surely, he concluded that Macedonio Fernández was a better converser than writer. This is a question of adjusting to a system of requirements. Sarmiento, as Macedonio, tends to flood the boundaries, to overflow. In any case, what is left is the internal tension of his sentences in which we recognize traits such as parallelisms; abundant, unbiased adjectivization; adverbialization; frequent diminutives; ample ellipses; comparisons and soliloquies. This is both product and vehicle of an energy that unfolds and constructs a totality from the experience of fragmentation. Its origin is not characterized by a formal compulsion, by a reduction of opposites.

In a second moment, the link between past and future, between unconscious and ideological motives, engenders a paradoxical result that I examined in an earlier study.[4] That which is ideological appears on the surface of the exposition as a defined project, that is, as a link to the future; that which is unconscious appears as dominated, conquered ground. This play lies inscribed at the heart of the construction of the text, based on what emerges from the action of the concept "civilization and barbarism" which, in not too indirect a fashion, incarnates the same tension between past and future.

This is not a question of the exaltation of barbarism over civilization (as if it were a conversion) but rather one of a barbarous past, invested with certain structural and economic explanations, that finally subverts the entire civilized schema to offer a new perspective. As noted in my earlier analysis, barbarism, with its territory in the pampa (where it re-

sides), gives way to the concept of "interior,"[5] those provinces characterized by economic activities of production that have historically been liq-
uidated or devoured by Buenos Aires, the home of "civilization." The
paradoxical program is a vindication of this plundered interior already
spoiled by the city ("Could Dorrego and his party have foreseen that the
provinces would come one day to punish Buenos Aires for having denied
them its civilizing influence; and that because of despising their backwardness and barbarism they would penetrate the streets of Buenos Aires,
establishing themselves there and placing their soldiers in the fort?"[6]).
This sort of conflict remains present in any formulation that attempts to
rescue a "national" existence whose basic expression is one of value—a
national existence that should be kept intact from adulteration by essentially urban, outside models—but that many will attempt to assign a current identity and relevance in language as the symbol of an identity still
being sought.

It is evident that these connections justify certain analyses made of the
person of Sarmiento as well as of his writing. In the first case, for example, a study has been made of his "provincial consciousness," to coin a
phrase, of his having been born in an unfavorable environment and of his
will to rise above it to the highest regions of culture.[7] His is a chained
spirit, struggling against his roots with any instrument he can find. It is
worth noting that this function could explain an identification Sarmiento
made early on in life between his person and his country ("I was born in
1811, nine months after the 25th of May!"), representing a gesture common to an entire generation of Argentine men, as seen in the memorial-
ists studied by Adolfo Prieto.[8]

From another viewpoint, this relationship between past and future, unconsciousness and ideology, can help make sense of the binary pact ro-
manticism/enlightenment and its paradoxical inversions. Romanticism is
acquired by reading: biographers underscore the role that the *library* of
Manuel J. Quiroga Rosas played in the formation of Sarmiento's ideas,
composed as it was mainly of Saint-Simonian, utopian, and romantic books
and reviews, traces of which are most visible in the epigraphs of *Facundo*.[9]
Thus, romanticism represents an ideological instrument for bringing to
light all that had been buried; it offers the author an expressive way to
rescue facts (e.g., the chapters of *costumbrista* detail, notably the tracker,
the guide, the singer, and the *gaucho malo*) and, in the end, offers a way
to bring about the productive economic recovery of colonial constitutions.
The Enlightenment, within this schema, and also in contradictory fashion,
incarnates the human unconscious insofar as it provides Sarmiento with
a system that he sees as natural, as proved by the identification of his

birth with the destiny of the Republic. This action informs the structuring of the entire text; and it surfaces, according to the reflections of Juan Luis Guerrero,[10] as a tripartition (physical aspect, the life of Juan Facundo Quiroga, and the unitarian government) that is not evident in the first edition (since the text published in 1845 in no way modified the *folletín* format as it appeared in *El Progreso* of Santiago de Chile) but only in its second version.[11] The tripartition, which could be translated as "milieu," "man," and "nation," corresponds to a modified enlightened order, but it is an order that Sarmiento already possessed in his spontaneous interpretation of the world. More important is the contradictory movement found in Sarmiento's schematic reasoning and in the explanations that diminish the depth of his wisdom as a result of his play of inversions and his alteration of instruments of thought.[12] Here, the Enlightenment regains its identity as a purely ideological incision, implying at the same time an ultimate contradiction: the future is projected as an ideological system, yet it pertains to the anachronistic past, to that which no longer works, its functions already exhausted. One can also reach this conclusion by looking at Sarmiento's judgments about Bernardino Rivadavia and the years of his presidency, generally conceded to be clear of encyclopedist thought.

Finally, these contradictions may be traced to Sarmiento's attitude toward the colonial heritage. From the standpoint of economics and production, Sarmiento reevaluates the colonial period (as archaic institution, as slavery, as elimination of the Indian) in terms of the Enlightenment's ideological "transcendence." Nevertheless, the Enlightenment arsenal (his defense of Jeremy Bentham and his ridicule of the seventeen volumes in folio of Cardinal de Luca in the description of Córdoba) bespeaks Sarmiento's decision to *distance* himself from the colonial past, to such a degree and with such effectiveness that the Enlightenment seems to cover everything and to define the ideology of *Facundo*. This contradiction emerges, for example, when Sarmiento invokes his triumphant ideology to fight against certain sectors of his own social class. We can accept this if we believe that the basic project of the text is to create a doctrine, "the" doctrine that will consolidate several dispersed, pre-bourgeois groups under the hegemony of one sector—which is not, one can easily observe, the indispensable group of Buenos Aires ranchers, although that group finally will triumph and Sarmiento will pursue its interests.[13]

3

The preceding discussion represents a parenthesis that we may now close in order to resume consideration of the lines that unfold from one's critical perception of rhythm. What now concerns us is a conception of literature as concrete practice. "Conception of literature" is here understood as an area in some way included in the "meaning" that rhythm prepares. In an inverted manner, "meaning" has to do with what the text offers in the specific area understood as literature.

Even when severed from this theoretical contact, it becomes immediately evident that the text is crossed by a preoccupation regarding *literature*. Sarmiento makes this explicit in the "Prologue to the Second Edition," with its famous letter to Valentín Alsina. It could be suggested that this gesture possesses two inflections, one definable as "motivational and/ or of literary behavior" and the other as "declarative." In the first, I would include the well-known problem of the suppression in the second and third editions (elimination of the introduction and of the two final chapters that give shape to the third part), explained in detail by Alberto Palcos in his essential La Plata edition. In this context, Sarmiento relegated the text to political circumstances, which, on the one hand, implies an act of subordination of literature to politics and, on the other, presupposes a magnified belief in the power of the literary word.

Regarding the "declarative" gesture, I believe it important to underscore what is said in Sarmiento's letter to Alsina: "I have literary ambitions, my dear friend, and in order to satisfy them, I have immersed myself in lucubrations, meticulous research, and meditated study. Facundo died in body in Barranca Yaco." In this sentence one observes the displacement: "to write" appears as an activity that tends toward an objective; from the methodology that defines a "practice," one moves to its justifying content. It is not odd that afterward he should finish this passage by giving it an exemplary meaning: "But there are other countries and men that should not remain free of humiliation and enlightenment." To sign and seal the synthesis of meaning, he declares: "There exists an exemplary justice to fulfill and a glory to acquire as an Argentine writer: to upbraid the world and humiliate the arrogance of great men, be they scholars or rulers."[14] In any case, a great unity exists between the "motivational" and the "declarative."

However, we may approach the issue from another perspective, that is, from the question of the "genre" to which *Facundo* might pertain. Palcos presents a detailed exposition of the issue: it is a novel, a history, an epic poem, a sociological essay, and so on, but it cannot be classified as any one of them in particular. I discussed this question in *Muerte y resurrección de Facundo*, where I wrote that the literary character of the text could not be defined from the angle of genres, but had to be discerned from the effects of the reading. *Facundo*, I concluded, is less a question of demonstrating than of convincing, for which purpose Sarmiento appealed to his public with every available means. According to Palcos, a great part of the value and permanent interest of *Facundo* lies in the fusion of so many dissimilar aspects into the production of the work. This permits us to consider two possibilities. On the one hand, there exists a certain free manipulation of current categories: one is immediately aware that the writer felt unconstrained by generic demands that organize an interpretation of reality (though, surely, this liberty has some remote relationship with what can be found in other genres, such as the "essays"—in the tradition of Montaigne—which, nevertheless, lacked a cultural presence in the Argentina of Sarmiento's time). At the same time, this fusion expresses the anxiety of one who is banished, the urgency of the alien to return to order, albeit thwarted and irrational in its force. As a source of anguish, it never recedes; rather, it evolves into what is habitually called "style," in the sense of a personal mark that characterizes expression.

I would not wish to leave this topic without adding one reflection: I do think that a structure exists that, despite its depth or range, opposes the resolution of "originality," a concept that seems superficial and subjective, that encloses and focuses on differences, because this not only fails to explain its genesis but also leaves no room for further thought. No less suffocating is the notion of "style" that appears as purely descriptive.

As a generational trait, the pursuit of originality was installed in the vital program of an entire period. According to Pedro Henríquez Ureña, this search appears to be obsessive—yet not necessarily framed within an individual horizon, as a substitute for postponed satisfaction, but rather as a vehicle of conscience or, perhaps more precisely, as that which permits one to become aware.[15] In *La literatura autobiográfica argentina,* Adolfo Prieto also discusses this psychological movement and compares it to the ideal of "fame" in medieval times; however, according to the corpus that he examines, the achievements of one's originality essentially lie in the political realm and not in literary production as sought by the romantics. From this kind of originality, the dream of social transformation could be generated. I believe that this schema, which could serve to explain a certain inflection in Sarmiento, can be located in a subconscious zone inasmuch as it might guide conduct and, at the same time, shape the conception of one aspect of the text, of a clear ideological source. Originality as both road and role fulfilled in the "great man's" history finds its only source in certain ideas processed by Sarmiento with the objective of a well-determined finality. This mixture of elaboration and finality is what allows me now to speak of the subconscious, a zone of mixture par excellence.

"Style," whose characterization holds the coexistence of different literary "genres" as a backdrop, is not exhausted as a problem in *Facundo*, but here it appears in all its dramatic complexity. Regarding its origin, one cannot help but consider what Ezequiel Martínez Estrada points out when writing that Sarmiento's works before 1852 "reflect an abundant stock of readings, his plan to achieve fame residing in the same terrain as Sir Walter Scott and Mariano [José de] Larra, James Fenimore Cooper and Benjamin Franklin."[16] This sentence synthesizes, without a doubt, my previous reflection concerning originality, but bespeaks an origin that all the same would be somewhat unilateral of the "mixture" that yields meaning to "style." Moreover, the "mixture" continues in subsequent works by Sarmiento, all linked by the same conception of "writing," though of course with less persuasiveness: the "style" (i.e., his verbal attitude) continues to be equal to his ideology, both in the political sense—whose projections begin to affect national reality—and in its literary dimensions.

In any case, for our purposes, this persistent "mixing" (whatever the source) defines, if not what *is* literature in the text of *Facundo*, at least the field that permits the emergence of what could be considered as literary in *Facundo*.

Clearly a specific path has taken control of our understanding of this line of argumentation: the "mixture" provides a schema that does not appear weakened from the coexistence of genres. If we consider that *Facundo* takes definition through many intersections—recall, for example, the overlapping concerns of "historiography" and "literature," characteristic of the eclecticism of the period, and itself the result of a series of accommodations and mixtures,[17] or concerns, of the written word and "action" through which everything written manifests an interweaving dominated by politics—we may observe that the "mixture" constitutes an essential trait that determines not only the general aspect of the text, but the structure of each clause and phrase.[18] An examination of the following quotes from *Facundo* will permit us to prove a point:

1. All of America has mocked those notorious Buenos Aires rallies, viewing them as the height of a nation's degradation; I see only the political intention they most successfully fulfill.
2. How can the idea of *personality* in government become embodied in a republic that has never known a king?
3. The red ribbon is a materialization of terror that accompanies us everywhere, in the street, in the bosom of the family; unavoidably, we think of it when dressing and when undressing.
4. And ideas become engraved upon us by association: the view of a tree in the countryside recalls a conversation occurring ten years before;

think of the ideas associated with the red ribbon, of its indelible impressions, always bound to the image of Rosas.

5.   Thus, in a communication from a high Rosas official, I recently read "that it is a sign his government has ordered us to wear in order to indicate conciliation and peace."

6.   The words *Death to the savage, disgusting, filthy unitarians* are certainly quite conciliatory, and only in exile or in the tomb will anybody dare to deny their efficacy.

7.   Rosas's henchmen in the Mazorca have been a powerful instrument of conciliation and peace; if this seems false, go see the result, and search the world for a better-conciliated and more peaceful city than Buenos Aires.

8.   At his wife's death, precipitated by one of his own brutal practical jokes, he decrees the honors due to a captain general, and orders the city and province to abide two years of mourning, during which all citizens must attach a broad crepe to their hats along with the customary red ribbon.[19]

In the above citations, the reader should note that the extract we are dealing with is unbroken, with no paragraph separation, thus allowing a continuum for scansion. The numbers indicate a division of segments; thus, between numbers, one can see an articulation that constantly changes signs: from 1 to 2, the articulation possesses a philosophic character; from 2 to 3, costumbrista; from 3 to 4, the articulation is scientific; from 4 to 5, journalistic; from 5 to 6, political; from 6 to 7, grammatical (joining); and from 7 to 8, historical and anecdotal. We have, if nothing else, a variety of inflections that gives us a notion of the correlative breadth of semantic planes, all amassed in the above-mentioned citation. If, moreover, we establish the phraseological unities of each segment, we will see, similarly, that the constructive direction of each differs from that which follows. Thus, from an initial objective ("All of America . . .") follows an adjective and subjective complementation ("viewing them as the height . . ."); what continues is now a simple subjectivization ("I see only . . .") that finally requires an objective and objectivized complement. In only one paragraph, as we can see, there are four levels that, added to all those which can register in the following segments, promote an image of vertiginous intersection and mixture.

One could conclude here that this "mixing" movement is so remarkable that it can be considered a generating pole, a force that, while present in the writing, explains at the same time its process of unfolding. Since this writing is presented as a "rhythm," the "mixture" (as force) can be defined as a marker of the rhythm, determining its production. However, another dimension exists: the "mixture" does not remain as a secret productive force but evolves into a design, a kind of sought-after, aesthetic ideal with a specific ideological project. This "mixture" simultaneously sustains two levels of theoretical definition that would mark in this passage a *literary* program, not only directing *Facundo* but, once transformed into a program of action, governing all natural production of writing. In other words, it comes to represent a model of a possible literature. United with this conclusion is what seems to be the "declarative" aspect of Sarmiento's preoccupation with literature: "I have a literary ambition," he writes on several occasions.

Leaving aside this "ambition" which is articulated within the concept of "mixture," and viewing it from the angle of a probable effect of reading, we could state that a certain "formlessness"[20] appears related to the set of "forms" that conventionally circulate in literature, in this case meaning literature as an activity understood by "schools," "aesthetics," or the interplay of reactions and actions. What might be the origin of such formlessness? What might its meaning be? The matter is related to the "plurality" that defines *Facundo*. Yes, plurality (of registers, of planes, of elements, of demands) is the source of this "lack of form," together with a desire to capture everything, an impulse somehow destructive, dialectically denied by its ideological proposal. For individuals such as Juan Bautista Alberdi and Paul Groussac, this formlessness responds to cultural gaps in Sarmiento's formation. From Martínez Estrada's perspective, this shapeless aspect of *Facundo* could be linked to "that constant line of his fate" which he receives as a forceful inheritance from his father and which is made manifest in a personal distortion: a talent for conceiving projects and an inability to fulfill them. Certainly, this speculation constitutes a positivist risk, but it is also true that what is called "style"—a concept that would explain these always chaotic beginnings—is inscribed upon both a *personal network* (organized by a set of interpolated models, lived and forgotten, but never alone in action, not even when one understands these models as being confused with even deeper motivations) and a *cultural network* (integrated by demands of the superego).

In any case, and without necessarily ending in an "explanation," this crossing of networks creates to a certain extent the basis of a system of determination that, albeit formless and plural, was nonetheless extraordinarily productive in Sarmiento, almost second nature. On certain occasions he attempted to regulate it—without success—through instruments linked to the will and related, at the same time, to responsibilities inherent in questions of power. Yet, if "formlessness" is an indelible mark as well as a source of activity and production, it also represents a counterweight to his more-than-evident inclination for touching up, correcting, or suppressing, a tendency that could be linked perfectly to his political opportunism. In order to rid this term of any leftist coloring, however, we might replace it with another, more generous word: empiricism. In this area, Sarmiento was by no means isolated or alone; yet in his own work it emerged as rending and conflictive, while in the texts of others it expressed calculated design and a more marked class consciousness.[21]

Seen from another angle, the "formlessness" is also an agitation—quite romantic and *Sturm und Drang*—against limits and barriers. It is individualism, but of a social type, given Sarmiento's singular identification with his country. These convulsive movements generally explain the appearance of a very personal engagement. Thus, the rupture of genre was preceded (in the case of *Facundo*) by Sarmiento's discussion in Chile of grammar and spelling and of the validity of romanticism.[22] At the same time, the coexistence of extremely acute social-psychological insights with superficial reductionism explains aspects we have already affirmed, such as Sarmiento's contrasting rhythms in prose (as a link between a nonrepressed unconsciousness and an ordering perspective) linked with some ideal form of society.

Romanticism, nevertheless, would take the lead insofar as it provided an up-to-date, applicable model, an interpretation of the world apt for thinking about that luminous future of a class destined to build power, the Republic, and civilization. The romantic impact is also justified for its contradictory facet, for the oscillation that it offers between the ideological and the unconscious, an oscillation that finally engenders a surprising inversion in the imposition of an Enlightenment rationality over the field that was to be overcome. Can this factor account for the origin of models and, at the same time, locate its roots in the "provincial" character that always hounded Sarmiento (i.e., his belabored resentment) or in the situation of the emigrant who finally appears compensated—as he vehemently shows in his 1843 pamphlet, *Mi defensa*[23]—by a conscientious perseverance founded on a clear idea of a national and social "project"? In any event, the situation of the "emigrant" of the nineteenth century merits reflection because, with differing traits and effects, the emigrant continues to exist today. The current massiveness of the phenomenon contrasts with the singularity of the cases at that time, leading to two consequences: on the one hand, concerning the individuals who emigrated, they more easily found protection, which made possible the reinforcement and authorization of the traditional and lax "right of sanctuary" of which Latin America boasted; on the other hand, this situation led to possibilities of self-analysis that favored both the emergence of personal conflicts and the production of texts as effective forms of action.

According to Groussac, who affirmed this tradition, much damage was done to Rosas by his exiles, which ratifies both the importance of the exile's situation and the perceived corrosiveness of writing. According to Alberto Palcos, Rosas attempted to silence Sarmiento by creating a newspaper in Mendoza, *La Ilustración Argentina*. One could also link this theme to the trite idea that Sarmiento wrote *Facundo* in order to discredit Rosas close to the arrival in Chile of Baldomero García, who demanded that the Chilean government contain the actions of the exiles. (However, it is also possible that García was sent to address the issue of borders, a perennial issue in relations between the two countries.)

4

The relationship between past and future—fundamental to the first schema I have identified in the *Facundo*—takes us to other areas of critical study. I refer to the position of the "intellectual" and the role he might perform.

It seems evident that the practice of literature, as it has been described, is subordinated to a more general idea of *action* through the written word. *Facundo* explicitly ratifies this concept and incidentally provides quite a timely image of the practice of intellectuals. In the letter to Alsina ("Prologue to the Second Edition"), Sarmiento writes: "Let us persevere, friend, let us die, you there, I here; but let no act, no word of ours reveal that we are aware of our weakness, and of the fact that we are threatened today or tomorrow by tribulations and dangers." He explains: "Vandalism has devoured us, in effect, and it is quite a sad glory to have prophesied so in a proclamation, and not to have made an effort to hinder it."[24] Note two things: first, Sarmiento's persistence, which presupposes faith in the mission of intellectual work, both as a legitimate practice and as an antidote to human debility; second, the intellectual's ineffectiveness in thwarting the blows of reality. Descriptively, this would be more of a verification of fact than a definition and/or a proposal. Beyond this, I can conceive of a definition and proposal giving rise to dual functions. As for the first aspect, Alexis de Tocqueville (*Democracy in America*) offers a model even more imposing in that it is recognized as "science" and as the essence of its historical development; a necessary model, since only through science will it be possible, as is claimed quite imaginatively in *Facundo*, "to sink one's vision into the shadows of the night." As Raúl Orgaz has pointed out (*Sarmiento y el naturalismo histórico*), Sarmiento possesses traits that Tocqueville noticed in writers during democratic times: a disregard for form, a quickness of execution that sacrifices perfection of detail, and a certain verbal agility, born of vehemence and spirit.

In regard to the second aspect, literature doubtless becomes an assistant to the "action," serving a determined content; for Sarmiento, this could have been the construction of a different society, although for some of his readers it might only have been the consolidation of a social class. In any case, the intellectual as such clears a path toward fulfillment, and upon bestowing power to himself, he invests it in his image and becomes a model: "Introduce me as the name most esteemed in these circles, of the Chilean and Brazilian governments, with which I am on intimate terms; in the army, among federals and unitarians, as the founder of a policy of party fusion. If this plan is followed, we shall achieve victory" ("Letter to Posse," April 10, 1852).[25]

The intellectual is then situated in a totality. From these heights, beyond class, he achieves a success that while rooted in his personal aspirations, is abstractly projected: "if one day intellectual powers will play a role in directing the affairs of the Argentine republic, many and quite complete figures of transformation will be found in this chosen pleiad, fully prepared by talent, study, travels, ill fate, and by the spectacle of errors and miscalculations that they have witnessed or committed."[26]

5

We are left with a question produced by the preceding topics: Does Sarmiento express a concern for literature as it evolves into a literary design for his own project? There exists, similarly, an idea about the intellectual who, on the one hand, produces a book and, on the other, presents himself as a social model. Might there also exist an idea about literature in general, that is to say, literature as it should be? What would its requirements be?

It does seem clear that *Facundo,* as Palcos imagined, can be seen as a primitive epic, the same characterization Leopoldo Lugones proposes for *Martín Fierro* in *El payador.* If this is so, it then contains all the appropriate elements for marking the rhythm of the birth of a nation and/or country (this observation could also be made of *Martín Fierro,* since the death of the gaucho would mark the painful emergence of the modern world). Literature, then, could be both epic in breadth and accumulative in detail. See, in particular, the last two chapters of *Facundo,* titled "Present and Future," whose programmatic elements, though in fact minimal, lead to a vision of epic proportions. However, let us offer a turn of phrase to this discussion of epic. Let us say that we have a totalizing and sweeping literature, but that it lacks certain mechanisms to fulfill its objective. "If one flash of a national literature can shine momentarily in the new societies of the Americas, it will be the result of the description of the grandiose, natural scenes, and, above all, the struggle between European civilization and indigenous barbarism'':[27] description and interpretation, nature and history; without a doubt, the model has been found in the U.S. literature of westward expansion.

A landscape for observation and a doctrine for application would then be the basis for establishing this national literature; in Sarmiento's view, the process is inaugurated with Esteban Echeverría's *La cautiva*. At the same time, the doctrinal basis of national literature is not presented as a recurring model but as an order of concepts having precise incarnations within the national landscape and, therefore, differing from the models that inspired the neoclassical generation before Sarmiento. The relationship between doctrine and nature is explosive, permitting the emergence of the suppressed or embryonic: "There exists, therefore, a well of poetry born of the natural accidents of the country and the exceptional customs that it engenders."[28] Literature, as a consequence, must take charge of this dynamism, and in its realization it should develop those elements awakened from the crossing of nature and doctrine.

What are those elements? Principally, customs. The answer is *costumbrismo*, which must attempt to capture and interpret curious local types that doubtlessly reveal, in the moment of description, their potential relationship to nature and doctrine. After all, nature engendered customs; but it is through the intellectual apparatus that we are able to observe them. In this relationship, writing encounters its principles and its justification.

The presence and influence of Mariano José de Larra are undeniable in this vein. It is possible that he represents merely a general orientation, since the regionalistic "portraits" (tracker, guide, singer, bad gaucho) in reality constitute the nucleus of something much greater: biographical form itself. This incidentally brings to mind an observation regarding these portraits and the elements employed in their sketches: there exists a literary intuition that justifies his energetic transpositions of nature. That is why his program opens up a way to others, why Sarmiento is concerned for the shape a national literature should take.

The most highly wrought model is that of biography which, as a practice, condenses nature and doctrine. Yet "biography," considered here in a generic perspective, is an instance, not a genre to return to after one has accepted the principles of "mixture" and "formlessness" as the basis of Sarmiento's *Facundo*. We find proof of this not only in the uncanny biographical beginning that initiates the *Facundo*, but also in the guiding concepts of the work. It begins, for example, with a "scene" (another form of "frame") and an episode, and not in the lineal perspective that justifies the biographic genre and survives (even in its modern variation) the "fictionalized biography," of which—according to Guerrero—*Facundo* would be a forerunner, as he has noted in *Tres temas*. The evasion of linearity is a constructive concept in this biography, and it is complemented by a mechanism of *selection* which, even if also present in classical biographies, here permits an essential displacement of *accent*. In reality, it produces a *montage*, in the modern sense of the word (of the sort that Eisenstein would grace with many examples and theories).[29] Selection and montage become articulated, and if on the one hand they authorize a certain discretionality (since one might well suppose that many situations of importance have been left out), they will on the other hand constitute a principle of energy that relativizes the "genre" once again and introduces a disconcerting, yet rich, element to the reading.

This is, perhaps, what *we* are able to read about biography in its production. Sarmiento, however, had a different idea: he accepted biography as genre and assigned it enormous moral significance. "It is the most adequate fabric for printing good ideas, and whoever writes it claims an almost judicial role, punishing triumphant vice and encouraging humbled virtue," he wrote in *Recuerdos de provincia*.[30] This moral finality lends, once again, function to literature—not in the philosophical but in the political sense, as an instrument for the construction of a modern society. Morals are thus politics for Sarmiento, and literature is an instrument that discovers in biography its maximum possibility.

Sarmiento was faithful to his viewpoint, one that he tried to generalize, thus offering himself as a model for national literature. He wrote several biographies, ending with his own, *Recuerdos de provincia*, in which moral judgment and its object are fused into one. If we disregard his theory of biography and limit ourselves to the question of how *Facundo* emerged within the textual process, we could perfectly well consider that what later happened in Argentine literature (the rise of the novel, the theater, and the sociological essay) constitutes a cultural regression, a distancing from vernacular production—and a submission to literary models that are themselves inscribed in other, more general models of submission.

However, if what Sarmiento wrote was "biography" in the classical European sense, we should also recognize that he anticipated a practice that in Europe would first emerge with positivism (I refer, of course, to that form known as "fictionalized biography"). From this, two consequences emerge. First, whether from Sarmiento's explicit theory or from our reading, *Facundo* proposes a model not only for Argentine literature but for world literature in general, thus offering a challenge that, after the growth of cultural colonialism, Latin America found itself unable to continue. Second, we must reconsider the false impositions of biographical genre upon an explosion of forms—one which rested on the desire for "originality" that possessed the Generation of 1837 and which implies a plain and simple adjustment to accepted cultural models, a necessary entry fee into "civilization" (with all it ambiguously involves).

In this context, one inevitably wonders about the production of cultural models from Latin America in a relationship of competition or submission to existing dominant cultures of the world (an issue that still poses problems today). But let me move to some final speculations about biographical form, in order to add an additional nuance to this look at the suggestions provided by *Facundo* concerning the issue of what direction the national literature should take.

Consider this: contrary to classical definitions of biography, let us assume that in *Facundo* biography is written by selecting elements that suggest a nonlinear order; in the same fashion, Sarmiento writes history, which seems to be, in his own view, one objective of his book that stands without refutation (except for the very limited comments of Valentín Alsina). From this understanding comes what some people accept as "true" in *Facundo* and what lies at the base of our liberal mythology. From the point of view of construction, then, our conclusions regarding biography can be applied to *Facundo* as history. Indeed, between biography and history a relationship exists that is based perhaps on a theory of literature's alliance with science, in vogue in Saint-Simonian thought. At the same time, and for this same reason, there exists an interlacing of the two: biography needs history; history is created through biography. This interlacing defines the textual process of *Facundo*; it is a writing whose laws would obey nonlinear rules—the bases for a reconstructing movement— and it is an interlacing that appears to be born from the need to clarify by example. This process reflects a literary intuition that proceeds according to a precise ideology, extracting the "secret" of nature and man while also building a text.

It is here that *Facundo*, through that extraction, reveals its minimal conditions of production, which, as they stand, generate a methodology involving a type of "American realism" and represent the possibility of writing. At the same time, these conditions spring from a permanent structure, or necessary models for action, which correspond to an idea of the nation. The second step consists in reconverting them, without making them disappear, by establishing a nonorthodox relationship regarding the production of the meaning. And if the "condition of production" in *Facundo* derives from this assumption, it is because the ideas—the "ideologies"—always carry a dual value; they help and subject at the same time, albeit without forming a single unit of meaning. From this network, one can grasp why *Facundo* offers considerable enticement for its images and relatively little as a field of ideas that demand to be embodied in ideological institutions.

By now, various points of discussion begin to reveal a common thread: the frames of *Facundo* constitute nuclei that allow us to construct an idea of biography. This possibility, at the same time, leads us to reevaluate the problem of those "models" *Facundo* followed and of *Facundo* itself as a model. If we leave aside the *substance* that the models attempt to impose upon us as readers, attending instead only to the demands that our relationship with them presents, we might consider the models as *instruments* of reference, as "telling." They represent known points on a circuit whose other extreme is marked by the event or object to be described, that unknown or concealed truth, the "secret" evoked on the first page of *Facundo.*

Between "models" and "total or partial ignorance" (the secret), a metaphorical relationship is virtually established that has general consequences for the text. The known, in this movement, is postulated; the unknown is brought forth as a problem; and even the formulation of this tension is metaphorized by means of comparisons that constantly traverse the text but never stop referring to the secret that the reader wants to reach: "I see [in Bolívar] an imitation of Europe and nothing that might reveal American essence to me." Exactly the same role is performed by the epigraphs to each chapter and by the quotations from myriad sources. I suppose that the intention is to "reveal" something, a "secret"; I suppose that Sarmiento's readings of other texts assist in this revelation. I am, however, more interested in describing how it is schematized and what instruments are required. Certainly, schematization and instruments are projected onto the entire text and register its articulation. Comparisons, for example, determine paratactic constructions that the stylists recognize and applaud; at the same time, grammatical subordination engenders an equally active hypotactic form and, between the two, a network takes shape that guides, perhaps, this "knowing how to tell" that we began with.

Yet, something more remains: to compare is to oppose, and to oppose presupposes terms that stand in opposition. We are faced with the embryo of the central idea—barbarism and civilization, black and white—which is naturally presented in the form of dilemma and, of course, directed options. In *Muerte y resurrección de Facundo,* I attempted to outline a constructive role for this formula which so clearly embodies an oppositional value. I even thought that "civilization and barbarism" offered a productive matrix of meaning. But can this formula have valid content? Or is it simply a catalyst within the text that permits us to imagine an "origin," a generative matrix whose only function is within the text itself, not exterior to it? As I have already addressed this problem in the aforementioned study, I would now like to point out how the opposition governs textual anatomy (in terms of syntax) by organizing each sentence and (on the semantic plane) by placing them in opposition and providing an option that simultaneously determines, if not the construction, at least certain internal structures of the sentences of the text.

However, I do not wish to immerse myself again in problems relating to construction of minimal units. On various occasions, I have already affirmed the role performed by opposition and contrast in textual dynamics. Now I want to refer to the "discourse" of *Facundo*, and I take as an example the opposition among units, an opposition of tone that evolves into a matter of semantics and becomes a model of the "orientation" intended to be given to the work as a whole.

We have, first of all, a striking declaration: "During his entire stay there, he lived under a tent in the middle of a corral with alfalfa, and he exhibited (for it was a meditated exhibition) his *chiripá!* Defiance and insult toward a city the majority of whose citizens rode with English saddles, and where the barbarian dress and barbarian tastes of the countryside were detested!"[31] We cannot help but sense, above all, the note of scandal that accompanies this evocation, a note that makes him appear solemn and antiquated, morally superficial, a *criollo* paterfamilias. A question could be asked of this excerpt: In what way might the meaning of Facundo's presence have changed had he resided in a house and donned a morning coat? Would he have stopped being a barbarian? Nonetheless, I should say that this is not a question of Sarmientine triviality, caused by a pressing need to continue condemning an individual already condemned; rather, there is a kind of vague optimism with respect to "sign," which opens the possibility for a structuralist reading that I refuse to perform in these pages. In their semanticization, these signs drift toward ethics, which is a political matter, or similarly define a policy based on stressing the semantic aspect of the signs.

Confronted with this fragment, let us cite another, related to Dorrego, which offers a semantic contrast: "Without a doubt, no one would assume the charge of defending the dead man at the expense of the survivors, those who survived thanks to having decided his death, save, perhaps, on the formal aspects of the event, doubtless the least substantial in a case such as this."[32] The total absence of a legal, or merely correct, judgment that might have influenced the fate of the leader at the hands of those who organized his defeat is here presented as a formality and not a substantive issue—the political aim of the upheaval—while the lack of a morning coat was presented in the case of Facundo as a matter of substance. The signs are directed in this mechanism of oppositions by semantic poles that correspond to an interpretation of *process,* which allows the opposition to be seen in two totally opposite ways simultaneously: one on the basis of textual generation and production; the other as a conceptual predetermination, which reduces the vertiginous richness of the text to a tracking of signs, leaving them unequivocal in meaning merely in order to ensure that they offer unequivocal confirmation of a political vision.

Facundo abounds in examples of this kind. In some instances, the system that was just described is enclosed within a single sentence, replete with lessons for the reader. In this respect, the following is full of current resonances: "The roles have been interchanged: the gaucho takes a house, the soldier of the Wars of Independence, a poncho; the first is triumphant, the second will die shot by a bullet from the passing *montonera.* If Lavalle had made his campaign in 1840 in an English saddle and carrying a French banner, today we would be at the shores of the River Plate arranging the navigation of steamers and distributing lands to European immigrants."[33] The historical results assumed by the confrontation of signs is clear. Also clear is the exchange produced between corresponding semantic aspects and their resulting inversions. And finally, the triumph of an emerging idea stands out, constituting, moreover, an essential nucleus of one of the organizing principles of Sarmiento's entire system—that of European culture itself—here less metaphorical than real. The current importance of these considerations takes shape in the relationship that we can establish between "populism" and "developmentalism," on the one hand, and between the "Left" and "populism," on the other. When populism—Juan Perón, for example, or the idea of Latin America, the masses, the "shirtless poor," or the montonera, in Sarmiento's sense of the word—becomes developmentalism (admiration for the "German miracle" or for "Spanish Europeanization"), what is proposed is the imposition of a metropolitan ("European") concept upon the present state of relations between imperialism and independence. Furthermore, when the Marxist Left (European in the best sense of the word) becomes populist (leftist Peronism, the "Montonera"), it is cut down by a European-style populism (union bureaucracy), albeit without a decisive battle, even more so when the military coup of March 23, 1976, "Western and Christian," sets out to exterminate this montonera combination, serving only to continue the preceding confrontation. Had anything else occurred, had leftist populism triumphed over developmentalism (populist until March 23; after which, perhaps not), we might have found ourselves before the definitive decline of the Sarmientine schema. We might have begun to think about a recuperation of signs and, therefore, about a society structured in another fashion.

6

We have come to the end of an elaboration of one possible model for a national Argentine literature as suggested by *Facundo*. I recognize that we have traveled far and that it is perhaps better to stop, lest we fall into what is currently known as "textual analysis," a possibility that always lurks when relationships between "sentence" and "totality" are admitted into the discussion. Every sentence, every segment, every contrast between sentences generates interpretations that impinge on one of the central concerns of the present essay: what we can understand as "current" in *Facundo*.

It is appropriate here to make a clarification that will unleash new modes of reasoning. To claim that a text is "current" affirms an order of prevailing structural problems that links old and new societies; it represents a symbolic possibility of "interpreting" contemporary phenomena in the light of phenomena described in a nineteenth-century text. *Current* is a way of seeing, even a way of seeing texts that should be included among the present problems—fundamental problems—of our society, our historical time. If this "way of seeing texts" can be translated by the concept of "reading," then I would say, by way of summarizing, that "reading" is not a purely interstitial activity; rather, it is an outlet for social activity at the moment when social engagements require codes and signs in order to reveal all their complexity. It is from this point that a "way of seeing," or rather a "way of reading," should be included among all that composes and defines our actuality. In this sense, I consider writing as production, and I see texts as moments in a chain of production that has close relationships with the chain of *social* production.[34] For a text to be produced, I believe, requires certain conditions, which are linked to conditions of general social production and which are neither simplistic nor reductive.

Another clarification: the relationship I propose is not one of social cause and literary effect favored by a positivist (or pseudo-Marxist) mechanism; rather, the idea is that between the text (as productive system) and society (as productive system) there exists a link in which the central element is *ideology*. In this sense, we wish to view *Facundo* in light of a general system of productivity whose principles are also those of the text. From this perspective, the text appears to be distorted in a way that, in the history of culture, is nevertheless surprising: if we recognize *Facundo* as a rich text, full of force and consequence that still challenges and sets forth multiple readings, yet still remains incomplete, how can we link this richness to the poverty of landscape, economy, and culture in which it was engendered? Perhaps the answer lies in the realm of contradiction: Buenos Aires drowned the interior and impoverished it. The need to understand the source of such ill-fortune creates, from the vantage of writing, conditions for reversing the tension: from the perspective of writing, we can see how an impoverished nation offers a rich text to a rich geographic area that seems only to engender poverty. This implies that the relationship between social production and textual production not only refuses linearity but is so contradictory as to be discerned from writing itself. In this way, writing is not the result of determined social forces, but presents itself as a source of social action, awakening the actors to future possibilities not yet reached in their current practice.

Several consequences emerge from this discussion, first and above all in the intellectual sphere. The relationship between an impoverished reality and an ebullient writing establishes the limits of what in modern times is known as the "anthropology of poverty": an abundance of observations that permits abstractions and generalizations, forged from meager material of little value, socially speaking. Furthermore, so as not to become a victim of the tendency to recognize in *Facundo* a new genre, one which will be a "forerunner," it is better to claim that the book first captures and then reveals the "culture of poverty," a concept we can also observe in José Hernández's *Martín Fierro*, where its elaboration cloaks other, equally subtle characteristics.[35] But does not this "culture of poverty," developed by both Sarmiento and Hernández, constitute one of the traits of an Argentine oligarchic culture that hides with its brilliance the indisputable fact of a deficient social structure in which unjust distribution of wealth transforms the dispossessed into mere objects (and never the agents) of cultural activity? Would not Lugones with *La guerra gaucha*, Enrique Larreta in *Zogoibi*, and even the Borges of *Evaristo Carriego* be heirs to this culture?

Moreover, it could be claimed that the means of literary production (though *Facundo* may be a unique case) might be more highly developed than the means of economic production. If this is acceptable, one might conclude that literature can be viewed as a possible model for productivity, one that carries over into the realm of ideological action. In other words, this wealth of productive, literary means derives from and engenders an ideological force, such that it soon will become embodied in social and economic forces.

Starting from a "literary" consideration, then, we finally enter the sphere of ideology, witnessing the birth of what really happened in history: namely, the reordering of an entire country and perhaps even a continent by liberal thought (thought—let us repeat—that needed to be vigorously formulated in order to achieve such monumental results).

Notes

1. Jean-Pierre Faye, "Théorie du récit," *Change,* no. 5 (1970): 5–15.

2. Sarmiento, "Letter to Calandrelli," August 12, 1881, in *Facundo,* critical and documented edition, prologue by Alberto Palcos (La Plata: Universidad Nacional de La Plata, 1938): ". . . having been brought up in a distant province and having been educated without structured studies, the tongue of the conquerors must have been preserved there for a longer time without noticeable changes" (p. 455).

3. Jorge Luis Borges, "Prologue" to *Recuerdos de provincia* (Buenos Aires: Emecé, 1943).

4. Noé Jitrik, *Muerte y resurrección de Facundo* (Buenos Aires: CEAL, 1968).

5. "You might believe that such mediocrity is natural to a city of the interior? No. Tradition is there to bear witness of the opposite" (*Facundo,* Palcos ed., p. 82).

6. Ibid., pp. 165–166.

7. Enrique Anderson Imbert, "El historicismo de Sarmiento," *Cuadernos Americanos* 4, no. 5 (1945): 158–177.

8. See Adolfo Prieto, *La literatura autobiográfica argentina* (Rosario: Facultad de Filosofía y Letras, Universidad Nacional del Litoral, 1963).

9. Alberto Palcos, *El Facundo* (Buenos Aires: Editorial Elevación, 1945); Allison Williams Bunkley, *The Life of Sarmiento* (Princeton: Princeton University Press, 1952).

10. Juan Luis Guerrero, *Tres temas de filosofía argentina en las entrañas del Facundo* (La Plata: Universidad Nacional de La Plata, 1945).

11. Alberto Palcos, "Prologue" to *Facundo* (see note 3, above).

12. The second note of Valentín Alsina is relevant here. Alsina observes in Sarmiento a certain "tendency toward systems," that is, toward imposing systems upon reality. Alsina's notes can be found in the Palcos edition of *Facundo* (note 3, above).

13. Jacques Lafaye, in *Sarmiento ou Marti? A propos de "D. F. Sarmiento, éducateur et publiciste, entre 1839 et 1852"* [by Paul Verdevoye], a reprint of *Langues Néo-Latines,* no. 172 (May 1965), maintains that the group countering Sarmiento's struggle is the "aristocracy," a characterization in which various notions converge: means of production, racial origin, customs, values, intentions, etc. The war between Dávilas and Ocampos in La Rioja exemplifies this characterization, which is taken from other conflicts between clans represented in literature. It would be more appropriate to consider that this distancing from some groups within the same class has an economic basis and is

centered, in the final analysis, on the opposition between pre-bourgeois sectors of the interior provinces and the more advanced sectors of Buenos Aires.

14. Letter to Valentín Alsina, in *Facundo,* Palcos ed., p. 25.

15. Pedro Henríquez Ureña, "Perfil de Sarmiento," *Cuadernos Americanos* 4, no. 5 (1945): 199–206.

16. Ezequiel Martínez Estrada, *Meditaciones sarmientinas* (Santiago: Editorial Universitaria, 1968), p. 18.

17. Raúl Orgaz, *Sarmiento y el naturalismo histórico* (Córdoba: Imprenta Rossi, 1940).

18. In the same manner of composition described in "Advertencia a la Primera Edición": "Coordinating different events that have taken place in differing and remote provinces, and in diverse periods, by consulting an eyewitness regarding a point, by revising manuscripts hurriedly written, or by appealing to one's own reminiscences" (*Facundo,* Palcos ed., p. 5).

19. *Facundo,* Palcos ed., pp. 258–259.

20. We should give the floor to Sarmiento himself, in his letter to Alsina ("Prologue to the Second Edition"): "If such an unformed work were corrected, both its primitive style and its poorly disciplined structure might disappear" (*Facundo,* Palcos ed., p. 24).

21. The entire episode of Alsina's notes and resulting corrections (along with the well-studied reasons for the suppressions in the second and third editions) shows, foremost, the influence of the changing conditions of the political struggle. Sarmiento makes concessions to Alsina in the midst of a general tendency toward utopianism that is counterbalanced through his will to become involved in a real sphere of action. I am convinced that, contrary to what is generally believed—as a concealed bourgeois myth—Sarmiento paid attention to *concrete* forces, particularly regarding politics, and negotiated with them (e.g., his choice of the Conservative party in Chile when everyone expected him to opt for the Liberal party). He did not intend to invent everything, but neither did he renounce the hope that this "everything" was moving forward. Here we find the play between opportunism and independence: the goal came first; and the goal, I repeat, was to constitute a class and a country simultaneously. If we compare him with Esteban Echeverría, who gladly assumes the limitations in the role of ideological founder, or with Alberdi, who chooses according to moral and political criteria similar to those of Sarmiento but perhaps with a mistaken sense of opportunity, we may conclude that within Sarmiento's action a concern with success is always present.

22. Norberto Pinilla, *La polémica del romanticismo en 1842* (Buenos Aires: Américalee, 1943).

23. This will be a permanent line in Sarmiento. In the "Prologue to the First Edition," first paragraph, he uses the word "banished," and he concludes: "Those who know of my conduct in Chile know whether I have fulfilled that protest" (*Facundo,* Palcos ed., p. 7).

24. *Facundo*, Palcos ed., p. 27.

25. *Epistolario entre Sarmiento y Posse* (Buenos Aires: Museo Histórico Sarmiento, 1946), 1:29.

26. *Facundo*, Palcos ed., pp. 282–283.

27. Ibid., p. 47.

28. Ibid., p. 49.

29. S. M. Eisenstein, "Structure, montage, passage," *Change*, no. 1 (1968): 15–41.

30. D. F. Sarmiento, *Recuerdos de provincia* (Buenos Aires: La Facultad, 1934), p. 55.

31. *Facundo*, Palcos ed., p. 209.

32. Ibid., p. 267.

33. Ibid., p. 191.

34. Noé Jitrik, *Producción literaria y producción social* (Buenos Aires: Sudamericana, 1975).

35. Noé Jitrik, "El tema del canto en el *Martín Fierro*," in *El fuego de la especie* (Buenos Aires: Siglo XXI, 1972).

11 The Unquiet Self: Mnemonic Strategies in Sarmiento's Autobiographies

SYLVIA MOLLOY

Toward the end of *Recuerdos de provincia*, speaking of the biographies he has written, Sarmiento declares that "biographies are the most original books South America has to offer in these times and the best material it can give to history." He then adds that *Facundo* and "these *Recuerdos de provincia* belong to the same genre."[1] Although debatable, both statements are revealing. Autobiography is taken here most literally: it is not necessarily an example of self-expression but a biography; a life, not of another, but of the self. As an example of a genre much valued at the time all over the world, and not only in Sarmiento's Argentina (suffice it to recall Disraeli's admonition: "Read no history: nothing but biography, for that is life without theory"),[2] autobiography seems a perfect vehicle for history and, concretely in the case of Spanish America, for the new history of the newly formed countries.

Now this generic adjudication (autobiography is biography is history), together with its specific characteristics (autobiography is not only history but new, national history), imposes a particular slant on the autobiographical text. Both autobiography and biography deal with lives in the past and imply, in whatever measure, a reassessment of those lives. However, whereas autobiography relies on memory for both its substance and its compositional thrust, biography fundamentally relies on documents. When writing the biography of the provincial strongman Juan Facundo Quiroga, Sarmiento only sporadically *remembers* his hero. He remembers, instead, the secondhand recollections others have shared with him, the information about Facundo that has been incorporated by that sector of public opinion on which he relies, and he remembers what he has read in documents. More than remembering, the biographer *records* a past in which he may be involved only tangentially. Sarmiento himself, a prodigious biographer and assiduous necrologist, wrote lives of people he knew in the past and lives of people he knew not at all. The ultimate goal of the recording, in which personal memory played or did not play a part, was not the pleasure of evocation but the preservation of knowledge and, one should add, the construction of a model.

Only in two of Sarmiento's biographies, and for different reasons, does this distanced approach—one that Sarmiento, quoting Abel-François Villemain, would call "impartial yet not impassive"[3]—work imperfectly. These are the two biographies in which, closely knitting the life of his subject into his own, Sarmiento cannibalized two mirror images: Quiroga, his "barbaric" shadow figure, in *Facundo*; and, in *Vida de Dominguito*, the son he would fashion into a copy of himself. While ostensibly biographical, these texts suffer from something akin to autobiographical unrest. I shall devote some attention to *Facundo* since, besides having been linked explicitly with *Recuerdos* by Sarmiento himself as another example of the "biographical" genre, it will allow me to consider the peculiar hybrid nature not only of *Recuerdos* but of many nineteenth- and some twentieth-century Spanish American autobiographies.

In the foreword to the 1845 edition of *Facundo*, Sarmiento, seeking to defend himself from his earliest critics, sought to justify his method:

> It was inevitable that some inaccuracies slip into a work composed in haste, far from the scene of action and on a subject on which nothing had been written until then. Having coordinated events that took place in different and distant provinces and in different periods, consulted eyewitnesses on some issues, searched through hastily written manuscripts or called upon my own recollections, I am not surprised if the Argentine reader finds I have left things out or disagrees on a name, a date that may be wrong or out of place.
>
> Regarding the noteworthy events to which I refer and which serve as a base for the explanations I set forth, I should stress that their accuracy is irreproachable and *is corroborated by the public documents that consign them.*
>
> Perhaps the moment will come when, free of the worries that prompted the composition of this little book, I shall recast it according to a new plan, stripping it of all accidental digressions and supporting it with *the numerous official documents* to which I refer only briefly for now. [*OC*, 7:6; emphasis added]

The first edition of *Facundo* in book form could well have corrected the errors found by critics when they first read the text in installments in *El Progreso*. It did not. Nor was Sarmiento ever to write the second, better-composed version he announces. Sarmiento did not correct: if he returned to what he had written, it was not to revise but to write another book. *Facundo*, then, stands very much on its own from the very beginning, faithful in spirit to the romantic tenets of inspiration and improvisation, acknowledging—even vaunting—its flaws.[4] Yet Sarmiento would have it both ways. Even as he praises the book's inspired untidiness, he claims documentary status for it. The need to validate the text in a historic light certainly haunts him in this insistent foreword: he hammers away at the reader that the events he writes about are accurate, not only because others, Sarmiento's informants, have witnessed them, but because they have been recorded, set down in manuscripts, committed to "public" documents, registered in—note the authoritarian crescendo—"official" documents. If, like his models Edgar Quinet and Jules Michelet, Sarmiento acknowledges the existence of other clues to the past besides the written word (a good portion of the second chapter of *Facundo* will be devoted to the unwritten historical archive amassed by local bards), when it comes to establishing the legitimacy of his project, he shows himself unusually reliant on that written word, not unlike those narrow-minded "dupes de l'écriture scellée" denounced by Quinet.[5]

A purportedly well-documented text, even in its hasty form, *Facundo* immediately becomes in Sarmiento's view a *document* in its own right. Five years later, in *Recuerdos*, he declares that the book has "provided publicists in Europe with the explanation for the conflict in the Argentine republic," and he adds that "many European publications are based on the facts and on the viewpoint of *Civilización y barbarie*" (*OC*, 3:225). For all its shortcomings, the biography of Juan Facundo Quiroga, as Sarmiento sees it, fits neatly into a chain of textual reference: it takes its authority from previous documents and becomes, in turn, a document, capable of authorizing subsequent texts.

"A fable decked out as a document," wrote Juan Bautista Alberdi of *Facundo*, drawing attention to the manner in which the purportedly "historical" nature of Sarmiento's text barely masked an exercise in personal vanity and oblique self-portraiture.[6] The expression could be applied just as aptly, if not more so, to *Recuerdos de provincia*, whose historical nature is infinitely more difficult to argue. Sarmiento claims the text belongs to the same genre as *Facundo*, that it is his own "biography." This time, however, there is no authoritative document, let alone "numerous official documents," to validate the self and attest to the accuracy of his tale. There is no previous record for that self except the unwritten text of its own memory; the only writing that supports it is the one performed in the autobiographical text itself. As a nineteenth-century biographer, though, Sarmiento is far from what, for the modern reader, is a self-evident fact. Instead, in a deliberate effort toward consistency that is as naive as it is revealing, he will set the stage for his life story in such a way that it will allow him to deal with it *as if* it were a biography. In order to fit this preconception, and also, perhaps, to avoid charges of self-centeredness, Sarmiento will fabricate a chain of documents for his "I."[7]

To satisfy his desire for objectivity and validate his (auto)biography for history, Sarmiento resorts to a ruse. Yes, there is a document on which to base the story of his self—it consists of the calumnies written about Sarmiento by his enemies. *Recuerdos de provincia* magnifies these written attacks which motivate his autobiographical response, a magnification that cannot be entirely credited to Sarmiento's egocentricity, nor to the self-defensive strategy that guides so many autobiographies. By attributing documentary value to the criticism leveled at him by the Argentine press, Sarmiento follows the pattern set in *Facundo:* he refers to a previous record to certify his project. There is, however, a disparity that even Sarmiento perceives. The documents consulted or alluded to in *Facundo* were supposedly truthful, worthy of continuation and elaboration. On the contrary, the "documents" sustaining the autobiographical project are— in the author's view—deceptive and, as such, in need of rectification. The autobiographer will not work with them but against them, striving to redress an injustice in an effort "dictated by truth and justified by need" (*OC,* 3:42). The resulting autobiographical text will then be the "good" document, whose incorporation into the dossier denounces the fallacy of the other pieces contained therein.

Once the spirit of *Recuerdos* is made clear—a document in a series of documents, a text written to inform readers and redress history—then its genre is justified for the reader: it may be called a biography. Not only does Sarmiento indicate this generic attribution at the end of *Recuerdos,* as I have mentioned, but he does so from the very beginning, in his preface. There, besides stressing its documentary nature, Sarmiento emphasizes another feature of his text; it is an exemplary piece, quite in keeping with the principles of nineteenth-century biography, a model endowed with moral and national value:

> I take delight . . . in biography. It is the most suitable canvas on which to set good ideas. He who writes it exerts a sort of judicature, punishing vice triumphant, applauding overshadowed virtue. There is something of the plastic arts in biography, capable of carving a piece of rough marble into a statue bequeathed to posterity. History would not advance if one did not attend to its prominent figures; ours would be extremely rich in characters if those who can would collect information on their contemporaries, as preserved by tradition, in a timely manner. [*OC,* 3:41][8]

These views increasingly condition the life story Sarmiento has to tell. It is a public document, a text endowed with historical and moral significance, an example for posterity and a national testimony. To be sure, all of these characteristics are present, in varying degrees, in a *Bildungsbiographie*, most especially in those written in Spanish America during the period of national reorganization. In Colombia, José María Samper, with his *Galería nacional de hombres ilustres o notables, o sea colección de bocetos biográficos*, is a good example of the genre.[9] So, in Argentina, is Bartolomé Mitre, who is clearly conscious of the ideological weight such biographies can have in the consolidation of national values and who plans his historiographic project accordingly. Mitre views his own "histories" of José de San Martín and Manuel Belgrano, together with the biographies he and others write for the *Galería de celebridades argentinas*, as integrating a textual pantheon and constituting an ideological matrix.[10] Sarmiento himself wields biography like a weapon, destined to defend the memory of worthy Argentines from evil or to doom the unworthy to oblivion. Eduardo Wilde tells how Sarmiento, at one point angered by an illustrious colleague, said excitedly, "I'll get my revenge, I won't write his biography."[11]

But if Sarmiento, mimicking the biographical process, "invents" documents to set autobiographical writing in motion, he very soon modifies his strategy. The very first chapter of *Recuerdos* is an eloquent evocation of his birthplace, San Juan, a city left in a state of near total decay by Spain's slothful colonial system. In San Juan, Sarmiento takes pains to assure us, there are no written signs of the past. All that remains to keep the record are three solitary palm trees that "had caught my attention early on. Certain trees grow as slowly as centuries and, when there is no written history, serve as reminders, as monuments to memorable events" (*OC*, 3:42). Besides those palm trees, Sarmiento salvages two other mementos as mute witness to the past: a Jesuit monastery door, from which the embossed lead lettering has been gouged out, and a file, labeled as containing the history of San Juan but emptied of its contents. "These, then, are the frail and deteriorated historical holdings on the first years of San Juan that I have been able to collect," writes a rueful Sarmiento, concerning all three wordless tokens of the past. The message is eloquent: San Juan is vacant, a barren place where there are no letters, where history has become mute.[12] It is at this point that memory, personal memory—the very memory that was considered secondary to the review of records, secondary to the collation of documents—saves the day, entering the picture as a valid source for (auto)biography. Resorting to individual recollection is necessary precisely because the file is empty and the palm trees mute. The exercise of memory is not so much a privilege of the solipsistic self as it is a civic duty: one remembers so that a communal past may not be lost.

This parallel between individual *bios* and a provincial, would-be national *ethos* is not devoid of epic overtones: Sarmiento harbors an heroic image of himself which he would gladly pass on to his readers. Yet the bond he stresses is of an even more intimate nature. It is not merely that Sarmiento pictures himself as an exemplary Argentine: he *is* the Argentine, forming with his country one inseparable body. "I was born in 1811, the ninth month after the 25th of May" (*OC*, 3:160), he writes, unambiguously establishing the genetic link, having the moment of his conception coincide with that of his newly independent country. If San Juan—a desert lost to unlettered barbarism, a blank page awaiting signs—is a synecdoche of the country, so is Sarmiento, as the remembering subject of his autobiography: he himself will be the document, the writing on the blank page.

This historical responsibility conferred on personal memory obviously imposes certain strictures on the way such memory is allowed to function within the text. I speak here not only of Sarmiento but of other autobiographers who have felt (or assumed) a similar obligation to recall. The short shrift given childhood is one possible consequence of this attitude.[13] The absence of speculation on memory itself—its workings, its range, its dependability—is another. Memory is viewed as a tool, one whose performance is as reliable as the perusal of a document, and not a subject for conjecture. A reflection on memory might indeed jeopardize the recreation of the past and its claims to veracity, opening it to doubt. The writer might be suspected of being less a historian writing down the dictates of truth, as Sarmiento fondly saw himself, and more of a fanciful fabricator, filling in the gaps left by his not-so-trustworthy memory. He might be considered a "fabulator," to use the term Pierre Janet would coin, one "who adds fabrication to his story *so as to give it order*" (emphasis added).[14]

Perhaps foreseeing such misgivings, which might render his whole enterprise suspect, Sarmiento takes pains to stress the accuracy of his account. Of *Mi defensa*, the autobiographical text antedating *Recuerdos* by seven years, he states that "this is not a novel, it is not a story" (*OC*, 3:5). Differentiating between fact and fiction, between precise recollection (what Pichon so admirably calls "le degré sec de l'évocation"[15]) and fond illusion, Sarmiento claims to be aware of the biased selectivity perpetrated by the "poetry of the heart" in the evocation of the past.[16] These signs of awareness are tenuous, however, as if Sarmiento thought any coupling of memory and imagination were better left unspoken. There are two passages that (more than the skepticism of any reader) question his claims to truth; yet he seems unaware of their corrosive potential. At the very end of *Mi defensa* (a text protesting truthfulness at every page), Sarmiento casually writes: "I have shown the man as he is, *or as he imagines himself to be*" (*OC*, 3:23; emphasis added). *Recuerdos* offers another, similarly jolting passage; again presented casually, it is barely elaborated upon. Sarmiento evokes Ña Cleme, an old Indian beggar in the San Juan of his childhood who was said to be a witch. Her interest as a character, Sarmiento notes, was that she not only assumed her reputation but reinforced it, increasing her notoriety by spreading stories about herself— "trabajaba en sus conversaciones." And he adds: "Decidedly, we have a need to call attention to ourselves. It turns those who can no longer stand being old, coarse, and poor into witches; those who are bold but incompetent, into cruel tyrants, and perhaps it is that very need that, God forgive me, leads me to write these pages" (*OC*, 3:151).

The intuition that self-portrayal, even in the name of truth, may lead to fabulation, and that the need to call attention to oneself may be synonymous with seduction or with authoritarianism was only that—an intuition. To pursue it lay beyond Sarmiento's possibilities, intent as he was on bequeathing a national statue, a well-composed patriotic whole. It is to his merit that, perhaps unsuspectingly, he included those fissures which constitute one of the chief attractions of his texts.

Like Ña Cleme, Sarmiento "works in his conversations" to preserve a gratifying image of self that he already counts on, the very image that sustains his autobiographical act. While the autobiographer's goal may appear to be the discovery or, even better, the construction of self, the process may also be seen, at the same time, to be the opposite. Self-image is an end product but it is also an initial *figure*, governing the unfolding of autobiography.[17] The past is re-created in order to suit the demands of the present—the demands of my own self-image, of the image I believe others expect of me, of the group to which I belong.[18] If some form of preconception invariably governs the unfolding of autobiography—that preconception which Gide called "un être factice préféré"[19]—dictating the rearrangement of the past, then one may say that Sarmiento's factitious being is the very country his text contributes to found.

However, this national factitious being, in Sarmiento, has more than one face. A look at *Mi defensa* in conjunction with *Recuerdos de provincia* is called for once again. In both texts, Sarmiento presents himself as a victim of slander, but the self-image that spurs his defense is different in each case. In *Mi defensa*, a text written early in his career when he has still to make a name for himself, the figuration to which the text responds is, not surprisingly, that of the self-made and self-taught hero. If autobiographical writing may be seen as an oscillation between dandyism and seduction—the desire, on the one hand, to inscribe the unique; on the other, the need to attract others to the autobiographical persona—then *Mi defensa* clearly stresses the first mode (while *Recuerdos* concentrates on the second). In *Mi defensa*, isolation is stressed at all times: the word *solo* recurs obsessively in the text. Faithful to his image as an autodidact, Sarmiento forgoes all reference to lineage, devotes a brief presentation to his immediate family, and then turns the focus on himself—and himself alone—as the self-taught head of the household:

> From the early age of fifteen, I have been head of the family. Father, mother, sisters, servants, all have been subordinated to me, and this distortion of natural relations has had a momentous influence on my character. I have never recognized any authority other than my own, and this subversion has its just reasons. From that age on, I have been charged with the care of all my relatives, am charged with it even today, and never was there a burden so gladly borne. [*OC*, 3:20–21]

This recollection—the fifteen-year-old becoming his own master and a precocious and watchful paterfamilias to boot—certainly befits the image of the self-made citizen that Sarmiento wishes to foster. Indeed, it increasingly patterns his self-writing, becoming manifest in one of the choice figurations representing his bond with Argentina: Sarmiento, Father of the Country. It is all the more surprising, therefore, that the one family tie which Sarmiento leaves unmentioned in his exemplary inventory of flattering roles and functions is, precisely, paternity—Sarmiento's own, biological paternity. When writing *Mi defensa*, Sarmiento is already the father of an eleven-year-old daughter, a fact he will never acknowledge directly in his autobiographical writings because, one suspects, it might tarnish the self-contained image he is trying to uphold. An illegitimate child, conceived during one of Sarmiento's trips to Chile and kept well out of the public eye, Ana Faustina will be integrated positively into her father's life only as an adult, when she is respectably married to the French printer Jules Belin who, let it be remembered in passing, was responsible for printing his father-in-law's *Obras completas*. For the moment, *Mi defensa* passes her over. Or very nearly. An oblique and none too gallant allusion—"There are in my life one or two moments of carelessness that I would gladly erase from the list of my deeds" (*OC*, 3:20)—might or might not refer to his daughter, indeed the product of one such careless moment. If it does, then the desired erasure, at least textually, is achieved.

Seven years later, Sarmiento rewrites his autobiography. In the new text, *Recuerdos de provincia*, the factitious being that triggers his memory has changed. Abandoning the role of precocious family leader and solitary hero accountable to no one, he now beholds himself not alone but *en famille*, a son many times over, heir to a distinguished patriotic lineage and the product of a community: "He querido apegarme a mi provincia" (*OC*, 3:41)—"I have tried to bond myself to my province." Thus, these new recollections, calculatingly dedicated "to my compatriots only,"[20] now emphasize family ties instead of short-circuiting them. In addition, far from limiting himself to the immediate family group, Sarmiento chooses to create an extended family out of prestigious figures from his native San Juan who came before him. Where once, in *Mi defensa*, he had needed to stand alone, now he must appear accompanied.

The genealogical concern at work in this new image once more bespeaks the autobiographer's need to establish himself as a historian. But it also responds to a conscious, ideological posture and to a new political plan.[21] The bellicose *Mi defensa*, written by a quite young Sarmiento, needed to sell the image of a relative newcomer on the national scene: thus the arrogant figuration of the maverick intellectual reading French books to which few had access; the self-styled young father who, single-handedly, brought order to chaos. Seven years elapse between *Mi defensa* and *Recuerdos*, years in which Sarmiento's reputation grows through his diligent efforts and, no doubt, through the publication of *Facundo* and *Viajes*. It is a more secure Sarmiento who writes *Recuerdos*,[22] one who allows himself to widen his scope, well aware that even when he speaks of others he speaks of himself; well aware, too, that while the image of the lonely, self-made intellectual with a privileged connection to European enlightenment might have helped project him onto the national scene, a less "original" figuration, as member of a family and, by extension, of a cultural community, might serve him better to achieve his goal, that of presidential candidate.

This new attempt at self-figuration is determined once more by what Martínez Estrada has so aptly called Sarmiento's "domestic sensibility,"[23] that is, the recasting of family romance in an ideological, precisely political mold. The approach is dexterous. Proceeding metonymically, Sarmiento works his way from remote ancestors to closer forebears to contemporary father figures to his parents (especially his mother) and finally to himself, their descendant. In so doing, he satisfies the biographical imperative set up for himself very successfully and many times over: each chapter, each section devoted to one of those worthy forefathers provides us with a short biography; each fashions a statue that becomes part of Sarmiento's personal gallery as well as part of a provincial, even national, pantheon.

However, these figures are linked by more than mere genealogical contiguity, as the reader finds out on reaching the striking declaration placed, quite literally, at the center of the text: "A mi progenie, me sucedo yo" (*OC*, 3:159). Marking a watershed, the phrase appears to announce, finally, Sarmiento's own (auto)biography, the last in the series. Yet the phrase is unusual, its syntax aberrant. Sarmiento does not say, as one would expect, "A mi progenie *la* sucedo yo"—"I am my progenitors' successor"—but, through a grammatical sleight of hand, dramatically breaks into the genealogical line and superimposes his "I" onto the chain of ancestors: he succeeds his progenitors but is also his own successor, his own creation. Like the two-faced Janus (a figure dear to him), Sarmiento's "A mi progenie, me sucedo yo" points at once to what precedes and what follows. If the remaining pages of *Recuerdos* do in fact trace Sarmiento's increasingly public figuration—the visible self to the detriment of a more private one—the series of minibiographies left behind may be seen, thanks to this statement, in another light. In a recuperative rereading, it becomes apparent that what links those ancestors (like Kafka creating his precursors) is, more than family ties, a powerful process of bonding (*apego*) enunciated by a very active "I."

Sarmiento intrudes in each minibiography and compromises its illusory independence by making his presence felt in the lives of his forebears; by reminiscing, evaluating, applauding, judging and, above all, in a process of deliberate affiliation, taking on the character traits, the innermost qualities, of the figures evoked. "There are young men who never knew their fathers and yet laugh, move, and gesture like them," he writes (*OC*, 3:138). Giving the statement a slight twist, one might say that Sarmiento laughed, moved, and gestured not merely *like* these "fathers" from the past on whom he modeled himself but, in his autobiography, quite literally *through* them. Paradoxically, Sarmiento's "I" seems much more present in those invasive appearances than in the second, more direct and univocal part of *Recuerdos*.

Sarmiento, whose claims to democracy are frequent, needs to insert himself nonetheless into a *privileged* lineage. These illustrious relatives or near relatives belong to what he terms "the nobility of patriotism and talent." The enlightened republicanism that Sarmiento had chosen previously to highlight in himself he now extends to his precursors. But these precursors also belong to what Sarmiento calls the "gente decente"—a social aristocracy to which he did not quite belong. (Sarmiento's position toward aristocracy is notoriously ambiguous. On the one hand, he salutes the passing of privileged castes like the Osunas and the Orléans, and he welcomes the advent of democracy which permits the rise of the self-made individual. On the other hand, when tracing his maternal family back to a twelfth-century Saracen chieftain, he pointedly compares the Albarracines to the Montmorencys—not by chance one of the most distinguished families in France.) In *Recuerdos*, Sarmiento expands his "I" to incorporate others, but he artfully directs that expansion upward. Patriotism and talent are viewed in conjunction with very real social power.

In addition, it should be stressed, most of these worthy precursors belong to the maternal side of Sarmiento's family. The series of portraits indeed culminates with an impassioned evocation of Sarmiento's mother. The emphasis on the maternal is not insignificant, ideologically speaking, if one considers the fact that the mother figure is perceived as a link to the Spanish colony throughout *Recuerdos*; a link not to the colonial *system*, constantly denounced by Sarmiento as the source of most Argentine evils, but to an idealized, ahistorical construct, a fantasy of origins embellished by "the poetry of the heart" and endowed with the charm of the *suranné*. Thus Sarmiento's precursors on his mother's side, while models of republican virtue, also bind him to the best of colonial tradition. Cunningly presented, these family ties make of Sarmiento, the future presidential candidate, a man for all (political) seasons.

Once again, in this second, carefully engineered recovery of the past, some things are worthier of being told than others and Sarmiento's family romance is subjected to fresh editing. A reader of *Recuerdos* who relied only on the text for information about Sarmiento—and let it be remembered that the informative function of this "biography" was highly prized by its author—would come away thinking that Sarmiento had benefited from the unique position of being the only male child in a family with four surviving daughters. Family records indicate that Paula Albarracín had fifteen children in all, several of which, male and female, died in infancy. There was, however, one other boy who survived. Honorio, Sarmiento's senior by three years, with whom Sarmiento appears to have been quite close, lived to the age of eleven. A charming memoir written by Sarmiento's older sister, Bienvenida, refers to that brother and to the interaction between the two boys: "A child of five, he [Domingo Faustino] was sent to school to keep an eye on an older brother who was being led astray by friends and made to miss school. Things went very well between the two; the little boy spurred the older one on and they both made great progress."[24] Even when extending the scope of his recollections to his kinsmen, Sarmiento has not renounced his claim to uniqueness; nor has the figure of the self-made hero completely disappeared. If the strategy of *Recuerdos* is to uphold the image of the worthy son, heir to the qualities of his forebears, it is clear that Sarmiento sees himself as the *only* heir: the presence of a brother (a potential rival, even at that early age) must then be sacrificed. Thus, when Sarmiento refers to his schooldays, *precisely to the same period evoked by his sister,* he edits out Honorio, presents himself as an isolated, precocious achiever, and alters the reasons why he was sent very early to school in a way that will both flatter him and fit his image:

> Barely had I begun to speak, when my eyes and tongue were made familiar with the alphabet, so great was the haste with which the settlers, who considered themselves citizens, hastened to educate their children in response to the decrees of the governing *junta* and of later governments of the period. . . . As soon as the Escuela de la Patria opened, I was one of the four hundred children, of all ages and all social classes, who rushed in to receive the only solid instruction that has been imparted in grammar schools in our midst. . . . I remained in that school for nine years, under no pretext ever missing a day, for my mother, with her unbending severity, was there to see that I fulfilled my duty by attending. At five I was able to read fluently out loud, with the intonations that come only with complete understanding of the subject, and so uncommon was this early skill at that period that I was carried from house to house to display my reading, reaping a plentiful harvest of buns, hugs, and praise that filled me with vanity. [*OC*, 3:160–161]

Erased from *Recuerdos*, Honorio seems to have also been deleted from Sarmiento's historical record.[25] Under the guise of "the dictates of truth," the book (as its author had hoped) inaugurated the "official" version of Sarmiento's life. With few exceptions, biographers and critics have perpetuated the fiction of the unique, precocious boy surrounded by four, hazily outlined sisters. And, most remarkably, those who do mention Honorio never stop to ponder his absence from Sarmiento's life story.[26]

Now, I am aware that I am venturing onto dangerous territory when pointing out these presumed "gaps" (absence of a daughter, absence of a brother) in Sarmiento's life stories, gaps that appear only when the autobiography is held up to a factual account of the individual's existence. My primary purpose, in pointing out these fissures, is not to seek correspondences or a lack thereof between what was and what is told, thus appearing to fall back on a simplistic view of the genre's purported referentiality—a referentiality that, as de Man has suggestively argued,[27] may be a mirage of the text itself. I find these absences striking not merely because they occur in *Mi defensa* and in *Recuerdos de provincia* but, more specifically, because they occur precisely *there* and not elsewhere. In other texts, especially in letters, Sarmiento occasionally mentions his daughter and (infrequently, it must be said) his brother.[28] There is no wholesale condemnation to oblivion: these figures *do* eventually get mentioned in some part of Sarmiento's self-writing. But there is definitely a diversion, from a text where their presence could prove bothersome, to a more innocuous place in Sarmiento's work where they live on, unnoticed. If, as Georges Gusdorf has noted, autobiographical memory is "always, to a certain degree, a revenge on history,"[29] it is also, in certain cases, a good excuse for housecleaning.

In other cases, memories connected with seemingly disaffected figures in the autobiographer's account may be put to a different purpose. This seems to be the case with women, those other phantom figures in Sarmiento's life, whom—with the exception of his mother and, to a lesser extent, his sisters—he likewise subjects to displacement. I use the word "figures" here advisedly: what Sarmiento seems to be blotting from one text and displacing to another is not so much an individual as it is a symbolic configuration. I am not, of course, unaware of the psychological import of the obliterations—a female child, a male sibling, and now, quite significantly, women in general. However, viewing those deletions as part of a figurative system may provide a better understanding of Sarmiento's selective memory and of the ways in which he uses it to achieve opportune (or opportunistic) representations. In the same way that Sarmiento incorporates texts to fashion his persona, he incorporates tropes (more than persons) to add to the image he has of himself as he writes. This image is, in itself, an amalgam of symbolic representations—*el hijo, el amigo, el militar, el hombre de partido*, and so on. Adopted figures of paternity and prestigious mentors will serve Sarmiento well; as vehicles of amplification, they conveniently magnify his persona. So will the mother figure serve him, in itself, for the importance it occupies in his life, but especially as a cultural figure whose tradition goes back through Lamartine to Augustine.[30] Instead, figures of contiguity that in some way would mirror him, even as inferior copies—the unplanned daughter, the unwanted sibling, the lover or spouse—rather than adding to his isolated monumentality, detract from it. And Sarmiento, it is clear, cannot tolerate the idea of expenditure, of diminution.

In the case of women, Sarmiento is notoriously cautious, not to say miserly, as to the place he awards them in his (written) life. His sisters, never referred to by name but as a group, "mis hermanas," are murky figures. If they come to life, as they do in the chapter entitled "The Paternal Home," they do so as foils for Sarmiento's *beau rôle* in the family struggle between old ways and new. Other women receive only circumstantial mention in *Mi defensa* and *Recuerdos de provincia*, and the ones who were linked erotically to Sarmiento, none at all. Differing considerably from one of his avowed models, Benjamin Franklin, who feels he can speak freely of "the hard-to-be-governed passion of youth [that] hurried me frequently into intrigues with low women"[31] without damaging the exemplary nature of his autobiography, Sarmiento glosses over any incident that might suggest sexual impropriety. Even the proper ties go unmentioned: Sarmiento is a married man when he writes *Recuerdos de provincia*, yet Benita Martínez Pastoriza, his wife since 1848, is never mentioned. The fact that there were signs of impropriety previous to the marriage might account for the silence, if only in part.[32]

Women are not entirely absent, however, from Sarmiento's self-writing. Much later, in the diary he keeps on his return trip from the United States in 1868, loosely written in the form of a letter to the woman he loves, Aurelia Vélez Sarsfield, and later published as part of his *Memorias*, Sarmiento includes a fairly long fragment entitled "Las santas mujeres" (the holy women). Under this self-serving title (the expression usually referring to the Virgin Mary and the other women who ministered unto Christ), Sarmiento celebrates the women in his life, prefacing his enumeration with the following remarks:

> In Paris I bought a statuette of the Venus of Milo and on its base wrote this inscription:
> TO THE HAPPY MEMORY OF ALL THE WOMEN WHO LOVED ME AND HELPED ME IN THE STRUGGLE FOR LIFE.
> The Venus de' Medici is all passion; the Venus of Milo is the woman ready to be a mother or a beloved, for she shows only her breast and is of serious mien, as if she felt the call of duty.
> There are the *Women in the Bible*, the women in the works of Shakespeare, the women in Goethe. Why would I not have the *Women in Sarmiento?* Not because I have created them in my fantasy but because they have all sheltered me under their maternal wing or helped me live during long years of ordeal.
> From the time I was born, my destiny has been woven by women, practically only women, and I can name them one by one, in a series in which, as in a chain of love, they pass the object of their affection from hand to hand.[33]

Just as he had established a formative chain of exclusively male intellectual mentors in *Recuerdos de provincia*, Sarmiento, more succinctly but no less admiringly, now rescues the links of another, no less formative chain of love made up exclusively of women. It begins with his mother, which was foreseeable, given his particular interpretation of the Venusian emblem that guides his evocation—a love not erotic but maternal, combined with a sense of duty. As in the case of Alberdi, who felt that in his letters he could rhapsodize freely about *La Nouvelle Héloïse*, even confessing to the physical attraction he felt for Rousseau as painted by Fantin-Latour, whereas in his autobiography he "remembered" only the author of *The Social Contract*, Sarmiento's recollections are tailored here to fit the image he wishes to give a precise recipient. If, in this passage from *Memorias*, a feminine "chain of love" that had no place in the more public, monumentalizing pages of *Mi defensa* or *Recuerdos* is salvaged and placed under the serene sponsorship of the Venus of Milo, it is because the text is addressed to a reader who herself is a woman and who is, in addition, the woman Sarmiento loves. The purpose of the autobiographer here is not to set an example but, more subtly, to charm and to woo.[34] A small act of seduction, it posits a different persona—the author surrounded by his many Venuses, wanting to be loved: "There must be something profoundly sad in my eyes that awakens maternal solicitude in women" (*OC*, 49:294). But if autobiography is indeed a vengeance on history, history, on occasion, gets its own back. Sarmiento allowed himself this portrait principally for Aurelia Vélez Sarsfield, not for posterity, to which he had already bequeathed the more solemn images of *Mi defensa* and *Recuerdos de provincia*. Posterity, in spite of Sarmiento, now reads all three pieces with an equal eye and delights in them.

Notes

1. Domingo Faustino Sarmiento, *Obras completas* (henceforth *OC*), 49 vols. (Buenos Aires: Imprenta y Litografía Mariano Moreno, 1896–1900), 3:224–225. All translations in this chapter are my own unless otherwise stated.

2. Quoted in A. O. J. Cockshut, *Truth to Life: The Art of Biography in the Nineteenth Century* (New York and London: Harcourt Brace Jovanovich, 1974), p. 9.

3. The full quotation, taken from Villemain's *Cours de littérature* and used as an epigraph to the first edition of *Facundo*, reads as follows: "I ask from the historian love of humanity and of freedom: his impartial justice must not be impassive. On the contrary, he must feel inspired, hopeful, pained or elated by what he writes" (*OC*, 7:7).

4. A celebrated letter to his friend and reader Valentín Alsina, published in the second edition of *Facundo* in 1851, shows Sarmiento to be cautious on the subject of revisions and well aware of the effect to be gained by leaving the book in its original, "ungainly" form: "I have used your precious notes with moderation, saving the most substantial ones for more auspicious times

and better-planned projects, fearful that in touching up such a shapeless work it would lose its primitive appearance and the robust and eager boldness of its undisciplined conception" (Domingo Faustino Sarmiento, *Facundo* [Buenos Aires: Ediciones Culturales Argentinas, 1961], p. 21).

5. Quoted by Lionel Gossman in his illuminating "History as Decipherment: Romantic Historiography and the Discovery of the Other," *New Literary History* 18, no. 1 (1986): 26.

6. Alberdi harshly criticizes both Sarmiento and Bartolomé Mitre for their highly personal, poorly documented attempts at historiography: "There are two ways of writing history: either following tradition and popular legend, which usually results in a history that is the product of vanity, a sort of *political mythology* with a historical base; or following documents, which is writing real history, something few dare do for fear of hurting the country's vanity with the truth" (Juan Bautista Alberdi, *Grandes y pequeños hombres del Plata* [Buenos Aires: Fernández Blanco, 1962], pp. 15–16).

7. Nonetheless, charges of self-centeredness were levied against Sarmiento. "Neither you nor I, as persons, are subjects substantial enough to attract public attention," admonished Alberdi (in Ricardo Sáenz Hayes, *La polémica de Alberdi con Sarmiento y otras páginas* [Buenos Aires: Gleizer, 1926], p. 39). Alberdi's reaction to *Recuerdos de provincia*, as the third of his *Cartas quillotanas* shows, was particularly strong. In 1849, a defensive Sarmiento writes to Vicente Fidel López, who presumably was trying to dissuade him from writing *Recuerdos:* "Have you noticed something remarkable— that in Chile I have won the right to speak of myself, of my own affairs, with the same openness as Rosas, in *La Gaceta?* They know that that is my defect, and they tolerate it" (Alberto Palcos, *Sarmiento. La vida. La Obra. Las Ideas. El Genio* [Buenos Aires: Emecé, 1962], p. 103). Others besides López, most notably Mitre and Félix Frías, tried to discourage Sarmiento (p. 102). Mitre "kept telling him that the book was a mistake" (Augusto Belín Sarmiento, *Sarmiento anecdótico (Ensayo biográfico)* [Saint-Cloud: Imprenta P. Belin, 1929], p. 45).

8. On Sarmiento's biographical approach to history, Ezequiel Martínez Estrada writes: "[A]ll his biographies, whether their subject be Argentine or American, condense . . . fundamental forms of his conception of history or, in the eloquent motto he himself coined, of that dialectical antithesis Civilization and Barbarism. Thus considered, biography . . . takes on the value of a symbol or, to put it more precisely, of a metaphor as a way of making the abstract . . . more comprehensible" (*Sarmiento* [Buenos Aires: 1946; reprint, Buenos Aires: Sudamericana, 1966], pp. 117–118).

9. Samper writes in his prologue: "The number of eminent men that my country can count on, in every party, is quite considerable. If I ventured to write biographies of all of them, beginning with the immortal Nariño, I would have to write a library, undertaking a task far superior to my capabilities and resources. It was not my intention to write *biographies,* but simple biograph-

ical *sketches*. If, given the quality of the artist's work, the Gallery they form is modest, it is great and luminous on account of the moral stature and the brilliance of the originals" (*Galería nacional de hombres ilustres o notables, o sea colección de bocetos biográficos* [Bogotá: Imprenta de Zalamea, 1879], p. vi). Like Sarmiento, the biographer Samper also wrote his autobiography, *Historia de una alma* [sic]. *Memorias íntimas y de historia contemporánea* (Bogotá: Imprenta de Zalamea Hermanos, 1881).

10. On this subject, I am indebted to Nicolas Shumway's "Bartolomé Mitre and the Gallery of Argentine Celebrities," in his *The Invention of Argentina* (Berkeley: University of California Press, 1991). Shumway perceptively analyzes this historiographic venture, authored by many (among them Juan María Gutiérrez, Tomás Guido, and Sarmiento himself) but unquestionably masterminded by Bartolomé Mitre, as an exercise in "officialist" historiography. In addition to paving a way to the future, the *Galería* strove to "legitimizie both his [Mitre's] aspirations as a national leader and Buenos Aires' grip on the country" (p. 194).

11. Eduardo Wilde, "Recuerdos, recuerdos," in Wilde, *Obras completas* (Buenos Aires: Lajouane, 1938), 5:134.

12. On the role of the romantic historian as interpreter of a mute past, see Gossman, "History as Decipherment," pp. 23–57. For Sarmiento's views on French historiography, see his "Los estudios históricos en Francia," in *OC*, 2:199.

13. Cockshut comments on the small amount of space allotted to childhood in nineteenth-century English biographies, remarkable at a time when, as he puts it, "Wordsworth was the idol of the intellectuals and Dickens of the crowd." He concludes that "the absence of childhood from the biographies is a fortuitous consequence of the fashionable method of composition," meaning by that an excessive reliance on documents (*Truth to Life*, pp. 17–18). Documents, needless to say, do not usually record childhood events.

14. Pierre Janet, *L'Evolution de la mémoire et de la notion du temps* (Paris: Editions Chahine, 1928), p. 461.

15. E. Pichon, "Essai d'étude convergente des problèmes du temps," quoted in Georges Gusdorf, *Mémoire et personne*, 2 vols. (Paris: Presses Universitaires de France, 1951), 1:51.

16. The following is an apt example of how lyrical evocation consciously corrects "objective" description in *Recuerdos de provincia*: "My mother's house, the fruit of her industry, whose adobes and fences could be computed in yards of cloth, woven by her hands to pay for its construction, has suffered some additions in these past years that make it merge with the other, average houses. However, its original form is the one that clings to the poetry of the heart, the indelible image that stubbornly comes to my mind" (*OC*, 3:147).

17. "When the autobiographer has gained that firm vantage point from which the full retrospective view on life can be had, he imposes on the past the order of the present. The fact once in the making can now be seen together

with the fact in its result. By this superimposition of the completed fact, the fact in the making acquires a meaning it did not possess before. The meaning of the past is intelligible and meaningful in terms of the present understanding; it is thus with all historical understanding" (Karl J. Weintraub, "Autobiography and Historical Consciousness," *Critical Inquiry* 1, no. 4 [1975]: 826). Georges Gusdorf, "Conditions and Limits of Autobiography" (1956), in *Autobiography: Essays Theoretical and Critical*, ed. James Olney (Princeton: Princeton University Press, 1980), pp. 28–48, had already explored the autobiographer's retrospective assignation of meaning to past events.

18. For useful comments about group pressure on an individual's retrieval of the past, see Charles Blondel, *Introduction à la psychologie collective* (Paris: Armand Colin, 1928), from which I extract the following: "It is evident that our recollections vary, become more precise, change or disappear according to the groups to which we successively belong. While we live within one group, our passions, our interests demand that we keep in mind facts belonging to the life of that group, to that of its members, to ours. . . . As soon as we leave that group, we begin to discard the assorted memories that had gathered in our minds for the use of that group, and the rapidity with which we do this is inversely proportionate to the time we have spent as members of the group" (p. 135).

19. André Gide, *Journal 1889–1939* (Paris: Gallimard, "Pléiade," 1955), p. 29. Gide adds: "One might say the following, which I see as a sort of inverted sincerity (in the artist): He must not tell his life in the way he has lived it, but must live it in the way he will tell it. In other words: so that the portrait of himself that is his life is identical to the ideal portrait he desires. More simply: that he be the way he wants himself to be" (p. 30).

20. Sarmiento cleverly summons two sets of readers here, readers who are to a point exclusive of each other; or, perhaps more accurately, he envisages two successive, quite different readings of his text. One set of readers is composed of those known compatriots to whom he personally dedicates the book; as his contemporaries, they will understand his precise references and sympathize with him. The others are those compatriots who will read him in the future; they will not really understand the references but will be touched by the exemplum, the "statue for posterity." These readers, I have argued, are foreseen by the two, divergent epigraphs to *Recuerdos*. See Sylvia Molloy, "Inscripciones del yo en *Recuerdos de provincia*," *Sur* 350–351 (1982): 131–140. For a discussion of the different kinds of readers an autobiographical text may summon, see (on Montaigne's *Essais*) Claude Blum, "La Peinture du moi et l'écriture inachevée," *Poétique* 53 (1983): 60–71.

21. Always eager to see through Sarmiento's alleged goals, Alberdi sees *Recuerdos* not as the fulfillment of public duty but as a self-serving venture:

> The telling of your story has not taught you anything that you did not know. Your work has been of no service to the Argentine republic, and I doubt that it has been of any service to you. In our country, so rich already

in noteworthy men, this is the first example of a citizen who publishes two hundred pages and a genealogical tree to relate his life, that of all the members of his extended family, and even that of his servants. San Martín did not allow his portrait to be painted. Rivadavia, Monteagudo, Passo, Alvear, and a hundred Argentine heroes are without biography and the Republic itself, all glory and heroism, is without history. . . . But your own biography is not just an exercise in vacuity, it is, in politics, a well-known, frequently used means of establishing one's name as a candidate to high position—a legitimate desire that turns you, however, into a tireless agitator. [Juan Bautista Alberdi, *Cartas quillotanas*, preceded by an explanatory letter by D. F. Sarmiento (Buenos Aires: Editorial La Cultura Argentina, 1916), pp. 133–134].

For an excellent analysis of the change in attitude from *Mi defensa* to *Recuerdos de provincia*, see Tulio Halperín Donghi, "Sarmiento: Su lugar en la sociedad argentina posrevolucionaria," *Sur* 341 (1977): 121–135. For additional, very insightful comments on *Recuerdos* as presentation of a political candidate, see Carlos Altamirano and Beatríz Sarlo, "Una vida ejemplar: La estrategia de *Recuerdos de provincia*," in their *Literatura y sociedad* (Buenos Aires: Hachette, 1983), pp. 163–208. My debt to both these texts is considerable.

22. In a letter to the historian Vicente Fidel López, he smugly declares: "I am preparing a fat book entitled *Recuerdos de provincia*, or something like that, in which, with the same candor as Lamartine, I compose my own panegyric. I assure you, my friend, that ridicule will shatter itself against so many good things, so worthy of being told, and that, willingly or by force, they will have to forgive this audacity" (Palcos, *Sarmiento*, p. 103).

23. Martínez Estrada, *Sarmiento*, p. 18.

24. *Rasgos de la vida de Domingo F. Sarmiento por su hermana Bienvenida*, introduction by Antonio P. Castro (Buenos Aires: Museo Histórico Sarmiento, 1946), p. 30.

25. In his *English Autobiography: Its Emergence, Materials, and Form* (Berkeley and Los Angeles: University of California Press, 1954), Wayne Shumaker mentions the not uncommon exclusion of siblings, children, spouses and (less often) parents in English autobiography (pp. 42–43), in particular in the *Autobiography* of John Stuart Mill (pp. 145–146). Shumaker's comments, rather too broad in scope, do not elaborate on these exclusions.

26. Palcos generally speaks of Sarmiento as an only male child (*Sarmiento*, p. 20) but does briefly mention the brother: "Another child, Honorio, died when he was eleven, leaving a strong impression on the mind of Domingo Faustino, who asserted, no less, that this brother was more intelligent than he" (p. 17). Manuel Gálvez refers incorrectly to him as Horacio (*Vida de Sarmiento. El hombre de autoridad* [Buenos Aires: Emecé, 1945], p. 18).

I add a personal anecdote to illustrate my point. In 1982, when doing research in the Museo Nacional Sarmiento in Buenos Aires, I asked the secretary for information on the elusive Honorio and was told emphatically that all of Sarmiento's male siblings had died at birth or very soon thereafter. Firm in my purpose, I asked to see the famous *libreta* where Sarmiento's mother kept her record of family births and deaths. In the shabby little notebook, written in crude script, I was gratified to find (and the secretary was disquieted to see) the dates that confirmed Honorio's short life.

27. Paul de Man, "Autobiography as De-facement," *Modern Language Notes* 94 (1979): 919–930.

28. In a letter sent from Chile in 1848 to José Ignacio Flores, a dear friend from childhood, Sarmiento alludes to his brother. While not naming him, he makes clear, by comparison, the importance Honorio had in his life: "For me you are a friend different from the rest, you are the inseparable childhood companion, the neighbor, the brother I once had. Now that so many impressions crowd my memory, I often return to childhood recollections, always so sweet, always so simple, and you are always a natural part of them" (Julia Ottolenghi, *Sarmiento a través de un epistolario* [Buenos Aires: Jesús Méndez, 1939], p. 41).

29. Gusdorf, "Conditions and Limits of Autobiography," p. 36.

30. For a thoughtful analysis of Sarmiento's interpretation of Madame de Lamartine, see Tulio Halperín Donghi, "Lamartine en Sarmiento: *Les Confidences* y *Recuerdos de provincia,*" *Filología* (Buenos Aires), 20, no. 2 (1985): 177–190.

31. *The Autobiography of Benjamin Franklin* (New York: Macmillan, Literary Heritage, 1967), p. 73.

32. Sarmiento had known Benita Martínez Pastoriza, a native of San Juan married to a much older Chilean businessman, for years. They married in 1848, a few months after the death of Benita's husband, and "Doña Benita's only son, Domingo Fidel, who had been born in the Chilean capital on April 25, 1845, took on the name of Sarmiento, who was his real father" (Palcos, *Sarmiento*, p. 92).

33. Domingo Faustino Sarmiento, *Memorias*, in *OC*, 49:293. A book on Sarmiento's women did in fact appear much later: César Guerrero, *Mujeres de Sarmiento* (Buenos Aires: n.p., 1960).

34. Another autobiography that might be read in the same spirit, as a winning gesture within the rhetoric of the *discours amoureux*, is Gertrudis Gómez de Avellaneda's autobiography, written in the form of a letter to the man she loves; see *Autobiografía y cartas*, 2nd ed. (Madrid: Imprenta Helénica, 1914).

12   Sarmiento:
Madness or Accumulation

DAVID VIÑAS

Let us remember, in this regard, the innovation proposed in
Algeria by Marshal Bugeaud, who, in order to combat the Arabs
successfully, overcame both the mobility of the guerrilla and the
superiority of the desert cavalry.
            —Sarmiento, *Los Catriel*, November 25, 1878

To leave untouched all children aged ten and older for fear that
they will suffer for loss of family is to perpetuate the barbaric
ignorance and ineptitude of the child, condemning him to the
moral and religious instruction of savage women. As soon as
possible, we must remove our children from this infectious
plague.
            —Sarmiento, *Las cartas de Catriel*, November 30, 1878

To lionize Sarmiento or to treat him as the Devil incarnate is one of the
most sportive debates engaging Argentine intellectuals. It belongs to a
Manichaean tradition that is marked in Argentina by an exhaustive and
repetitious circularity. Reaching an almost autistic self-absorption, the
debate about Sarmiento reminds me of the nation's historical stagnation
and its ever-increasing blindness to dialectical reason.

Such a diagnosis is hardly edifying; moreover, as a writer, I even find
myself drawn into the polemic, which eventually colors all my opinions
about Sarmiento. These observations notwithstanding, I will attempt in
the following pages to open two points of discussion: first, to trace the
itinerary of Sarmiento as it corresponds to Charles Morazé's now classic
study of the nineteenth century, *Les Bourgeois conquérants* (1957), in
order to establish a contextual frame for discussion; and, second, to propose a diachronic guide to the activity of the Argentine statesman as it
emerges symbolically from his inaugural newspaper, *El Zonda* (1839),
through to his final periodical publication, *El Censor* (1885).

From Morazé's *Les Bourgeois conquérants*, one might infer at least
three defining characteristics of nineteenth-century intellectuals: an overwhelming attraction to figures of force; general exaltation of the entre-

preneurial spirit; and a passion for men of science. In the case of the Argentine statesman, these attractions often accompany his ideas on nation building and modernity. Consider, for example, Sarmiento's permanent fascination with Bugeaud, the French marshal who in 1834 repressed the artisans of Paris with gunfire and cannon and then moved on to become the ruthless conqueror of Algeria and the founder of a modern empire along with Lyautey and Gallieni. Sarmiento met Bugeaud in Algeria and cited him reverentially in the *Viajes*; he repeatedly signals his admiration whenever he participates in or comments upon Argentine military campaigns. Thus Sarmiento proposes the tactics of Bugeaud even before Rosas's final defeat at Caseros, and later he puts them into practice: in La Rioja, during Argentina's war with Paraguay, and at the time of the uprisings in Entre Ríos headed by Ricardo López Jordán. But Sarmiento's French military models prove even more relevant in 1879, when General Julio Roca finishes his conquest of Patagonia and successfully exterminates the indigenous population.

This orthodox military approach, inspired by the example of the marshals of the Restoration and Second Empire, is corroborated in another Sarmientine activity. And this brings me to my second example: the repeated exaltations, volunteered by Sarmiento in *Educación popular*, of that paradigm of the "conquering bourgeois," Ferdinand de Lesseps, the international entrepreneur who traced his roots to the Saint-Simonian brotherhood. Sarmiento met de Lesseps in Barcelona and repeatedly referred to him as an archetype. Especially when Sarmiento portrayed himself as an entrepreneur in Argentina and abroad (recall the self-portraits as miner, printer, farmer, and tourist), de Lesseps, the triumphant bourgeois, provided a rigorous model.

As a third inflection in Sarmiento's choice of models in the bourgeois world to which he aspired, we might include Samuel Morse, the North American inventor whom Sarmiento mentioned on several occasions and especially on his journey through the United States. Morse is tied specifically to the *writing style* of Sarmiento, particularly if we consider three fundamental aspects: velocity, economy, and penetration. Sarmiento is tantalized by the mighty seduction of those long and frenetic sheets of perforated paper, the product of Morse's telegraph. Indeed, that invention carries several connotations: punctuality; the inexorable demands of the clock (a metaphor that recalls the discursive rhythms of *Argirópolis* and reminds us of Sarmiento's subtle alliance with the hero of Jules Verne's *Around the World in Eighty Days*); and the relationship of the metallic pen with the white surface of the page. In order not to belabor a discussion about a few dots on a sheet of paper as a metaphor for Sarmiento's telegraphic style, let me recall a more pressing image that draws Sarmiento's project into line with emerging visions of modernity. Consider, then, the metaphoric significance of the stock market, with its breathless financial churning or, even better, the urgent, categorical convocations of the expeditions against the Indians, whether Mapuche, Toba, or Sioux.

Benjamin Franklin, with his *Poor Richard's Almanack* and his references to the spinning wheel and his sister, marks the fourth promontory affording us a better view of Sarmiento in a world that extended from the "conquering bourgeois" inward, toward Sarmiento himself. In this encounter with Franklin—condensed metaphorically by Sarmiento in *Recuerdos de provincia* via his references to the loom and to the image of his mother—we can trace his fascination for "invention," his legendary negligence and austerity in dress, and his undaunted talents in diplomacy.

For the moment, however, let me return to the vision of Morazé in connection with the fundamental journalistic circuit that defines Sarmiento's activity throughout the whole half-century that separates *El Zonda* from the years of *El Censor*. From his earliest periodical publication, *El Zonda*, whose verbose and aggressive critiques were inflected by folkloric gestures and by an almost tumultuous spontaneity, to his late journalism which, inevitably, is marked by his role as General of the Nation, Sarmiento's writing is rich in its display of the workings of the nineteenth-century imagination: from the inauguration of the military academy to the blazing swords, the blustering and crested arrogance, the chests draped with medals, the drum majors, cavalcades, and lances and, from his own collection, the insistent distribution of blurred photographs of himself in full military regalia, always gallant yet obstinate, and bearing his energetic signature. This is a penultimate reading of a nation shifting from romantic culture to a liberal state in formation.

In this context, one cannot ignore the last decade of Sarmiento's life, his persistent attacks on the political oligarchy led by Presidents Julio Roca and Miguel Juárez Celman, and the scandals linked with the private appropriation, after the mythical "Conquest of the Desert," of 15,000 square leagues of Indian territory. Beyond this, we should also decipher in the pages of *El Censor* Sarmiento's demands for the concession of land near Carhue lagoon or his opinions about immigrants and socialists in late-nineteenth-century Argentina. It is commonly known that Sarmiento's positivism developed into the social Darwinism he expressed in *Conflictos y armonías de las razas* (1883). But we should also recall that the racist premises of *Situación del extranjero* coincides with the logic of a series of Argentine novels that includes Eugenio Cambaceres's *En la sangre* (1887) and Julián Martel's *La Bolsa* (1891). Taken as a whole, these books corroborate Sarmiento's xenophobia and anticipate, as part of a wider "corpus" of texts, the Argentine Law of Residence of 1902. In this respect, we should also consider the connection between Sarmiento and the right wing of the Generation of 1880, represented by Sarmiento's grandson, Augusto Belín (a veritable disciple and editor of the master; the real "Dominguito" invoked so often by Sarmiento as his chosen heir), who refashions the texts of his grandfather with an approach comparable to the editing activities of Nietzsche's sister (or, better yet, the devoted wife of Mark Twain) and who later writes an especially instructive text entitled *Una república muerta* (1892).

But let us return to the route that extends from *El Zonda* to *El Censor*. At the center of these texts, we see reminiscences of the master narrative that sets the tone for Sarmiento's *Facundo* (1845). These most productive years of Sarmiento's life—signaling his greatest flow of ideas and, critically, marking his most clearheaded and aggressive period—comprehend the publication of *Facundo*, weave in the *Viajes* and *Recuerdos de provincia*, and close with *Campaña en el Ejército Grande* (1853) and the polemic sustained with Juan Bautista Alberdi in *Las ciento y una*. The illumination produced by Juan Manuel de Rosas's defeat at Caseros casts a historical and conceptual halo over Sarmiento's writing, motivated by his struggle against a system of rule that has become sadly anachronistic. We might claim that these eight years, saturated by the logic of *Facundo*, articulate the early condition of a man on the road to power. Indeed, they are for Sarmiento a period of forcefulness and lucidity not to be seen again after his arrival in Buenos Aires.

In addition, two major events of 1848 necessarily condition Sarmiento's writing: in France, the revolution that subverts the bases of support for the "bourgeois conqueror"; in Argentina, the assassination of Florencio Varela. Here, Sarmiento realizes the power of *style*; he has identified his audience and he knows how to seduce his readers. Moreover, he senses that, more than anyone, he can track the essential rhythms of mid-century and condense, as Borges might say, the spirit and rule of the times, absorbing the writings of Varela and José Mármol, while also touching upon the style and logic of Félix Frías, Alberdi, Andrés Lamas, the junior López, José Rivera Indarte, the senior Cané, Bartolomé Mitre, and many others. In this network of overlapping styles and inflections, Sarmiento manages to capture the emerging social production of his generation while he also sees himself for the first time in a clear and unambiguous public role: as the heir to Varela's towering presence in the field of journalism; as an eventual candidate for the presidency.

Through this wide range of experiences, *Facundo* remains a center of gravity for Sarmiento, a pivotal point for the articulation of his ideas and for the constant reshaping of national narration. Through *Facundo,* we are confronted once again with the unavoidable question of "genre." Whether *Facundo* is a novel or essay is a matter not simply for erudite scholars. After all, with the hybrid form that *Facundo* ineluctably suggests, Sarmiento satisfies two goals at once. If, on the one hand, *Facundo's* rational exposition of ideas allows Sarmiento to withdraw from the fermenting hotbed of *madness* that shapes the modern novel and allows him to experience the dispirited *chill* that envelops essayistic form, on the other hand the work as a whole finds its raison d'être in tracking the prodigal fury of Facundo Quiroga. Posed another way, we might claim that the madness ascribed to Quiroga is the basis of the text's unrestrained productivity; and when Sarmiento bridles this unharnessed narrative form and pulls it in the direction of the essay, he adopts an economy of thrift and restraint consonant with the bourgeois morality he admired. In this respect, Sarmiento's *opus magnum* reads like a compendium of minuscule details, an exhaustive scrutiny of objects and events, all designed to counter the effusive storm created by Quiroga. Put differently, Sarmiento's eye for detail coincides with the common bourgeois obstinacy of the mid-century Victorian mind, which finds its pleasure in itemizing itineraries, prognostications, ancestors, and economic transactions ranging from stakes in a gambling parlor to the debts and credits given to servants. This form of *accumulation* depends for its very success on a persistent curbing of excess and a repression of lavish indulgence, signs of narrative pleasure that mark the fictions of Sarmiento's age. Ironically, the very form of *Facundo*—a "stack" of uneven pages with random episodes and digressions—depends upon a peculiar bourgeois law of accumulation in order to reveal its totalizing contents to the public.

Reckless extravagance and accumulation: this emblem casts an overarching shadow upon the range of texts extending from *El Zonda* to *El Censor.* The dissipation evoked by Sarmiento is, of course, "barbaric" just as the economy of thrift and accumulation portends the grandest symbol of "civilization" belonging to such bourgeois conquerors as Franklin and de Lesseps.

From this productive nucleus of images, we can finally speculate about Sarmiento's two-tiered project located in his *moral* and *immoral* biographies of distinguished men. The positive element is embodied in the lives of Franklin, Lincoln, Antonio Aberastain and Christ, and even his son Dominguito. In this context, even Sarmiento himself becomes the subject of flattering inquiry in the *Recuerdos de provincia.* On the opposite track, Sarmiento follows the *caudillos:* Quiroga, Félix Aldao, José Gervasio Artigas, and "El Chacho" Peñaloza, men whose dissolute lives suggest waste and unmanaged expansion.

In the world of providential men, Morse, de Lesseps, and the Victorian bourgeoisie assume a special place, defined by their progressive ideologies, their accumulative instincts, their morals and moralizing discourses, and their ability to thwart the madness of *caudillismo* and the lure of gambling.

Let us give a final twist to this picture. Ponder the progress of history from 1852 to the triumph of 1880, the setback of 1890, and the recuperation in the two centennials of 1910 and 1916. Sarmiento's style will acquire its political definition through an efficient centralization of power; he accompanies this progress with systematic calls for war to the death against Paraguayans, Indians, and *montoneras* in the years between 1863 and 1879, followed by healthy interventions against an obdurate clerical conservatism contemporary to his first signs of defensiveness before the growing "corruption of national language"; he answers this problem by returning to a defense of Greek and Latin, a project that will be incorporated later, in 1896, as part of the program of the national university's Faculty of Philosophy and Letters on the eve of its inauguration. Finally, recall Sarmiento's exorcism of the contaminated immigrant, debased in Law 4144, the infamous Law of Residence, which banned the foreigner from civic engagements and left him powerless in the eyes of the state. Thus Sarmiento, an organic intellectual of the Argentine bourgeoisie, casts a mold in the 1880s whose presence will continue to be felt well into the twentieth century.

In view of these provisional questions which inform my reading of Sarmiento's journey and his voyage toward a bourgeois morality defending work and order, let me allude to one final feature of Sarmiento's cunning legacy to national culture. While the example I provide may appear abstract, think for a moment of the line of continuity extending between Sarmiento and Roberto Arlt. Almost one hundred years (not exactly of solitude) separate *Recuerdos de provincia* and Arlt's *El juguete rabioso*, yet they signal the official itinerary of Sarmiento—in all its lucidity, arbitrariness, expanse, and limitation. Boht texts tell the history of poverty in Argentina, describe the importance of labor, celebrate discovery and invention. If the nineteenth-century figure initiates a journey that carries him through the history of the printing press, through agricultural programs, and labor in the mines, the twentieth-century writer dreams of exploding homemade cannon, metallic roses, and dry-cleaning services for dogs. In transition from Sarmiento to Arlt, we also pass from a *moral* history to a fiction about *immorality*. Within this configuration, compare the figures of the mother. Sarmiento's Doña Paula implores her son to study; she commends him to the virtues of economy and reason, and urges providential thrift. In Arlt's novel, the maternal figure appears as an antithesis of the mother of *Recuerdos de provincia*. Indeed, she challenges the liberal project designed by the Argentine statesman. Thus, when the symbolic mother appears in Arlt as reticent and exhausted, she distrusts the bourgeois conqueror who invades the space of the text; she calls into question his morality, his labor, his desire for accumulation, his greed. *El juguete rabioso* was published in 1926, but Roberto Arlt's delirium—a response to the orderly society envisioned by Sarmiento—was not to reach its pagan fury, its unbridled urge against order, until 1930 when, in the shadow of José F. Uriburu and the birth of an alternative national project, he expands those early suspicions and strikes a decisive blow against the culture of his illustrious predecessor. In this respect, a cycle is closed; a liberal project is brought to completion. The odyssey of the conquering bourgeois is halted by national madness.

13 A Lost World Rediscovered: Sarmiento's *Facundo*

ROBERTO GONZÁLEZ ECHEVARRÍA

> An English traveler at the beginning of the nineteenth century,
> referring to the journey by canoe and mule that could last as long
> as fifty days, had written: "This is one of the most miserable and
> uncomfortable pilgrimages that a human being can make." This
> had no longer been true during the first eighty years of steam
> navigation, and then it became true again forever when the
> alligators ate the last butterfly and the maternal manatees were
> gone, the parrots, the monkeys, the villages were gone:
> everything was gone.
> —Gabriel García Márquez, *Love in the Time of Cholera*

The opening sentence of Esteban Echeverría's "El matadero" is ambiguous, but at the same time clearly programmatic: "A pesar de que la mía es historia, no la empezaré por el arca de Noé y la genealogía de sus ascendientes como acostumbraban a hacerlo los antiguos historiadores españoles de América que deben ser nuestros prototipos" ("Although the following narrative is historical, I shall not begin it with Noah's ark and the genealogy of his forbears as was wont once to be done by the ancient Spanish historians of America who should be our models").[1] This is quite a portentous beginning for a mere novella, but Echeverría's is a very ambitious text. The Argentine writer wanted to depict in his story the ruthless repression to which opponents of Rosas's dictatorship were being subjected. The explicit scenes of mayhem are presented in the clinical tone of a scientific observer describing natural phenomena. In the story, a young man who is very clearly a projection of the author is assaulted by the rabble who work or just assemble at the Buenos Aires slaughterhouse. These thugs represent the barbaric supporters of dictator Juan Manuel de Rosas, who ruled Argentina from 1829 to 1852. The young man is slain as if he were just another animal. "El matadero" is a political allegory, but also much more. Echeverría's statement about history is important for two reasons. First, it acknowledges a desire for continuity of purpose in Latin American history. The historians to whom Echeverría refers are obviously the chroniclers of the discovery and conquest of America. Like them, he wishes to place the New World within a large historical outline, hence his allusion to the Bible. Writing the narrative of Latin America involves writing about the beginning of history. But, at the same time that Echeverría invokes the chroniclers as his models, he signals a break with them. This break is evidence of the emergence of a new masterstory in the narrative of Latin America. The story will not depend on a providentialist design reaching back to biblical events for coherence and meaning, like the Spanish chronicles did, yet it will have a beginning just as powerful as theirs in determining the unfolding of Latin American history. Echeverría's history will be of the present. After the sentence just quoted, Echeverría writes: "Tengo muchas razones para no seguir ese ejemplo [that of the chronicler's], las que callo por no ser difuso. Diré solamente que los sucesos de mi narración pasaban por los años de Cristo de 183 . . ." (pp. 12–13) ("Numerous reasons I might adduce for not following their example, but I shall pass them over in order to avoid prolixity, stating merely that the events here narrated occurred in the 1830's of our Christian era" [p. 210]). In the vast expanse of time encompassed by the Christian era, within which the chroniclers assembled their capacious historical machines, Echeverría's own time in the present is privileged as the start. That present is distinctive and historical because Latin American nature endows it with the power to break with the past and create a new and distinct sequence. The break is represented by violence in "El matadero," the violence whose victim is the educated young observer, who could not remain detached enough from the phenomena that he watched. The violent present is its own antecedent, its own start. Echeverría's novella marks the beginning of a new Latin American masterstory, mediated by the most authoritative discourse produced in the West since the eighteenth century: modern science. "El matadero" may very well contain all of the most important elements in that masterstory.

It is not by chance that Echeverría should be the writer to signal in such a clear fashion a break with the previous masterstory, which was based on the relationship between writing and the voluminous legal production of the Spanish Empire. The decadence of the Spanish Empire since before the eighteenth century is a fact that need not be belabored here. What is important, however, is that powers such as England, which were taking a forward leap to modernity through the Industrial Revolution, came increasingly into contact with territories in the Spanish Empire. Spain, which had obviously lagged behind in the development of science and technology, was either being replaced by independent republics, or its control was so weak in the territories it did hold that communication with other European powers via contraband was extensive.[2] Illegal commerce with England and France was a fact of life in Spanish colonies from the beginning of Spanish rule, but as the Spanish Empire lost its grip, smuggling increased or was replaced by outright takeovers, as in the case of the English occupation of Havana in 1762 and that of Buenos Aires in 1806. Contacts such as these with Spanish territories were often decisive in changing colonial societies, propelling them sometimes ahead of Spain into the new mercantilist world created by the Industrial Revolution.[3] In a sense, whether the territory in question was independent of Spain or not, it was often entangled in a web of commercial and cultural relations with other European powers that turned it into a neo-colony of such growing empires. In Spain itself, after the accession to power of the Bourbon dynasty, and particularly during the reign of Charles III, a sizable elite, sometimes with the support of the Crown, tapped into the sources of the Enlightenment, and attempted to bring about radical reforms. The gyrations of Spanish law became ever more abstract, increasingly less concerned with the reality of the new societies, except where it constrained the native, creole oligarchy, which was European- and U.S.-oriented. Hence a new kind of hegemonic discourse emerged. Perhaps the last important work to emerge from the law–narrative relationship was Alonso Carrió de la Vandera's *El Lazarillo de ciegos caminantes* (1773), which turns out to be about the circulation of documents in Spanish America, and where the complex games of authorship lead to the inescapable conclusion that the book is its own picaresque protagonist, as Karen Stolley has brilliantly shown.[4]

Given the kind of relationship the former Spanish dominions established with the new powers, one in which furnishing raw materials was the most important role, it is not surprising that nature should be the focus of such discourse, though this is not the only motive. And given the advancement of Argentina with respect to the rest of Latin America as well as its apparently boundless natural resources, it should come as no surprise that Argentine writers should be the focus of attention, though similar examples abound in the rest of Latin America. This new master-story does not derive its cogency from a direct observation and imitation of Latin American nature, but from the mediation of works by numerous scientific travelers who should rightly be considered the second discoverers of the New World. If the first discoverers and settlers appropriated Latin America by means of legal discourse, these new conquistadors did so with the aid of scientific discourse, which allowed them to name again (as if for the first time) the flora and fauna of the New World. This discourse had its own rhetoric, which differs considerably from what we identify as scientific today. These travelers wrote accounts in the form of diaries and travelogues that did not fall entirely outside literature. There was, in fact, a promiscuous complicity between literature and scientific reportage that made it relatively easy for Latin American writers to assimilate these narratives. The new Latin American narrative absorbs this second voyage, this pilgrimage in search of Latin American historical uniqueness through the textual mediation of European science.

But the law does not disappear altogether from these narratives. Echeverría's scene of frenzied lawlessness also reveals the transformation of legal discourse in this second masterstory, and how it continues to appear as an important vestige until the present. I refer to the law in the literal sense, as legal codes, not in the more abstract sense of a hegemonic discourse that mediates the narrative; the law which, under different guises, serves as the model the narrative follows. The law as penal code appears again through individuals who are outside of it, who have committed an infraction that isolates them from the norm, like the thugs in Echeverría's story. Whereas in the colonial period lawlessness centered on questions of legitimacy—bastardy, adultery, secession—now violence is the issue, a violence that excludes yet does not threaten legitimacy. Being outside the law in the sixteenth century meant one did not exist in a civil sense. In the nineteenth century and after, lawlessness does not exclude; the criminal other is an "other within," created by the split of Latin American society into urban and rural worlds as a result of modernity. That other is within a law that includes the observer, an observer who, in the case of the narrative, both fears and desires to be like him. This inclusiveness does not mean, of course, that the "other within" will be given a place in Latin America's stratified society, but rather that he represents a nature which, newly interpreted by science, beckons as an all-inclusive law that will explain the otherness of the New World as a whole. From now on the Latin American narrative will deal obsessively with that "other within" who may be the source of all; that is, the violent origin of the difference that makes Latin America distinct and, consequently, original. This problematic will remain as a strong vestige not only in obvious texts such as Horacio Quiroga's stories, but also in more recent ones like Julio Cortázar's "Axolotl." Facundo Quiroga, Antonio Conselheiro, Doña Bárbara, Demetrio Macías, become the central characters of their respective books because they are lawless and violent in some way. Their grandeur is a measure of their otherness, of their straying from the norm; in their cases, literally from the law. The Latin American self both fears and desires that "other within," because of his lawlessness, and travels to meet him. But the only way to apprehend him is through the mediation of a hegemonic discourse, which is now that of modern science, as disseminated by the naturalists who turned the New World into their living laboratory.

As with legal discourse, the new is a dialectical process of imitation and distortion, a process that itself becomes the subtext or true masterstory. No book exemplifies this operation more dramatically, and no book leaves a deeper imprint on Latin American narrative, than Sarmiento's *Facundo* (1845), a near contemporary of "El matadero," perhaps even its full-blown version.

1

Facundo is a book that is impossible to pigeonhole; it is a sociological study of Argentine culture, a political pamphlet against the dictatorship of Juan Manuel de Rosas, a philological investigation of the origins of Argentine literature, a biography of the provincial *caudillo* Facundo Quiroga, Sarmiento's autobiography, a nostalgic evocation of the homeland by a political exile, a novel based on the figure of Quiroga; for me it is our *Phenomenology of the Spirit*. Whatever one makes of the book, *Facundo* is one of those classics whose influence is pervasive and enduring and which is claimed by several disciplines at once. The fact that Sarmiento rose to become president of Argentina and put into practice policies that had such a tremendous impact on the course of his country's history adds to the canonical status of his book. The most recent evidence of *Facundo*'s lasting relevance are the debates around the figure of Caliban as symbol of Latin American culture, a polemic whose origin is found in Sarmiento.[5] Another, perhaps more durable resurgence is the proliferation of dictator-novels in Latin America, all of which have their source in *Facundo*.[6] Alejo Carpentier's *El recurso del método* (1974) pays the most explicit homage to the Argentine, not only in such thinly veiled allusions as giving the name of Nueva Córdova to the provincial town in which part of the action takes place. Carpentier's novel is a critical reflection of the mimetic process between European and Latin American texts that *Facundo* sets in motion. That process is one of the reasons for its continued presence in the Latin American literary imagination. It is, therefore, not by accident that *Facundo* centers on the issue of authority and power.

Facundo o civilización y barbarie en las pampas argentinas was written while Sarmiento was in political exile in Chile, fleeing from the dictatorship of Rosas. As with many classics, much to the frustration of positivistic critics, the text evolved through various editions, so that it is really impossible to say which is the definitive version of *Facundo*. When it first appeared in 1845 in Santiago de Chile, the book was called *Civilización y barbarie. Vida de Juan Facundo Quiroga y aspecto físico, costumbres y hábitos de la República Argentina*. The second edition dropped the pair *civilización y barbarie*, a formula that would spawn a progeny of commentators and become a topic of Latin American literature and thought. The book is now called *Vida de Facundo Quiroga y aspecto físico, costumbres y hábitos de la República Argentina, seguida de apuntes biográficos sobre el general Fray Félix Aldao* (1851). There are several other editions in Spanish, including one printed in New York in 1868 and one in Paris in 1874. Whatever the changes, the core of Sarmiento's book continued to be the life of Facundo Quiroga, a caudillo, or strongman, from the Argentine pampas, whom Sarmiento wishes to study in order to better understand Rosas and the genesis and exercise of political power in his country. By studying Facundo Quiroga, Sarmiento hopes to isolate an early stage in the development of dictatorship, its seed, as it were. Although he was Sarmiento's contemporary, Facundo Quiroga's violent present harks back to the origin—a present origin. The study of Facundo Quiroga leads Sarmiento to his description of the pampas and the society of gauchos from which the caudillo emerged (though, strictly speaking, Facundo was from Llanos de la Rioja). Power and authority are somehow lodged in the seminal figure of Facundo Quiroga, a barbaric product of the land who, Sarmiento knows, is at the contradictory core of Argentine and, by extension, Latin American culture (what Hegel, when he spoke of Napoleon, called a world-historical individual).[7] Yet he, Sarmiento himself, is also a part of that culture; the part that will be, he hopes, its civilized future. It is with fascination and repulsion that Sarmiento approaches Facundo Quiroga, like someone delving into the darker recesses of his or her own subconscious. The grandeur of the book is predicated on this antithetical origin, a cauldron of warring contraries in which author and protagonist embrace like Dioscuric twins, joined and separated by their correlative differences.

Facundo Quiroga was not, of course, the only caudillo, nor was he necessarily the most ferocious. He was one of many who emerged after independence, and who vied with each other in a struggle for life that certainly appeared to be based on the survival of the fittest. (Their wars reappear in those of Colonel Aureliano Buendía in *Cien años de soledad*.) By 1819 the caudillos with their gaucho bands were the lords of much of the countryside: Estanislao López was master of Santa Fe, Francisco Ramírez controlled Entre Ríos, Bernabé Aráoz ruled Tucumán. Quiroga was the strongman of Rioja, where he had been born to a family that prospered, but he had wandered off to war, winding up in a Chilean cell, where he is reported to have killed the Spaniard who helped him escape. Though notorious, Facundo Quiroga was not necessarily unique. It was the group of outlaws, of caudillos, not Facundo Quiroga himself, who eventually gave one of them, Rosas, power. (*Stricto sensu* Rosas's title continued to be Governor of the Province of Buenos Aires, though the other governors delegated to him the power to represent them abroad.) But when he was ambushed and killed at Barranca Yaco, reportedly on direct orders from Rosas, Quiroga's life acquired a neatness that elevated him from mere type to legend.[8] To understand him Sarmiento needs the aid of science.

Sarmiento's relationship to Facundo Quiroga is homologous to the one his book establishes with the discourse of scientific travelers and thinkers whose names he mentions and whose texts he quotes or uses as epigraphs throughout. The role of this web of texts—some placed in liminal positions, others quoted in the body of the work—is to lend authority to Sarmiento's discourse, to serve as a model, and to give Sarmiento legitimacy as author. For Facundo Quiroga to be intelligible (i.e., to be legible), he has to conform to the scientific categories and rhetoric of modern science; yet, to be compelling and worthy of attention he has to fall out of them. To be readable to Europeans or to those steeped in European culture, Sarmiento has to write a book that conforms to their discourse; yet, to be himself and hence interesting to them, he has to be different and original. As established by the relationship between the discourse of the law and narrative in colonial times, the mimetic act will serve as a form of liberation, both because of the formal compliance implicit in the very act of representation and because of the self-annulment that takes place in that process of compliance, in the absorption and denial of the authoritarian relationship established. The dimensions and reach of this subtext increase from Sarmiento to Euclides da Cunha. But let me first turn to the mediation or model.

2

To be able or not to perceive the distinctive hues of that which is creole [i.e., Latin American] may be insignificant, but the fact is that of all the foreign travelers (not excluding, by the way, the Spaniards), no one perceives them better than the English: Miller, Robertson, Burton, Cunningham, Graham, Hudson.
—J. L. Borges, *La Nación*, August 3, 1941

Travel literature has been a mainstay of writing about the New World and, in fact, a good many of the colonial *relaciones* were *récits de voyage*, beginning with Columbus's *Diario*. The discovery and conquest of America gave rise to a great deal of travel literature, much of it concerned, even if at times incidentally, with scientific reportage. The *cronista cosmógrafo* was expected to tally as much information as possible about natural phenomena, such as volcanic eruptions and storms. Travel literature, as Percy G. Adams has shown in his compendious book, has been an important part of European letters since Herodotus, and has evolved according to changing historical conditions without ever becoming a genre, or even being confined to prose. Adams has also shown how travel literature may have influenced the emergence of the modern novel, mostly through parody.[9] The fact that parodies of travel books as influential as *Gulliver's Travels* and *Candide* appeared already in the eighteenth century (with the latter including a journey to South America) is evidence of the influence of travel literature in the period that I am concerned with, and of its being one of the forms the novel assumes. The travel literature relevant to my purposes here, however, is specifically related to the rise of modern science. Hence, while the history furnished by Adams, which reaches only to the end of the eighteenth century, is relevant as background, scientific travel to Latin America in the modern era has characteristics of its own, determined by the new conception of nature formulated by modern science.

The importance of the copious travel literature produced by the numerous scientific travelers who crisscrossed Latin America in the eighteenth and nineteenth centuries has not been totally overlooked, though as a body of writing it has yet to be systematically studied. To date Edward J. Goodman's is the best general introduction to the subject.[10] In Latin America, the only important work on the travelers is that of Carlos J. Cordero, whose *Los relatos de los viajeros extranjeros posteriores a la Revolución de Mayo como fuentes de historia argentina* is much more than the title announces.[11] The relevance of travel literature to Latin American literary history has all but been ignored. The overall import of travel literature in the general context of Latin American culture was established in 1944 by Mariano Picón Salas, who wrote, with his customary perspicuity:

> The growing interest of European countries, notably England and
> France, in assuring the freedom of the seas for their own international
> trade, together with the spirit of research in natural history character-
> istic of the age, made the eighteenth century a period of scientific ex-
> peditions. . . . Commercial and political advantage was thus identified
> with scientific curiosity. Some of these eighteenth-century travelers,
> Louis de Bougainville for instance, cleverly combined a scrutiny of na-
> ture with adventure and brought back information of interest to both
> their monarchs and their academies of science. With specimens from
> so many distant places, botanical gardens, mineralogical collections,

and museums of "curiosities" were established in European capitals from Madrid to Saint Petersburg.[12]

The combination of economic interest, scientific inquisitiveness, and desire for adventure characterized the travels of European scientists for nearly two centuries. Picón Salas lays out most of the major characteristics of European scientific travel literature in the modern era. Modern imperial powers, through institutions charged with acquiring and organizing knowledge (scientific institutes, *jardins des plantes*, museums of natural history, *Tiergarten*), commission individuals possessing the scientific competence to travel to their colonies or potential colonies to gather information.[13] Once there, these often colorful individuals engage in a variety of adventures in the pursuit of knowledge and profit. The result is thousands of books describing, analyzing, and classifying the flora, fauna, landscape, social organization, ethnic composition, fossil formations, atmosphere, in short, everything that could be known by nineteenth-century science. The equation between power and knowledge, between collection and possession could not be clearer, particularly when one takes into account that many of the travelers, as in the case of Captain Francis Bond Head, were representatives of corporations involved in some sort of economic exploitation, such as mining. In many other instances the exploration and research carried out by the travelers had a direct or indirect military application and, in fact, travelers like Captain Richard Burton were military men. The various attempts that the British Empire made to occupy territories vacated by the Spanish are less-mediated manifestations of this relationship between knowledge and power, as were those by the United States when it emerged on the world scene as an economic and military power in its own right (there were quite a few travelers from the United States).[14] This means, paradoxically (given that they were often active agents in fierce economic exploitation), that these scientific travelers were more often than not agents of progress, and that their efforts had in some instances a revolutionary impact on Latin American societies. The case of Alexander von Humboldt is, of course, the best known in this regard.

Backed as they were by the might of their empires and armed with the systemic cogency of European science, these travelers and their writings became the purveyors of a discourse about Latin American reality that rang true and was enormously influential. Their entire discursive activity, from traveling itself to taxonomical practices, embodied truth and exuded authority through its own performance. The influence of this travel literature was immense, not only on political developments within the very reality they described, but on the conception of that reality that individuals within it had of it and of themselves. A crucial component in that creole mind was the scientific knowledge of Latin American nature, which was in many cases made available or possible by scientific travelers. Strong evidence of the enduring influence of scientific travel books in Latin America since the beginning of the nineteenth century can be found in a journal such as *El Plantel*, published in Cuba by Domingo del Monte and the group of romantic writers who first conceived the notion that there could be a Cuban literature. In addition to poetry, essays and history, the journal contained long pieces by the Cuban naturalist Felipe Poey, accompanied by drawings of animals and plants much like those found in the travel books.[15]

The obsolete legal discourse of Spanish colonization was replaced by scientific discourse as the authoritative language of knowledge, self-knowledge, and legitimation. This scientific discourse became the object of imitation by Latin American narratives, both fictional and nonfictional. Conventional literary history, which focuses on works that fall within the sphere of influence of European literature, such as Jorge Isaacs's *María* (1867) and José Mármol's *Amalia* (1851, 1855), hardly take into account the powerful influence of scientific travel books on those very novels and on Latin American narrative of the nineteenth century in general. The mediation of travel books is present as much in Sarmiento's *Facundo* and Lucio V. Mansilla's *Una escursión a los indios ranqueles* (Argentina, 1877) as it is in Cirilo Villaverde's description of sugarmill life in *Cecilia Valdés* (Cuba, 1880) and Euclides da Cunha's *Os Sertões* (Brazil, 1902).[16] It is the hegemonic model in Latin American narrative until the 1920s and appears as a strong vestige in archival fictions from *Los pasos perdidos* to *Cien años de soledad* and *Yo el Supremo*.

Although one would look in vain for traces of it in manuals of literature and specialized journals, the sheer volume of books about Latin America by European and U.S. scientists is staggering. Thousands of these books are listed in the recent bibliography published by Thomas L. Welch and Myriam Figueras, *Travel Accounts and Descriptions of Latin America and the Caribbean 1800–1900: A Selected Bibliography* (1982), and I am sure that many more could be added if the temporal span were broadened backward and forward. I am also certain that research in the publications of the various learned institutions of France, Germany, Belgium, England, and the United States would reveal many more names and texts that were not published separately as books. This proliferation is comparable only to that of legal documents during the first two hundred years of Spanish domination, or until the famous *Recopilación* of 1681.

The travel books play a similar role in relation to the narrative, though the differences are also quite significant. To begin with, these scientific texts obeyed no anonymous rhetorical rules, nor were they penned by notaries. The scientific travelogues had authors with resounding names, like Charles-Marie de la Condamine, Louis de Bougainville, Alexander von Humboldt, Charles Darwin, Peter Wilhelm Lund, Captain Francis Bond Head, Robert and Moritz Richard Schomburgk, Captain Richard Burton. Not all the books were written by scientists in the strict sense, or even in the more inclusive sense prevalent in the nineteenth century. As S. Samuel Trifilo says with reference to English travelers in Argentina: "The accounts were written by a wide cross-section of British society— soldiers, merchants, naturalists, diplomats, businessmen, engineers, miners, missionaries, adventurers, tourists, and many others."[17] Again, as opposed to the humble formulas of the Spanish bureaucracy or even the sophisticated histories written by humanists, the scientific travelogues are literary by almost any standard.

These scientists were as much imbued with literature as the poets of the era were fascinated and influenced by science (Goethe, for instance). Besides, the travelogues gave an account not only of the objects found but also of the process by which they were found; that is, the story of the traveler's life as he journeyed in search of the secrets of nature, which of course also turns out to be a voyage of self-discovery. These travelers were powerful writers, and the stories they told are fraught with dangerous and droll adventures. Their passion for nature, as intense as that of the poets, produced compelling examples of the romantic sublime.[18] This is true not only in the masterworks, like Humboldt's *Voyage aux régions équinocciales du Nouveau Continent*, but also of the minor ones, like *Reisen in Britisch-Guiana in den Jahren 1840–1844*, by his disciple Moritz Richard Schomburgk. In addition, some of the travelers were themselves artists or carried artists in their retinue for the purpose of drawing or painting the landscape or the specimens under scrutiny—in some cases because they could not be preserved, in others so that the reader could "see" them in their natural habitat. The practice appears to have its remote antecedent in the so-called Drake Manuscript of the sixteenth century, which contains a remarkable array of drawings in color.[19] As a result, the books these travelers produced were remarkably valuable objects, containing beautiful illustrations of the flora, the fauna, geological formations, human types, and occasionally the party of scientific adventurers.

The prevalence of journeys of this type during the nineteenth century was such that they became a topic in Western popular fiction up to our times, when, almost as a subgenre, travel adventures have invaded the cinema and television. In the nineteenth century the most notable examples are, of course, the novels of Jules Verne and, closer to our time, Sir Arthur Conan Doyle's *The Lost World* (1912), which some have mentioned as a possible source of Carpentier's *Los pasos perdidos*. Professor Challenger's journey in search of living specimens from the prehistoric era takes him to a plateau, deep in the South American jungle, where plant and animal life have been kept outside of the evolutionary process.[20] The scientific result of the expedition consists not only of the account we read, but also of some pictures of the prehistoric monsters, needed to convince the general public as well as the properly skeptical scientific societies. The scientific traveler's human and technical probe into the uncharted regions of the colonial world was literary not only in his own perception of nature but, increasingly, as a literary topic as well.

If one were to single out the most important element in the scientific travelogues and the one that had the most powerful influence on narrative, their own and others modeled after it, it would have to be time, or more precisely history, and even more specifically natural history.[21] Latin American nature had been a source of wonder to Europeans since the discovery, and the Spanish chronicles are filled with quaint descriptions of natural objects, beings and phenomena that were strange, or out of the ordinary to the author, and for which there was no word.[22] The stranglehold of Neo-Scholastic philosophy was too tight to allow the Spanish to conceive of Latin American nature as a system obeying a different history, to think actually that Latin American nature could in fact be "other." A great deal of intellectual energy was spent forcing divergent natural phenomena into Aristotelian categories, as in the case of Father José de Acosta's monumental *Historia natural y moral de las Indias* (1590). It was like fitting a square peg into a round hole, and the results not surprisingly were monstrous, as parts from various classifications were invoked to account for animals that seemed to have been put together with pieces from different puzzles. An animal was not the result of a unique history, but a collage of parts drawn from other creatures, out of whose unchanging shape a wing, a leg or a claw had been borrowed. Much of the charm and power of baroque Latin American literature is based on the tropological contortions required to describe the New World as a set of reshuffled bits from the Old. The European travelers brought an idea of history that would allow Latin American nature to provide the basis for an autonomous and distinct Latin American being; this, along with the truth-bearing power of their discourse, is their lure to the Latin American imagination. On the political side, the result was independence from Spain.

On the narrative side it provided a new masterstory, the one Sarmiento attempted to write.

The elements of that masterstory are determined as much by science as by the voyage. The voyage of scientific or quasi-scientific travelers was part of the romantic *Bildungsreise*. Traveling is the emblem of time, both personal and historical. Not only is natural history a kind of clockwork ticking away the complicated periodicity of evolution, but the observing self of the traveler is also swept along in the swirl of time. This double movement of subject and object creates an asymptote whose expression is the romantic topic of longing for a lost unity of self and cosmos, an organicity that would include the observing self. In Europe the poets always traveled south, preferably to Italy, like Goethe, Byron, or Musset, to regions where nature, together with the ruins of a splendid pagan past, could kindle or rekindle inspiration, and actually transform the self. As Goethe writes in his *Italian Journey:* "Above all, there is nothing that can compare to the new life a reflective individual experiences when he observes a new country. Though I am still always myself, I believe I have been changed to the very marrow of my bones."[23] That symbolic South is analogous to the world of nature found elsewhere in Africa or Latin America in that it is outside the modern world that the poet flees; a modern world whose most bewildering and perverse feature is that it determines that flight from itself and absorbs it. Within that "visionary South," as Wallace Stevens would call it many years later, poets traveled to the provinces, as in the case of the Spaniard Mariano José de Larra, Echeverría himself, or Villaverde in his *Excursión a Vuelta Abajo*.[24] Extremely revealing figures in this respect are those Latin Americans, or descendants of Latin Americans, who return to their countries of origin and write travel books in languages other than Spanish. One is Ramón Páez, a son of Venezuelan caudillo José Antonio Páez, who was educated in England and wrote *Wild Scenes in South America; or, Life in the Llanos of Venezuela* (New York, 1862), after an 1847 journey, a book that would influence Venezuela's most important fiction, *Doña Bárbara*. Another is María de las Mercedes Santa Cruz y Montalvo, Countess of Merlín, a Cuban aristocrat married to a French general in Madrid during Bonaparte's occupation, who wrote *La Havane* in 1844.[25] For these travelers, the predicament of scientific travel becomes literal—they wind up being both subject and object of their gaze, and the language they use detaches them artificially from who and what they are in the same way that scientific discourse presumably establishes a distance between naturalists and the world they study. The narrator of *Los pasos perdidos* is their anguished descendant.

Traveling was an ordeal, a detachment from the world known to the traveler in search of knowledge of nature and of himself. The ideal was, of course, a self-discovery in which nature and the self would be one, in which the luxurious and even somber beauty of the natural world would be in harmony with the soul in search of its secrets. Thomas Belt intones, in his remarkable *The Naturalist in Nicaragua:* "Alone on the summit of a high peak, with surging green billows of foliage all around, dim misty mountains in the distance, and above the blue heavens, checkered with fleecy clouds, that have traveled hundreds of miles from the north-east, thoughts arise that can be only felt in their full intensity amid solitude and nature's grandest phases. Then man's intellect strives to grapple with the great mysteries of his existence, and like a fluttering bird that beats itself against the bars of its cage, falls back baffled and bruised."[26] The rhetoric of scientific travel narrative is permeated by the figure of this narrator-hero who undergoes trials for the sake of knowledge. These trials were not trivial, given the primitive means of transportation available, the weight, volume, and fragility of the cumbersome scientific instruments, the epidemics to which the traveler was exposed and to which his body was far from immune, and the difficulties in communicating with the "natives" of the various regions visited. Many European scientists succumbed to disease; others lost their reason. Belt, for instance, died in Denver, Colorado, at age forty-five, of a "mountain fever," while Joseph Juissieu, a botanist who accompanied La Condamine, lost his mind when, according to Goodman, "the collection of plants he had so laboriously gathered with the greatest of effort was lost through carelessness."[27] To these difficulties one might add those involved in securing specimens of plants, rocks, or animals, preserving them through taxidermy or some other method if necessary, and sending them back to the metropolis for analysis, classification, and eventual display. Humboldt's many trunks filled with desiccated specimens made long and circuitous voyages of their own. Some still have not arrived at their destination.

The most arduous trial, however, was for the traveler to retain his sense of self at the same time as he searched for knowledge—and not any kind of knowledge, but one with cosmic implications, for it involved the origins of time and the innermost secrets of a natural world to which he too belonged. Specialization had not yet dulled the sensibility of scientists, and their awareness of the literary dimensions of their enterprise made them receptive to their personal involvement in the reality they observed. Hence, it was not easy to be detached from the reality described and at the same time not distort it, and it was difficult to write with detachment in the midst of a world that threatened to unveil secrets that could conceivably jolt the traveler out of his identity. This was particularly so in the case of travelers like Francis Bond Head, whose exploits as a horseman made him akin to the gauchos, in such a way that one feels that he was becoming one with them. But, to write for a European public, scientific or otherwise, the traveler had to remain European, had to persevere in his identity in spite of the lures of the wild. His discourse demanded it. The rhetorical strategy that kept this distance was the constant expression of wonder, of surprise, achieved through repeated comparisons between the European and the colonial world. But distance was created mostly by the practice of classification and taxonomy (for which Linnaeus had provided a whole new language). The other world, or the world of the other, is classifiable, apt to become the object of a taxonomy. The soul, the spirit of the traveler, interposes the grid of classification between his desire to fuse with the object of his study and that object itself. In these books, Latin America becomes a museum of living natural history, a zoological and botanical garden in which, in contiguous enclosures, animals or plants live separated sometimes by centuries of evolutionary history.

In some of the voyages this perseverance in European identity is manifested in a spectacular fashion, as when the Schomburgk brothers, who are traveling under British auspices, fire salvos in the midst of the jungle to celebrate the Queen's birthday. Their expedition into Guiana and Venezuela is like a capsule of European time within the vast time machine of nature. In popular fiction this element of the voyage is expressed in the elaborate preparations that the travelers make to carry with them a European environment. In Jules Verne's *La Jangada,* a novel about the Amazon, for instance, the huge raft built by French travelers becomes a Noah's ark for European life, an island of civilization floating downriver through the deepest jungle. European paraphernalia insulate the traveler from the reality outside but, as in Verne's contrived vehicles, ornate windows are built to observe and classify flora, fauna, and human samples. "Civilized" impedimenta are both a form of isolation and a point of view; both instruments and means of travel are representations of method, emblems of the travelers' discourse. Hence Captain Nemo's observatory-like window in the *Nautilus,* which allows him to view rare fish and plants in the depths of the ocean.

The image of Captain Nemo peering into the depths at unusual specimens allows us to posit the characteristics of travel narrative derived from science, the previous ones having been derived from the very activity of travel itself. The notion of depth expresses the conception of reality as natural history; an unfolding or, of course, an evolution in time, which accounts for differences in flora and fauna because evolution took diverse paths in different regions. Time, in other words, is not the same in every place. A given evolutionary path leads to a different set of species. Travelers journeying through the colonial world searched for those differences in the hope of finding a master combination, the key to history, or the beginning or beginnings of it all. But Nemo is also looking at animals that belong to a prehistory, animals that were somehow left out of the evolutionary process and either became extinct or very rare. In the nineteenth century Latin America became the field of study of a significant group of paleontologists who hoped to find the secrets of evolution in prehistoric animals preserved by a quirk or accident of history. This is what Professor Challenger—the protagonist of Sir Arthur Conan Doyle's *The Lost World*—searches for on that fictional plateau in the South American jungle, a plateau which, given its elevation, owing to a violent upsurge of the earth, isolated its flora and fauna from the rest of the jungle, creating some sort of natural genetic laboratory. (The model for Conan Doyle here is obviously the Galápagos Islands and the role they played in Darwin's observations and theories.) This "splendid isolation," as George Gaylord Simpson described it in one of his fascinating books on the subject, preserved the origins in the present.[28] Scientific travelers in Latin America looked not only for current specimens of flora and fauna, but for specimens that represented a backward leap into the origins of evolution. Hence, to travel to Latin America meant to find history in the evolution of plants and animals, and to find the beginning of history preserved—a contemporary, living origin. It is the present depicted in Echeverría's "El matadero" as the violent time of the narrative.

3

Nos instruments de physique et d'astronomie excitaient à leur tour la curiosité des habitants.
                                                                —A. von Humboldt, Cumaná, November 16–18, 1799

Sarmiento's fascination with the work of European travelers is well known. He quotes them often, and even states: "A la América del Sud en general, y a la Argentina sobre todo, ha hecho falta un Tocqueville, que, premunido del conocimiento de las teorías sociales, como el viajero científico de barómetros, octantes y brújulas, viniera a penetrar en el interior de nuestra vida política, como en un campo vastísimo y aún no explorado ni descrito por la ciencia, y revelase a la Europa, a la Francia . . ." (p. 10) ("South America in general, and Argentina in particular, has needed a Tocqueville who, armed with the knowledge of social theory, like the scientific traveler with his barometers, octants and compasses, would come and penetrate into the depths of our political life, as if it were a vast territory still unexplored by science, and reveal it to Europe, to France . . .").[29] (These instruments that Sarmiento longs for and that travelers lugged through Latin America will appear in *Cien años de soledad* as part of Melquíades' equipment.) Sarmiento's fascination with the methods and practices of modern science was undeniable and unabashedly expressed in other writings. What is revealing here, however, is that he equates social and natural science. He believes that the instruments of both are alike. Hence this is not an empty pronouncement on the part of Sarmiento. Given the significance of the instruments as a representation of method, Sarmiento's pronouncement is like a methodological profession of faith and an identification of the model of his discourse (in a sense the instruments play a role analogous to that of the notarial arts in the colonial period). Tocqueville's gaze upon North American social life is the optical perspective— the instrument mediated or enabling point of view—that Sarmiento wishes to attain to look at South America. He is himself the Tocqueville that he claims "South America" needs. Tocqueville, however, is a mere emblem of the scientific travel book that determines *Facundo* as a text. How do the characteristics of scientific travel narrative sketched above appear in Sarmiento's book?

Sarmiento's journey away from Argentina may have had a political motive, but it is also analogous to the ordeal of separation discussed in reference to the travel books. It is the trial that leads to writing. In fact, the very act of leaving Argentina, which appears in a kind of prologue or epigraph (not included in the English translation), is directly linked to writing. Sarmiento scribbles a political harangue, in the form of a French quotation:

A fines del año 1840 salía yo de mi patria, desterrado por lástima, estropeado, lleno de cardenales, puntazos y golpes recibidos el día anterior en una de esas bacanales sangrientas de soldadesca y mazorqueros. Al pasar por los baños de Zonda, bajo las armas de la patria que en días alegres había pintado en una sala escribí con carbón estas palabras: ON NE TUE PAS LES IDEES.
El gobierno, a quien se comunicó el hecho mandó una comisión encargada de descifrar el jeroglífico, que se decía contener desahogos innobles, insultos y amenazas. Oída la traducción: "¡Y bien!—dijeron— ¿qué significa esto?" Significa simplemente que venía a Chile, donde la libertad brillaba aún, y que me proponía hacer proyectar los rayos de las luces de su prensa hasta el otro lado de los Andes. Los que conocen mi conducta en Chile, saben si he cumplido aquella protesta. [n.p.]

Toward the end of the year 1840 I was leaving my homeland, exiled by pity, beaten up, full of welts and cuts inflicted upon me the pre-

vious day by the blows of the soldiery and government thugs. On
passing the Zonda Baths I wrote the following words in charcoal beneath the national coat of arms, which in happier times I myself had
painted on the wall of one of the rooms:
ON NE TUE PAS LES IDEES.
Informed of the deed, the government sent a committee charged with
interpreting the hieroglyphic, which was reputed to contain vile im-
pudences, insults, and threats. Upon hearing the translation they said:
"So what? What does this mean?" It means simply that I was on my
way to Chile, where freedom still shines, and that I intended to project
the rays of Chile's bright press upon the other side of the Andes.
Those who are familiar with my activities in Chile can say whether
I have been true to my intention. [Translation mine]

It is revealing how much Sarmiento here resembles the hero of Echeverría's "El matadero," and how much his leaving is the result of an act of
violence. Leaving and writing are violent acts inscribed in this liminal
text, not quite yet in the book, but projecting upon it the reason for beginning it. Leaving and writing are linked in *Facundo* as they are in the
travel books. They represent an ordeal, a separation. Sarmiento will discover his own self and delve into Argentine culture by moving away and
seeing it from afar. He has been routed away from it, as if he were the
issue of a violent and bloody rebirth. Of course, he is at once moving
from his own culture and to it as object of study, as opposed to the travelers who move from their culture to an alien one which they will study.
This difference is crucial because it denotes one of the productive contradictions in *Facundo:* the terrain actually to be traveled is not that of Argentina but that of the texts by the European travelers. It is a known fact
that Sarmiento's acquaintance with the pampa came mostly through books,
particularly the one by Sir Francis Bond Head, *Rough Notes Taken during
Some Rapid Journeys across the Pampas and among the Andes,* a work
he quotes in French.[30] The self-discovery in *Facundo* is thoroughly mediated by texts, just as the texts of the travelers are mediated by scientific
discourse. This double mediation is Sarmiento's version of the perseverance in a European self, the equivalent of the scientist's European impedimenta. Only here the manifestation of that perseverance is textual and
corresponds to the intertextual web of quotations, epigraphs, and allusions in the book. Legitimation, self-recognition, power, authority are all
invested in the chameleon-like ability of Sarmiento's text to blend in, not
with the land, but with the European texts about the land. Discourse and
its object are one, because the object is always already discourse.
    The literary character of that mediation is also revealed in a curious

feature of Sarmiento's discourse: He often compares gaucho life to various oriental societies as they are described by European orientalists.[31] If the gaucho is the origin of Argentine culture, the deep stratum of the Argentine self, that origin is the solidly literary figure of a gaucho dressed in the garb of a bedouin as described by French, German, and British travelers. At times the gaucho is compared to unabashedly literary texts by the likes of Victor Hugo. The congruence of European science is to the discourse of the scientists what this textual prisonhouse is to Sarmiento's: the grid that presumably keeps him from becoming one with his object of study, which, paradoxically, becomes his object of study because he too is a product of that construct. The origin, the self, and the history of the self are literary figures, fictions of the European literary imagination as much as products of scientific inquiry.

There is a sense in which Sarmiento's mixing of European texts from scientific and literary origins unveils the profound complicity between those forms of discourse, disavowing the possible objectivity and scientific truth-bearing quality of the scientists' books. Surely the scientists project onto their object of study a vision as charged with values and desires as that of literature itself. The European gaze is one, whether it be scientific or artistic; its object is an "other" created out of its longing for an origin and organicity, an other that it depicts, classifies and describes as it creates a discourse of power predicated on the adequation of scientific discourse and an object that it has molded for itself. It is in this circularity that science and modern literature reflect each other, as Sarmiento's use of both kinds of texts reveals because of his ambiguous position as both subject and object. It is by revealing this circularity that *Facundo* breaks free of the mimetic bond out of which it was created as a text.

There are other characteristics drawn from scientific travel books in *Facundo* beyond this double mediation, most notably Sarmiento's classificatory practices, particularly of the gaucho. Among the most memorable pages in *Facundo* (the ones that most Latin Americans remember from elementary and high school) are those devoted to the description of the various kinds of gauchos: the minstrel, the pathfinder, the track-finder, the outlaw. Each of these types is described minutely, from his attire to his daily routines. The gaucho is to Sarmiento like a species of vegetable or animal life whose various families he finds, describes, and classifies for the European observer. The same taxonomical compulsion is carried over to larger blocks of Argentine life, as when the various kinds of cities are analyzed and contrasted: for instance, Córdoba versus Buenos Aires.

What is remarkably modern about this classification is that it holds simultaneously multiple layers of time, that it reflects depth in the sense discussed before. Buenos Aires and Córdoba occupy the same time in the present, but belong to two different eras separated perhaps by centuries. The pampa may be the remote origin of all and, if so, is contemporaneous with later manifestations of Argentine culture that it has determined. Facundo Quiroga is an earlier stage of Juan Manuel de Rosas, though they are contemporaries (they were both born in 1793, but the caudillo was cut down in 1835, while the dictator lived a long life in exile until 1877):

> Desenvolviéndose los acontecimientos, veremos las montoneras provinciales con sus caudillos a la cabeza; en Facundo Quiroga última-mente, triunfante en todas partes la campaña sobre las ciudades y dominadas éstas en su espíritu, gobierno y civilización, formarse al fin el gobierno central, unitario, despótico del estanciero don Juan Manuel Rosas, que clava en la culta Buenos Aires el cuchillo del gaucho y des-truye la obra de los siglos, la civilización, las leyes y la libertad. [pp. 54–55]

> As events succeed each other, we shall see the provincial monto-neras headed by their chiefs; the final triumph, in Facundo Quiroga, of the country over the cities throughout the land; and by their subjuga-tion in spirit, government, and civilization, the final formation of the central consolidated despotic government of the landowner, Don Juan Manuel Rosas, who applied the knife of the gaucho to the culture of Buenos Ayres, and destroyed the work of centuries—of civilization, law and liberty. [p. 55]

Another significant feature of the book's temporality is the way in which the origin is conceptualized. Although Sarmiento often alludes to the Spanish and even the Indian history of Argentina, the origin is the pampa, which appears as an absolute beginning, prior to history, represented by the topic of nomadic, shepherd societies, an origin shared with other cul-tures, such as the Oriental ones. In Argentina, however, that origin is present at the same time as the history that has followed it. *Facundo*, like the books by the travelers, purports to display the dynamics of history in a spatio-temporal display, a kind of arrested-animation exhibition, high-lighting the various shapes that the accidents of evolution have created in the specific region described. The book is like a gallery of types and ep-ochs, held in synchrony by the machinery of scientific discourse.

Perhaps the best way to visualize this kind of representation is through a painting. In 1859, the U.S. artist Frederic Church unveiled his enor-mous canvas *Heart of the Andes*, based on two expeditions to South America, but mostly inspired by Alexander von Humboldt's writings. Church followed Humboldt's perception that, in the Andes, "at a single glance, the eye surveys majestic palms, humid forests. . . . [T]hen above these forms of tropical vegetation appear oaks and sweetbriar, and above this the barren snow-capped peaks." A disciple of the renowned artist Thomas Cole, Church was a member of what is known as the Hudson River school of painting, which delighted in portraying the beauty of the North American landscape. In *Heart of the Andes*, however, he attempted to give an all-encompassing view of nature's history in the manner of Humboldt's ambitious *Cosmos: A Sketch of a Physical Description of the Universe*.[32]

Sarmiento, of course, is not missing from that picture. Like the travelers, his life is part of the narrative, as we saw in the quotation from the book's prologue or epigraph. Sarmiento weaves himself in and out of the picture as observer, classifier, and commentator as much as author of the account. His authority is bolstered not only by the extensive quotations from scientific and literary texts, but by the sense of his having been there, of his having a special knowledge garnered through the ordeal of travel and observation. He often refers to his life in Chile, where, as a foreigner, he is naturally the object of attention. The sense of being out of his home country, often expressed by the travelers, appears in these vignettes in which Sarmiento recounts how Chileans dealt with him, and what is of interest to them about him because he is different and foreign.

These laborious preparations—a propaedeutic—lead Sarmiento to his specimen: Facundo Quiroga, whose life is set in the center of the book like an odd insect trapped in a glass paperweight. The story of Facundo Quiroga's life obeys no conventional rhetorical rules for writing a biography. Life, biography, has the emphasis here on the *bio*—life is biological. Life is a concept much in vogue in nineteenth-century science, and the debate between organicists and mechanicists is well known. It is a concept that left a deep imprint on European thought and literature, culminating perhaps in Nietzsche or in Unamuno, and the Hispanic versions of *Lebensphilosophie* called *vitalismo*. Sarmiento accounts for Facundo Quiroga's character and fate in scientific terms. The caudillo is motivated by an excess of life, a thrust that leads him inevitably and tragically to Barranca Yaco, where he knows he will be slain. Facundo Quiroga's surfeit of life is visible in the shape of his head, in his stoutness, and in his fiery eyes. These are biological accidents that determine his fate, that make his life conform even more to a tragic pattern. Just as Facundo Quiroga's originality is the result of accidents, so is the whole of gaucho culture, a serendipitous accumulation of random events. The *pulpería*, the social nucleus of gaucho life, develops from the chance meetings of gauchos:

> Salen, pues, los varones sin saber fijamente a dónde. Una vuelta a los ganados, una visita a una cría o a la querencia de un caballo predilecto, invierte una pequeña parte del día; el resto lo absorbe una reunión en

una venta o pulpería. Allí concurren cierto número de parroquianos de los alrededores; allí se dan y adquieren las noticias sobre los animales extraviados; trázanse en el suelo las marcas del ganado; sábese dónde caza el tigre, dónde se le han visto rastros al león; allí, en fin, está el cantor, allí se fraterniza por el circular de la copa y las prodigalidades de los que poseen . . . y en esta asamblea sin objeto público, sin interés social, empiezan a echarse los rudimentos de las reputaciones que más tarde, y andando los años, van a aparecer en la escena política. [pp. 50–51]

The men then set forth without exactly knowing where they are going. A turn around the herds, a visit to a breeding-pen or to the haunt of a favorite horse, takes up a small part of the day; the rest is consumed in a rendezvous at a tavern or grocery store [pulpería]. There assemble inhabitants of the neighboring parishes; there are given and received bits of information about animals that have gone astray; the traces of the cattle are described upon the ground; intelligence of the hunting-ground of the tiger or of the place where the tiger's tracks have been seen, is communicated. There, in short, is the Minstrel; there the men fraternize while the glass goes around at the expense of those who have the means as well as the disposition to pay for it . . . yet in this assembly, without public aim, without social interest, are first formed the elements of those characters which are to appear later on the political stage. [pp. 48–49]

Even the nature of the gaucho's poetry is due to accidents of the terrain, irregularities like those of his body: "Existe, pues, un fondo de poesía que nace de los accidentes naturales del país y de las costumbres excepcionales que engendra" (p. 36) ("The country consequently derives a fund of poetry from its natural circumstances [accidents] and the special customs resulting [being engendered] from them" [p. 27]).

The notion of "accident" is decisive because it determines Facundo Quiroga's freedom, his flight from the norm, his originality. When he defeats regular armies he does so because he is free to use nonconventional tactics that befuddle his enemies. An accident is inaugural by definition: it is an event independent of the past which becomes a unique form of present violently broken off from history, a new form of temporality, like the series of tumultuous acts narrated in Echeverría's story. An accident is a beginning like those that paleontologists hope to find in caves and digs; Facundo Quiroga's penchant for brutality is an expression of his freedom. As an origin in the present, he validates Rosas's inclination to violence, and Sarmiento's own escape from the model furnished by the scientific travelers.

When Sarmiento finally arrives at the beginning of his *life* of Facundo Quiroga, we read:

Media entre las ciudades de San Luis y San Juan un dilatado desierto que, por su falta completa de agua, recibe el nombre de *travesía*. El aspecto de aquellas soledades es, por lo general, triste y desamparado, y el viajero que viene de oriente no pasa la última *represa* o aljibe de campo sin proveer sus *chifles* de suficiente cantidad de agua. En esta travesía tuvo lugar una vez la extraña escena que sigue. Las cuchilladas, tan frecuentes entre nuestros gauchos, habían forzado a uno de ellos a abandonar precipitadamente la ciudad de San Luis, y ganar la *travesía* a pie, con la montura al hombro, a fin de escapar a las persecuciones de la justicia. Debían alcanzarlo dos compañeros tan luego como pudieran robar caballos para los tres.

No eran por entonces sólo el hambre o la sed los peligros que le aguardaban en el desierto aquel, que un tigre *cebado* andaba hacía un año siguiendo los rastros de los viajeros, y pasaban ya de ocho los que habían sido víctimas de su predilección por la carne humana. Suele ocurrir a veces en aquellos países en que la fiera y el hombre se disputan el dominio de la naturaleza, que éste cae bajo la garra sangrienta de aquélla; entonces el tigre empieza a gustar de preferencia su carne, y se le llama *cebado* cuando se ha dado a este género de caza; la caza de hombres. El juez de la campaña immediata al teatro de sus devastaciones convoca a los varones hábiles para la correría, y bajo su autoridad y dirección se hace la persecución del tigre *cebado*, que rara vez escapa a la sentencia que lo pone fuera de la ley.

Cuando nuestro prófugo había caminado cosa de seis leguas, creyó oir bramar el tigre a lo lejos y sus fibras se estremecieron. Es el bramido del tigre un gruñido como el del cerdo, pero agrio, prolongado, estridente, y que, sin que haya motivo de temor, causa un sacudimiento involuntario de los nervios, como si la carne se agitara ella sola al anuncio de la muerte.

Algunos minutos después el bramido se oyó más distinto y más cercano; el tigre venía ya sobre el rastro, y sólo a una larga distancia se divisaba un pequeño algarrobo. Era preciso apretar el paso, correr, en fin, porque los bramidos se sucedían con más frecuencia, y el último era más distinto, más vibrante que el que le precedía.

Al fin, arrojando la montura a un lado del camino dirigióse el gaucho al árbol que había divisado, y no obstante la debilidad de su tronco, felizmente bastante elevado, pudo trepar a su copa y mantenerse en una continua oscilación, medio oculto entre el ramaje. De allí pudo observar la escena que tenía lugar en el camino: el tigre marchaba a paso precipitado, oliendo el suelo y bramando con más frecuencia a medida que sentía la proximidad de su presa. Pasa adelante del punto en que ésta se había separado del camino y pierde el rastro; el tigre se enfurece, remolinea, hasta que divisa la montura, que desgarra de un manotón, esparciendo en el aire sus prendas. Más irritado aún con este chasco, vuelve a buscar el rastro, encuentra al fin la dirección en que va, y, levantando la vista, divisa a su presa haciendo con el peso balancearse el algarrobillo, cual la frágil caña cuando las aves se posan en sus puntas.

Desde entonces ya no bramó el tigre; acercábase a saltos, y en un abrir y cerrar de ojos sus enormes manos estaban apoyándose a dos varas del suelo sobre el delgado tronco, al que comunicaban un temblor convulsivo que iba a obrar sobre los nervios del mal seguro gaucho. Intentó la fiera dar un salto impotente; dio vuelta en torno al árbol midiendo su altura con ojos enrojecidos por la sed de sangre, y al fin, bramando de cólera se acostó en el suelo, batiendo sin cesar la cola, los ojos fijos en su presa, la boca entreabierta y reseca. Esta escena horrible duraba ya dos horas mortales; la postura violenta del gaucho y la fascinación aterrante que ejercía sobre él la mirada sanguinaria, inmóvil, del tigre, del que por una fuerza invencible de atracción no podía apartar los ojos, habían empezado a debilitar sus fuerzas, y ya veía próximo el momento en que su cuerpo extenuado iba a caer en su ancha boca, cuando el rumor lejano de galope de caballos le dio esperanza de salvación.

En efecto, sus amigos habían visto el rastro del tigre y corrían sin esperanza de salvarlo. El desparramo de la montura les reveló el lugar de la escena; y volar a él, desenrollar sus lazos, echarlos sobre el tigre, *empacado* y ciego de furor, fue la obra de un segundo. La fiera, estirada a dos lazos, no pudo escapar a las puñaladas rápidas con que en venganza de su prolongada agonía le traspasó el que iba a ser su víctima. "Entonces supe qué era tener miedo", decía el general don Juan Facundo Quiroga, contando a un grupo de oficiales este suceso.

También a él le llamaron *Tigre de los Llanos*, y no le sentaba mal esta denominación, a fe. [pp. 71–73; emphasis in original]

Between the cities of San Luis and San Juan, lies an extensive desert, called the Travesía, a word which signifies *want of water* [on the contrary, it means a watercrossing]. The aspect of that waste is mostly gloomy and unpromising, and the traveler coming from the east does not fail to provide his *chifles* [canteens] with a sufficient quantity of water at the last cistern which he passes as he approaches it. This Travesía once witnessed the following strange scene. The consequences of some of the encounters with knives so common among our gauchos had driven one of them in haste from the city of San Luis and forced him to escape to the Travesía on foot, and with his riding gear on his shoulder, in order to avoid the pursuit of the law. Two comrades were to join him as soon as they could steal horses for all three.

Hunger and thirst were not the only dangers which at that time awaited him in the desert; a tiger that had already tasted human flesh had been following the track of those who crossed it for a year, and

more than eight persons had already been the victims of this preference. In these regions, where man must contend with this animal for
dominion over nature, the former sometimes falls a victim, upon
which the tiger begins to acquire a preference for the taste of human
flesh, and when it has once devoted itself to this novel form of chase,
the pursuit of mankind, it gets the name of *man-eater*. The provincial
justice nearest the scene of his depredations calls out the huntsmen of
his district, who join, under his authority and guidance, in the pursuit
of the beast, which seldom escapes the consequences of its outlawry.

When our fugitive had proceeded some six leagues, he thought he
heard the distant roar of the animal, and a shudder ran through him.
The roar of the tiger resembles the screech of the hog, but is prolonged, sharp, and piercing, and even when there is no occasion for
fear, causes an involuntary tremor of the nerves as if the flesh shud-
dered consciously at the menace of death.

The roaring was heard clearer and nearer. The tiger was already
upon the trail of the man, who saw no refuge but a small carob-tree at
a great distance. He had to quicken his pace, and finally to run, for the
roars behind him began to follow each other more rapidly, and each
was clearer and more ringing than the last.

At length, flinging his riding gear to one side of the path, the gaucho turned to the tree which he had noticed, and in spite of the weakness of its trunk, happily quite a tall one, he succeeded in clambering
to its top, and keeping himself half concealed among its boughs which
oscillated violently. Thence he could see the swift approach of the tiger, sniffing the soil and roaring more frequently in proportion to its
increasing perception of the nearness of its prey. Passing beyond the
spot where our traveler had left the path, it lost the track, and becoming enraged, rapidly circled about until it discovered the riding gear,
which it dashed to fragments by a single blow. Still more furious from
this failure, it resumed its search for the trail, and at last found out the
direction in which it led. It soon discerned its prey, under whose
weight the slight tree was swaying like a reed upon the summit of
which a bird has alighted.

The tiger now sprang forward, and in the twinkling of an eye, its
monstrous fore-paws were resting on the slender trunk two yards
from the ground, and were imparting to the tree a convulsive trem-
bling calculated to act upon the nerves of the gaucho, whose position
was far from secure. The beast exerted its strength in an ineffectual
leap; it circled around the tree, measuring the elevation with eyes red-
dened by the thirst for blood, and at length, roaring with rage, it
crouched down, beating the ground frantically with its tail, its eyes
fixed on its prey, its parched mouth half open. This horrible scene had
lasted for nearly two mortal hours; the gaucho's constrained attitude,

and the fearful fascination exercised over him by the fixed and bloodthirsty stare of the tiger, which irresistibly attracted and retained his
own glances, had begun to diminish his strength, and he already perceived that the moment was at hand when his exhausted body would
fall into the capacious mouth of his pursuer. But at this moment the
distant sound of the feet of horses on a rapid gallop gave him hope of
rescue.

His friends had indeed seen the tiger's foot-prints, and were has-
tening on, though without hope of saving him. The scattered fragments of the saddle directed them to the scene of action, and it was the
work of a moment for them to reach it, to uncoil their lassoes, and to
fling them over the tiger, now blinded with rage. The beast, drawn in
opposite directions by the two lassoes, could not evade the swift stabs
by which its destined victim took his revenge for his prolonged tor-
ments. "On that occasion I knew what it was to be afraid," was the
expression of Don Juan Facundo Quiroga, as he related this incident
to a group of officers.

He too was called "the tiger of the Llanos," a title which did not ill
befit him . . . [pp. 73–76]

Sarmiento has encrypted in this story, on the threshold of Facundo Quiroga's life, the central tropological mechanisms of his book. The story can
be read as an allegory not only of the caudillo's life, but more interestingly of the life of *Facundo* the book; of its existence in relation to Sarmiento and the books by the scientific travelers. This quasi-liminal text,
on the verge of the full story, is a version of that masterstory of the
narrative of Latin America whose kernel is Echeverría's "El matadero":
both center on violence and sacrifice. Here, however, the internal dialectics from which the story issues are more forcefully present.

It is a curious fact that the first sentence of the life of Facundo Quiroga
already contains a trope that announces the mastertropes of the story, as
if beginnings always had to contain in embryonic form middles and ends.
The desert between San Luis and San Juan is called a *travesía* because of
its absolute lack of water; yet one normally calls a *travesía* the crossing
of a body of water. Hence the name means, in this specific context, the
opposite of what it ordinarily does; it is a kind of natural catachresis, as if
language communicated in a mysterious, nonrational way, by doing violence to conventional relationships between signifier and signified. To understand language we have to be able to master a code that is not the
universal one, which we presume to be based on a layered memory of
human exchange. The desert is called a watercrossing because of its absolute lack of water; therefore, we must be ready to read the opposite of
what words appear to mean. We know from Amado Alonso and others,

of course, that a term like *travesía* entered Argentine Spanish as far back as 1575; borrowed, like many other words, from the language of seafaring that the colonists brought with them after the inevitable crossing of the ocean, a linguistic phenomenon common to the Spanish of the Americas.[33] Be that as it may, the inversion remains, whether it is a historical retention or a renewed misnomer.

The watery metaphor is continued when we are told that travelers must store up water before embarking on a journey through the desert at the last *represa*, that is to say, the last dam or lock. Now, *represa* is given here as synonymous to *aljibe*, a well or cistern, which does contain water but which gets its name, it seems, because it marks the boundary of the desert, not because it provides water. The metaphoric body of water to be crossed is fenced in by dams where the traveler must load up on that which is missing from the area thus contained. If we remember that the vast wastes of the pampa are often compared to the sea in *Facundo*, we can understand better that, within the tropological system of the text, which seems to be made up of a series of inversions, the earth can be water. What all these inversions have been preparing the reader for is the unusual, the out-of-the-ordinary, the "strange scene" about to be narrated, one in which man is the object of the chase, not the other way around. Strangeness, uniqueness, pervades the story of Facundo Quiroga, the singular specimen, the mutant that is going to explain a distinct Latin American strain.

The singularity of the gaucho, his existence outside the norm, is expressed by the fact that he is often an outlaw. This gaucho in particular flees the city because he has stabbed a man to death in one of the frequent outbursts of violence against fellow men and animals that punctuate the life of a gaucho. The gaucho's violent nature makes him both a man of nature and a man outside the law. Like the catachresis that describes his habitat, the gaucho lives in a world of transgressions, of rupture, of breaks. This condition is further emphasized in this particular case by the gaucho having to travel on foot. The horse was the gaucho's way of life, practically from birth. The "strange story" is not only about an individual who functions outside the law, but about one who is, at this specific moment, outside his own law, where he can be prey to an accident like the one that in fact befalls him. The story is about an instance, original and unique, hence capable of engendering an individual as exceptional as Facundo Quiroga.

The tiger enters the "strange scene" also under the banner of a misnomer. We are dealing here not with a tiger, of course, but with a species of jaguar, "tiger" being one of the approximations used by Europeans to name American natural phenomena that did not quite conform to their categories. Be that as it may, like the gaucho, the tiger is running away from the law because he kills men. This is no ordinary tiger. He belongs to a special kind that is partial to human flesh. Once he has tasted a human, the tiger acquires a predilection for humans, a predilection that is based on a very intimate, secret, and forbidden knowledge. To be *cebado* means to be "primed," to have a foreknowledge that incites desire; already to have or to have had a morsel of what one desires, a teasing, partial sampling. This knowledge and desire for more of the same—a same that is already part of one, being inside, consumed—is the aesthetic counterpart of the scientific curiosity of the travelers; the literary aspect that Sarmiento unveils through the pell-mell mixing of textual tidbits from science and literature. The tiger's ability to capture humans, his technique in following a scent, his hermeneutic power to interpret the signs of human presence, are predicated on this foreknowledge. Like the textual doubling in the mediation of discourses, knowledge is predicated on foreknowledge, on capturing an object that discourse has itself molded. There is, precisely, a sense in which this knowledge exceeds the norm, goes beyond the mere need for food. To be *cebado* means not only to be primed but to be fat, to be satiated. One can *cebar* an animal, fatten him for the kill and the table. Hence the taste for human flesh on the part of the tiger is a forbidden knowledge in that it is like a vice, a desire that exceeds need. There is in the beautiful descriptions of the animal—particularly of his violent acts and his perseverance in pursuit of his prey to the point of giving his life in the effort—a reflection of this doubly vicious character, at once meanness and addiction to pleasure. To be *cebado* is to have a penchant for extravagance, for luxury, to be driven by an excess of life, like Facundo Quiroga. This foreknowledge acquired through the taste of flesh is in consonance with the communication established between the tiger and the gaucho, which is not merely a digestive one.

The gaucho learns of the tiger's presence through the roar of the animal, in reaction to which "sus fibras se estremecieron," meaning, of course, his muscle fibers, his flesh. Taste is not the only sense through which the flesh of the gaucho and the tiger communicate. It is explained in the next line that the roar of the tiger is like the grunt of a pig, but shrill and long. Even when there is no "reason" for fear (*motivo* here has to be translated thus), it causes one's nervous system to shudder involuntarily, as if the flesh itself became agitated "al solo anuncio de la muerte" ("by the mere announcement or threat of death"). The tiger's roar establishes a communication with the gaucho's flesh that bypasses language. Later on, the same kind of understanding is established when the tiger communicates a tremor to the tree that acts directly upon the nerves of the gaucho. As opposed to the vagaries of communication through language and its tropological relays, delays, and detours, the language the tiger speaks to the gaucho communicates directly, producing in him a contradictory feeling of fascination and mortal fear. Tiger and gaucho understand each other subliminally, that which is being communicated being itself sublime: terror and desire. This identification and communication between tiger and gaucho by means of a sublime language says much about the masterstory embedded in Sarmiento's book.

The language of the pampa, as shown, breaks with the received language of social communication; words often mean, irrationally, against history, the opposite of what they normally signify. That language is like the one the tiger and the gaucho speak. Meaning is not conveyed by the established code but by a given feeling, a feeling that stands at the threshold of the need to trope, at the very origin of language. The pampa is not merely a plain—a blank page—but a silence whose vastness provokes, like the sea, a feeling of the infinite that incites both fear and longing. The "strange story" narrates an accident; an accident cannot have an antecedent, otherwise it would not be one. Since it does not have anything prior that explains it, the accident has to be narrated in a catachretic language, whose odd signs are like the unique specimens involved. The fact that Facundo Quiroga acquires his nom de guerre from this scene is a clear indication of how naming proceeds in this language. The gaucho steals from the animal his already mistaken name. By killing the tiger, the gaucho names himself. Naming is a violent activity, a break with the norm, with the law. This would be of no particular interest if the story were narrated with detachment by the voice Sarmiento uses for classification, the rhetoric of the travelers that allows him to hold up as distinct, strange, and uncivilized that which he is describing. But this is not the case.

Until Facundo Quiroga breaks in to explain that it was then that he learned about fear, the reader does not know that it was *the caudillo himself who was telling the story.* Sarmiento has almost imperceptibly surrendered the narrative voice to the protagonist himself. This prosopopoeia creates an identification between Facundo Quiroga and Sarmiento that is parallel to the one just established between the tiger and the gaucho. The gaucho cannot evade the bloodthirsty stare of the tiger, which both attracts him and threatens him, drawing him toward the animal's enormous mouth. A mouth with a voice, but with no articulate language, a language that is also spoken through the eyes, as if being deflected, monstrously, through another organ. A language of gazes, of looks, that returns the inquisitive stare of the gaucho, that classificatory, affixing glance of man.

The gaucho cannot speak out of fear. The mouth of the tiger has stolen his voice, like Facundo Quiroga stole Sarmiento's. Is Sarmiento the detached, civilized observer, or is he, like the gaucho up in the tree, vibrating with the sublime language of fear? Or, again, like the tiger, drawn in opposite directions by the two lassoes, pulled by fear and desire toward certain annihilation? If one takes into account that time and again Sarmiento insists that Rosas commands through fear, then the chain of identifications becomes even more interesting: the tiger is like Facundo Quiroga, who is like Juan Manuel de Rosas, who is like Domingo Faustino Sarmiento. The language of the text is not that of the scientific travelogue but the accidental language of literature, a subliminal language whose system is that of breaking the system, and whose aim is to be unique like the gaucho and the tiger, to partake of their violent beauty.

Sarmiento or, better, Sarmiento's discourse is like the tiger's, made up of misnomers, of violence represented as catachreses, motivated by a desire for the object that turns him into the object, as Facundo Quiroga's and the tiger's voice blend one with the other. Sarmiento's discourse is *cebado,* primed, satiated, yet desirous for more, and reveals at the same time this quality to be the fundamental one in the scientific traveler's discourse. It is the artistic, the aesthetic excess in those books, which Sarmiento feeds on to create an outlaw discourse, beyond the taxonomies of science. For to capture that unique, monstrous prey, that mutant which marks the foundation of Latin American narrative discourse, his own discourse has to be unique and monstrous, the product of a different time. It is for this reason, and for no other, that *Facundo* is a founding text in Latin American narrative; it contains in a dramatic fashion the second masterstory, one that will prevail until the *novela de la tierra,* and remain a strong vestige until the present.

But there is more, of course, for in killing the tiger the gaucho is killing himself, or at least prefiguring his own death in Barranca Yaco. Facundo Quiroga's life is the stuff of tragedy. His excess of life, like a tragic hubris, leads him to the grandeur of his power as well as to his death, about which he is warned on several occasions. He cannot escape his fate because, in order to be free, his life has to be determined by accidents that release him from the norm. Fear, the language he knows, can make his flesh shudder in anticipation of death, but fear cannot tell him what to do to avoid death; if anything, fear leads him to death. Sarmiento, the omniscient narrator in the book, is caught in the same trap. Given his identification with Facundo Quiroga and Rosas, their demise is his own demise. He too is blind to his own fate, which is to be like them. In literary history Sarmiento lives because of Facundo Quiroga. What Sarmiento has found in his voyage of discovery and self-discovery is a present origin, one that speaks through him, hollowing out the voice of his scientific language. His authority will not be attained by it, but by the tragic sacrifice of his protagonist, which he reenacts in the text. This tragic fusion is a reflection of the linear time introduced by the evolution of nature, which brings everything to an end, inexorably, so that it will be reborn in a different guise. Fusion with the object of analysis is the escape from the hegemonic discourse, the subplot of this second masterstory, a flight into the abyss of time. Escape from mediation is figured in nineteenth-century narrative by this joining with the object of observation, which is a fusion with mutability. This vertiginous sense of time will remain in Latin American fiction in the endings of novels like Carpentier's *El reino de este mundo* and García Márquez's *Cien años de soledad*, narratives in which the action is brought to a close by a violent wind that blows everything away. That wind first swept across the pampas in Sarmiento's *Facundo*.

Notes

1. Esteban Echeverría, "El matadero" in *El cuento hispanoamericano. Antología crítico-histórica*, ed. Seymour Menton, 3rd ed. (Mexico: Fondo de Cultura Económica, 1986), p. 13; "The Slaughterhouse," in *The Borzoi Anthology of Latin American Literature*, ed. Emir Rodríguez Monegal (New York: Alfred A. Knopf, 1977), 1:210. The story was probably written about 1838.

2. C. H. Haring, *The Spanish Empire in America* (New York: Harcourt, Brace & World, 1963 [1947]); Jorge I. Domínguez, *Insurrection or Loyalty: The Breakdown of the Spanish Empire* (Cambridge: Harvard University Press, 1980); T. Halperín Donghi, *Politics, Economics, and Society in Argentina in the Revolutionary Period* (Cambridge: Cambridge University Press, 1975).

3. Manuel Moreno Fraginals, *El ingenio: Complejo económico-social del azúcar* (Havana: Ciencias Sociales, 1978); translated as *The Sugarmill* (New York: Monthly Review Press, 1976).

4. Karen Anne Stolley, "*El Lazarillo de ciegos caminantes:* Un itinerario crítico" (Ph.D. diss., Yale University, 1985).

5. See "The Case of the Speaking Statue: *Ariel* and the Magisterial Rhetoric of the Latin American Essay," in my *The Voice of the Masters: Writing and Authority in Modern Latin American Literature* (Austin: University of Texas Press, 1985), pp. 8–32.

6. I have written about the dictator-novel in terms that may be relevant to the discussion here in "The Dictatorship of Rhetoric/The Rhetoric of Dictatorship," in *The Voice of the Masters*, pp. 64–85.

7. "Such are all great historical men—whose own particular aims involve those large issues which are the will of the World-Spirit. . . . Such individuals had no consciousness of the general Idea they were unfolding, while prose-

cuting those aims of theirs; on the contrary, they were practical, political men, who had an insight into the requirements of the time—*what was ripe for development.* . . . When their object is attained they fall like empty hulls from the kernel. They die early, like Alexander; they are murdered, like Caesar; transported to St. Helena, like Napoleon." G. W. F. Hegel, *The Philosophy of History,* introduction by C. J. Friedrich (New York: Dover Publications, 1956), pp. 30–31. Napoleon is one of Sarmiento's most frequent references.

8. For the poetic, legal, and narrative versions of Quiroga's death, see Armando Zárate, *Facundo Quiroga, Barranca Yaco: Juicios y testimonios* (Buenos Aires: Editorial Plus Ultra, 1985).

9. Percy G. Adams, *Travel Literature and the Evolution of the Novel* (Lexington: University of Kentucky Press, 1983), p. 275.

10. Edward J. Goodman, *The Explorers of South America* (New York: Macmillan, 1972). See also his *The Exploration of South America: An Annotated Bibliography* (New York: Garland Publishing Co., 1983). Another charming and entertaining book on the subject is Victor Wolfgang von Hagen's *South America Called Them: Explorations of the Great Naturalists La Condamine, Humboldt, Darwin, Spruce* (New York: Alfred A. Knopf, 1945).

11. Carlos J. Cordero, *Los relatos de los viajeros extranjeros posteriores a la Revolución de Mayo como fuentes de historia argentina. Ensayo de sistematización bibliográfica* (Buenos Aires: Imprenta y Casa Editora "Coni", 1936). Cordero provides reliable bibliographic information on each book, a biographical sketch of the author, and a table at the end with information about the professional expertise, purposes of the trip, and nationality of each author. His book gives ample evidence of the importance of these travel books at the time they were written. Their translations were sometimes commissioned by the Argentine government.

12. Mariano Picón Salas, *A Cultural History of Spanish America: From Conquest to Independence,* trans. Irving A. Leonard (Berkeley: University of California Press, 1962 [1944], pp. 155–156. There are also the following works on travel literature: Lincoln Bates, "En pos de una civilización perdida: Dos audaces viajeros del siglo XIX exploran la América Central," *Américas* (OAS), 38, no. 1 (1986): 34–39; Chester C. Christian, Jr., "Hispanic Literature of Exploration," *Exploration* (Journal of the MLA Special Session on the Literature of Exploration and Travel), I (1973): 42–46; Evelio A. Echeverría, "La conquista del Chimborazo," *Américas* (OAS), 35, no. 5 (1983): 22–31; Iris H. W. Engstrand, *Spanish Scientists in the New World: The Eighteenth-Century Expeditions* (Seattle: University of Washington Press, 1981). Engstrand's superb book should be read in conjunction with María de los Angeles Calatayud Arinero's *Catálogo de las expediciones y viajes científicos españoles siglos XVIII y XIX* (Madrid: Consejo Superior de Investigaciones Científicas, 1984). Continuing the list: Jean Franco, "Un viaje poco romántico: Viajeros británicos hacia [sic] Sudamérica: 1818–1828," *Escritura* (Caracas),

4, no. 7 (1979): 129–141 (this article is one of the few, and perhaps the first in recent times, to notice the importance of travel accounts as writing; there was no contradiction, however, as Franco assumes, between the economic motivation of the journeys and the romanticism of the writers); C. Harvey Gardiner, "Foreign Travelers' Accounts of Mexico, 1810–1910," *The Américas* 8 (1952): 321–351; Gardiner was the editor of a series of travel books called Latin American Travel. His introductions to the following two volumes are important: Francis Bond Head, *Journeys across the Pampas and among the Andes* (Carbondale: Southern Illinois University Press, 1967), pp. vii–xxi, and Friedrich Hassaurek, *Four Years among the Ecuadorians* (Carbondale: Southern Illinois University Press, 1967), pp. vii–xxi; Ronald Hilton, "The Significance of Travel Literature with Special Reference to the Spanish and Portuguese Speaking World," *Hispania* (AATSP), 49 (1966): 836–845; Sonja Karsen, "Charles Marie de la Condamine's Travels in Latin America," *Revista Interamericana de Bibliografía/Inter-American Review of Bibliography*, 36, no. 3 (1986): 315–323; Josefina Palop, "El Brasil visto por los viajeros alemanes," *Revista de Indias* 21, no. 83 (1961): 107–127; Mary Louise Pratt, "Scratches on the Face of the Country; What Mr. Barrow Saw in the Land of the Bushmen," *Critical Inquiry* 12, no. 1 (1985): 119–143, and her "Fieldwork in Common Places," in *Writing Culture: The Poetics and Politics of Ethnography*, ed. James Clifford and George E. Marcus (Berkeley: University of California Press, 1986), pp. 27–50. Though these articles are essentially about Africa, there are useful observations about Latin America. Arthur Robert Steele, *Flowers for the King: The Expedition of Ruiz and Pavón and the Flora of Peru* (Durham: Duke University Press, 1964); Samuel Trifilo, "Nineteenth-Century English Travel Books on Argentina: A Revival in Spanish Translation," *Hispania* (AATSP), 41 (1958): 491–496. See also Clifford Geertz, *Works and Lives: The Anthropologist as Author* (Stanford: Stanford University Press, 1988), p. 35ff.

None of these works approaches the depth and beauty of Paul Carter's *The Road to Botany Bay: An Exploration of Landscape and History* (New York: Alfred A. Knopf, 1988), which is about the founding of Australia. Marshall Sahlins's superb *Islands of History* (Chicago: University of Chicago Press, 1985) centers on Captain Cook's travels through the South Pacific.

13. There were, in fact, quite a few Spanish travelers also, particularly in the first years of the Bourbon dynasty. See the books by Calatayud, Engstrand, and Steele (note 12, above). At the same time, Spain had been the object of travel accounts since the seventeenth century. The latest update on the topic is by R. Merrit Cox, "Foreign Travelers in Eighteenth-Century Spain," *Studies in Eighteenth-Century Literature and Romanticism in Honor of John Clarkson Dowling*, ed. Douglas and Linda Jane Barnette (Newark, Del.: Juan de la Cuesta, 1985), pp. 17–26.

14. There were also U.S. travelers who explored what would become, or

what already was a part of, their country, as is the case of William Bartram (1739–1823). His *Travels through North & South Carolina, Georgia, East & West Florida, the Cherokee Country, the Extensive Territories of the Muscoulges, or Creek Confederacy, and the Country of the Chactaws* (1791) "caught the imagination of the Romantics and influenced, among others, Chateaubriand, Coleridge, Emerson, and Wordsworth," according to Edward Hoagland, the general editor of the Penguin Nature Library, to whom I owe this information, as well as a copy of the 1988 edition of Bartram's *Travels*, with an introduction by James Dickey (New York: Penguin). See also A. Curtis Wilgus, "Viajeros del siglo XIX: Henry Marie Brackenridge," *Américas* (OAS), 24, no. 4 (1972): 31–36. Melville, of course, not only traveled to Latin America, but left in *Benito Cereno* a literary record of that experience. See Estuardo Núñez, "Herman Melville en la América Latina," *Cuadernos Americanos* (Mexico), 12, no. 9 (1953): 209–221.

15. *El Plantel*, 2nd ser. (October 1838). On the foundation of the Royal Botanical Garden in Mexico City, see Engstrand, *Spanish Scientists*, pp. 19–21.

16. The tendency known in conventional literary history as *costumbrismo* is not free from the traveler's influential gaze. Costumbrismo, or the description of the quaint and unique, often the vestiges of colonial times, is in a way a description from the outside. That outside is the one furnished by a point of view that feels superior because of its knowledge of something else. That something else, if not always science, was at least a method, a way of looking.

17. Trifilo, "Nineteenth-Century English Travel Books on Argentina," pp. 491–492.

18. Miguel Rojas-Mix, "Las ideas artístico-científicas de Humboldt y su influencia en los artistas naturalistas que pasan a América a mediados del siglo XIX" in *Nouveau Monde et renouveau de l'histoire naturelle*, présentation M. C. Bénassy-Berling (Paris: Service des Publications Université de la Sorbonne Nouvelle, 1986), pp. 85–114. Rojas-Mix studies the influence of Humboldt on painters like the ones mentioned in the next note. Humboldt was himself an artist, as Rojas-Mix reports, and even wrote one volume of poetry, *Die Lebenskraft oder der rhodische Genius*, which has been studied, in conjunction with his scientific ideas, by Cedric Hentschel, "Zur Synthese von Literatur und Naturwissenschaft bein Alexander von Humboldt" in *Alexander von Humboldt: Werk und Weltgeltung*, ed. Heinrich Pfeiffer (Munich: Piper, 1969), pp. 31–95.

19. I am guided here by Verlyn Klinkenborg's description of the manuscript in the exquisite exhibition catalogue *Sir Francis Drake and the Age of Discovery* (New York: The Pierpont Morgan Library, 1988). It seems that Drake was not only accompanied by artists in his travels but was himself a deft painter of natural phenomena. On the artists, see Donald C. Cutter and

Mercedes Palau de Iglesias, "Malaspina's Artists," in *The Malaspina Expedition* (Santa Fe: Museum of New Mexico Press, 1963); Donald C. Cutter, "Early Spanish Artists on the Northwest Coast," *Pacific Northwest Quarterly* 54 (1963): 150–157; Iris H. W. Engstrand, *Spanish Scientists;* Barbara Stafford, "Rude Sublime: The Taste for Nature's Colossi . . ." *Gazette des Beaux Arts* (April 1976): 113–126; José Torre Revello, *Los artistas pintores de la expedición Malaspina* (Buenos Aires: Universidad de Buenos Aires, Instituto de Investigaciones Históricas de la Facultad de Filosofía y Letras, 1944). There is an anonymous note on an exhibition of prints from travel books in *Americas* (OAS), 5, no. 10 (1953): 24–26. In Cuba the books by La Plante and Irene Wright became classics. It is quite possible that a book such as Neruda's *Arte de pájaros* was inspired by some of the works of artists contained in travel books. Nicolás Guillén's *El gran Zoo* appears to follow the same format. Though not normally considered as part of art history, the works produced by these artists were often of superb quality and should be recognized for shaping an artistic vision of the New World. Gabriel García Márquez avers that he looked at drawings from travel books when writing *El amor en los tiempos del cólera;* see Raymond Leslie Williams, "The Visual Arts, the Poetization of Space and Writing: An Interview with Gabriel García Márquez," *Publications of the Modern Language Association of America* 104 (1989): 131–141.

20. Rob Rachowiecki writes, in an article relating a journey to Mount Roraima, in the area of Guayana visited by Carpentier when he was writing *Los pasos perdidos:* "The plateau summits of the *tepuís* are separated from their surroundings by almost impenetrable cliffs, and they harbor a flora and fauna that is not only distinct from the lowlands, but is different from mountain to mountain. Indeed, so remote are the summits that 19th century scientists debated the possibility of prehistoric dinosaurs surviving atop the isolated massifs. This idea was popularized by Sir Arthur Conan Doyle's science fiction novel, *The Lost World*, published in 1912. The book is said to have been based on Roraima and the 'lost world' tag has stuck to this day." "The Lost World of Venezuela," *Américas* (OAS) 4, no. 5 (1988): 46.

21. I am guided here, above all, by Michel Foucault's *Les Mots et les choses* (Paris: Gallimard, 1966) and Arthur O. Lovejoy, *The Great Chain of Being* (Cambridge: Harvard University Press, 1936).

22. Antonello Gerbi, *Nature in the New World from Christopher Columbus to Gonzalo Fernández de Oviedo*, trans. Jeremy Moyle (Pittsburgh: University of Pittsburgh Press, 1985 [1975]).

23. "Überhaupt ist mit dem neuen Leben, das einem nachdenkenden Menschen die Betrachtung eines neuen Landes gewärt, nichts zu vergleichen. Ob ich gleich noch immer derselbe bin, so mein'ich, bis aufs innerste Knochenmark verändert zu sein." In *Italienische Reise, Goethes Werke* (Hamburg: Christian Wegner Verlag, 1950 [1967]), 12:146. I have learned much about this "grand tour" from a paper by my dear friend Giuseppe Mazzotta,

which centers on W. H. Auden's poem "Good-bye to the Mezzogiorno" and reviews the works of travelers through Calabria in the nineteenth century. The paper is entitled "Travelling South" and is unpublished.

24. Larra casts a critical view on his own country in his famous essay "La diligencia," which is a kind of travel account of his journeys through the provinces of Spain. He had spent a good deal of time in France and looked upon Spain from the perspective of a foreigner. Fernán Caballero, in her novel *La gaviota* (Madrid: Espasa Calpe, 1960 [1849]), includes a footnote to justify a lengthy description of a convent. Her reason is that such a description "tendría interés para los extranjeros que no conocen nuestros bellos y magnos edificios religiosos" (p. 33). In a sense her book, along with much of costumbrismo in both Spain and Spanish America, appears as a travelogue for foreigners and city dwellers.

25. Villaverde's book is modeled after those of the European travelers and narrates an experience that in some ways anticipates the plot of Carpentier's *Los pasos perdidos*. See Antonio Benítez Rojo's chapter in *La isla que se repite* (Hanover, N.H.: Ediciones del Norte, 1989). There is a modern edition of Villaverde's book (Havana: Editorial Letras Cubanas, 1981).

The most advanced work on the countess is Adriana Méndez Rodenas's "A Journey to the (Literary) Source: The Invention of Origins in Merlín's *Viaje a La Habana*," which I have read in manuscript thanks to the kindness of the author.

26. Thomas Belt, *The Naturalist in Nicaragua*, foreword by Daniel H. Janzen (Chicago: University of Chicago Press, 1985), p. 147. The first edition is from 1874. Belt was an English engineer whose work was much admired by Darwin.

27. Goodman, *The Explorers of South America*, p. 191.

28. George Gaylord Simpson, *Splendid Isolation: The Curious History of South American Mammals* (New Haven: Yale University Press, 1980) and *Discoverers of the Lost World: An Account of Some of Those Who Brought Back to Life South American Mammals Long Buried in the Abyss of Time* (New Haven: Yale University Press, 1984). Sarmiento, who seems to have had time to read everything, knew the work of some of these paleontologists well, above all that of Argentine Francisco J. Muñiz, whose biography he wrote. It is now collected in vol. 43 of *Obras de Domingo F. Sarmiento* (Buenos Aires: Imprenta y Litografía Mariano Moreno, 1900).

29. I quote from *Facundo o civilización y barbarie en las pampas argentinas*, fijación del texto, prólogo y apéndices de Raúl Moglia; xilografías de Nicasio (Buenos Aires: Ediciones Peuser, 1955). The translation in this case is mine. Unless otherwise indicated translations are from *Life in the Argentine Republic in the Days of the Tyrants; or, Civilization and Barbarism*, with a biographical sketch of the author by Mrs. Horace Mann; 1st American from the 3rd Spanish ed. (New York, 1868; reprint, New York: Hafner Library of Classics, 1960).

30. I have used C. Harvey Gardiner's edition (Carbondale: Southern Illinois University Press, 1967). The original is from 1826.

31. Edward W. Said, *Orientalism* (New York: Vintage Books, 1979).

32. I take the information and the quote from Mary Sayre Haverstock, "The Cosmos Recaptured," *Américas* (OAS), 35, no. 1 (1983): 41.

33. Amado Alonso, *Estudios lingüísticos: Temas hispanoamericanos*, 3rd ed. (Madrid: Gredos, 1976), p. 55.

3

SARMIENTO: HIS MODELS AND HIS RECEPTION

14 Sarmiento: Casting the Reader, 1839–1845

ADOLFO PRIETO

When Mariano José de Larra wrote for *El Pobrecito Hablador* in 1832, he was so familiar with the contemporary journalistic practice of occasionally probing into the nature of the readership who supported the press that, rather than elaborating a personal version of this practice, he limited himself to freely transcribing Victor de Jouy's article "Le public," written some twenty years before in Paris. Larra's blatant appropriation of de Jouy's text indicates that he intended to probe into the same subject, and to venture into a field that knew no boundaries other than those provided by linguistic peculiarities and local customs.[1] In his article ("Who Is the Reading Public and Where Can It Be Found?") Larra will characterize those boundaries via references to several Madrid social spots: the church, the salons, the cafés, and the theater. Also, by reference to the occupations and customs of the local residents. Such references did not mar the general flow of the text.[2]

Just six years after this exercise in discursive montage, Juan Bautista Alberdi, in Buenos Aires, was poised for a similar repetition. At least the use of the pseudonym "Figarillo" with which Alberdi signed his articles in *La Moda*, bespoke both admiration for the model and a commitment to apply it to the specific sociocultural context of Buenos Aires. Nevertheless, the modest impact of the weekly's first issues prompted Alberdi to try to understand his readership. His attempt underscored the distance between the journalistic practices of *El Pobrecito Hablador* and *La Moda*. "Figaro" (Larra) had set out to prove the diversity, complexity, and elusive character of the readership. "Figarillo" practically set out to verify its nonexistence. Larra had sought and found the local elements that fitted his discourse; Alberdi went about proving both the difficulty of visualizing the components of the Buenos Aires readership as well as his own incompetence with respect to defining the terms of his search.

In his articles "Predicar en desiertos" and "Un papel popular," Alberdi addressed both the difficulty and the incompetence. He admitted that the frivolity of the first issues of the weekly was owing to their appeal to the business community. He further added that the readership targeted was that of "girls and young men inclined toward business." In the first of these articles, he concluded that "to write for businessmen, peasants, herders, craftsmen, and workers of any type is to preach in the desert. They do not read nor have they ever." But he then added that one should write for the people in order to enlighten them. The people he referred to, however, had to be differentiated from the masses, from the multitude, from the conglomerate of people that neither know nor think.[3]

In order to establish this distinction, Alberdi chose as examples a woman, a merchant, a general store and tavern owner, and a shoemaker. To the vague and abstract categories of businessman, peasant, herder, and worker he now added an arbitrary and incoherent new formula. These "four persons representative of the most populous classes in society" were, in principle, "a population in miniature." Nevertheless, when he proceeded to examine each component, he concluded that because of their common proclivity toward the grossest materialism, and their shared ignorance, they represented not the people, but the masses. "The people" thus remained undefined as an idea for the future. The masses would be able to achieve the status of people only by means of instruction. The writer, Alberdi concluded, should persist in his mission of addressing the crowd anyway; it was the duty of the moment, the contribution of the present to the future. Therefore, "one should write for a woman, a shoemaker, a merchant, or grocer," he stated, "without paying any attention to what they may say. They have no voice in the matter. They are the masses."

Larra's model had a substantially different effect on the pages of *El Zonda*, published in San Juan a little more than a year after the termination of *La Moda*. One of *El Zonda*'s writers, Quiroga Rosas, had contributed to the now-defunct Buenos Aires weekly. This link further reinforced the close affiliation between the two projects as well as the community of political and cultural interests that characterized their respective supporters. Another member of its founding group, Sarmiento, had written to Alberdi in order to salute him as one of the intellectual promises of the Republic. With these many connections, then, it is not surprising that some of the topics and expressive codes of Larra's journalism utilized by *La Moda* would freely circulate in the columns of *El Zonda*. What *is* surprising is the pragmatism with which these topics were elaborated and the intensity with which some of these expressive codes were charged.

Thus Sarmiento, the irrepressible writer of the July 20, 1839, editorial, set out to examine the nature of his readership. He began by estimating the potential size of the readership on the basis of the total population of San Juan. Then he estimated the size of the actual readership, in relation to the practice of reading and, only secondarily, in relation to such factors as social condition, sex, or occupation. Hence, in a population of some thirty thousand, twenty-five thousand are excluded because they are illiterate. Of the five thousand who are literate, four thousand have virtually lost this skill for lack of use. Of the one thousand remaining, our editorialist considers it prudent to cut a further six hundred, since not everyone will be interested in the material the weekly may publish. Now there are four hundred, half of whom are not the kind of people who would be interested in *El Zonda*. Of the two hundred people who survive this Sarmientine scrutiny, one hundred and fifty will certainly read the periodical, but many of their copies will have been borrowed, which means that the effective number of readers—that is to say, subscribers—can be reduced to fifty.

Nevertheless, the inverted pyramid sketched by Sarmiento did not cause him to follow Alberdi's recommendations for *La Moda*. These fifty inhabitants for whom the practice of reading presupposed the habit of supporting the press were perceived by Sarmiento as a mere statistical fact.[4] Of course, these calculations seemed appropriate for the cloistered society of San Juan. It is also true that the breakdown of this population into fifty subscribing readers made this figure suspiciously close to the number of contributors needed to cover the costs of printing the paper. Although such a fact was of little relevance to the young professionals who defrayed the costs of *La Moda*, it was of primary importance for the journalists of *El Zonda*, and in particular for Sarmiento. He was concurrently Director of the Official Press of San Juan, where the weekly was published under the condition that all printing costs would be reimbursed to the provincial treasury.[5]

Whatever the circumstances surrounding the mapping of the readership, it is clear that these calculations revealed the modus operandi of Sarmiento the writer. They showed his need to insert himself in the context of a tangible and verifiable readership, as well as his need to identify a group on which to test his writings and hear the echo of his own voice.

Surely, no one knew as well as Sarmiento that his domestic audience contradicted both his less-than-modest aspirations to recognition and his professed faith in the universal dissemination of the press. No one knew, as Sarmiento himself hastened to admit, that his own self would become a collective audience of tremendous scope. Optimistically he wrote that

> the advertisements, the announcements, the subscriptions outside San Juan and . . . furthermore, the practice of reading will restore those 4,000 we calculated as having forgotten [how to read]. Curiosity will tempt the other 600 who would not bother with our publication; of the 200 that are left, some will die, some will find reading less improper and, finally, schoolchildren will have grown up with a love for reading . . . which will increase our readership to such a degree that we are filled with pride and pleasure just imagining all of those people engulfed in the reading of El Zonda.[6]

The long-term effect that the schools could have on the recruitment of readers for El Zonda, a periodical that existed for barely six weeks, is indicative of great expectations concerning the role of education in training a readership. While that training was in progress (as part of a vast enterprise in which Sarmiento reserved for himself a prominent role), the circle of domestic readers had to broaden, then, in numbers proportionally higher than those already available, by means of a persuasion generated by the press itself.

The writer of El Zonda, with an optimism that will characterize his most personal endeavors, took for granted the success of this recruitment operation. As could be expected, however, in six issues the weekly was unable to demonstrate its power of persuasion. Nor was Sarmiento able to do so during his early contact with the Chilean press, even though his numerous articles written between 1841 and 1842 for El Mercurio and El Nacional of Valparaíso won him sufficient professional prestige to make him, as of November 1842, the visible head of El Progreso, the first daily newspaper in the Chilean capital.[7]

It was in Chile that Sarmiento resumed the journalistic practices so abruptly interrupted in San Juan, and he did so in ways that reflected his previous experience. As in the case of El Zonda, he assumed direct responsibility for the success or failure of this journalistic endeavor. Yet his first journalistic experience took place in his native community while the second had to be realized in a foreign country. As with El Zonda, the main task was to build a readership that could financially support the paper; in contrast to the experience of El Zonda, however, this readership did not exist as a mere fact of reality, but rather as a hypothesis to be verified by a no less hypothetical process of familiarization. To the fifty readers considered necessary to ensure the survival of El Zonda, Sarmiento had to add the larger number of potential readers from San Juan. To the two hundred considered essential to fund the publication of *El Progreso*, he had to add the larger potential readership of Chile. But while he had only a month and a half at *El Zonda* to prove his first hypothesis, he would have almost three years and nine hundred issues of *El Progreso* to prove the second. This is an important period not only in terms of time but also in terms of writing, for this is the extended moment when Sarmiento wrote and published the *Facundo*.

The problems of attribution that surround a good part of Sarmiento's journalistic writing have been acknowledged by the author himself or by the editor of his complete works. The resulting uncertainty does not, however, appear to affect most of the articles that define the editorial policy of *El Progreso*, those with which Sarmiento sought to build a Chilean following. After the predictably enthusiastic announcement of the paper's prospectus, after considering the impact that the first daily of Santiago should have over the eighty thousand inhabitants of the city, after feeling justified, after all his calculations, in expecting the spontaneous appearance of hundreds (if not thousands) of subscribers, Sarmiento faced reality in the fifth issue (November 14, 1842) by accepting the actual size of his readership and by preparing himself to initiate a process of mutual acquaintance.

In that issue of *El Progreso*, Sarmiento described a meeting with a French lithographer residing in Santiago. His interlocutor had attempted to establish a price range for lithographs based on the number of subscribers:

> "[A]ssuming that you might not have more than four thousand subscribers," said the lithographer . . . "this city has so many inhabitants. In France, four thousand subscribers can be counted for *Le National*, thirty thousand for *Le Quotidien*, fifty thousand for *Le . . . Le.*"
>
> "Quiet, man," interrupted the writer, "stop talking nonsense. Four thousand subscribers in Santiago!"
>
> "But you will have two thousand at least?"
>
> "Not that many either."
>
> "A thousand."
>
> "Less."
>
> "*Alors*, five hundred."
>
> "Not even close."
>
> "Oh, you are joking, *ça* is not possible."
>
> "Well, believe it or not . . . I'll bet you can't guess how many subscribers we have?"
>
> "In that case you must have no fewer than three hundred."
>
> "Bah! not even close, lower your sights."

"Two hundred and fifty?"

"Lower."

"Two hundred?"

"Even lower, as low as you want . . ."

"Well, then, what shall we do to make the illustrations inexpensive?"

"By barely pressing the plate, so that little ink is wasted and the price can go down. Oh, it is magnificent! You print your design so softly, so superficially that it can barely, just barely be distinguished by the subscribers. In this way, the crane-necked reader that gets within a half a yard of a man reading his *own* paper, cannot see more than a white spot, even if he squints his eyes or puts on glasses."[8]

In this street scene, which makes suggestions for the punishment of readers who indulge in the habit of reading papers without buying them, one can observe how Sarmiento admitted the crudeness of his own calculations, adjusting to the actual size of an audience that could share his identification—and mockery—of the crane-necked reader, that strange species which read borrowed papers in a community of sparse readers. Sarmiento made sure that this voyeur of the Chilean press could not but be recognized by the brotherhood of subscribers to *El Progreso*.

Sarmiento addressed this brotherhood again two days later, in order to inform them of how slowly the list of members was growing. He also announced the good news that eight hacienda owners in Maipó had discussed "measures for providing for their daily delivery of *El Progreso*" and that, the previous evening, the paper had received the subscription of "a poor shoemaker in association with a neighboring wine trader. We hasten to announce this," he added, "because it demonstrates that the day the barrier between our working classes and the movement of ideas and public interest will fall is close at hand."[9] In the issue of November 18, he communicated to the members of that same brotherhood (dispersed throughout the city of Santiago and in the villas of the surrounding area) that the dissemination of the paper required that they visit those neighbors who were not acquainted with it and convey to them the benefits of learning about it. To this end, Sarmiento provided them with the following script:

"How are you, neighbor? Is your little girl better? She's come down with scarlet fever? Say, neighbor, has your copy of *El Progreso* been delivered?" "What do you mean, 'What *Progreso*?' " (you must look astonished). "Neighbor, my God!" (put your hands on your head in a gesture of shame). "What is it I'm hearing? You do not subscribe to the first daily of Santiago! What, then, can be expected of unenlightened, ignorant men who live with no knowledge of what goes on or what is being thought and said. I wouldn't have believed that of you, neighbor."

"But neighbor, I truly don't know what you're talking about; I just returned from my hacienda, and I'm not in touch . . ."

"Well listen, a magnificent newspaper has begun to be published. It is as big as this table and is written with huge letters. It talks about everything, and it intends to speak about much more, if it finds enough subscribers to finance it all . . . Everyone who's anyone in Santiago has subscribed, except the merchants, the judges, the clerks, the notaries, the military, the young people, the old people, and one or two more . . ."[10]

In the issue for November 26, Sarmiento wrote in a more conventional tone, perhaps to prevent any upset provoked in some individuals by the familiarity of some of the allusions, about the necessity of gathering at least two hundred subscribers in order to cover printing costs.[11] However, a few days later, on a separate page addressed to "those not subscribing to El Progreso," he reproduced a large image of two feminine figures and two angels who, in tears, are guarding a catafalque bearing the following inscription: "Would you want to see me in the Pantheon for not having given two pesos?" In the text that accompanied this sharp graphic demonstration, Sarmiento returned to the reprimands against the potential reader who, out of habit or plain meanness, refused to pay for the paper he read: "The fact is that this illustrious city has very bad habits regarding subscriptions. The wealthy cream of society approaches just anyone to read the newspaper: as if this anyone had paid nothing for it."

The inflection of the voice that declares the necessity of incorporating such dawdlers into the readership of El Progreso becomes recomposed only when those addressed are the established subscribers. After five months of publication, in the April 10, 1843, issue, an editorial note apologized for the distribution problems of the previous evening. "Yesterday, more than one hundred subscribers, that is to say, nearly all of them, failed to receive their papers," admitted the writer of El Progreso. In an effort to explain what happened, he frankly stated that two of the paper's distributors had killed some time in a tavern, consuming more alcohol than the fulfillment of their obligations permitted. He proceeded to beg forgiveness by stating that there was no way to keep those in charge of distribution from "killing time where time is exchanged for liquor."[12]

It should be noted that the expectations of fast growth declared in the "Prospectus" were justified at least during the paper's initial months of circulation. Indeed, the regular inclusion of serials translated from the most famous European books, a fashion page, statistics, lithographs—all intensely promoted in the first issues—were used as lures in the manner of the great newspapers of Europe and the United States. The frank presumption of the effectiveness of these lures is apparent in issue no. 45, where it was anticipated that in the immediate future *El Progreso* would increase its circulation to fifteen hundred copies in order to distribute in the provinces. This expectation was never fulfilled.[13] Still, in 1849, upon returning from his travels in Europe and the United States, Sarmiento believed it fitting to emphasize the public acceptance of his new newspaper, *La Crónica*, by printing in capital letters on its editorial page the number THREE HUNDRED AND SIXTY-EIGHT SUBSCRIBERS, a figure proposed as an approximate ceiling for the newspapers of Chile throughout the decade or, at least, a reliable parameter.[14]

Although the expectations of expansion were disappointing, financial support for *El Progreso* did materialize, despite the modest size of the readership. Government support in the form of subscriptions to the paper, as well as through the printing of official announcements, helped redress the paper's economic woes. On August 28, 1843, an article signed by "The Editors" defended such support against attacks on the part of an opposition congressman. To assist the press financially is not the same as to hire it, argued the editors; it is merely to permit the existence of the press in a society that will not support it with subscriptions. Ten years later, the same argument was made in a much more sensitive context: the dispute that followed Alberdi's publication of the first of his *Cartas quillotanas*.[15]

Long before the newspaper had completed a single year of existence, Sarmiento had no doubts about the limits of its expansion, nor about the relative stability of its assumed domestic readership. And under these conditions, the process of familiarization that was part of the creation of such a readership began to manifest clear signs of reversion. The familiarization of the reader implied, in effect, a relationship between reader and writer. During this process, Sarmiento never failed to register the progress of this identification mechanism or to promote its utilization.

As early as March 1843 (that is to say, in the fifth month of the newspaper's circulation) an editorial note responding to attacks against a previously published article stated:

> It is well known that *El Progreso* was born one day in Santiago at noon, and no one has greater rights to nationality than it has. However, one of its writers who did not have such luck and whom, for this reason only, we are all tempted to throw out, has acquired at an unfor-

tunate moment something that is not precisely fame, and unde-servedly so. We will call it *publicity* because it is the only word that can characterize the misfortune that has become him. When *El Progreso* says something that does not set well with the opinions of some-one or another, it is not the paper that is attacked, but rather the evil member on the staff.[16]

Perceived from the outside, the foreigner Sarmiento was viewed as a jour-nalist with an established readership who could, or should, influence pub-lic affairs. This clout, whether it helped or hindered the editor or the paper itself, was sharply resented by those sectors opposing the official line of *El Progreso*. The militancy of these opposition sectors soon made a change advisable. On March 21, 1844, an editorial note signed by Antonio Vidal announced changes in format and graphic design as well as the introduc-tion of a new body of writers whose names would not be disclosed; im-plied was the exclusion of Sarmiento, founder and main writer for *El Progreso*.[17]

The exclusion, it became clear, was only cosmetic. It was neat enough to prevent the opposition press from attributing everything expressed in *El Progreso* to Sarmiento, yet lax enough to permit Sarmiento, this time using his own name, to continue writing as a special collaborator. This change, of course, strengthened the mechanisms of identification with the readership by suppressing the unnecessary overlap of anonyms. It also helped to promote the idea that Sarmiento was much less interested in performing a role in the internal politics of Chile than he was in con-structing the image of a political, moral, and literary personality.

It may seem paradoxical, after the consolidation of his public image, that Sarmiento would continue to use such old strategies as making room in the pages of *El Progreso* for the grossest diatribes contrived by his opposition. Yet these diatribes, exemplified by the article "The Stable of Progress," were less a sign of the journalistic habits of the times than they were a part of the publicity that "the evil writer" required in order to gather the support of his readership.[18] Given the substance and abun-dance of these insults, it is possible to determine some aspects of Sarmien-to's public image. The ire stirred by his linguistic reform project among certain conservative groups illustrates one aspect.[19] Another is exempli-fied by the political campaign in which his name appeared in association with that of Minister Manuel Montt. Sarmiento, as was his custom, re-produced some of the texts printed in the opposition papers, commenting on them with a vehemence that already distinguished his polemical prose. Clearly, Sarmiento did not have as much influence in Chilean politics as his adversaries believed; however, in the association that the opposition press established with the powerful government minister, he surmised the resentment caused by his relationship to Montt.[20]

In the heat of debate Sarmiento launched the following war dispatch: "Are there personalities against us? In those cases we will resort to the truncheon. They do not exist? We will assume that they come in disguise." The opposition press responded with its own attacks, as summarized in Sarmiento's version:

> Nothing more was needed by the liberal *La Correspondencia* and other decent, moderate, and energetic papers to pull out the truncheon and thwap! thwap! thwap! thrash the man who was going to play each personality against another. . . . *El Siglo* . . . hurls its editorials at Sarmiento, whom it refers to as no-account, rancher, Sargento Pino, imbecile, madcap. One challenges him in the press, another recommends he be spat upon; and all for what? For the horror of personalities harbored by these souls. Never will *La Correspondencia* nor *El Siglo* tolerate the existence of personalities in the press![21]

Despite all the egotistical preoccupation offered by this material, one can observe that the war of communiqués coincided precisely with the final installments of *Facundo* in *El Progreso* in June 1845. In the intersections of this chronology, personality also signified for Sarmiento the backing that the *Facundo* needed in order to justify his intervention, not in Chilean matters but in those of the River Plate region. Sarmiento concluded that the success of the campaign of the opposition press could achieve two objectives at that time: namely, making him leave *El Progreso* and "serving the interests of Rosas, who, unable to find anyone in Chile willing to defend his government, would be happy at least if such a wily writer could be removed from the press."[22]

Notes

1. Because of the French Revolution and the Industrial Revolution, the notions of "public sphere," "audience," or "reading public," so long established in Europe, suffered profound alterations. It is not, therefore, surprising to find that in the late eighteenth and early nineteenth centuries efforts were made to understand the nature of these alterations, to measure the growth and the internal fragmentation of the new audiences, and even to localize a social setting for reading. See Jon P. Klancher, *The Making of English Audiences, 1790–1832* (Madison: University of Wisconsin Press, 1987); James Smith Allen, *Popular French Romanticism: Authors, Readers, and Books in the 19th Century* (Syracuse: Syracuse University Press, 1981).

2. In the edition of this article presented in *Larra. Artículos de costumbres*

(Madrid: Clásicos Castellanos, 1942) and in *Obras de D. Mariano José Larra* (Madrid: Real Academia Española, 1960), the following appears as a subtitle: "Artículo mutilado, o sea refundido. Hermite de la Chaussée d'Antin." In *Obras de D. Mariano José de Larra* (Barcelona: Biblioteca Clásica Española, 1885) and in another, updated edition from Garnier that alone reproduces the prologue from the complete works published in Madrid in 1843, the subtitle changes to: "Artículo robado." This second version textually responds to what Larra himself said in "Dos palabras," which precedes *El Pobrecito Hablador*: "So there will be articles that are someone else's cloak with new concealments. Today's will be of this sort. Furthermore, who is to deny that similar articles do not pertain to us after we have stolen them? Undoubtedly they will be ours by right of conquest." A simple comparison with the text of de Jouy, published on May 2, 1812, illuminates these statements: the idea of "homage" seems to capture the intent of the procedure. See also Susan Kirkpatrick, *Larra, un laberinto intrincado* (Madrid: Gredos, 1977).

3. *La Moda*, Buenos Aires, March 10 and 17, 1838, respectively.

4. *El Zonda. Periódico semanal*, San Juan, no. 1, Saturday, July 20, 1839.

5. Regarding this point, see Paul Verdevoye, *Domingo Faustino Sarmiento, éducateur et publiciste (entre 1839 et 1852)* (Paris: Centre de Recherches de l'Institut d'Etudes Hispaniques, Institut des Hautes Etudes de l'Amérique Latine, 1963.

6. *El Zonda*, no. 1 (see n. 4, above).

7. In the "Prospectus," a leaflet that would be reprinted in the first issue of *El Progreso*, November 10, 1842, the following is highlighted: "To establish a newspaper in the capital of our Republic is the same as elevating the rank it deserves by merit of the culture of its inhabitants, the industriousness of the city, and the influence it exercises over the rest of the nation."

8. *El Progreso*, no. 5, November 14, 1842.

9. *El Progreso*, no. 6, November 16, 1842. At various times during his journalistic career, Sarmiento had the opportunity to sharpen his vision of social issues. In the passage quoted, apart from his obvious propagandistic intention, it is possible to observe a clear articulation of the concept of "working class" and the implicit formulation of a program of education designed to incorporate that class into the "movement of ideas and public interest." The events of 1848 in France reinforced both his interest in social issues and his exclusive faith in the mechanisms of political control and popular education. In any case, during the Chilean upheaval of 1851, novelized by Alberto Blest Gana in *Martín Rivas*, Sarmiento showed no sympathy for the rebels; he even participated actively in the repression of the uprising. See Luis Alberto Romero, "Sarmiento, testigo y testimonio de la sociedad de Santiago," *Revista Iberoamericana* 143 (April–June 1988): 461–475.

10. *El Progreso*, no. 8, November 18, 1842.

11. *El Progreso*, no. 15, November 26, 1842. In order to attract subscribers to the newspaper, Sarmiento reports on the readership of other Latin Ameri-

can cities: "There are in Buenos Aires, and there have been for the past twenty years, two and three thousand subscribers to the different papers. In Montevideo the figure stands above a thousand for the Spanish, French, English, and Italian papers; even in Lima, El Comercio has more than eight hundred; and in Santiago we cannot secure enough subscribers to support a fledgling publication whose length, interest, and importance always stand in relationship to the number of subscribers."

12. El Progreso, no. 127, April 10, 1843.

13. In the collection of El Progreso at the National Library of Santiago de Chile, there is no trace of the actual existence of a "Fashion Page." In any case, its mere mention, together with the material included in the brief series of "Letters to Rosa" (its attribution to Sarmiento should be carefully examined), is evidence of an effort to recruit female readers, a group whose potential readership probably exceeded that of men.

14. La Crónica, May 13, 1849.

15. In the course of this debate, Alberdi repeatedly accused Sarmiento of being a government-paid hack, and it is probable that no other accusation was so intensely resented as this one. Three years earlier, as if anticipating this attack, Sarmiento published in La Crónica an article about press subsidies in which he admitted that without the support of the government, neither Valparaíso's El Mercurio nor Santiago's El Progreso, founded by him, could have survived, at least during their initial periods. "Until 1842, there was no daily paper in Chile except the newspaper of Valparaíso which had eighteen subscribers in Santiago. The government, therefore, wanted to anticipate the habits of the population by favoring the publication of a paper that could not survive by its own means. Upon attempting to establish a daily in the capital, it was necessary to keep in mind the same rationale, especially since a similar attempt had failed once before. But the paper filled a void, already acutely sensed by public men" (La Crónica, no. 24, July 17, 1849).

16. El Progreso, no. 110, March 20, 1843. In the same year, it should be remembered, El Progreso published the serial Mi defensa.

17. El Progreso, no. 420, March 21, 1844.

18. El Progreso, no. 473, May 21, 1844. Under Sarmiento's signature, the editors of El Progreso are invited to reproduce, for four consecutive days, an "announcement" published the day before in El Siglo. The announcement, titled "The Stable of Progress," read as follows:

All coachmen who wish to buy a good selection of horses from the Cuyo region, which, in addition to their characteristic qualities, are educated with modern methodology under the direction of a highly civilized native of Cuyo, can come by the offices of El Progreso because someone there will be able to help. These horses know how to read and write with the American spelling system designed with glory and honor by Monsieur Sarmiento, or "maestro" as he is called by El Progreso. They run backward and forward like few others; they whinny with the mastery that their fellow parrots use in their speaking and writing; and, finally, they are good little animals even for pulling carts carrying the heaviest loads produced in Argentina: their writers.

Sarmiento justifies his request to reproduce the announcement in this fashion:

> There are certain things that do not deserve to be answered, and persons from whom it would be exorbitant to expect justice or restraint. They are made this way and are beyond polishing.
> Concerning the judgment passed by Mr. Espejo on the American spelling system: as with all my poor literary works, it is the same one to which the press has accustomed me. My name has never appeared in it, if not marinated with the juices of vexation and insults.

19. The report by Sarmiento on the spelling reform was approved by the Faculty of Philosophy and Humanities in April 1844. In the letter of approval, all newspapers are invited to adopt the system. Sarmiento, of course, did so with great enthusiasm, but the opposition papers refused—at times, quite noisily. In *El Progreso*, no. 469, March 16, 1844, a note from *El Siglo* is humorously transcribed in the new spelling: "and if *El Progreso* and *La Gaceta* have done it, that is because of the intruding and idiotic pretension of the former to claim the reform as its own, and because the latter has believed itself obliged to do so in light of its close relations [with *El Progreso*]. *El Siglo*, which represents Chilean ideas and interests, has found itself as a stranger in the field of journalism." [TRANSLATOR'S NOTE: The transcription demonstrates the standardizing modifications attempted by the spelling reform, which attempted to suppress silent h's and accent marks, change y's to i's, and soft g's to j's. Thus: "i si el *Progreso* y la *Gaceta* lo an echo, es por la intrusa y necia pretensión del primero de mirar la reforma como suya, y porque la segunda se a creído obligada a virtud de las relaciones de paisanaje que la ligan con aquel. *El Siglo*, por representar ideas e intereses chilenos, se a encontrado extranjero en el campo de la prensa."]

20. *El Progreso*, no. 806, June 13, 1845.

21. *El Progreso*, no. 810, June 18, 1845.

22. *El Progreso*, no. 806, June 13, 1845.

15 Sarmiento and the Woman Question: From 1839 to the *Facundo*

ELIZABETH GARRELS

In 1839, with the founding of the Santa Rosa school for girls in San Juan, Argentina, Sarmiento inaugurated his lifelong public commitment to the education of women. A few texts of an institutional nature still survive from this early project: the *Prospecto de un establecimiento de educación para señoritas* (Prospectus for an Educational Establishment for Young Ladies); the *Constitución del Colegio de Señoritas de la Advocación de Santa Rosa de América* (Constitution for the School for Young Ladies of the Appellation of Saint Rose of America); and five speeches delivered by the director (Sarmiento) and four of his colleagues at the opening ceremony on July 9.[1] Of the three texts attributable to Sarmiento, the first two are the most substantial with regard to the subject of women and their ideal education. Seen within the entire corpus of Sarmiento's writings on the female sex during the period from 1839 to 1845, these texts—the most pragmatic, in that they attempt to institutionalize a specific educational experience—are also among the most conservative, since they emphasize, above all, the limitations or restrictions that should characterize a woman's life and training. Curiously, this markedly repressive quality will reappear toward the end of the period under consideration, while certain of the intervening texts will create a more permissive space in which to reflect upon even such a daring proposal as the possible emancipation of women in some distant future.

The *Prospecto* already sets forth a number of themes that will remain constant throughout these years. For example, it states that a principal goal of women's education is "to predispose them to be tender and tolerant wives, enlightened and moral mothers, diligent and thrifty heads of households," and it insists upon the influence that women exert upon men in the home and, more important still, the influence that they exert as mothers upon future generations: "Nothing is more evident than the way in which a man's character, his habits, likes and inclinations, show signs in adult life of the impressions he has received in his first years, in that age wherein education is confided to the tenderness of mothers."[2] This influence is considered so profound as to hold young ladies responsible for the backwardness "of youth in general" and to blame bad mothers for the misconduct of their sons in adult life: "nothing is more pernicious, nothing brings more transcendent consequences than the pampering, weakness, and indulgence by certain mothers who are too tender, too affectionate."[3]

What does in fact distinguish this text, though hardly rendering it unique among those studied, is its acceptance of the need to subjugate women, to deny them the same freedom of movement etc. that society allows men. "It is never too early," one reads, "to give habits of order, cleanliness, thrift, docility, and submission to a sex which, because of its needs and weakness, as well as our customs and institutions, must always be subjugated."[4]

Written by a man who would always show remarkable sensitivity to the ways in which social institutions and practices form the social subject, the *Constitución* proposes to materialize in an openly disciplinary manner the philosophy of subjugation that informs the *Prospecto*. Owing to its exceptional authoritarian rigor, the *Constitución* is a unique text among those consulted for this essay, and the reader should not lose sight of it when considering the less severe ideas that Sarmiento will express, always on a more abstract level, in later years.

The spirit of the *Constitución* is summed up in the following sentence:

> Good order depends on subordination, and therefore it is of the utmost importance that the boarders respect and obey their superiors, without contradicting them or opposing their orders, this infraction being considered one of the greatest that can be committed and therefore meriting the most severe punishments that the school can administer.[5]

The boarders shall submit to a highly regimented schedule and will be granted very few days to visit their families. "Prohibited" activities include "Reading any book whatsoever without the knowledge of the Headmistress," "All touching games," and "Undressing in the presence of roommates." In short, there is a concerted effort to control thought, body, and sexuality; however, prohibitions such as those against "All familiar forms of address" and "The use of nicknames," besides inculcating obedience, aim also at infusing the boarders with the abstract and homogenizing concept of republican citizenship.[6] Such a project reverberates throughout the speeches given at the school's inauguration ceremony, and all concur that the "republican mother" is the desired product of the new establishment. Idalecio Cortínez, for example, exhorts the students to "execute faithfully all they are ordered to do" because "then we will have enlightened matrons who produce grateful sons, solicitous fathers, industrious citizens, edifying preachers, men of great wisdom, and firm pillars of the nation's independence."[7]

Interestingly enough, a speech by Manuel José Quiroga Rosas criticizes the excessive dependence of women on their husbands and recommends that they be educated not to live in a cloister but in society, that they be inculcated with an idea of the fatherland, and that they acquire "those talents of industry" needed to secure their own subsistence. Although this relative liberality anticipates the tone of some of Sarmiento's later articles, it is no less true that these will also echo Quiroga's warning that the emancipation of the American woman must be gradual and not sudden "as some modern systems have attempted."[8] In fact, reading these speeches from 1839, one realizes that many of the ideas about women that Sarmiento developed in his journalism between 1841 and 1845 were already present within that circle of provincial friends (some of whom had studied in Buenos Aires), who for two years met in the evenings to discuss recent French publications belonging to the personal library of the young Quiroga Rosas.[9]

Saint-Simonianism, Women, and the Generation of 1837

Both *La Moda* (Buenos Aires, 1837–1838) and *El Iniciador* (Montevideo, 1838–1839), the two most representative organs of the fledgling Argentine Generation of 1837, show a sustained interest in the dignification of women in their dual role as wife and mother. On this issue, their main inspiration derives from France, in particular from Saint-Simonianism. Esteban Echeverría, who was both a member and a mentor of this generation, returned from France in mid-1830 "ready to propagate the philosophy of the Saint-Simonians." According to Juan Marichal, however, the two disciples of Saint-Simon who perhaps exercised the greatest influence on the young Argentines were Pierre Leroux and Jean Louis Eugène Lerminier, both dissidents who "abandoned Saint-Simonianism near the end of 1831."[10] Marichal does not specify the reason for this separation, but (at least in the case of Leroux and very possibly in that of Lerminier, since there were a number of defections for the same reason) it boils down to differing interpretations of the woman question.

The French Revolution had given rise to a brief but important flourishing of feminist activism, quickly suppressed by the Jacobins themselves. Shortly thereafter, the Napoleonic Code (1800–1804) served to institutionalize this antifeminist reaction, and in 1816 the law permitting divorce (passed in 1792) was finally repealed. According to Claire Goldberg Moses, who has written on French feminism in the nineteenth century, one would have to look to the novels of Madame de Staël (*Delphine*, 1802; *Corinne*, 1807) to find an expression of feminist aspirations during the first three decades of the new century in France.[11] It was not until around 1830 that feminism reemerged in the public sphere, and this was principally owing to the Saint-Simonians, now grouped under the leadership of Prosper Enfantin.[12]

The philosopher Saint-Simon, who died in 1825, had written extremely little on the female sex, but by 1831 the woman question had become a central preoccupation among his followers. Unlike Mary Wollstonecraft of England and other eighteenth-century feminists imbued with Enlightenment rationalism, Enfantin was a romantic. Also unlike Wollstonecraft, yet like the majority of his romantic contemporaries as well as most writers of the previous century, Enfantin believed that emotion and sensuality (matter and flesh) constituted the essence of woman, while reason (spirit and intelligence) defined the essence of man.[13] He was, however, distinct among his contemporaries in supporting the rehabilitation of sensuality and the flesh. A pacifist, he extolled the role of women in an imagined future where universal love and harmony would reign. Inspired by a phrase attributed to Saint-Simon—"l'homme et la femme voilà l'individu social"—Enfantin believed that the social nucleus of the future would be the couple, not the individual, and that within this ideal couple man and woman would fulfill different, sexually specific functions, though equal in value. Such complementarity rested on a belief in the equality of the sexes.[14] What prompted other Saint-Simonians to oppose Enfantin was his insistence that this equality would demand a new sexual morality, seen by many as a call to promiscuity. This proposal for sexual liberalization is what motivated Pierre Leroux and others to withdraw from the group at the end of 1831. A year later Enfantin, along with an associate, was jailed on charges of corrupting public morality.

The pages of *La Moda* and *El Iniciador*, full of ideas and attitudes consistent with Saint-Simonianism, cite the group and its members frequently. However, the young Miguel Cané begins one of his essays in *El Iniciador* by insisting on his differences with them:

> The disciples of Saint-Simon have said man and woman are the social individual; we declare that this opinion does not conform to our own. We do indeed think that woman needs an emancipation lifting her from the lamentable condition in which uses and customs less republi-

can than those necessary for our society have placed her, but we are
far from espousing that the female occupy the space that among us the
male himself does not know how to fill.[15]

Perhaps even more revealing is the comment made by Sarmiento in *El
Mercurio* of Valparaíso, Chile, in 1841. In a series of four articles in which
the young Argentine tries to elaborate something like a philosophy of
history by summarizing woman's condition throughout all of history and
prehistory, he inserts the following observation about Saint-Simonianism: "With Saint-Simon, philosophy and the restless spirit of progress
attempt to break with all the moral traditions and to emancipate woman
all at once from any dependence on man."[16] Some paragraphs later he
adds: "Woman will have to respect and submit herself to the ideas of the
historical period in which she lives; our age has watched the comedy that
Enfantin and the Saint-Simonians wished to represent fall apart amidst
the public's hisses, and it should not expose itself recklessly to new mock-
eries."[17]

An identification with many Saint-Simonian positions, including some
but not all of those concerning women, and a clear disavowal of the new
sexual morality espoused by Enfantin: such appears to have been the posture assumed by the young Generation of 1837 and by Sarmiento in particular, at least until his trip to Europe in 1845. The four *El Mercurio*
articles mentioned above are in fact a gold mine for evaluating the young
Sarmiento's ideas about women. His opinions on this subject, despite their
contradictions and even opportunistic shifts in emphasis, do not seem to
evolve during the four-year period that culminates in the publication of
the *Facundo* and Sarmiento's departure for Europe.

Sarmiento on Women:
El Mercurio, *August 20, 1841*

In the first of the four articles, Sarmiento defines his purpose as follows:
"We propose to dedicate some pages to the vindication of woman's right
to a serious cultivation of her mind, pointing out the objective toward
which her education should be directed, as well as the false path down
which it is presently led."[18] In the second article, he will state three other
purposes, one of which comes to dominate the rest of the series:

> To properly determine the moral rules that ought to guide the conduct
> of women in modern societies, it would be necessary, in addition to
> undertaking the study of the nature and instincts of her sex, to gauge
> precisely the degree of importance that she holds in the opinion of
> men and the role that this opinion has assigned her in civil society.[19]

The first of these objectives is prescriptive: to determine the moral rules that ought to guide the conduct of the modern woman. The second relates to an eagerness, already characteristic of a good many writers in the eighteenth century, to define the nature and instincts of the female sex.[20] Both these objectives reveal a singular confidence on the part of the male writer to define and classify women and then to make prescriptions regarding their conduct. The third objective, which determines the greater part of the remaining articles, also follows a convention rooted in the eighteenth century: that of reflecting on the role assigned to women in different types of societies. Sarmiento is encouraged to review the situation of women in what he calls the savage, the barbaric, and the civilized states, since the "opinion that man has formed of women has not been the same in all the various degrees of civilization among peoples."[21]

But let us look separately at each of the four articles. The first, as has already been noted, defends a woman's right to an education that will prepare her for "her high mission in contemporary society."[22] This mission is defined as "fulfilling the duties of motherhood . . . these being of such great importance since from the lap of the mother comes the man fully formed, with inclinations, character and habits which his first education molds."[23] Such primacy conferred upon motherhood in no way distinguishes Sarmiento from the immense majority of those writing about women in Europe and the Americas during these years. On the contrary, there seems to have been a consensus among conservatives and feminists alike that woman's primary social mission was precisely that of motherhood.[24]

Within this consensus, however, there were differences in emphasis, and it is undeniable that Sarmiento did not identify with the more progressive formulations. During these years, Sarmiento makes no distinction like that found in Mary Wollstonecraft's *Vindication of the Rights of Woman* (1792): "speaking of women at large, their first duty is to themselves as rational creatures, and the next, in point of importance, as citizens, is that, which includes so many, of a mother."[25] And he falls quite short of his North American contemporary Margaret Fuller, who, in her book *Woman in the Nineteenth Century* (1845), hardly mentions motherhood at all when speaking of a woman's right to education.[26] In like manner, it is fair to note that although Sarmiento and the others of his generation make reference to the Saint-Simonians, they remain silent about the female disciples of the movement, many of whom were published writers. One of the most radical, Claire Démar, went so far as to declare the end of motherhood as a career. She said that in order to emancipate herself, woman had to work, and that it was not possible for her to successfully combine work with child rearing. It was therefore necessary that the state, by hiring wet nurses, assume responsibility for child care.[27] Obviously this position, characteristic at best of a tiny minority, would have seemed scandalous to the youthful Generation of 1837.

If Mary Wollstonecraft's book represented a more extensive debate between Rousseau and those who defended woman's capacity for reason, Sarmiento tended to take sides with Rousseau. The first article in the 1841 series has a fairly eighteenth-century and conservative flavor with respect to what Sarmiento says about "the nature and instincts" of woman and "the false path down which [her education] is presently led." His condemnation of the latter echoes many of the complaints that appear in *La Moda* and *El Iniciador,* which in turn sound rather like those found in *La Quijotita y su prima* (1818) by the Mexican José Joaquín Fernández de Lizardi, or in Rousseau's *Emile:* namely, the denunciation of feminine attachment to luxury and fashion and of the danger posed by poorly educated women.[28]

Sarmiento and Louis Aimé Martin

The second article of the series begins with an epigraph from Louis Aimé Martin's book *De l'education des mères de famille,* originally published in France in 1834.[29] This book is of central importance in shaping Sarmiento's views on women during these years. Although the epigraph is the only explicit reference in the 1841 articles to Aimé Martin's book, Sarmiento borrows a good deal from the French moralist, including ideas and quotes from other authors. In his writings on women up through 1845, Sarmiento will return to Aimé Martin's book repeatedly, and in December 1842 he will publish translated passages from it in his Chilean newspaper *El Progreso.*[30]

Aimé Martin appears to have had much in common with the Saint-Simonians: he believed in uninterrupted progress; he was a pacifist and sought to regenerate humanity through the promotion of religious sentiment; he attacked materialism and egoism. The first part of Aimé Martin's book maintains that a woman's role as mother, and thus as transmitter of moral and religious sentiment to future generations, is the most important and sacred of missions. He claims that woman has the power to regenerate the world. His book is an apotheosis, so to speak, of woman as wife and mother. His two most evident masters are Fénelon and Rousseau, whom he considers pioneers for having recognized the need to educate women and for having understood the social importance of the family. However, unlike Rousseau and his "livre divin" (the fifth book of *Emile*), Aimé Martin does not mention women's defects, nor does he permit himself the misogynist sorties of his master. In sum, he suggests that his purpose is to modernize Rousseau for the nineteenth century.

The Second Article: El Mercurio, August 22, 1841

As stated above, Sarmiento's second article opens with an epigraph by Aimé Martin:

> Man cannot lower woman without himself falling into degradation; and by elevating her he improves himself. Societies are turned to brutes in her arms, or they are civilized at her feet. Let us take a look around the globe: we observe these two great divisions of the human race, the Orient and the West. Half of the ancient world remains motionless and without thought, under the weight of a barbarous civilization: women there are slaves. The other half marches toward equality and light: women are free and honored.[31]

In Aimé Martin, Sarmiento finds a congenial Orientalist mentality. Yet, the greater part of this article does not deal with the Orient, but rather with America and Africa. Sarmiento wants to present a panorama of the condition of woman throughout the evolutionary stages of the human species. His thesis, which finds ample support in the writings of Aimé Martin and a number of eighteenth-century writers is that "the level of importance that women enjoy among a given people always results from the level of that people's civilization; without fear of error, each measure of progress in the condition of the weaker sex can be attributed to an advance in civilization."[32] Such a thesis is consistent with the belief in uninterrupted progress so firmly rooted in the young Sarmiento, and it tends to foster a certain satisfaction with the present order of things. This complacency, which will be clearly expressed in the fourth article of the series, is at heart conservative in that it reduces the urgency of the need for change. Moreover, it undermines—and possibly contradicts—the protests in the first article against the deplorable education of contemporary women.

In this second article, Sarmiento focuses on the condition of women in what he considers to be the most primitive stage of the human race. He sums up this condition as follows: "[In savage life] *woman is seen by man as a degenerate member of his species.*"[33] Sarmiento starts from the idea, circulated in eighteenth-century travel writing, that the discovery of America revealed for the first time to the civilized world the nature of the primitive life of the species, since the American Indian supposedly continued to exist at the earliest stage of human evolution. For his discussion of the American Indian and the condition of women in the primitive state,

Sarmiento quotes extensively from the Scottish writer William Robertson, in particular from the fourth book of his *History of America* (1777).[34]
In fact, Sarmiento lifts about thirty lines from Robertson's text, or roughly
half of section 52 of book 4. We read:

> In America, their [women's] condition is so miserable, and so cruel the
> tyranny exercised over them, that the word "slavery" is not suffi-
> ciently expressive to give a just idea of their lamentable status. In
> some tribes woman is considered a beast of burden, destined to all la-
> bors and all hardships; while man spends the day in dissipation or
> idleness, woman is condemned to continual work.[35]

This vision, adapted to the supposed barbarism of the Argentine countryside, will be activated four years later when Sarmiento describes the life
of the gaucho woman at the end of the first chapter of the *Facundo*. Before
going on to consider woman in the state of barbarism, Sarmiento looks at
Africa, where he finds "pitiful displays of the degradation of women,"
including a practice incomprehensible to Europeans: "He [a Euro-
traveler] saw [the African queens] join together to form an impressive
bodyguard, and their majesties performed the office of messengers
throughout the whole monarchy."[36] Sarmiento concludes this section by
establishing a hierarchy that will function in his writing at least throughout the 1840s: "The black person of central Africa is not in every respect
as savage as the American Indian."[37] This is because he does not "still
wander through forests. . . . [H]e has a fixed domicile, and he has distributed and taken control of the land."[38]

The final part of the second article along with the first section of the
third article treat the subject of woman in the state of barbarism. Here
barbarism is Asia; Asia is the entire Orient; and the Orient is little more
than the harem. Like his mentor Aimé Martin, Sarmiento develops a vision of the seraglio that vacillates between fascination and censure—censure because monogamy does not exist in the harem and because woman
continues to have "a relative existence." Thus: "Let us not forget that
she is a simple ornament of man's life; the sort of happiness she will enjoy
will not be, then, in relation to the moral necessities of an intelligent
being working by itself for itself, but only relative to the man who has
found her good for his pleasures and has appropriated her."[39]

The Third Article: El Mercurio, *August 23, 1841*

The third article of the series briefly continues the discussion of Asia.[40] It
momentarily shifts its gaze from the harem to India, expressing horror

that for "the noble wife of a Hindu" it is not "honorable to survive her dead husband."[41] Then the text turns to consider certain "capital events" in the history of women within European civilization. The third article gets only as far as "the chivalric spirit" of the Middle Ages, but Sarmiento promises that these "capital events, judged in terms of their influence on woman, will suffice to lead us to her present condition, which in itself contains the elements of the future that awaits her."[42]

Sarmiento starts his journey through European history with a rather unenthusiastic vision of Greece and Rome: "The history of Greece and that of Rome, its successor in civilization, does not present sufficient facts for appreciating the social position of woman in detail; indeed, in those societies, she participated, insofar as it was compatible with civilized life, in the disadvantages of a more primitive stage of development."[43] However, he praises the Roman woman's vocation for republican motherhood and suggests that it was this female strength that "alone perhaps, laid the groundwork for Rome's greatness, inspiring its daughters with maternal virtues, like the mother of the Gracchi, who instead of jewels, proudly displayed the two sons she was rearing to be tribunes of the people."[44]

In those remote times, "a great step" was taken toward woman's ennoblement—the establishment of monogamy: "this fact, which distinguishes European civilization, henceforth assigned woman the high rank of man's companion, and called her at last to occupy the place to which nature had destined her."[45] In describing this seemingly natural place, Sarmiento articulates an entire political theory about the family, which is in fact the one he considers appropriate for his own century:

> In charge of the domestic hearth, adapting her occupations to her strengths and ability, and guiding the first steps of her progeny, she will give birth to the family, that is, that compact body, that embryo of society which reciprocally links its members by mutual affections and gives rise to ideas of authority, obligation, rights, along with the affections of the heart which are its strongest tie.[46]

From here, Sarmiento turns to Christianity's role in determining the position of women. Consistent with the Generation of 1837, Sarmiento defends a Christ of the masses—of the poor, the weak, the oppressed and, therefore, of women, whose equality with men Christ came to reveal. Sarmiento also eulogizes Mary, whom Christianity converted into an exalted symbol of the characteristics and emotions that he considers most admirable in women: "the young girl's love, love in marriage, mother's love, pity, intercession, tears, and supplications."[47] The eulogy ends with an emphasis on woman as bearer of the future: "Mary is the greatest mystery of Christianity, because within her is enclosed the future of the world."[48]

Sarmiento maintains that Christ's repudiation of the Jewish practice of divorce contained one of his most important teachings on the equality of the sexes; it represented a major step forward, one that Europe was able to take only centuries later. Sarmiento presents the indissolubility of marriage as progressive because he sees it as protecting women against abandonment. Many writers in the first half of the nineteenth century held a similar view, including a good number of feminists and in particular many women. However, there were those who defended divorce as a means of freeing women from abusive marriages. In France, divorce had been legalized by the Revolution in 1792, and it had survived the establishment of the Napoleonic Code until 1816. Between 1832 and 1834, Saint-Simonian women who wrote for the *Tribune des Femmes* called for the reinstitution of divorce. In 1837 Flora Tristán submitted a petition for a return to the 1792 law; and the trial in 1835–1836 in which George Sand tried to gain a legal separation from her husband, had drawn international attention to the issue of matrimonial reform. In Sarmiento's Chile, in 1844, the young Francisco Bilbao, adopting a position that would earn him excommunication and disgrace, exalted George Sand as the "priestess" of "matrimonial democracy" and called for the reform of marriage laws, without discounting divorce as a viable legal solution.[49] It is worth noting that given the historical possibility of various reactions to the question of divorce, Sarmiento seems to have adopted a position which, however much it belonged to the majority, was in fact conservative.

The Final Article: El Mercurio, August 24, 1841

The first paragraph of the fourth article, like the last paragraph of the third, deals with the advances women made during the Middle Ages. According to Sarmiento, woman's situation benefited substantially from the practices of chivalry and courtly love, but also from the "reconcentration of the family."[50] With a characteristically nineteenth-century bourgeois vision, Sarmiento once again promotes female domesticity.

In the passage from the Middle Ages to the modern period, Sarmiento reasons, if woman remains inferior to man, that is because she has not participated, like him, in "the rapid development of the intellectual faculties. . . . [T]he man of our day has become all intelligence," and only with difficulty can he respect a woman incapable of comprehending his intellectual restlessness: "Woman, then, needs to have ears to hear the thoughts that ferment in the soul of man, who even in the domestic sanctuary, needs witnesses for his intellectual labors, for his musings and opinions."[51]

Disregarding the contradictions in his argument, Sarmiento now recognizes that women have indeed participated in the intellectual ferment of the day. With this, he embarks on a discussion of two women writers whom he clearly admires: Madame Roland, whose *Mémoires* were posthumously published in 1820, and Madame de Staël, who published novels and essays until her death in 1817. In Madame Roland, whose memory will inspire him to frequent effusions of praise during the decade of the forties, he celebrates "the seductive womanly graces, the maternal tenderness and conjugal fidelity" as well as a "most astounding genius and [a] . . . most pure and lofty love of freedom."[52] His first words about her recall her political activity "at the head of the Girondist party."[53] Similarly, he stresses Madame de Staël's political influence, crediting her with a good deal of "the sad glory" of having overthrown Napoleon. For the first and last time between the years 1839 and 1845, Sarmiento acknowledges politics as a legitimate terrain for women.

Before initiating his overview of human history, Sarmiento had alluded to woman's future. Indeed, he considers it possible that this future will offer her a radical alternative to the present. Sarmiento sees in Corinne, the fictional heroine of Madame de Staël, a possible promise of things to come:

> Corinne, traveling neither with companions nor guardians, passing triumphantly through the streets of the ancient capital of the world, crowned with her literary talents like Tasso and Petrarch; following the instincts of her heart, without concern for the forms and conventions of the world which seem not to exist for her; Corinne, superior to the man whom she has distinguished with her affection, and creating alone her happiness or misfortune; might she not be a prophesy of the future position afforded to woman by centuries more ordered, more perfect, more egalitarian for the weak and the strong, for men and women, than ours? Regarding the illustrious author of this sublime female creation, has she not with her penetration and talents, guessed the future of her sex? And . . . without revealing her thought in its entirety, has she not wanted to laugh at the disbelief with which her century views a woman who is as free as man? . . . Would she have dreamed for her sex the fourth and final step left to be taken in society, the aspiration to equality and freedom, to emancipation and rights?[54]

At this point, Sarmiento contains his evident enthusiasm and writes:

> Aside from this, let us refrain from trying to pull aside the veil of the future. Woman has already made enough conquests for the present, and assuming with dignity the place that society offers her, she herself will be able to open the road to new forms of progress.[55]

On the one hand, a conservative satisfaction with the present but, on the other, a recognition that woman herself—and not man working paternalistically on her behalf—can open the road to her future.[56] Indeed, in an attempt to defend the present, Sarmiento adds that "freedom is not everywhere an empty word for her" and explains that in the United States women enjoy freedom of movement.

The fourth article ends by resounding the conservative and somewhat eighteenth-century note of the first article. "Woman will have to respect and submit herself to the ideas of the moment in which she lives," Sarmiento writes, going on to recall the public outcry at the unfortunate experiments of Enfantin and the Saint-Simonians. Again, he emphasizes woman's mission as daughter, wife and, above all, mother. And once again he chastises ignorant women who fail to recognize the weighty responsibilities of motherhood.

From 1842 to Facundo

References to brilliant or exceptional women, including women writers, grow scarce between the years 1842 and 1845. Now it is Aimé Martin's saccharine female who predominates: an eminently bourgeois image of woman as mistress of the household and guardian angel, comforter of the afflicted, safekeeper of religion, and symbol and consumer of aesthetic refinements in a world where men, ever more exclusively, dedicate themselves to pragmatism or, as Sarmiento clearly states in an article from 1844, to wealth and power.[57] Consistent with this image is Sarmiento's increased insistence upon naturally determined feminine instincts and conservatism:

> Piety is woman's inherent gift; faith, her reason; and religion, the sacred repository confided to the purity of her heart. Woman is charged with the conservation and transmission of sanctioned traditions and beliefs. Man thinks, doubts, discusses, alters and reforms; ideas change and institutions and laws are successively modified. But custom moves at a slower pace, and in the traditions that woman maintains through the mild dominion she exerts over the family is one of the principles of order that slow the movement of ideas, which without this healthy counterbalance, could be too sudden and harsh.[58]

In a series of articles that he publishes in December 1844 and February 1845 (when he is already working on the *Facundo*), Sarmiento is much more explicit about the importance of woman's faith and her incapacity for abstract thought. In these articles, grouped under the title "Polémica con la Revista Católica sobre la obra de Aimé Martin" (Polemic with the *Catholic Review* regarding the Work of Aimé Martin), Sarmiento makes his most conservative statements about women since his arrival in Chile in 1840. For example:

> . . . being those who form customs and maintain them, they should receive ideas that have already been translated into facts and that are outside the realm of discussion. Woman was born to believe, and not to doubt or inquire, and it would be a sad gift, indeed, to place uncertainty and doubt in her head, impotent as it is to embrace abstract truths. . . . [S]he does not think, but practices, and her faith in received ideas serves her instead of reason.[59]

It is possible, and I suggest it is probable, that the conservatism of such statements is a defensive tactic used by Sarmiento to protect himself against his powerful adversaries in this polemic (the Chilean clergy) as well as to distance himself from the recent scandal that had erupted around Francisco Bilbao's "Sociabilidad chilena."[60]

Irrespective of his motives for doubting woman's capacity for abstract thought, the education Sarmiento recommends for them during this period is quite limited and certainly distinct from that which he would have recommended for men. For the women of the popular classes, whom he hoped to see transformed into laborers, he advocates a training that will enable them to produce "artistic handiwork."[61] Such training is expected to inculcate "carefully calculated and rationalized work habits," which will contribute to "the creation of domestic customs of a new type, customs that we regretfully lack, founded on work, on positive interests; that is, on monetary gain, as in North America."[62] This sort of education has two objectives: to make women capable of "securing their own well-being," thus keeping them from poverty or prostitution, and to socialize them according to the particular model of national capitalist development that Sarmiento envisioned during these years.[63]

For the upper-class woman, he considers "reading, writing, arithmetic, religion, grammar, geography, French" and "exercises in epistolary style and other [unspecified] branches of learning" to be sufficient.[64] To these he adds the "ornamental arts, which are so important for the gentle sex, and the pretty manual labors that serve to cover with flowers the voids left in her life by comfort and the lack of serious obligations."[65]

There is yet a third category of women whose education Sarmiento does not specifically address: those middle- and upper-class women whose

lives are *not* characterized by "comfort and the lack of serious obligations." As a group, they will receive more attention in his 1849 book *De
la educación popular* (On Popular Education) and in his 1853 article "Escuela normal de mujeres" (Normal School for Women), where he advocates a much more rigorous professional training than the one he had
considered adequate for the woman of leisure eight years before.[66] However, already in 1843 he speaks of teachers as a social category when he
writes that "a woman is the only competent teacher of her sex" and the
best instructor in early childhood since, "simply by instinct and the admirable disposition of her nature, she knows how to bend to the condition
of a child."[67]

In this text from 1843, Sarmiento presents instinct as the ally of education, although elsewhere the two are treated as adversaries, instinct being
the very thing that education must control. This becomes particularly
clear in the "Polémica con la Revista Católica" of 1844–1845:

> Might one doubt that a woman ought to be educated so that she in
> turn can educate her children well? . . . Whoever doubts it, let him
> read the work of Aimé Martin, and you will see there that if the ef-
> forts taken to exterminate the vices and immorality of the multitudes
> have been impotent up to now, that is because the wound deep within
> the body of the family has not been probed: the inability of women,
> abandoned to their instincts and without the help of instruction and
> moral education, to form the heart and customs of men.[68]

The connotation of danger that Sarmiento now gives to the instincts is
even more noteworthy when one reflects on the dates of this so-called
polemic: they correspond to the period during which Sarmiento was preparing the *Facundo*. Indeed, in the same article from which the last quote
was taken, one also reads the following: "Only fifty years ago our matrons did not know how to read, and even today the immense majority of
mothers who prepare the popular masses, on whom the industry and morality of the nation depend, live in the most complete barbarism."[69] One
begins to discern that, for Sarmiento, "women abandoned to their instincts" have a lot in common with the "popular masses." These are two
groups which in their present state constitute a danger, for they are both
too close to nature and too far from civilization.

Epilogue: The Facundo of 1845

Although this is not the place for a detailed consideration of women in
the *Facundo*, I should like to point out how that text recycles and affirms
some of the notions about women that Sarmiento had expressed in his

earlier writings. At first sight, the mere idea of discussing women in the *Facundo* may come as a surprise, for in this most masculine of books they are conspicuous by their near absence. The only woman in the text who could be called "memorable" is Severa Villafañe. Yet it is precisely this relative absence of women in a book which aspires to be both a political attack and a biography of an important historical figure that confirms the prejudice (already articulated in the article dated August 24, 1841) that woman does not "exert a visible . . . influence on life" or, rather, that "the mild dominion" she exercises is "over the family"—in short, within the domestic but decidedly not within the public sphere.[70] A book that seeks to illuminate historical change by focusing on battles, presidential administrations, and political alliances is likely to assign only a marginal or accessory role to one who has been relegated to the dark corners of tradition and the home. The result is that the overwhelming majority of women who pass so quickly through the text are figured in the roles of mother, spouse, daughter, sister, beloved, betrothed, or victim of male concupiscence. In other words, they are presented as appendages to men.

However, since woman provides the first moral education "to the tender child, who later will become a man who forms society," the responsibility for what happens in history falls, in the final analysis, to her.[71] Thus, the mother of Sarmiento's political enemy, Juan Manuel de Rosas, comes in for particularly harsh treatment in the text. Twice Sarmiento insinuates that the excesses of the tyrant are in part owing to the rigidity and Spanish fanaticism of his mother. This conviction that mothers determine the behavior of their sons also helps explain the reverential portrait that Sarmiento will paint of his own mother in his self-promoting autobiography *Recuerdos de provincia* (Provincial Recollections).

Woman, then, as adjunct to man, provides a standard by which to judge him: the good man has a good mother, and the civilized man treats women with respect. This last point is an analogue to the argument made by Sarmiento in 1841 that a society can be deemed civilized or barbarous by how it treats its women. In terms of individual conduct, both Rosas and Quiroga fare poorly in the *Facundo*. Rosas is accused of having precipitated his wife's death with a brutal joke, and the whole text wallows in Quiroga's repeated abuse of women.[72] As for social systems, that of the gaucho and the rural pastureland is condemned, in part, owing to the position it assigns to the female sex. The first chapter concludes with a discussion of the division of labor between men and women in the Argentine countryside. Although the text generally identifies the gaucho with barbarism, the description we read here of the enormous inequality between the sexes, in which the rural woman does almost all the work and the man leads a free and idle existence, recalls William Robertson's discussion of savagery, which Sarmiento had reproduced in his article of 1841.

Finally, it remains to be asked whether women in the *Facundo* fall under the rubric of barbarism, along with the gaucho and his idols Rosas and Quiroga, the blacks who supported Rosas, and at times even the execrated Indians (that is, when these are not relegated to the category of savagery). Fundamentally, there are two types of women in the *Facundo*: the supposedly civilized ladies, both married and single, who tend to be figured as the prey of barbarism (e.g., the young girls from Tucumán), and the evil and/or humble women who somehow form a tie with—or are part of—barbarism itself (e.g., Rosas's mother, Santos Pérez's treacherous mistress, the black women who support Rosas).[73] But beyond this obvious dichotomy, which clearly betrays political, racial, and class prejudices, there is an identification (perhaps unconscious) with a long misogynist tradition that has taken shape in a metaphorical/mythological language associating women with the terrors of an uncontrolled nature. I refer to the Harpies, who are associated with both Quiroga and Rosas, and to the Medusa, whose snaky head is compared with Quiroga's curly locks. Above all I refer to the Sphinx, the symbol of Rosas, whose frightful shadow stretches across the whole of the book. The famous Argentine Sphinx in the first paragraph of the introduction—"half woman, owing to its cowardice; half tiger, owing to its thirst for blood"—inaugurates the book with a powerful image of how women, if unredeemed by civilization, can enter into a monstrous alliance with the most destructive forces of nature.

Notes

This essay was originally written in Spanish. It was translated for this volume by Gwen Kirkpatrick and the author.

1. These speeches are reproduced, at least in part, in the first two issues of the short-lived San Juan newspaper *El Zonda*, available in facsimile reprint (Buenos Aires: Guillermo Kraft, 1939). In order of appearance, they are by Sarmiento, Manuel José Quiroga Rosas, Antonio Aberastain, Idalecio Cortínez, and Dionisio Rodríguez.

2. *Prospecto*, Memorias del Museo de Entre Ríos no. 18 (Paraná: Impresora Argentina: 1942), pp. 6, 2. For the location of this difficult-to-find text, I am grateful to Donna Guy. I should also mention the generosity of Alfredo Rodríguez and Marta Gutiérrez de Platero, both with the Library of the Central Bank of Argentina, who helped me consult the material (catalogued under Historia Argentina no. 821) which forms part of the Tornquist Library, at present closed to the public for lack of funds.

3. *Prospecto*, pp. 2, 3.

4. Ibid., p. 3.

5. Facsimile reprint: Museo Histórico Sarmiento 4, 1 (Buenos Aires: Guillermo Kraft, 1939), p. 17.

6. This imposition of uniform modes of respectful address recalls the protocol of the Rodríguez brothers' school that Sarmiento attended in his youth and that he would praise in the first edition of the *Facundo*: "Where today is this great source of morality, good manners, and solid instruction that were distributed to an entire people, without distinction between rich and poor, black and white, since all of us walked together and treated one another as *gentlemen?*" (ed. Alberto Palcos [Buenos Aires: Ediciones Culturales Argentinas, 1961], p. 77). This passage would be deleted from all subsequent editions. For another discussion of the *Constitución*, which makes the claim that this text is representative of the pedagogical philosophy of the entire youthful Generation of 1837, see Mark Szuchman, *Order, Family, and Community in Buenos Aires 1819–1860* (Stanford: Stanford University Press, 1988), pp. 159–161.

7. *El Zonda*, July 27, 1839, p. 3.

8. *El Zonda*, July 20, 1839, pp. 4, 3.

9. Sarmiento speaks of these publications in his *Recuerdos de provincia* (Barcelona: Editorial Ramón Sopena, 1967), pp. 139–140.

10. Juan Marichal, *Cuatro fases de la historia intelectual latinoamericana (1810–1970)* (Madrid: Fundación Juan March and Ediciones Cátedra, 1978), pp. 51, 57.

11. Claire Goldberg Moses, *French Feminism in the Nineteenth Century* (Albany: State University of New York Press, 1984), p. 14.

12. Ibid., p. 41. On Saint-Simonianism and women, I have followed Claire Goldberg, chaps. 3 and 4, as well as Maite Albistur and Daniel Armogather, *Histoire du féminisme français du moyen âge à nos jours* (Paris: Editions des Femmes, 1977), pp. 270–273, and Richard K. P. Pankhurst, *The Saint Simonians, Mill and Carlyle: A Preface to Modern Thought* (London: Lalibela Books, n.d.), chaps. 6 and 8.

13. On the eighteenth century in Europe, I have followed in part the first chapter of Jane Rendall's *The Origins of Modern Feminism: Women in Britain, France, and the United States, 1780–1860* (New York: Schocken Books, 1984).

14. Enfantin stated that God was androgynous, and that women as well as men were made in God's image. The equality of the sexes followed logically from this thesis of God's androgyny. See Pankhurst, *The Saint Simonians*, p. 107.

15. Miguel Cané "Educación," *El Iniciador*, July 15, 1838, in facsimile reprint (Buenos Aires: Guillermo Kraft, 1941), p. 182.

16. Sarmiento, "De la educación de la mujer," August 24, 1841, in *Obras* (Santiago de Chile: Imprenta Gutenberg, 1886), 4:242.

17. Ibid., 4:244. Another disavowal of aspects of Saint-Simonianism appears in a text published by Juan Bautista Alberdi ("Boletín cómico," *La Moda*, March 17, 1838, in facsimile reprint [Buenos Aires: Guillermo Kraft, 1938], p. 175). There, writing under the pseudonym "Figarillo," he adopts a satiric tone which to a certain degree, I think, should be taken literally: "I do not go along with Saint-Simon that woman needs to be emancipated. She is already much too emancipated, and would that she were not so much so."

18. Sarmiento, "De la educación," in *Obras*, 4:231.

19. Sarmiento, "La mujer y la civilización," August 22, 1841, in *Obras* (Buenos Aires: Mariano Moreno, 1896), 12:195.

20. See Rendall, *Origins of Modern Feminism*, pp. 8–21.

21. Sarmiento, "La mujer," in *Obras*, 12:195.

22. Sarmiento, "De la educación," in *Obras*, 4:231.

23. Ibid., 4:233.

24. Rendall, *Origins of Modern Feminism*, pp. 9, 34.

25. (Middlesex: Penguin, 1978), p. 257.

26. When Fuller does mention motherhood, it is in the following context: "Earth knows no fairer, holier relation than that of a mother. It is one which, rightly understood, must both promote and require the highest attainments. But a being of infinite scope must not be treated with an exclusive view to any one relation. Give the soul free course, let the organization, both of body and mind, be freely developed and the being will be fit for any and every relation to which it may be called" (Columbia: University of South Carolina Press, 1980), p. 84.

27. Goldberg, *French Feminism*, pp. 73–74.

28. Sarmiento, "De la educación," in *Obras*, 4:232, 233. As far as I know, the young members of the Generation of 1837 never mention Lizardi. I name him because, as a liberal rationalist of the generation preceding Sarmiento, he is a good point of comparison. Particularly useful for this discussion are Jean Franco's "Women, Fashion and the Moralists in Early Nineteenth-Century Mexico," in *Homenaje a Ana María Barrenechea*, ed. Lía Schwartz Lerner and Isaías Lerner (Madrid: Editorial Castalia, 1984), pp. 421–430, and Joan B. Landes's *Women and the Public Sphere in the Age of the French Revolution* (Ithaca: Cornell University Press, 1988).

29. Rendall has described Aimé Martin as "extraordinarily influential throughout Europe and the United States" in the mid-nineteenth century (*Origins of Modern Feminism*, p. 123). In 1843 Sarmiento will emphasize the book's international acclaim throughout the "civilized world." See his "Colejio de las monjas francesas," *El Progreso*, February 16, in *Obras*, 4:279.

30. Aimé Martin, "Lectura instructiva: Escuela y métodos. El verdadero maestro de los niños," *El Progreso*, December 28, 1842, pp. 2-3.

31. Sarmiento, "La mujer," in *Obras*, 12:195. This is the translation of a passage appearing in Aimé Martin, *De l'éducation des mères de famille ou*

de la civilisation du genre humain par les femmes (Brussels: Meline, Cans et Comp., 1837), p. 55.

32. Sarmiento, "La mujer," in *Obras*, 12:196. In regard to the eighteenth-century writers with whom Sarmiento's thesis concurs, Rendall mentions Turgot and Helvetius in France and Adam Smith, Adam Ferguson, William Robertson, and John Millar in Scotland (*Origins of Modern Feminism*, pp. 21–28).

33. Sarmiento, "La mujer," in *Obras*, 12:196.

34. William Robertson, *The History of America* (Albany: E. & E. Hosford, 1822), 4:255.

35. Sarmiento, "La mujer," in *Obras*, 12:198.

36. Ibid., 12:199.

37. Ibid.

38. Ibid.

39. Ibid., 12:201.

40. For the third as well as for the fourth article in the 1841 series, there exist two slightly different versions in the *Obras:* one in vol. 4, under the title "De la educación de la mujer" (On the Education of Women), which includes articles 1, 3, and 4; and one in vol. 12, under the title "La mujer y la civilización" (Woman and Civilization), which includes articles 2, 3, and 4. In those cases where there is a discrepancy between the two versions, I have composed a third version that seems to make sense given the general context. This means that in some instances the version that I quote in translation is a combination of the two and does not correspond exactly to either of the originals. When this occurs, I indicate it in the notes.

41. Sarmiento, "De la educación," in *Obras*, 4:235.

42. Ibid., 4:239, 236.

43. Combination of versions from *Obras* 4:236 and 12:203.

44. Sarmiento, "De la educación," in *Obras*, 4:236.

45. Ibid.

46. Ibid., 4:237.

47. Ibid., 4:238.

48. Ibid., 4:239.

49. Francisco Bilbao, "Sociabilidad chilena," in *Obras completas*, ed. Pedro Pablo Figueroa (Santiago de Chile: Imprenta de "El Correo," 1897), 1:69–71. Although Sarmiento seems not to have identified himself publicly with George Sand's position on the dissolution of marriage, he does create a space for her in the feuilleton of his newspaper *El Progreso.* On December 16, 1842, he announced that during the next few days he was going to hand over the feuilleton to an aficionado of this "mother of two lovely children . . . who has written the loveliest things and who has engaged in fierce polemics with the top writers of France." He also announced his intention to publish a novel by the notorious Frenchwoman entitled *Matea* (see Sarmiento, "Al oído de las lectoras," in *Obras* [Santiago de Chile: Imprenta Gutenberg, 1885], 2:79–

80). And, indeed, three anonymous articles soon appeared that applauded George Sand and her battles against male discrimination. These were followed by a translation of the novel *Matea*, which, though certainly not one of the author's most daring (e.g., it defended marriage), did speak for a woman's right to choose a husband as well as for equality and active economic collaboration between spouses. The very sexual moderation of this novel might indeed be a sign of the limits that Sarmiento set himself in his defense of the emancipation of the contemporary woman.

50. Sarmiento, "De la educación," in *Obras*, 4:240.

51. Ibid., 4:242.

52. Ibid.

53. Ibid.

54. Ibid., 4:242–243. In reality, the judgment that Corinne is "as free as a man" is questionable. The most notable forms that her social rebellion takes are her desire to have a public life as an artist and her insistence on living alone, far from the unbearable vigilance of her stepmother. In her confession to Oswald (which, given her superiority of character, can be assumed to be true), Corinne reveals a chaste past—that is to say, a considerably more controlled sexual conduct than would have been permitted a man of the same social class. This is particularly interesting when one considers the freer sexual behavior of some of George Sand's heroines. I have consulted a new rendition into English: *Corinne; or, Italy*, trans. Avriel H. Goldberger (New Brunswick: Rutgers University Press, 1987).

55. Sarmiento, "De la educación," in *Obras*, 4:243.

56. This recognition recalls a similar point made by Quiroga Rosas in his speech at the inauguration of the Santa Rosa School for Girls in 1839. See *El Zonda*, July 20, 1839, p. 4.

57. Sarmiento, "El trabajo de la mujer," *El Progreso*, December 3, 1844, in *Obras*, 12:214.

58. Sarmiento, "Colejio de las monjas," in *Obras*, 4:280.

59. Sarmiento, "Polémica," *El Progreso*, December 3, 1844, in *Obras*, 2:230–231.

60. As a result of the publication of his essay in June 1844, Bilbao was tried and found guilty of blasphemy and immorality in the third degree. When the essay appeared, its author was employed as a teacher in the Liceo, or high school, founded a year earlier by Sarmiento and his friend Vicente Fidel López. Bilbao quit his job to avoid implicating the school's directors, but the gesture came too late: Sarmiento and López had to close the Liceo when scandalized parents withdrew their sons. In his article dated December 26, 1844, Sarmiento clearly tries to distance himself from Bilbao, calling the latter's essay an "undigested mixture of folly and heresy." However, he also accuses the civil courts of engaging in "a mindless persecution" of the young author ("Polémica," in *Obras*, 2:244).

61. Sarmiento, "El trabajo," in *Obras*, 12:215.

62. Ibid.

63. Ibid., 12:216.

64. Sarmiento, "El colejio de la señora Cabezón," *El Progreso,* January 24, 1845, in *Obras,* 4:326.

65. Ibid.

66. See chap. 3, "De la educación de mujeres," in *De la educación popular,* in *Obras* (Buenos Aires: Mariano Moreno, 1896), vol. 11, and "Escuela normal de mujeres," *Monitor de las Escuelas Primarias,* February 15, 1853, in *Obras,* 4:420–425.

67. Sarmiento, "Colejio de las monjas," in *Obras,* 4:278–279.

68. Sarmiento, "Polémica," in *Obras,* 2:235.

69. Ibid., 2:236.

70. Sarmiento, "De la educación," in *Obras,* 4:242.

71. Sarmiento, "Colejio de las monjas," in *Obras,* 4:280.

72. For a more detailed discussion of some of these themes, approached from a slightly different perspective, see my article "Layo y Edipo: Padres, hijos y el problema de la autoridad en el *Facundo,*" *La Torre,* n.s. 7 (July–September 1988): 505–526.

73. There are exceptions to the equation "good women = victims." For example: the ladies of the Sociedad de Beneficencia de Buenos Aires (The Buenos Aires Charitable Society), Madame de Roland, etc.

16   The Wiles of Disputation: Alberdi Reads *Facundo*

DIANA SORENSEN GOODRICH

The present essay is part of a project on the history of the reception of *Facundo* that attempts both to stage the life of that book through its readings and, perhaps more ambitiously, to explore ways of redefining the historicity of a text. Rather than attempting to recover an intended meaning embedded in it, I prefer to look at a text through the layers of readings that have accumulated on it along the diachronic axis and to underscore the ways in which readings are charged with the remnants of others, thus providing an archaeological base of sorts and an intertextual dimension of which we may be more or less aware. To clarify the question of redefining a text's historicity, I borrow the notion of "unhitching" from Janusz Slawinski in order to suggest a shift away from the following contextualizations which might be provided for a literary work:

> a specific phase in the writer's biography, a moment in the evolution of the collective consciousness of a social group, the state of the literary system (tradition) which is receptive to a given creative initiative, the body of related initiatives that grow out of analogous tendencies, and, finally, the literary scene in which the writer plays his part. "Hitching" a text to a situation defined by such coordinates means that in each of the mentioned relationships the text provides, so to speak, the closure for a certain sequence of experiences, the final link in a chain.[1]

Instead, the productivity of a work resides in the varied and often unexpected readings to which it gives place, the new structures of reception that result from different interpretations. The "life" of a work embraces the life of its producer as well as that of its readers on the synchronic axis: the act of "unhitching" it from the contexts of production and tradition seeks to undermine the possibility of closure in its study and to open it up to the multiple relationships that might obtain as different readers read.

Sarmiento's *Facundo* exacerbates this productivity because it has engendered a plurality of often conflicting readings that point to the unstable nature of the text itself. Far from being a homogeneous bearer of meaning, it is a web of differential relationships that is not limited by the physical boundaries of the book; rather, it spreads over a vast network of readings claiming to canonize it, question it, or undermine it. Because of its controversial nature, *Facundo*'s readings produce a vast discursive field on which the struggle for power is staged.

One interesting moment in this struggle is what we can quite loosely call its "initial reception,"[2] conceived not as a point at which its meanings were stabilized or definitively established, of course, but—to return to the archaeological metaphor—as the first and founding layer in a long process of accumulation and cross-fertilization. The initial reception is merely a point of discursive departure; in the case of *Facundo*, at least, it had a certain founding effect because its early readers started off some of the major controversies that were to surround the text.

As a preliminary step, the context of reception must be brought to bear on the different interpretive positions. The early readers of *Facundo* were deeply influenced by the struggles that preceded and followed Juan Manuel de Rosas's dictatorship, and their views sprang from their relationship to the struggle for interpretive and political hegemony. The nature of the texts that record their readings varies, but for the most part they are pieces that appeared in newspapers or journals: the reviews published in 1845 by *El Mercurio* and *El Progreso*, by Demetrio Rodríguez Peña and Carlos Tejedor, respectively; the one written by Charles de Mazade for the *Revue des Deux Mondes* in 1846; the "Notas" sent to Sarmiento by his friend Valentín Alsina. This essay is an attempt to deal with one of the most heated episodes of what I am calling, in a broad sense, the contemporary reception of *Facundo*: the long, drawn-out polemic between Sarmiento and his rival Juan Bautista Alberdi. While this polemic does not deal exclusively with *Facundo*, it is of significant interest to the study of its readings. Alberdi's challenge to Sarmiento's book is the most powerful, not only because of the weight of his arguments and his conceptual framework but also because it soon becomes evident that this is the terrain on which they are waging the struggle for discursive and political supremacy. As he sets down his disagreements with the book's assertions, Alberdi deploys them to show that Sarmiento is altogether mistaken, that he fails to understand Argentine reality, that he misrepresents conflicts—

to show, in other words, that on account of his duly demonstrated cognitive incapacity, Sarmiento does not deserve either his readers' trust or, more important still, access to political power. It is an interesting episode in the richly woven relationship between discourse and power.

Reading a Polemic

[I]t is the act of analysis which seems to occupy the center of the discursive stage, and the act of analysis of the act of analysis which in some way disrupts that centrality. In the resulting asymmetrical, abyssal structure, no analysis—including this one—can intervene without transforming and repeating other elements in the sequence.
> —Barbara Johnson, "The Frame of Reference: Poe, Lacan, Derrida"

Why does reading an epistolary polemic like the one that occupies me here subvert any possibility of attaining what Barbara Johnson calls "a position of analytical mastery"? It seems to me that what we have here is a system of multiple gazes (metareadings) that are superimposed upon each other, producing a somewhat distorting effect. Some of Alberdi's texts (the ones I will be rereading here) are essentially his transcriptions of his act of analysis of *Facundo*. Because of their argumentative thrust they radicalize the inevitably positional nature of interpretation, the space that a text opens up for dialogue, difference, or disputation. Our own reading is somehow housed within that same space, for how do we reach a point beyond the text of the polemic, a verdict of sorts that might unravel the play between truth and fiction, message and feint, so as to proclaim a victor? Even if some critics have confidently granted the victory to Alberdi because of his calmer, more rational stance, it seems to me that such a proclamation entails a certain blindness to the critic's own act of analysis, to his sense of values and interpretive priorities. In fact, at the root of a polemic's discursive formation lies a certain contradiction: while it is underpinned by the dichotomy between truth and imposture, right and wrong (with which Western discourse has been obsessed), it stages the very impossibility of deciding between them. In a polemic such as the one that involved Sarmiento and Alberdi, the purely cognitive and referential elements (what might be "knowable") are overshadowed by the constant negation and by the will to argue, to dispute. As readers we are caught up in a complex mechanism of wills that problematizes our own interpretive moves. Yet, confronting a polemic and the issues it raises seems relevant not only from the point of view of Sarmiento studies but also as one more way of broadening the field of literary studies by not restricting them to their belletristic manifestations. Studying this genre through the famous dispute between two such founding figures as Sarmiento and Alberdi may help throw light on what some call the "literature of ideas." My essay will focus on one of the two disputants, Alberdi, as a reader of Sarmiento.

As we take up the reading of Alberdi's reading, we confront a deceptively simple question: How should we read it? What texts make up the discursive entity that criticism has called "la polémica entre Alberdi y Sarmiento"? When does it start? To borrow a term from Gérard Genette, what are its "seuils" (thresholds), what constitutes its paratext,[3] how do we demarcate reading contexts that help us understand why the dispute arose? This kind of polemic seems to spill over the textual domain, not in a naively referential sense but in a clearly pragmatic one: Sarmiento and Alberdi resort to writing as a way of talking about acting in the world. Their writing is therefore trammeled with the problems of doing: in an Austinian way, we might say that this is discourse heavily laden with illocutionary and perlocutionary forces. In order to grapple with these problematic demarcations, editors of Alberdi's and Sarmiento's works have resorted to supplementing the publication of the two central bodies of the polemic (Alberdi's so-called *Cartas quillotanas* and Sarmiento's *Las ciento y una*) with what one of them aptly called "documentos explicativos." The polemic does not produce its own reading contexts; it begs to be contextualized as if it could only stand in the center of a complex web of concentric circles—it is not a self-sufficient text.[4] Let me clarify my point with examples. In the *Quillotanas* there is a significant paratext entitled "Breve noticia para informar al lector," which attempts to create a meaningful reading context for the letters that follow by citing the following relevant texts: Sarmiento's "Ad Memorandum," written when he left Justo José de Urquiza and dealing with the events preceding the Battle of Caseros; his "Carta de Yungay," addressed to Urquiza on October 13, 1852; his *Campaña en el Ejército Grande* of 1852, preceded by a letter to Alberdi through which he dedicated the book to him.[5] Sarmiento's text is thus incorporated into Alberdi's: the *Cartas* are preceded by Sarmiento's letter of November 12, 1852, dedicating *Campaña en el Ejército Grande* to Alberdi. Thus, Alberdi's *Cartas quillotanas* are framed by Sarmiento's dedication of one of his own works to Alberdi—a text whose prefatory force was actually directed to the *Campaña* and not to the *Quillotanas*. In a similar attempt to significantly frame and contextualize the two main texts that constitute the body of the polemic, the editors of Sarmiento's *Obras completas* named volume 15 *Las ciento y una* but included before them more than one hundred pages of what they called "Preliminares." While the pieces are heterogeneous in nature (some are journalistic, others are letters or are proclamations signed jointly by Sarmiento and other Argentine expatriates living in Chile after Caseros—such as Juan Gregorio de Las Heras, Gabriel Ocampo, and Juan Godoy), they are strung together by one common theme: the post-Caseros struggle for national organization, the political scene upon which the polemic is staged.

What I hope to show with these examples is the extent to which a polemic can present, in a somewhat radical, exacerbated manner, a problematic of the limits and demarcations that texts often pose. If, as Michel Foucault argues in *The Archaeology of Knowledge,* the frontiers of a book are never clear-cut,[6] then as we approach the struggle enacted in these complex textual configurations, we are dealing in more or less intense ways with crucial aspects of the discussion on texts, their identity, their circulation, and the ways in which their mode of existence constitutes a preamble for the act of reading. What is called today, in shorthand form, *Cartas quillotanas* was not originally constituted as a unified book: the first four letters were published in 1853 in Valparaíso by the Imprenta del Mercurio, under the title *Cartas sobre la prensa y la política militante de la República Argentina.* A supplementary text was published later that same year: *Complicidad de la prensa en las guerras civiles de la República Argentina.* The 1853 edition of Montevideo lacked this second text, but all later ones subsumed both under the shorter title *Cartas quillotanas.*[7] Indeed, the "system of references" is particularly rich in the case of this polemic because the textual concatenation extends over a vast diachronic span: aside from the *Quillotanas* and *Las ciento y una,* surrounded by the supplementary texts I have discussed above, there are other books which continue the polemic. After the Constitution of Santa Fe was approved, Sarmiento's negatively critical *Comentarios* were published, followed by Alberdi's *Estudios sobre la Constitución Argentina de 1853 en que se restablece su mente alterada por comentarios hostiles y se designan los antecedentes nacionales que han sido base de su formación y deben serlo de su jurisprudencia.* All this in 1853.

But the flexible frontiers of the debate were extended through the decades: in the 1880s Alberdi continued the struggle in *Facundo y su biógrafo,*[8] published in his *Obras póstumas* in 1895. This is a discursive phenomenon with unstable boundaries at the beginning and at the end, and hence lacking a "last word" to mark a point of closure. Inasmuch as it pertains to the reception of *Facundo,* it has contributed to the controversies surrounding it. As I focus on Alberdi's *Cartas quillotanas,* I do so with an awareness of the somewhat artificial and arbitrary nature of the choice. Yet I hope it will suggest points of departure for productive discussion of other sections of the polemic.

One of the most striking features shared by both the *Quillotanas* and *Las ciento y una* is the strong dialogic function that underscores the communicative aspect inherent in any text. Since they are letters, they have a strong pragmatic thrust derived from the kind of speech situation they presuppose: writing fulfills a mediatory function between the addresser and his or her addressee, who are separated by time and space.[9] The "I" and the "you" that underlie the dialogic situation are markedly present here, but not in their conventional manifestations. The disputational nature of the genre promotes interesting deformations that lead to what Catherine Kerbrat-Orecchioni has called "un dialogue de sourds," in great part owing to the ways in which the "I" constitutes itself as the founding subject.[10] Alberdi's *Cartas quillotanas* take skillful advantage of the dialogic movement of the letter and of the mediation provided by the physical absence of his opponent in order to invoke him, question him, and yet remain as the sole source of discursive authority. He both asks and answers the questions, thereby silencing Sarmiento's voice and proclaiming his own opinions:

> Caído Rosas y llegada la oportunidad de fundar la "autoridad" de crear el gobierno regular de la República, ¿qué ha hecho usted? Olvidar sus máximas de 1845, para ir más lejos en atraso político que los unitarios de 1829, condenados por usted en ese tiempo.[11]

> ¿Qué son sus servicios de diez años en la prensa? Voy a estimarlos, no con el fin de negar su mérito, sino con el de estimarlo tal cual es, para sacar una conclusión de justicia y de paz, a saber, que sus escritos no lo hacen a usted presidente de la República Argentina por derecho natural. . . . Sus trabajos de "diez años" contra Rosas son hoy documentos que obran contra usted. [pp. 50–51]

> Once Rosas had fallen and there arose the opportunity to found the "authority" to create the government of the Republic, what did you do? You forgot your maxims of 1845 and went beyond the 1829 unitarians, whom you had condemned at the time, in matters of political backwardness.

> What are your ten-year-old services to the press? I will evaluate them, not in order to deny their merits, but to appraise them for what they are, to draw a conclusion of peace and justice: namely, that your writings do not make you President of the Argentine Republic by natural right. Your "ten-year-old" works against Rosas are documents that act against you today.

Obviously, Alberdi presents himself as reading Sarmiento's texts and actions more acuitously than the author himself might be able to: the "I" overwhelms the "you" and turns him into a mere rhetorical device. But there is more: this "you" has a slippery identity, the result of a doubling whereby at times it refers to Sarmiento and at times it is a gesture that implicitly invokes a third party who is witnessing the discursive process and sharing Alberdi's points of view:

> Ese libro [referring to *Facundo*] es el más imparcial de cuantos ha escrito el señor Sarmiento. [p. 53]

> Llevó la exageración el señor Sarmiento hasta definir a Quiroga: "el tipo más ingenuo del carácter de la guerra civil de la República, la figura más americana de la revolución." El cree explicar la revolución argentina con la vida de Facundo Quiroga, porque cree que él explica suficientemente una de las dos tendencias. [p. 53]

> El señor Sarmiento explica esta verdad histórico-política, que él desconoce hoy, con un éxito de expresión y de sentido que lo hacen digno de reproducción textual. [p. 54]

> That book [referring to *Facundo*] is the most impartial of all those written by Mr. Sarmiento.

> Mr. Sarmiento was led by exaggeration to the point of defining Quiroga as "the most naive type of character of the Republic's civil war, the most American figure of the revolution." He thinks he is explaining the Argentine revolution with Facundo Quiroga's life, because he thinks Quiroga sufficiently explains one of the two tendencies.

> Mr. Sarmiento explains this historico-political truth, which he ignores today, with such felicitous expression and meaning that he deserves to be quoted.

Here Sarmiento becomes a third person who is observed and evaluated by Alberdi and his implicit reader; together they constitute a sort of communal "we," which points at a "him," who is silenced in the process and powerfully discredited. In this shifting relationship it becomes clear that the dialogue is fictive, that the identity of the participants depends on the suasive rhythms regulated by an ever-present "I." This is, in a way, the mechanism that ensures the survival of the polemic: the dialogue seldom "takes," except for a few common points that the debaters touch upon as points of departure. A polemic like the one that engaged Alberdi and Sarmiento so intensely rests for its survival on the mediatory powers of writing, for an oral encounter would force them to address their disagreements in more direct ways.[12]

The Uses of the Author

As he manipulates the dialogic situation, Alberdi deploys interesting strategies to evoke Sarmiento the author. The "you" he is addressing in his third "carta quillotana" (which I will be examining more closely now) is primarily constituted as the author of *Facundo*, since the letter focuses on this key text in order to posit a mimetic relationship between the author and his book: "el *Facundo o civilización y barbarie* . . . lo representa a usted más completamente que ninguno de sus escritos. Es su publicación más célebre en la realidad y a los ojos de usted mismo" (p. 52) (*Facundo o civilización y barbarie* depicts you more completely than any of your writings. It is your most famous publication both in real terms and in your own eyes). In a reversal which characterizes Alberdi's debating style, he unexpectedly goes on to declare that while the letter was originally written against Rosas, "viene a servir hoy contra usted por haberse puesto en oposición con su libro" (p. 52) (it ends up working against you because you have placed yourself in opposition to your book). This amounts to subverting the author's intentions and, in a general sense, illustrates how interpretation can cut itself off from authorial intentions: here is an instance in which Derrida's vision of the "orphaned text" can be materialized.[13] Indeed, Alberdi goes on to read *Facundo* against the grain, making it "say" things its author would not have accepted. Moreover, as he is discussing the text almost eight years after its publication, he judges it on the basis of the events that followed Rosas's fall in 1852, thus radically modifying the contexts of production and reception. Alberdi sets out to read not only "la historia de la barbarie y el proceso de los caudillos argentinos" (the history of barbarism and the Argentine chieftains), but also "la historia y el proceso de los errores de la civilización argentina representada por el 'partido unitario' " (p. 52) (the history and the proceedings of the mistakes made by Argentine civilization as represented by the 'unitarian party' ")—the very party Sarmiento was trying to praise and defend.

Alberdi's (man)handling of Sarmiento's authorial persona can be addressed in Foucault's terms, centered on the "modes of circulation, valorization, attribution, and appropriation of discourses."[14] What marks the reading performed by the "Tercera carta" is that even as Alberdi quotes extensively from *Facundo* (sometimes strategically praising its assertions), Sarmiento never really remains the source of its significations: they are modified and reappropriated by Alberdi for his own purposes. A case in point is the following commentary, which follows the transcription of an early passage in the book dealing with the nature of the "caudillo Facundo" as "expresión fiel de una manera de ser de un pueblo":

> Presentar a Facundo Quiroga—uno de los mayores malvados que presenta la historia del mundo—como . . . el espejo fiel de la República Argentina, es el mayor insulto que se pueda inferir a ese país honesto y bueno. . . . Pero el insulto está solamente en la exageración de un hecho que tiene algo de verdadero en el fondo. Quítese la exageración

del autor de *Facundo*, y quedará una verdad histórica que otros antes que él habían señalado ya, a saber, que el caudillaje y su sistema son frutos naturales del árbol del desierto y del pasado colonial. [p. 54]

To present Facundo Quiroga—one of the most wicked men in world history—as the faithful mirror of the Argentine republic, is the greatest insult that can be directed at that good and honest country. But the insult lies only in the exaggeration of a fact which contains some truth. If you remove the author's exaggerations, you are left with an element of historical truth that others had already pointed out: namely, that the system of chieftains is a natural fruit borne by the tree of the desert and the colonial past.

Two mutually reinforcing strategies are deployed here: the devalorization—even condemnation—of Sarmiento's cognitive claims, followed by the appropriation of their salvageable residue as something that others (perhaps Alberdi himself) had already pointed out. In the process, Sarmiento's authority is undermined: as an author, he is "used" as a target whose statements, having been made public through the mechanisms of publication, are open to question, disagreement, and condemnation.

The strongest blows are reserved for Sarmiento's valorization of himself as an author—in fact, a major portion of the third letter attempts to debunk the authorial figure from the position of superiority it may have claimed for itself. Adolfo Prieto has recently published an insightful study of this very aspect of the polemic as observed from the angle of Sarmiento's response in *Las ciento y una*, and in many ways what can be added is of minor importance.[15] As Prieto has amply demonstrated, Alberdi accuses Sarmiento of arrogating to himself the status of a political myth and of postulating himself as a candidate for the nation's presidency. What I would like to examine here is the double-edged sleight whereby Alberdi modulates his attack on the writer so as to avoid disqualifying himself from the position of authority that is at issue in the polemic. The discursive insertion of the writer resorts to the age-old opposition between word and action, arms and letters:

No hay duda que haber escrito diez años contra el tirano de la República es un título de gloria; pero es mucho mayor el de haberle volteado en campo de batalla. ¿Quién confundiría la gloria de Mme. de Staël con la de Wellington, como vencedores de Napoleón? . . . ¿Quién ha igualado la gloria de la palabra a la gloria de la acción? Pues bien: usted que atacó a Rosas de palabra sin bajarle del poder, usted ha olvidado en un instante la gloria del que le derrocó, no de palabra, sino de obra. [p. 49]

There is no doubt that there is glory in having written against the Republic's tyrant for ten years; but there is much more glory in defeating him at the battlefield. Who would confuse the glory of Mme. de Staël with that of Wellington, as Napoleon's victors? Who has made the glory of the word equal to the glory of the deed? Thus, you who attacked Rosas with the word, without overthrowing him, you forgot in an instant the glory of the one who overthrew him, not with the word but with the deed.

Other similarly eloquent passages could be cited to illustrate this opposition, and several of them also usefully demonstrate Alberdi's proficiency in the field of European culture. At first, then, it would appear as though he is disqualifying the writer as such—and therefore himself—from access to political power: "¿la gloria literaria es antecedente de gobierno en ninguna parte? . . . El escritor prepara, pero nada concluye" (p. 50) (Is it anywhere the case that literary glory is an antecedent for a position in government? The writer prepares, but he finishes nothing). Soon, though, it becomes clear that Alberdi has in mind a restricted kind of writer, and he masterfully works out an unstated opposition between the deserving and the undeserving writer. The undeserving one is the "escritor de prensa periódica," the journalist, as epitomized by Sarmiento himself, of course. (A reading of *Las ciento y una* immediately reveals that such a professional categorization stung Sarmiento to the quick, for it reduces his authorial status in several ways.) In the first place, Alberdi performs a sweeping operation of reduction: he minimizes Sarmiento's contributions to the affairs of their country by reminding him that as a journalist working for the Chilean press, only in a secondary way could he deal with the problems of a foreign nation:

> Representaría una quinta parte de la redacción colectiva, la parte consagrada a los asuntos argentinos. De los diez años hay que deducir los que ha viajado usted en Europa. Tenemos, según esto, que los diez años de trabajos periodísticos de usted sobre la República Argentina, largamente computados, se reducen a dos. [p. 51]

> The part devoted to Argentine affairs would represent a fifth of the collective writing. Of the ten years, one has to subtract those you spent traveling in Europe. According to this, what we have is that your ten years' journalistic work on Argentina is reduced to two.

This is one of the few instances in which Alberdi sets aside his heavily charged rational tools and turns to humor in order to undermine his enemy's insistent claims of long years of service to the nation through his writings, for it is obvious that the kind of computing proposed in the passage quoted above has no claims to any kind of mathematical verisimilitude. Having reduced the length of the service, Alberdi goes about reducing its quality: as a journalist Sarmiento received a salary from the Chilean press. Implicit here is the presupposition that he was inserted in a system of dependencies that deprived his work of the disinterested nature assumed to be the hallmark of patriotic writing. It is eloquent that Alberdi should tacitly suggest, as he moves about the arena where the articulation between discourse and power is worked out, that the power of a journalist's assertions is undermined by his subordination to the owners of newspapers: he is still a considerable distance away from the professionalization of the writer that was to cause such considerable anxiety in the latter part of the century:

> No negaré su patriotismo, pero no me negará usted tampoco que siempre ha escrito periódicos por su sueldo, como medio honesto de ganar el sustento de su vida. Ellos expresan, pues, a la vez que patriotismo, necesidades satisfechas. [p. 51]

> I will not deny your patriotism, but neither will you deny to me the fact that you have always written newspapers in exchange for a salary, as an honest means of earning a living. They therefore express needs met as well as patriotism.

The final blow is reserved for the kind of writing that is produced by the journalistic activity. Alberdi argues that it lacks the carefully meditated qualities required of a statesman:

> La reserva, la meditación detenida, la espera, que son las cualidades del estadista, serían la ruina de un periodista, que no tiene que pensar al paso que escribe, por no decir después. [p. 66]

> Reserve, sustained meditation, the ability to wait, which are a statesman's qualities, would be a journalist's ruin, for he does not have to think while he writes, let alone after.

Sarmiento's standing as an author has by now been totally discredited by assigning it to the category of journalism. What remains to be seen is how Alberdi manages to safeguard his own standing as a writer as well as his own public stature. To be avoided is any debunking of the authorial function in general. He proceeds by referring rather obliquely to writings that deal with what he calls "la ciencia pública," turning to the term "ciencia" in order to suggest the serious, carefully thought through nature of its assertions, and to suggest an opposition with the rash practices of journalistic discourse. It is not a far cry to see which ideas are to be inferred from this opposition: if the "public science" (i.e., political science), provides, as Alberdi claims, the competence a statesman needs, who is more suited to enact such competence than the author of the *Bases* himself? Through oppositional pairs—think/write (political scientist) versus *not* to think/write (journalist)—Alberdi is in a way presenting his own credentials as an author who does indeed bear the mark of authority. It is tempting to repeat Alberdi's handling of Sarmiento's claims by applying them to him as well, suggesting the possibility that in the empty space left by a discredited journalist we can instate a different kind of author: the careful, professionally trained political scientist. In this instance, it can be said that as we read Alberdi reading Sarmiento we encounter a degree of self-transparency that opens up the possibility of reading Alberdi. One particularly significant passage finally vindicates the writer precisely as it points to the kind of text that Alberdi himself has produced:

> La ciencia política no le debe un libro dogmático, ni un trabajo histórico de que pueda echar mano el hombre de Estado o el estudiante de derecho público. [p. 66]
>
> Political science does not owe you either a treatise or a work of history which could be of use to the statesman or to the law student.

This statement carves out a prominent place for the author of such works as the *Fragmento preliminar al estudio del Derecho* (1837), *La República Argentina a 37 años de su Revolución* (1847), and the influential *Bases y puntos de partida para la organización política de la República Argentina* (1852), which played such a central role in the drafting of the Constitution of 1853. In a subtle way, Alberdi has both established the direction in which discourse and power can fit into each other and canceled out the claims put forth by his enemy's writing. Indeed, not even *Facundo* is spared, for it is neither a history book nor a "libro de política" (book about politics): "Es una biografía, como usted mismo lo llama; casi un romance, por lo que tiene de ideal, a pesar de su filosofía, que no falta hoy ni en los dramas" (p. 66) (It is a biography, as you yourself call it; almost a romance, because of what is idealized in it, which, in spite of its philosophy, is not even lacking in today's plays).

The Wiles of Disputation

In this final section, I propose to examine the devices whereby Alberdi's argumentation is emplotted and whereby the refuted discourse is incorporated into the refuting one. Alberdi's reading of the *Facundo* in the third "quillotana" is in many ways an aggressive reappropriation of Sarmiento's text designed to discredit its cognitive claims. Despite his hostile slant, Alberdi reveals a difficulty inherent in critical work: namely, how to weave one discourse into the other. In Barbara Johnson's terms:

> The question of how to present to the reader a text too extensive to quote in its entirety has in fact long been one of the underlying problems of literary criticism. Since a shorter version of the text must somehow be produced, two solutions constantly recur: paraphrase and quotation. Although these tactics are seldom if ever used in isolation, the specific configuration of their combinations and permutations determines to a large extent the "plot" of the critical narrative to which they give rise.[16]

As Alberdi reads *Facundo*, obsessively probing its—to him—totally mistaken conception of the unitarian party, and of the distribution of civilization and barbarism in Latin America, he often resorts to quotation in order to present both Sarmiento's text and his own conclusions. He thus emplots his interpretation in a double weave, leading his reader through an intricate texture which is framed and controlled by his own designs. I will briefly consider one particular instance of this procedure. When Alberdi discusses the question of the "caudillaje" as a natural consequence of the colonial past and what he metonymically calls "the desert"—a shorthand for the negative influence of the environment—he introduces a long series of quotations whereby he presents significant portions of chapters 1, 2, and 3.

It is interesting to observe how Alberdi culls from these three chapters passages that produce a coherent exposition of Sarmiento's ideas while at the same time directing the discussion for purposes of his own. One could actually read Alberdi's "collage" paying no attention to the typographical marks that acknowledge the absent portions and find an almost seamless text that can be read without the trace of omissions. And yet, while not doing violence to Sarmiento's argument, Alberdi is performing a series of reductions that have the effect of underscoring the presentation of one of *Facundo*'s theses: namely, that the geographic environment has conditioned the forms of human development and socialization on the plains. He omits anecdotes and examples, as well as the descriptions of *el baqueano*,[17] *el rastreador* (the tracker), and *el gaucho malo* (the bad gaucho) in order to focus on what he calls "a philosophic truth" (p. 57). Moreover, Alberdi reminds us of his controlling presence not only by framing Sarmiento's discourse with his own, but also by inserting parenthetical commentaries that weaken the claims of Sarmiento's presentation. Thus, after the comparison between the loneliness of the Argentine plains and the area between the rivers Tigris and Euphrates—couched in rather lofty,

spiritual terms, because Sarmiento is taking himself very seriously here—
Alberdi inserts the following destabilizing comment: "(bueno es recordar
que el autor no conocía entonces ni la 'Pampa' ni la llanura asiática)" (p.
54) (it behooves us to remember that the author did not at the time know
either the pampa or the Asiatic plains). In another case, he interrupts a
passage in order to underscore the relevance of the point he is leading up
to with a "Let's not forget that . . ." directed to an implicit reader who is
guided along deliberately.[18] The framing devices deserve mention as well.
Alberdi takes on a magnanimously objective and even laudatory voice as
he goes about borrowing from Sarmiento's text:

> El señor Sarmiento explica esta verdad histórico-política, [alluding to
> the influence of the environment] que él desconoce hoy, con un éxito
> de expresión y de sentido, que lo hacen digno de reproducción textual.
> [p. 54]

> Mr. Sarmiento explains this historico-political truth [alluding to the
> influence of the environment], which he ignores today, with such fe-
> licity of sense and expression that he deserves to be quoted.

Likewise, at the end of the unusually long transcription from the first
three chapters, he announces less convincingly:

> He ahí la pintura que el señor Sarmiento hace del suelo, del hombre,
> de la vida, de la sociedad normal de la República Argentina. No res-
> pondo de la exactitud de las apreciaciones; pero reconozco que hay in-
> finito talento y mucho de verdadero en ellas. [p. 57]

> Here is Mr. Sarmiento's depiction of the terrain, of man [*sic*], of life in
> the Argentine republic's normal society. I do not answer for the accu-
> racy of his evaluations, but I acknowledge that there is endless talent
> and a good bit of truth in them.

Read together, these passages suggest that what is being privileged is fe-
licity of expression, at the expense of the cognitive claims.[19] Their validity
is frontally attacked through a rhetorical maneuver of counterargumen-
tation.[20] Having presented Sarmiento's views, Alberdi proceeds to draw
quite different conclusions from those envisaged by their author, moving
out of the field demarcated by the events Sarmiento's book deals with (the
Wars of Independence, the life of Facundo Quiroga, the Rosas dictatorship) and into the aftermath of Rosas's ouster. Alberdi uses Sarmiento's
theory of environmental influence to advance the following conclusion:
"Esa filosofía conducía derecho a la adopción de una política tolerante,
paciente, moderada." (p. 58) (That philosophy led directly to the adoption
of tolerant, patient, and moderate politics). From this point on, he is free

to jump out into the scene of the issues addressed not by *Facundo* but by the polemic: namely, how to deal with Urquiza and with the question of national organization after the Battle of Caseros. Alberdi wishes to condemn the policies of the old unitarian party, which believed that the "caudillaje" could be annihilated not with the moderate, patient policies advocated above, but in a sudden, violent way: "se quiso remediar el despotismo del atraso con el despotismo de la violencia: la violencia con la violencia" (p. 58) (The attempt was made to remedy the despotism of backwardness with the despotism of violence: violence with violence). Having traced his opponent's thinking in careful detail, Alberdi has carved into it his own opinions, adding to them the weight of a meticulous reading. Here we see the workings of interpretation and the points of articulation in which the freedom of reading is embedded: in this case, they are located where space is made for diverging conclusions which, in turn, produce semantic dissonance in the text.

There is another instance that illustrates Alberdi's artful appropriation of Sarmiento's book, one that I will touch upon briefly. Once again, Alberdi is quoting from *Facundo* (reinforcing the authority of his reading), but this time the form of emplotting the quotations is more elaborate. Resorting to a complex syntactical orchestration of subordinate adjective clauses, he strings together short descriptive passages taken from the same first three chapters, but linked by his own conjunctive and subordinating elements. The accumulation is effective; it builds an anticipatory momentum that culminates in Alberdi's formulation of a question which, while having the status of a veiled conclusion, carries the added advantage of allowing a categorically negative answer from the man who, inexorably, has the last word. Here is a brief sample of this artful operation:

> Y, en efecto, sobre esas llanuras, "que según los filósofos preparaban las vías del despotismo"; que en materias de camino "recibirán por largo tiempo la ley de la naturaleza salvaje"; cuya "extensión imprime a la vida cierta tintura asiática", [I omit seven clauses here.] ¿Intentó el partido hostil al "caudillaje" establecer un gobierno que tuviese algo de asiático como el suelo de su aplicación? . . . Nada de eso. [p. 60]

> And, indeed, on those plains which "according to the philosophers," prepared the way for despotism"; which in terms of roads "will be subjected to the laws of savage nature for a long time"; whose "vastness lent life a certain Asiatic tint" . . . [I omit seven clauses here.] Did the party that was hostile to the chieftains try to establish a government with some Asiatic qualities, like the land it was ruling? Not at all.

This final "nada de eso" has its illocutionary effect reinforced by a preceding question, which claims to stem from the very tenets of the book.

What it denounces, in many ways, is the gap Alberdi is observing between a way of decoding national reality and the forms of political action that spring from it. In this particular instance, having quoted Sarmiento's text, he is not so much disagreeing with its conceptual edifice as with its distance from the actions taken under its aegis.

While Alberdi manipulates the uses of quotation to disagree with the conclusions or the pragmatic implications derived from his opponent's text, he turns to paraphrase and elliptical allusion when he categorically declares him to be wrong. In these instances, emphatic assertions immediately follow statements that invalidate Sarmiento's claims:

> Usted pone en los "campos" la Edad Media y el antiguo régimen español, y en las "ciudades" el siglo XIX y el moderno régimen. La vista nos enseña que no es así. [p. 65]

> You place the "country" and the old Spanish regime in the Middle Ages, and in the "cities" the nineteenth century and the modern regime. What we see teaches us that it is not so.

What follows is a thorough refutation of the polarity that underpins the *Facundo* and that constitutes the basis for the deepest philosophical disagreement between Alberdi and Sarmiento. In a cogent discussion that will be taken up again in *Facundo y su biógrafo*, Alberdi advances the first materialist explanation of the forces at work in nineteenth-century Argentina. While not a reader of Marx or Hegel, he reached their thinking through Herder, Savigny, Lerminier, and Cousin. The materialist theories of Saint-Simon and the economic writings of Adam Smith exerted a powerful influence on Alberdi's thinking, and thanks to them he was able to propose an interpretive paradigm that was not bound to Sarmiento's powerful formulation. In a process of conceptual accumulation, Alberdi piles up the arguments that set out to vindicate the country and its people from the standpoint of their contribution to the Wars of Independence and of what he calls "la existencia nueva de esta América" (p. 65) (this America's new existence). As he discusses these ideas, the refuted discourse is temporarily bracketed, pushed aside so as to be overcome by the refuting one. In the process, Alberdi succeeds in articulating a view of the continent that powerfully foreshadows José Martí's brilliant and programmatic "Nuestra América" (1895), written when the relationship between the hegemonic countries and Latin America was altering the civilization/barbarism dichotomy and the values assigned to it. This is Alberdi's 1853 version:

> Y el buen sentido en Sud América está más cerca de la realidad inmediata y palpitante, que de los libros que nos envía la Europa del siglo XIX, que será el siglo XXI de Sud América. Así el gaucho argentino,

el hacendado, el negociante, son más aptos para la política práctica que nuestros alumnos crudos de Quinet y Michelet, maestros que todos conocen, menos Sud América. [p. 59]

In South America good sense is closer to immediate, throbbing reality than to the books sent to us by the Europe of the nineteenth century, which will be the twentieth in South America. Thus the Argentine gaucho, the landowner, the merchant, are more competent for practical politics than our raw students of Quinet and Michelet, masters known by everyone except South America.

We hardly need to be reminded of the intertextual ring of Martí's propositions: "Por eso el libro importado ha sido vencido en América por el hombre natural"; "Con un decreto de Hamilton no se le para la pechada al potro del llanero"; or "el buen gobernante en América no es el que sabe cómo se gobierna el alemán o el francés, sino el que sabe con qué elementos está hecho su país"[21] (That is why the imported book has been defeated by natural man in America. . . . With a decree by Hamilton one cannot stop the push of a plainsman's horse. . . . In America the good ruler is not the one who knows how to govern the German or the French, but the one who knows what elements his country is made up of). While in his *Cartas quillotanas* Alberdi is not developing these ideas as thoroughly as he does in *Facundo y su biógrafo,* where he maps out a distinctly materialist account of the role of the countryside as representing civilization, "expresada por la producción de su riqueza natural, en que la riqueza del país consiste"[22] (expressed by the production of its natural wealth, which constitutes the country's wealth), it is within the frame provided by his attacks on *Facundo* that he launches his inverted version of the interpretive formula.

No matter how meticulously critical of Sarmiento's book Alberdi remains, he is always willing to grant *Facundo* a hegemonic standing in the studies of Argentine affairs, and in Sarmiento's oeuvre. And yet, as is clear by now, there is a certain degree of *mauvaise foi* in the relevance bestowed upon it. Earlier I referred to the change Alberdi brings about between the context of production and that of its reception: by reading *Facundo* in 1853, Alberdi can make it say things against its author. Indeed, it is claimed to be a condemnation of Sarmiento and of "los errores de la civilización argentina representada por el 'partido unitario' " (p. 52) (the mistakes of Argentine civilization as represented by the unitarian party). Wittingly or unwittingly, Alberdi falls prey to the contradictions of his own game: having praised the book for its ability to unmask the errors of the "unitarios" (a gesture that obviously implies letting the author's intentions go by the wayside), he then finds himself condemning it as "el catecismo de esa falsa doctrina" (p. 66) (the catechism of that false doctrine). Of course, rather than viewing this as a contradiction, we might attribute it to the rhythms of disputation, carefully regulated so as not to be overwhelmed by its perpetually negative thrust. For Alberdi metes out criticism in different guises—one of which is a disguise of the negative tucked into the folds of praise. The final effect reminds us of his legal training, which allowed him to deal his blows with the procedural modes of a court case.

In many ways, Alberdi's polemical reading of *Facundo* metonymically inscribes the trace of future readings, prefiguring many of the controversies that have traversed it since. As part of a study of the book's initial reception, it enacts and transcribes the workings of interpretation: it enacts them because, by dint of its very generic nature, it is writing that wants to transgress its own boundaries in order to reach the realm of doing; it transcribes them because, in order to do and fight, Alberdi records his reading—the elusive act of analysis Barbara Johnson was problematizing above. Toward the end of his life, Alberdi gave away the main secret of his wiles:

> El *Facundo* es, en cierto modo, el más instructivo de los libros argentinos, pero a condición de saberlo leer y entenderlo. El que no lo entiende al revés de lo que el escritor pretende, no entiende el *Facundo* absolutamente.[23]

> *Facundo* is, in a certain way, the most instructive Argentine book, provided one knows how to read it and understand it. He who does not understand it in a way that is opposite to what the author means, does not understand *Facundo* at all.

Notes

1. Janusz Slawinski, "Reading and Reader in the Literary Historical Process," *New Literary History* 19, no. 3 (Spring 1988): 526.

2. This is one of the many concepts I borrow from Hans Robert Jauss. For his fundamental ideas, see *Pour une esthétique de la réception* (Paris: Gallimard, 1978). Two very useful volumes by Jauss are available in English: *Toward an Aesthetic of Reception* (Minneapolis: University of Minnesota Press, 1981) and *Aesthetic Experience and Literary Hermeneutics* (Minneapolis: University of Minnesota Press, 1982).

3. See Gérard Genette, *Seuils* (Paris: Editions du Seuil, 1987). Genette defines the paratext in the following way: "The paratext is that by which a text becomes a book and presents itself as such to its readers, and more generally to the public" (p. 7). The forms of presentation include "a certain number of productions, themselves verbal or not, such as the author's name, a title, a preface, illustrations, . . . which surround and extend it precisely in

order to present it, in the usual sense of this verb, but also in its stronger sense: to make it present, to ensure its presence in the world, its reception and its consummation, in the shape, today at least, of a book" (p. 7).

4. In a certain sense, this illustrates a point that Derrida advances in his polemic with John Searle: namely, that "a context is never absolutely determinable, or rather . . . its determination is never certain or saturated" (Jacques Derrida, *Margins of Philosophy* [Chicago: University of Chicago Press, 1982], p. 310). Derrida's claim is philosophical in nature; the polemic validates it in a concrete way.

5. It is interesting to note the titling devices that present this text: "Carta explicativa de Domingo Faustino Sarmiento / Advertencia / Bueno será que el lector empiece por instruirse de la siguiente carta, que ha motivado la presente publicación: Dedicatoria de la campaña en el Ejército Grande" (Explanatory letter by Domingo Faustino Sarmiento / Notice / It will be good for the reader to become cognizant of the following letter, which has motivated the present publication: Dedication to the Campaign in the Great Army).

6. Trans. A. M. Sheridan Smith (New York: Harper Colophon Books, 1976), p. 23.

7. The third edition was brought out in Buenos Aires in 1873, toward the end of Sarmiento's presidency. It was introduced by a preface signed anonymously by "Un liberal" and was intended to undermine the president's image—another illustration of the pragmatic dimensions of the polemic.

8. This book was published in Buenos Aires in 1964 by Ediciones Pampa y Cielo with an eloquent title change: *La barbarie histórica de Sarmiento*.

9. For a cogent discussion of the generic attributes of the letter, see Ana María Barrenechea's "La epístola como problema genérico," *Dispositio* 15, no. 39 (1990): 51–66.

10. Catherine Kerbrat-Orecchioni, "La Polémique et ses définitions," in *Le Discours polémique* (Lyon: Presses Universitaires de Lyon, 1980), p. 39.

11. *Cartas quillotanas* (Buenos Aires: Ediciones Claridad, n.d.), p. 62. All further quotes are from this edition.

12. Some oral encounters acquire institutionalized forms of mediation, with effects similar to those of writing. I am thinking of the case of a political speech, in which the person who is being attacked cannot resort to interrupting in order to truly actualize the dialogue without a breach in protocol, or of that highly coded situation of enunciation which permitted a Cicero to address Catiline as he did.

13. For an incisive study of how Derrida himself can get trapped into reading others "with regard to their intentions" and into wanting to be read that way himself, see Robert Scholes's "Deconstruction and Communication," *Critical Inquiry* 14, no. 2 (Winter 1988): 279–295.

14. See Michel Foucault, "What Is an Author?" in *Textual Strategies*, ed. Josue Harari (Ithaca: Cornell University Press, 1979), pp. 141–160.

15. Adolfo Prieto, "El escritor como mito político," *Revista Iberoamericana* 143 (April–June 1988): 477–489.

16. Barbara Johnson, "The Frame of Reference: Poe, Lacan, Derrida," in *Literature and Psychoanalysis. The Question of Reading: Otherwise,* ed. Shoshana Felman (Baltimore: Johns Hopkins University Press, 1982), p. 459.

17. The *baqueano* is a kind of topographer who knows every detail about the land, the rivers and where to cross them, the trees and grasses, and anything necessary to orient the individual in the vastness of the Argentine landscape.

18. In other cases Alberdi resorts to footnotes in order to correct Sarmiento and supplement his attacks: see p. 60, n. 1, and p. 62, n. 1.

19. As one studies the history of *Facundo*'s reception it is striking to take stock of the frequency with which this strategy is deployed: even as Sarmiento's powerful language is being praised, his ideas are undermined. For more on this, see my "*Facundo* y los riesgos de la ficción," *Revista Iberoamericana* 143 (April–June 1988): 573–583, and "Ricardo Rojas, lector del *Facundo*. Hacia la construcción de la cultura nacional," *Filología* 12, no. 1 (1986): 173–181.

20. Marc Angenot designates this strategy "retorsion": "One will take up again the data and the principles of one's adversary (while one declares not to adhere to them), but that will be in order to reach new conclusions in the antagonized terrain, conclusions which will be unfavorable to the one who is being refuted and favorable to the one who is refuting: one is dealing, then, with 'retorsion.'" See his *La Parole pamphletaire* (Paris: Payot, 1982), p. 215.

21. José Martí, *Conciencia intelectual de América,* ed. J. Ripoll (New York: Las Américas, 1970), pp. 225 and 226.

22. Alberdi, *La barbarie histórica,* p. 26.

23. Ibid., p. 25.

17   The Latin American Romance in Sarmiento, Borges, Ribeyro, Cortázar, and Rulfo

MARINA KAPLAN

[Y] así la humanidad va amontonando leyes, principios,
monumentos inmensos, sobre estas oscuras bases cuyos orígenes,
cuyas cavidades están ocupadas por un error, por un misterio, por
un crimen.

— Joaquín V. González, *La tradición nacional* (1888)

Domingo Faustino Sarmiento's essay, *Facundo, Civilización y barbarie* (1845), analyzes the causes of civil strife in Argentina during the period following the country's independence from Spain. Sarmiento's thesis is that the Argentine struggle, usually couched in conventional political terms (such as "federalism" and "unitarianism"), was in reality a fight between two ways of life: that of the Europeanized, cultured inhabitants of the cities and the primitive, autochthonous, "American" life-style of the rural gauchos. The eloquence of his arguments, his vigorous style, his colorful scenes depicting native "types" and the vast, mysterious pampas, as well as the very passion of his political project, all contributed to the influence that his work had on successive generations of Latin American writers. Indeed, *Civilización y barbarie* established the discursive parameters within which the social sciences and the novel operated until, roughly, 1930. Thus, for example, both in terms of liberal ideology and of prominence of the telluric element, Rómulo Gallegos's *Doña Bárbara* and the "novelas de la tierra," written in the first quarter of this century, can be read as the direct descendants of *Facundo*.

My purpose in this essay is to explore a different, less documented continuity between Sarmiento's text and more recent works of literature. In order to do so, I will suggest a genre for *Facundo* and will trace the persistence of similar generic traits in some contemporary narratives that belong, with the exception of Julio Ramón Ribeyro's novella, to the realm of fantastic or "magic realist" writing. It is a truism that *Civilización y barbarie* is a romantic hybrid as far as its genre is concerned; nevertheless, by bracketing its generic heterogeneity, I hope to bring into strong

314

relief a particular narrative configuration whose singular endurance in the Latin American imaginary is what I consider culturally significant.

Two constitutive elements of genre will interest me in this analysis: the structure of the plot and the *fabula*. The latter is the Russian formalists' term for the summary (the amalgamation of a single level of sense) of a narrative. As Umberto Eco points out, the construction of such a microstory involves an interpretation on the part of the reader, who will perform selections or semantic activations in order to arrive at his particular summary of what a text is really about. The result is that a plot can validly yield more than one *fabula*.[1] A quick example from the *Facundo* might illustrate this last point, by concentrating on a secondary incident that can yield divergent readings. When the conquest of Tucumán is achieved, Facundo Quiroga, triumphant, confiscates goods and money from the inhabitants. This is in keeping with his despotic nature and, I should add, with the customs of the time. But Quiroga also takes part in the auction of goods: "Facundo himself sells shirts, women's petticoats, children's clothes, unfolding and displaying them to the crowd. Half a *real*, one *real*, any bid was welcome."[2] How is the reader to reconcile the titanic image of the *caudillo*, which the text reinforces throughout, with this one of a street vendor? The reader can do so in at least two ways. He can ignore or "narcotize" the scene because, though part of the plot, it is incongruent with a more abstract significant whole. This is what I have chosen to do. Alternatively, he can acknowledge the scene and then conclude, as does Noël Salomon, that the figure of Quiroga illustrates the romantic mixture of the sublime and the grotesque.[3]

The repetition of a narrative structure and a fabula creates, in turn, a literary genre and its concomitant "horizon of expectation." In other words, a genre is an inductive construct based on a study of literary works along their synchronic and/or diachronic axes.[4]

The above-mentioned hybrid generic nature of the *Facundo* (it is a biography, a historical and sociological essay, a political pamphlet) includes an important literary aspect traditionally associated with the novel. "If *Facundo* is a novel," writes, for example, Salomon, "it is above all a romantic novel" ("Valores románticos," p. 154). "*Facundo* is the paradigmatic example of the historical novel," concludes William Katra for his part.[5] My aim here is to propose a different generic filiation for Sarmiento's text, not in order to accomplish a totalizing new reading of a classic but, rather, to highlight those organizational parameters that are the deeper way in which literature speaks about history. It is the semantic values of the structure and the fabula that interest me, as well as their persistence along the diachronic axis of Latin American literature. Consequently, the genre proposed in this essay is to be understood as a heuristic tool and a construction of meaning, not as a prescriptive or formal label.

My thesis is that *Facundo*, read as a work of fiction, resembles a romance more than it does a novel. Since this is an English distinction which does not exist in Spanish criticism,[6] I will first explain it and then discuss how it relates to Sarmiento's text. In modern literature, the difference between romance and novel is essentially one of degree: of verisimilitude, of precise naturalistic causality. While the novel is concerned with plausibility, the romance indulges in extravagance, a reminder of the unrestricted fantasy of its medieval models.[7] To a modern sensibility this can appear as problematic, especially in the case of those nineteenth-century romances where codes are mixed in unclear proportions: in them, within a realist fable, traces of an older, mythic imaginary can either delight or disconcert the careful reader. Criticisms will then stem from an expectation of naturalist portrayals of events which the romance, faithful to a different generic code, frustrates. This need on the part of the reader for a clear demarcation between fact and fiction, this desire that the text unhesitatingly throw in its lot with either reality or magic, is satisfied by fantastic literature, the twentieth-century heir of the romance (Jameson, "Magical Narratives," p. 145), but it is neglected in many earlier works. The issue can be particularly disconcerting in those cases in which the text proposes itself as "history."

Such a troubled response on the reader's part does not occur solely with regard to modern works. Ezra Pound, for example, complained that sentimentality, lack of common sense, and exaggeration were blemishes of the *Chanson de Roland*, which, as a "geste" (i.e., as a poem rooted in historical facts) was unsatisfactory, not up to the robust realism of the *Poema de Mio Cid*. His remarks, which are standard objections to any uncertain mixture of fact and fantasy, will serve to clarify right away what English criticism understands by romance in the medieval sense. "Whatever the 'Cid' owes to the 'Roland,' " writes Pound,

> it is an immeasurable advance in simplicity; it is free from the striving for effect, as in the two trees and four white stones of marble: it is free from any such exaggerations as a horn heard at thirty leagues distance. Indeed, the "Roland" is either too marvellous to be natural or too historical to allure by its mystery. In the realm of magic, the land of the "Romances," one expects, one demands, the delight of haunted fountains, bewitched castles, ships that move unguided to their appropriate havens; and the Breton cycle, the cycle of Arthur, was already furnishing them to the mediaeval audience and supplanting the semiverities of the "Matter of France."[8]

"Striving for effect," "exaggerations," the "marvellous," and the stylization of the "two trees and four white stones" are all elements of the genre; their appearance in the *Roland* weakens it as an epic, without, however, being marvelous enough to define the work as a romance. If we may grant this for medieval times—i.e., if, as Pound suggests, there is a minimum amount of "marvel" required for a work to be a romance—we may nevertheless consider that the situation is much more flexible in the nineteenth century in Latin America. In this latter case, what is significant is that there should be any "marvel" left at all, given that during this period of national projects the secular reason of the Enlightenment strove to prevail against anything reminiscent of irrationality, obscurantism, or fantasy. As such, reason was a censor of unbounded imagination.[9] Consequently, in a programmatic essay such as Sarmiento's, the domain of fantasy that Pound expected to find in a romance is restricted to descriptive details or, more interestingly, is hidden in the structural organization of the work and in its denouement. The fact that the "marvellous" was not eliminated, but rather preserved, even if camouflaged, is what I consider important.

Pound's strictures immediately recall Bartolomé Mitre's objections in the case of Sarmiento's text: no gaucho could perform the feat of lassoing a bull from a distance of forty *pies* because no lasso is that long. This is an unrealistic "exaggeration," just like Roland's horn heard at thirty leagues.[10] The same lack of realistic proportion is also criticized by Valentín Alsina, who reminds Sarmiento that hyperbole is appropriate only to poetry, to "a romance, or an epic"—in other words, to fiction. "You did not intend to write a romance, or an epic," he admonishes, "but a true social, political, and even military *history*" (*Facundo*, Palcos ed., p. 364). What it was that Sarmiento had wanted to write we will return to later. First I want to sketch what I consider the specific romance traits of his work.

The central conflict occurs between two orders of the real which, traditionally, had been the divine and the demonic, white and black magic, or the civilized castle and its opposite: the enchanted forest (the site of adventure par excellence). In the Latin American examples that I will discuss here, that enchanted forest where adventure takes place is the mysterious pampa, in *Facundo*; an isolated farm on that same pampa, in "El Evangelio según Marcos" by Jorge Luis Borges; a modern Paris where nothing is what it used to be, in "La juventud en la otra ribera" by Julio Ramón Ribeyro; a silent aquarium in the Jardin des Plantes, in "Axolotl" by Julio Cortázar; and the land of the dead, in Juan Rulfo's *Pedro Páramo*. Thus isolated from the world of everyday events, the characters in these stories, like modern knights-errant, engage in combats where modernity and the past fight a battle to the death over the meaning, or the meaninglessness, of history. Stylization proposes their confrontation as a transcendent adventure.

This exemplary division of the narrative world is a defining trait of the medieval romance, whose reappearance in romantic texts such as Sarmiento's suggests the following hypothesis: in its modern form, the genre represents an attempt to recover the possibility, or lament the impossibility, of absolute affirmations or negations in a now desacralized world.[11] In other words, by positing a narrative world constituted exclusively of antagonistic moral landscapes, which are mirror images of each other, the text harks back to an earlier ethic of unqualified truths. In doing so, it brackets the modern absence of a metaphysical substratum for such truths. That is why the romance, unlike the novel, keeps its distance with regard to reality.

In the realist novel, which I consider here as paradigmatic of the genre, the genesis of characters and events obeys a rational, progressive causality and there are multiple points of view. Characters and readers share an *Umwelt*, fictionally reinforced by anaphora and redundancy, which allows them to judge the course of the action apparently without direct intervention from the author. The novel, consequently, can afford gray areas. In the romance, on the other hand, characters and events can appear readymade (an old man with wings can fall in somebody's backyard, as in Gabriel García Márquez's "Un hombre muy viejo con unas alas enormes") and the point of view is the author's, who supplies the fictional world with an idiosyncratic coherence: he legislates what is possible or impossible (time can stand still for a year, as in Borges's "El milagro secreto") and he presents us with a causality that is realistic at times (a man has to put on a sweater), magical at others (when the same man desperately manages to get his head through the neck of the sweater, his own hand attacks him and he dies, in Cortázar's "No se culpe a nadie").[12] The romance shuns the grayness of realism. By thus relaxing the demands of verisimilitude, it can approximate the myth or the fairy tale.

These narrative options work jointly with the divided landscape of the genre: in the enchanted forest strange things happen. Thus in *Facundo* (pp. 69–70), beyond the obvious mystery of the pampas, the province of La Rioja itself, birthplace of Quiroga and the stage of his early actions, is compared to Palestine, its inhabitants to the hermit of Engedi. The scenery is colored with magic because La Rioja is a chosen, or a cursed, land. As such it is admonished, with biblical language, and reminded that its suffering is an atonement for the evils that the province has unleashed on the Republic: "In truth I say to you that Sodom and Gomorrah were better treated than what you shall be," concludes Sarmiento (p. 70). This hallowed, or damned, environment in turn allows the reader to accept that Quiroga, in consonance with the demonic landscape of his origin, should be someone beyond rational explanation, simply "born" to be great (pp. 60, 63, and 168), predestined to be a scourge of his country (p. 105). (One should keep in mind that this contradicts the geographic determinism of the essay.) The discourse betrays a similar dream of a mythic genesis ("born" great, predestined, etc.) in the urgency with which the establishment of civilization is envisioned: Bernardino Rivadavia, we are told, would have poured Europe's laws onto the American lands *all at once* ("de golpe," p. 91; also pp. 63 and 185). "The Argentine republic," we read elsewhere, "finds itself today in the situation of the Roman Senate which, by decree, would order five hundred cities raised, and *the cities would appear in response to that call*" (p. 223; emphasis added). Magic in this last example is projected onto the dimension of political utopias, and the word is, consequently, a "decree." Civilization achieved "de golpe," or cities that spring up in response to a call, are emblematic of the thrust of the essay. At work in these figures of speech is a remnant of more archaic epistemological constructs in which words could conjure up realities. Such dreams of omnipotence are also glimpsed, to show but one last (and different) example, in the description of Quiroga attacking La Rioja: "Quiroga ardently accepts [the one hundred men offered by Carlos Aldao], marches toward the city, takes it, apprehends the government officers, sends them confessors and the order to prepare themselves to die. What purpose does he pursue in this revolution? None; he has felt strong, has stretched his arms and defeated the *city*. Is it his fault?" (p. 73) Quiroga destroyed La Rioja through an excess of vitality, Sarmiento seems to say, and not through any ulterior motive. The physical movement of the caudillo toppled the city, as if he were not a man but a giant.

Such a narrative world is an idealized one, whose miracles and giants coincide with the dream images of its society: expressions of serenity or horror, the realization of desires, or the exorcism of threats. As Gillian Beer summarizes this, the romance "offers a peculiarly precise register of the ideals and terrors of the age" (*The Romance*, p. 58); the latter in turn represent, beyond the surface narrative, the social instability that accompanies the rise of the genre, which flourishes in periods of consolidation of new social formations (p. 78). Unlike realism, which relishes its immediate context by re-creating it, the romance withdraws, through stylization, to the topography of the imaginary, where the author can sketch with greater vigor and less ambiguity the world either feared or longed for by his contemporaries.

From this ensues another important characteristic of the romance which I want to discuss in some detail with regard to *Facundo:* idealism. John Stevens concludes that this is the genre's fundamental trait: "The 'claim of the ideal,' I have argued, is the central experience of romance, and all the basic conventions have emerged, crystallized, to express it—not only conventions of setting and location, but conventions of plot and action (including the usual 'happy ending'), of characterization and of motive" (*Medieval Romance*, p. 169). In the *Facundo*, that "claim of the ideal" is summarized in the concept of "civilization." The term appears to function as a Lacanian name-of-the-father: it generates a symbolic order and underpins an ideological discourse by means of which Argentine anarchy, ultimately equated with the state of nature, is explained, condemned, and transcended.[13] What is important to point out, though, is that this father is an ideal one. Argentines, Sarmiento tells us in *Facundo*, had searched in Europe for "their ancestors, their fathers, their models" (p. 211). Even though the real France and the real England had disappointed them, they had found their model in the "ideal" France, which they had learned to love in books (p. 214). Thus understood, this name-of-the-father is not, as it is in the case of the European novel, the reality principle. It is not the rigor of the real which awakens heroes from their dreams and forces them to accept the existing social order (the paradigmatic example here would be *Don Quijote*). On the contrary, Sarmiento's "civilization" is only a desired state which coincides with the designs of Providence and infuses the text with a utopian impulse characteristically romancesque. The envisioned reign of order in *Facundo* is both a social blueprint and an incantation; this latter quality ends up overpowering the real events narrated and produces a magical (i.e., contradictory) denouement.

The first example of these contradictions is the final reconciliation, which is disconcerting because it is not a logical outcome of the plot. Critics of Sarmiento's text have been conscious of this problematic resolution, which they have variously labeled as Machiavellian, conciliatory, or as a "mortal leap of logic."[14] In the last chapter in particular, "Presente y porvenir," the regeneration of a fallen society occurs as if that society had been magically seduced by order. It is a "happy ending" stubbornly rescued from among the fatal consequences of violence. Indeed, after so much horror, writes Sarmiento, Rivadavia's goal, hindered for so long by fighting and fragmentation, has finally become a reality: the country is now united and ready to embark on a progressive course.

Let no one assume that Rosas has not managed to bring progress to the Republic which he is tearing apart. No. He is, in fact, a great and powerful instrument of Providence, that fulfills everything that is of import to the future of the nation. See how: there existed before him and Quiroga a federal spirit in the provinces, in the cities, among the *federales* and among the *unitarios* themselves; he extinguished it, and organized for his own self-benefit that unitarian system which Rivadavia wanted for the good of all. Today all those petty *caudillos* from the interior, degraded, debased, tremble at the thought of displeasing Rosas and hardly breathe without his consent. The ideal of the unitarios is now realized; only the tyrant is beside the point; the day when a good government is established, it will find local resistances defeated and everything in place for unity. [*Facundo*, p. 217]

If the reader can distance himself from the persuasive force of this passage, he can then remember that in 1845, when the text was written, civilization had lost the battle. Sarmiento had fulminated against such an outcome up to this point. No matter, though. In this last part, he managed to rescue positive values from the country's ordeal and to find something good even in the omnipotence of his enemy. More than shrewd, "Machiavellian" thinking, as Alberdi charged, what we have here is a set of conclusions overdetermined by faith in progress. Superimposed upon the fable, forcing it to serve optimistic ends, a teleological conception of history interprets events—even the most negative ones—as indices of mankind's unstoppable march toward harmonious polities. This is the linear and positive view of history that had come into being during the Enlightenment and that was adopted by romantic historiography.

At the inception of this new, secularized view of the meaning of history, Immanuel Kant had acknowledged and defended the fact that such a view, such an optimistic lens through which to read the past, was bound to shape the resulting narrative in the form of a "romance." "It is strange and apparently silly," wrote Kant, "to wish to write a history in accordance with an Idea of how the course of the world should be if it is to lead to certain rational ends. *It seems that with such an Idea only a romance could be written.* Nevertheless, if one may assume that Nature, even in the play of human freedom, works not without plan or purpose, this Idea could still be of use."[15] Kant correctly anticipated the effect that the concept of progress, in its function as a masterplot, would have on historiography. The belief in the "rational ends" in store for mankind, equated with historical providentialism (elsewhere Kant, just like Sarmiento, speaks of Providence), functions like ancient magic. This last provocative term of comparison is only metaphorically implicit in Kant's reference to the romance, but it is directly, and mischievously, spelled out by Fredric Jameson with regard to Alessandro Manzoni's *I promessi sposi*—a representative text in this regard. In it, observes Jameson, the notion of foreordained progress serves as a teleological force capable of bringing about miracles in a world that is incompletely secularized ("Magical Narratives," p. 143). Lionel Gossman finds similar structural elements in the case of Augustin Thierry's history of France. "Thierry emplots history as a romance, or a divine comedy," he concludes.[16]

This "salvational logic," as Gossman calls it, appropriates unto itself even the realm of evil. The manner in which this is brought about is peculiar to romances: the bearers of evil abruptly change their sign and join the good society. This is the second mechanism that accounts for *Facundo*'s contradictory resolution. In the last part of Sarmiento's essay there is a veritable avalanche of such sudden transformations, whose aim is to show that social regeneration is now absolute. Thus the gauchos, at the end of the narrative, have begun to become true "citizens"—either through contact with civilized people exiled from Buenos Aires by Rosas's policies (p. 212), or by becoming familiar and eventually sympathizing with the cause of the cities they have invaded (p. 217). *Federales, unitarios,* and the young have deposed their antagonisms in order to unite in the struggle against Rosas (p. 229). The earlier irreducible antinomies have dissolved, and the country which had been in danger of fragmentation is now united: "The fight of the countryside against the cities is over" (p. 217). Even the *mazorqueros,* those sinister lackeys of Rosas, may perhaps hide, under the "exteriorities of crime, virtues that some day will be rewarded" (p. 226).

These changes ensure rather hastily the triumph of a social cohesion whose fracture the text has until then denounced. What I want to stress is that this harmony is recovered not by the victory of one group over the other (indeed, if anything has triumphed in *Facundo* it is the barbarism of the countryside) but, rather, by the surprising change of value of the antagonists. The bad guys have become good. This is a characteristic of romance intimately related to those mentioned earlier: the polarized ethical landscapes, the utopian ideal, and the magical force that watches over the affairs of men. Romances deal with emotional and moral extremes not subordinated to the conventions of realism.[17] However, good and evil, personified in characters without nuances, are not exclusive to romance: the "Western" film and, at the other distant end of time, the *chanson de geste* (which, as a genre, precedes the romance) share what Jameson calls a "positional notion" of good and evil. But in these latter cases the enemy, the "other," the "bad" one, remains so until the end. In the romance, on the other hand, the antagonist surprises both the protagonist and the reader when, after innumerable adventures, he reveals his true identity and discovers that he is not the villain. His wickedness turns out to have been mere appearance, and he ends up being a member of the good group.

Jameson, whom I am following here, considers this type of surprising conversion to be a fundamental trait of the genre which, in its origins, adopted a traditional literary structure—that of the enemies of the chanson de geste—and adapted it to a new social reality: the emergence of feudal nobility as a universal class ("Magical Narratives," p. 161). He who was an enemy in earlier times is now another nobleman, and the texts reflect this in the sudden transformation of the antagonist into a member of the normative group. An appropriate illustration, in addition to those mentioned by Jameson, is the anonymous late-fourteenth-century English romance *Sir Gawain and the Green Knight*: at the end of his adventure, Sir Gawain and the reader discover that the terrible giant of the title is but a mask behind which is disguised Gawain's elegant host. The peril of the anticipated fight against the monstrous green knight is dissolved, and the characters celebrate the reestablished harmony of peers. The last section of the *Facundo* brings us close to this manner of portraying social reintegration by means of universalizing the domain of the positive characters. In summary, this rapid change of sign, in which the green knight turns out to be a nobleman—or, to give two other common illustrations, the destitute heroine discovers her aristocratic parents, and the beast proves to be the prince—is similar to the revelation that Rosas is a tool of Providence and that even the mazorqueros may hold some good. Such a swift reversal partakes both of wishful thinking (the true realm of the imaginary and the romance) and of an ideology in the process of asserting itself. The romance, more than the novel, camouflages the complexities of reality and, through magic, suppresses difference by means of miraculous, last-minute revelations of sameness. In Sarmiento's text, this conversion of the bad characters serves to universalize liberal ideals, proposed throughout the work as the exalted domain of the good.

In the case of Quiroga himself, this change of value (which, it should be recalled, was one of the contradictions that so angered Alberdi) has an additional meaning and broader implications. In the last chapter devoted to the character's life, "Barranca Yaco," Sarmiento turns the whole country into a stage for the silent duel between Quiroga and Rosas. In the description of Quiroga's trip, all his actions raise his stature and contribute to change his sign: the comparison of Facundo's premonitions with those of Napoleon (*Facundo*, p. 173); his ghostly carriage, in which he speeds across the country with death always behind; his obstinacy in continuing to travel to an encounter with his murderers, about whom he has had repeated warnings; the dignity with which he confronts them, and the tragedy to which he drags his unfortunate companions—all this rounds off the portrait of a hero. If until then Facundo, of black locks and glaring eyes, has incarnated Evil, in the death scene he suddenly changes, in a reversal whose distant antecedent is the unmasking of the antagonists of medieval romance. Facundo the monster who, frustrated in his desire, had bathed in blood the young woman that rejected him, Facundo who had broken her skull with his heel (p. 126), Facundo "the bad gaucho of the Llanos," ends up dying with grandeur.

Before continuing with this motif, which is a structural permutation of values, it is important to remark that Facundo's death represents, at the symbolic level, the death of an older world—glimpsed in the code of values that his final actions embody. When confronting his assassins the caudillo behaves like a feudal lord, sure of his place in the world, and opens the door of the carriage in order to control his enemies by his mere presence. He expects individual hierarchies, those based on strength, valor, and fame, to be respected and privileged. But his enemies no longer respond to such norms: a hired killer treacherously shoots him down. His death signals the passing away of the gaucho aristocracy of courage, defeated by a now impersonal and cowardly efficiency. This end of a world, suggested through images, is reinscribed into a more explicitly historical frame by the subsequent comparison of Quiroga's assassin to Danton (*Facundo*, p. 179). Facundo's death is thus the Argentine version of 1789, the moment when the pampean old regime gives way to a new order. (We will see this allusion to the French Revolution acquire an inverted meaning in Ribeyro's story.)

Facundo's stay in Buenos Aires, prior to his trip, serves to prepare the reader for the caudillo's metamorphosis. Like a knight-errant in the city, he is subjected to a test: that of *porteño* civilization, its laws and its comforts. He emerges transformed and he doubts, for the first time, that physical force is the absolute source of power (*Facundo*, p. 169). This loss of his earlier assurance foreshadows both his imminent ruin as a protagonist and his change of value as an actant. His earlier "barbaric" traits begin to wane in Buenos Aires, so that it is his superior bravery, stripped of contradictions, that is exalted when he undertakes his last, rash, and fatal act of daring. In the episode of "Barranca Yaco," the creature of nature, as Sarmiento had called him, acquires his mask, his social persona: specifically his heroism, in which his identity will now be fixed and for whose sake, we may suspect, he will repress his common sense and lose his life.

(Of course, I am speculating on the motivations of a fictional, not an empirical, character.) He dies like a hero, and this allows Sarmiento to change his sign: for someone of Facundo's newfound stature there is a place in the pantheon of Argentine history. There he enters, having acquired, in the words of Sarmiento years later, "the sculptural forms of the primitive heroes, of Ajax and Achilles."[18]

This returns us to the question left open at the beginning of the present essay: how Sarmiento saw his own work. When writing about it in the eighties (*Facundo* was written in 1845, some forty years earlier), he referred without ambiguity to the importance of his text as a romance. His words are worth quoting in full, since they are usually repeated only fragmentarily. *Facundo*, he tells us, is comparable to Sallust's account of the war against Jugurtha, because both are books without subject matter. This is so because the adventure they narrate leaves no "mark in history; it is merely an inconsequential episode." In other words, it is not their historical content that makes these books great, but rather their exotic landscapes, the grandeur of their scenes, and all those other qualities that Sarmiento himself had defined, in the text of *Facundo*, as being traits of romances. In the case of the Latin treatise,

> What Rome saw was a book, and what students and Latin scholars see is the figure of Jugurtha the Numid, with his white burnoose, on a black horse, making *razzias*, fancy charges, or marauding in front of the Roman legions. It is Sallust, the painter of Africa, of the desert.

Naturally, the implication is that all these features are the enduring literary qualities of the *Facundo*, too. Precisely because the value of his work is literary, Sarmiento goes on to defend it against the demands of strict historical realism which, in his opinion, miss the point:

> Let not the historian, who searches for graphic truths, wound with his scalpel the flesh of *Facundo*, which is alive. Do not touch it! As it is, with all its flaws, all its imperfections, the book was loved by its contemporaries, honored by all foreign literatures; it haunted those who read it for the first time, and the Argentine pampa is as poetic today around the world as are the mountains of Scotland portrayed by Walter Scott for the solace of men's minds.[19]

The elderly Sarmiento thus disagrees, indirectly, with the reading of Valentín Alsina and with that of the majority of his present-day readers in the social sciences: the value of his *Facundo*, he affirms, is poetic. His account, like Sallust's, is "a book" and not history.

Of course this is only one reading among several. (Sarmiento knew this when, in the same article, he congratulated himself on the ideological success of his book, saying that it had been "a veritable rock" thrown at the head of one titan by another.) However, if we pursue this single fabula, we will notice that it is Quiroga's abrupt change from destroyer to destroyed, from enemy to hero, from bad to good, that makes possible all the ensuing transformations of "Presente y porvenir." His final tragic nobility seems to unleash a change in the whole society and initiates the recovery of harmony of the last two chapters. After "Barranca Yaco," the social body appears to have been purged. This organization of the narrative suggests a causal connection between the end of the caudillo and the subsequent reconstitution of society. We could then say that the assassination of Facundo is similar in its function to that of the victim of ritual sacrifice in primitive religions: like the immolation of the pharmakos studied by René Girard, the elimination of Quiroga is the catalyst that converts an "infectious violence into positive cultural values."[20]

This was Joaquín V. González's intuition concerning order, as expressed in the epigraph to the present essay.[21] Speculating on Facundo's death, González wrote that society erects its laws and monuments on obscure foundations whose hollow core encloses a crime. This hollow core, this "cavity," is also an "origin." Inside it, a mystery, a murder. The genesis of the social order—genesis with its maternal cavities and its paternal monuments, their union a "doubtful formula," their offspring "un delito"—is thus apprehended in all its painful ambiguity, as if anticipating modern formulations of the sacrifice imposed by the symbolic order, or the violence of arche-writing.[22] Facundo's immolation represents, for González, that error, mystery, or crime which makes possible the founding of institutions.

Here, it seems to me, is the primal scene of several future Latin American romances: the death of the pharmakos as the pivot on which hinges the fortunate or impossible resolution of the constitution of society. Unlike all the other characteristics already mentioned, this is not a typical trait of earlier European romances. I will therefore discuss how this scene reappears in two contemporary texts, uncertain heirs of the founding model, and will then offer some remarks on the recombination of the constitutive elements of Facundo's genre in texts of Cortázar and Rulfo.

The assassination of the hero is the primal scene of Jorge Luis Borges's "El Evangelio según Marcos," and of Julio Ramón Ribeyro's "La juventud en la otra ribera." In Borges's story,[23] the events occur in the magic landscape of otherness. The ranch is a ritual space: it is at the center of four roads and, flooded, it imposes on the protagonist the strict isolation required by a rite of passage. In that solitary place, the urban intellectual and the gaucho, traditional antagonists, confront each other. With these similar initial elements, the text constructs an antithesis of Sarmiento's romance.[24] The denouement is inverted, since the victim is Espinosa, the representative of modernity. His killers, with their red hair and Indian features, are a caricature of the old gauchos—and a satire of naturalism, I should add, since the final crisis is brought about by the inevitable workings of the fanaticism "in their blood." These gauchos now represent intellectual barbarism, which for Borges consists in mistaking the text for reality. In this sense, the whole story is a mockery of literal readings and, therefore, a criticism of romances. Like *Don Quijote*, it is an antiromance or, more specifically, a satiric parody, as Alberto Julián Pérez has proposed:[25] in it, what I have called the primal scene now serves to foreground the impossibility of meaning. Espinosa's death does not initiate a new reign of order but highlights instead the absurdity of the whole ordeal. It inverts, parodically, the function of its two models: the sacrifices of Christ and of Facundo.

In conflict with this fabula, however, a sudden change of register insinuates itself in the very last lines of the narrative, as if the parody and its model were one. I am referring to the moment when, as the door to the shed is opened, Espinosa sees "the firmament" and recognizes the cry of a bird:

> The girl wept. When they opened the door, he saw the heavens. A
> bird cried; "A goldfinch," he thought.

This is my translation of the corresponding lines in the first book edition of this story, in *El informe de Brodie* (p. 136), published in 1970. This ending was modified in the English translation of 1972; part of that modification was later retained in the Spanish-language *Obras completas* of 1974. Concerning these changes, it is of interest to my argument that the serious, and spare, original diction of "vio el firmamento," which is left intact in the 1974 Spanish edition, is carefully avoided in English in 1972: "firmamento" is replaced by a more chatty "patch of sky." In Spanish, "firmamento" differs from "cielo" in that the former is elevated, indeed mannered, in tone, and it has no religious connotations; "cielo," for its part, can mean either "sky" or "Heaven." The studied choice of diction, the artificiality of "firmamento," on the one hand, and the apparently contradictory feat of baring this neoclassic term of its customary declamatory resonance, on the other, call attention to the very process of paradigmatic selection, with the result that the attempted repression becomes instead a revealing denial *(dénégation)* of a potentially transcendent signified. The latter, "cielo," is legible under erasure, precisely because it

has been so self-consciously avoided, and also because the paratactical juxtaposition of the girl weeping and the door that opens onto Heaven is a
scene that has an iconic quality—and a long tradition in religious Western
art, in which the clouds and rays of sunlight that connect earth and Heaven
in so many Renaissance and Baroque "glories" are, symbolically, a "door."
While suspended briefly on that threshold, the hapless protagonist and
the model of the parody, Christ, coincide. The fact that the English rendering is not simply "sky" underscores what (both, I assume) author and
translator may have considered as the disruptive potential of such an
archetypal image of liberation within the sustained parodic tone of the
narrative. In English, this tone is preserved, and the colloquial "patch of
sky" dissolves the *point de capiton* into a naturalistic description, traduc-
ing the tension of the Spanish original into the opaque materiality of a
"patch," ensuring that even at the imagistic level, the painterly fragment
of sky shall not be mistaken for signification.[26]

In Spanish, however, the vision of the sky and the recognition of the
bird by its song—a knowledge acquired by the protagonist when it is too
late—constitute a tragic pause that momentarily scuttles the parody, leading both character and reader away from the preceding ridiculous humiliation to face the vastness of the sky. For our purposes, what is interesting
is the reappearance of the contradictory movement of the death of the
pharmakos: from barrenness to Eden, from meaninglessness to transcendence, which is here glimpsed in the swift permutation of a grotesque
humor into the lyricism of an epiphany. In this sense, the opening of "the
door" is a hesitant reminder of Dahlmann's crossing of "the threshold"
("el umbral") in Borges's much earlier "El Sur." In both cases, the protagonist traverses what amounts to being a ritual boundary between the
agony of the real—i.e., of history—and the transcendence of myth. "El
Evangelio" is more austere than "El Sur," but even its parody is not
immune to the brief intrusion of the old romance mechanism of transformation, reintroduced in a vision that salvages from the wrecks of meaning
a minimal form of interiority in a subject threatened with annihilation.
Parody and romance, disturbingly juxtaposed, are the rhetorical constructions that correspond, respectively, to history and myth. And myth (within
modernity) is the poetic word, with its long intertextual life and its de-
votions. Thus "firmamento": meaning both sky and foundation, equally
distant from the conventions of religion and from those of positivistic
naturalism, this term introduces a Parnassian stillness in the worldly disorder of satire.

At this point, it is appropriate to recall that such a final disjunction of
the narrative characterizes other stories of Borges. In "Tlön, Uqbar, Orbis

Tertius," for example, the narrator (like Espinosa) does not fight against the new world that is supplanting reality. Instead, in the last paragraph, he rejects it by turning his back on it, in order to translate Sir Thomas Browne's "Urn Burial." In doing so, he opposes to the "symmetries with an appearance of order" (i.e., to modern reason and its psychosis) the mystery of salvation through grace exalted by Browne.[27] Comparing the two stories, we can propose a similar dichotomy for "El Evangelio": history is an absurdity, but there is a reference, however ambiguous, to "a secret miracle" at the end. Espinosa's final resignation can then be understood as an illustration of moral stoicism—it is futile to fight against history (and this is a constant in many of Borges's stories)—while the sight of the firmament becomes a symbol of transcendence, albeit one of a spiritual and not, as in Sarmiento's text, one of a social kind. The door that opens onto Heaven is the structural and semantic equivalent of the "indecisive translation" of "Urn Burial," as well as of Hladik's secret year of grace in "El milagro secreto" and of alternate, "other" deaths, such as Dahlmann's in "El Sur." Through these scenes, the text attempts to withdraw from the ultimate consequences of a history that is absurd by resorting to the old "salvational logic" of romance. Meaninglessness is momentarily sidestepped by an inversion reminiscent of the transformations characteristic of the genre.

The "claim of the ideal" encoded in the last lines of "El Evangelio" is, however, too ironic to impose a romance resolution on the narrative. When the symbolism of Christ's death and the absurd rite of passage of the protagonist coalesce, for example, the model itself becomes tinged with parody (could Christ's death have been as absurd?) even as the parody acquires, in tentative fashion, the dignity of the original. In general, the denouements of all these narratives are ironic aporias, as befits their ostensible skepticism. Consequently, while we believe that the green knight is a disguise for the lord of the castle, or that barbarism is all but extinguished after Quiroga's death, we respond with ambivalence to the miracles in Borges's stories. The final epiphany is a nostalgic mnemonic sign, predictably presented *sous-rature*. Why is it there at all, though? Why does the free thinker Espinosa see heaven? Why does Villari, in "La espera," turn toward the wall to "dream" his imminent execution? Why does the protagonist of "Tlön" undertake a useless translation when he realizes that all is lost? The significant vision (in "El Evangelio"), the dream (in "El Sur" or in "La espera"), and the book (in "Tlön"), all of which appear as abrupt disjunctions of the narrative line, are there as the "secret" *peripeteia* by means of which the text refuses to surrender the subject's interiority to the forces of external destruction. If the adventure that overwhelms these protagonists is the equivalent of history, then the vision draws a magic circle around the self, preserving it from the inevitable contamination of the modern absurd. Consequently, these final scenes can be read as a trace of the old dream of the Latin American romance: to magically transcend a history portrayed as a grotesque nightmare.

In "La juventud en la otra ribera," the protagonist is a middle-aged Peruvian on vacation in Paris—the dream city of Latin American culture. But the Paris he finds is a place where everything is spurious, from the tavern set up to dupe tourists to the pseudo-artists who are Solange's friends. Of Sarmiento's "ideal France" there only remain now, significantly, certain historical places: Versailles, Notre Dame and Fontainebleau. In this way, the typically split geography of the romance places the possibility of authenticity on the "other side," which in this story is the other side of history: peaceful museums or bucolic prairies belonging to the world prior to 1789. The rest, the center of the city and of the narrative, is the barbarism of Solange's friends.[28]

The names of these criminals, curiously enough, harken back to the romanticism of the first half of the nineteenth century. The instigator of the crime, Petrus Borel, has the same name as the outlandish and unhappy member of the Jeune France who, in 1832, in his preface to his *Rhapsodies*, had proclaimed that his passion for freedom went beyond republicanism: it was a form of lycanthropy. "I am a republican because I cannot be a Carib Indian," he had added defiantly.[29] The second friend is Paradis, whose name alludes to Baudelaire's *Artificial Paradises*. With Solange as bait, they and their companion Jimmy rob and, at the end, in Fontainebleau, murder Plácido Huamán. The protagonist also has a significant name: Plácido (peaceful? a dreamer who is more curious than passionate?) and Huamán, a typically Quechua name. America, then, a placid, middle-class America with roots in its Indian past, is the bearer of civilization here; barbarism resides in the heart of modern Paris.

The first complication in this allegorical reversal of the foundational model is introduced by the fact that the three men occasionally communicate in a language that is not French. It is probably Arabic, since Jimmy is Moroccan—and since the historical Borel ended his life as a bureaucrat of sorts in the new colony of Algeria. The three, then, represent the former colonial world, the periphery, which has now invaded the center. Briefly, the center (i.e., the *logos*) has disappeared; it is a museum piece.

Criminals who masquerade as radical bohemians (with roots in a certain nineteenth-century literature which, like Borel's stories, is plagued with horror and crimes) assassinate this classic example of a provincial bourgeois. It is as if through his death, in symbolic and now grotesque fashion, were completed the unsuccessful revolution mourned by the original Borel in 1830. Therefore, like Espinosa's death, Huamán's also repeats elements of an originary mythic event—here the French Revolution and its aftermath—in degraded form.

Further complications are inscribed in Ribeyro's text by the complexity of the historical and the literary allusions. Unlike Sarmiento's romance, in which the comparison of Facundo's murderer with Danton served to underscore the end of the world of personalism and the birth of harmony, in Ribeyro's story Fontainebleau and Versailles are the uninhabited reminders of a project gone awry. Borrowing Terry Eagleton's phrase,[30] we could say that it is "the Enlightenment's grand narrative of emancipation" that is alluded to indirectly in the references to the Ancien Régime. The allusion is then broadened to include the subsequent historical split between the bourgeoisie and "the people," encoded in the name of Petrus Borel (in 1830, Borel was one of "the people's" artistic, contradictory defenders). And the whole is brought up to date in the tired rhetoric of an old avant-garde that now serves as a mask for crime. (It is tempting to think here of recent acts of terrorism in general and, more specifically, of the mixture of populist-revolutionary rhetoric and crime in some members of the Andean drug cartels.) Without straining the allegorical possibilities excessively, we might read in the annihilation of the bourgeois hero an image of the fear evoked by a spurious impersonation of the Left, which is presented as a doubling of its original, already problematic, 1830s self. In the end, the true enemy is the lure of the romantic trap—just as in Borges the true antagonist is the seductive power of "a" final meaning.[31]

In Ribeyro's novella, the dangers of the romantic trap are political (and these are allegorically encoded in the work) as well as existential. In the latter sense one recalls Champavert, in Borel's story of the same name, raging against monotony in true romantic fashion. Nature, perhaps, can save us from the theatrical farce of history, because it attaches us to existence, he concedes. However, what tedium!

> Nothing is more boring than fixity, an immutable fashion, a perpetual almanac. Every year, the trees are green and forever the trees are green; Fontainebleau! Who will deliver us from the green trees? How that irritates me! . . . Why no more variety? Why could not the leaves take in succession the colors of the rainbow? Fontainebleau! how dumb this greenery is! [*Champavert*, p. 200]

The site of Huamán's death, Fontainebleau, which is an inscription in the text of the demise of a historical order, can now also be linked to the romantic exasperation with repetition and desire for novelty, as expressed by Borel's Champavert. Both the farce of history that Champavert despised and the monotony of tradition (i.e., of nature) that elicits his sarcasm, can be circumvented or alleviated by the romancesque adventure—which is what Huamán does. Attracted by the possibility of something new, outside his colorless routine, he ventures into the enchanted forest—but this turns out to be an artificial paradise. In spite of this, he persists in his wanderings (to the reader's dismay), not out of love for Solange but because of his increasing attachment to what I am equating with the old code of the knights-errant: once begun, the travails, the arbitrary tests, are pursued wherever they may lead. However (and this returns us to the political subtext), since this Peruvian in Paris is a modern (i.e., post-1789) and a Latin American knight, his adventure retains elements of the ritual combat for social legitimacy found in *Facundo*. In both texts, the split landscape overlaps with a generational conflict. This is implied in Sarmiento's essay and clearly represented in "La juventud." Specifically, there are Oedipal allusions which can be read in both cases as a literary encoding of a historical struggle for power. In *Facundo* (p. 241), the author (i.e., the "civilized" hero) proposes himself as a modern Oedipus capable of resolving the riddle of the Sphynx and, by extension, destroying the monster's Argentine avatar, Rosas. In "La juventud," Paradis, one of the three "barbarians," is Oedipus: he wears dark glasses and limps.[32] (Huamán himself responds to this tension by becoming progressively more engaged in rivalry with the criminals.) The implications of this reversal, which is an inversion of both point of view and historical context, are obvious: in *Facundo*, Oedipus = Sarmiento / the positive hero = order and liberalism on the ascendant; in "La juventud," the bourgeois hero, the old representative of liberalism, is threatened and eventually murdered at the hands of a new Oedipus = Paradis / a criminal = disorder and terrorism. Borel's monsters have invaded reality.

This suggested struggle for legitimacy is, in turn, generalized into the ordeal for meaning, as in Borges's "El Evangelio." Huamán blindly cooperates with his assassins as he tries to outsmart them (akin in this to Lönnrot, the doomed detective in another story by Borges, "La muerte y la brújula"). This shifts the semantic weight away from a representation of fraudulent romanticism and away from what I read as its implied concomitant, modern terrorism, and ends up displacing meaning onto the broader universal absurdity of man's tragic, or irrelevant, fate.

All this notwithstanding, Ribeyro's concluding line once again indulges in the sudden reversal of romances by suggesting a last-minute form of individual transcendence: when Huamán falls to the ground, mortally wounded, he looks up and sees, "this time at last, nightingales and larks flying by" (*La juventud*, p. 309). The birds' absence had been noted three times before, first in the opening sentence of the story: "They were not nightingales or larks, but a poor autumn pigeon delousing itself on the window sill." The prairie in Fontainebleau where Huamán is killed is described as a clearly ritualistic place, so that, as in "El Evangelio," death is a rite of passage. In the case of "La juventud" the passage to "the other bank" (of the Seine and of the Styx) is from fraudulence (the pigeon) to truth (the nightingale). Or should we say from sordidness to beauty? There is a strong aestheticizing element in this story. Opposed to a history that is a travesty of old myths, death appears in both stories as the only redeeming absolute. If the latter is ironic in relation to the surface narrative, it is nevertheless raised to an archetypal, serious level by the symbols of Heaven and birds.

A quick comparison with the ending of Gustave Flaubert's *Un Coeur simple* will confirm this. Félicité, who, unlike Espinosa and Huamán, dies of natural causes, has, like them, a vision of a bird in her last moments. What she sees, however, or rather what she *thinks* she sees, is a giant parrot: "et, quand elle exhala son dernier souffle, elle crut voir, dans les cieux entrouverts, un perroquet gigantesque, planant au-dessus de sa tête."[33] I read this as one last textual refusal to yield to any ostensible form of idealization. It is psychologically reasonable that poor Félicité, who has come to confuse her stuffed parrot with the Holy Spirit (p. 75), should see its gigantic image in the end. The words "dans les cieux entrouverts" insinuate an opening up of a vertical dimension, a sudden link with transcendence in a life that until then has had none. But this parenthetical phrase is overwhelmed by the subsequent grotesque effect of the enormous and unconventional bird. The novel ends with this image, calculatedly stifling the contrary romantic impulse. In Borges's and Ribeyro's stories, the two protagonists are also two simple hearts, if observed from the inexorable vantage point of what Borges would call "narrative magic" (*Obras completas*, p. 230). Unlike Félicité, however, they are pitted against violence (i.e., against one of the forms of the demonic of romance) and their last visions suggest epiphanies that free what was constrained in Flaubert's lines.

Such epiphanies problematize the reading of these stories exclusively as parodies—as Alberto Julián Pérez, for example, suggests for "El Evangelio." Pérez stresses that, in general, Borges prefers what Mikhail Bakhtin defined as the satire of the Menippean variety (*Poética*, pp. 276–279), or the carnivalized serio-comic genres (p. 222). I agree with his fine readings, but I think it is important not to overlook the longing for a center that, in my view, is a mark, however faint, of the romantic absolute. Sylvia Molloy alludes to this longing for stability as a "foreseeable trace" within the broader essential *instability* of Borges's prose writings.[34] In her recent study of modern parody, Linda Hutcheon defines the genre as "imitation characterized by ironic inversion, not always at the expense of the parodied text." In other words, what used to be called the "target" of parody need not, and usually is not, parodied in the common sense of ridiculed or mocked but, on the contrary, serves as "an ideal or at least as a norm from which the modern departs."[35] Indeed, Borges's and Ribeyro's stories allude to origins as an ideal, or a myth, precisely in order to dramatize the distance separating their protagonists from meaning and to construe history as radically absurd. "La juventud" wants to leave no doubts about this: Huamán's body will be burned, as if the text wanted to emphasize that there will be no archive, no museum left for any future re-creation of significance. As I have attempted to show, there remains, nevertheless, a departure from the protocols of parody that should be acknowledged: in the last scenes, the customary discontinuity between the parallel codes of the "target" and the parody proper collapses. It is the protagonists themselves, and not some archetypal models, who have the vision. (Even when the coincidence is ambiguous, as is the case in Borges's story, the asymptote follows the positive movement of desire. It is the longing for coincidence that, so to speak, bends the line.) Borrowing psychoanalytic terminology, we could say that meaning, whose absence is parodied in the fabula, is not foreclosed but is, on the contrary, subject to a sudden return of the repressed, whose symbols are Heaven and the birds. These symbols are a minimalist trope through which plenitude reasserts itself as the eternal antagonist of barrenness.

"Perhaps it may not be redundant to point out," wrote Borges and Adolfo Bioy Casares in their prologue to *Los orilleros*, "that in ancient books, searches were always successful: the Argonauts found the golden fleece, and Galahad the Holy Grail. Nowadays, on the other hand, we find mysteriously pleasing the concept of an infinite search, or of the search for something that, when found, has deadly consequences. . . . [T]he white whale is the doom of him who finds it in the end."[36] Baltazar Espinosa and Huamán are modern versions of knights-errant: they are now bourgeois heroes, myopic readers, simple hearts. Unlike the chivalrous knights and their ancestor, old Ulysses, these modern characters take off never to return again. The land of otherness into which they venture is the textual locus of class conflicts rooted in the past—the antagonists are rough and very dumb gauchos or criminal con artists. In this sense, the meaningless destruction of the protagonist can be read as a metaphor for the Latin

American terror of the "shades" that did not find their final rest in Barranca Yaco. This failure of the quest perhaps is mysteriously pleasing, as Borges and Bioy propose. Or perhaps, as Borges laments in a later, revised version of the above statement, the hero's defeat is the product of modern man being "so poor in valor and faith" that he cannot believe in Heaven, only in Hell (Obras completas, p. 1128). This lost spiritual dimension (or white magic, if the Jamesian reader prefers) is precisely what the pharmakos' last vision reintroduces. Its effect is not to conflate history and Providence, as in Facundo, but, more modestly, to contest the hegemony of history as modernity's single interpretive code. In doing so, it redraws the textual battlelines to reveal a new enemy beyond the nineteenth-century problems inherited by Latin America. Indeed, it is the integrity of the classical unified subject that is now at risk. Against the uncontestable threat posed by the anonymous fragment of postmodernity (Espinosa's crucifixion, Huamán's burned body), the text resorts to magic to preserve the interiority of the self. In this sense, what Eagleton calls the modernist "struggle for meaning" drives both stories towards "classical styles of sense-making" (Against the Grain, p. 143)—here, the traditional absolute of romance, which defies the invasive nihilism of the parody.[37]

In Julio Cortázar's fiction, the transformation of the function of the name-of-the-father makes many of his stories inversions of Sarmiento's text.[38] Frequently we are presented with two absolutely heterogeneous realities—the axolotl and the man, the motorcyclist and the Moteca Indian, the familiar sweater and horror—which function like the old antagonists of the romance, since they end up being one entity. The denouement is as surprising as that of Sir Gawain and the Green Knight, and for the same reason: it is brought about by an unexpected change of sign—the dead man (in "Cartas de mamá") or the dream (in "La noche boca arriba"), for example, invades, i.e., becomes reality. But unlike Sarmiento's text, in these stories, under the mask of the fantastic is problematized a name-of-the-father whose salient trait is the exact opposite of that which infuses a utopian element to Civilización y barbarie: the "ideal" father of Sarmiento has turned into an inexorable and destructive reality principle. Two examples will suffice to make this clear: in "La noche boca arriba," the adventure (i.e., history, providential in the nineteenth century) now destroys both the contemporary motorcyclist and the ancient Moteca Indian; in "Axolotl," literature (i.e., civilization) appropriates the Aztec-faced salamander of the title, uses it, and abandons it to its solitude. Thus, writing, the equivalent of the symbolic order posited with such conviction by Sarmiento, is now a faute de mieux: the nineteenth-century celebration has become a resigned "consolation" for Cortázar's axolotl, a "mask" troubled by its bad faith in the story of "El perseguidor."

The "bloodied dust" of Facundo's remains, rising again from the past, can annihilate Borges's and Ribeyro's civilized heroes. In some of Cortázar's stories, more realistic in this respect, the past reasserts itself in order to replay its defeat—as we witness in the death of the Moteca, or through the entrapment of the tiny avatar of Xolotl, the Mexican god who had refused to comply with the sacrifices imposed by culture, and whose animal form is now labeled and on display in the aquarium.[39] In other stories by Cortázar, Facundo's legacy, modernized into the class conflict dormant in Sarmiento's text, can awaken desire and compassion in a bourgeois protagonist that longs for union with her/his double. Beyond the anecdote, though, in the textual unconscious, this fusion turns out to be a threat, that of setting in motion previously static social differences and thus initiating in the heart of the socius a dangerous fibrillation. This disruptive potential, however, the story hastily and successfully arrests. Indeed, the mapping of longing comes to a sudden halt after the fantastic encounter. In the story "Lejana," for example, economic otherness, initially foregrounded, is a double conjured up by guilt and by the desperate vacuity of the protagonist's middle-class life. The wealthy Alina Reyes dreams of a beggar; just like Espinosa and Huamán, she confronts her mirror image across social discontinuities. This notwithstanding, she differs from those heroes in a substantial respect: namely, that while they walk straight to their own destruction, she, perennially elegant, manages to wrest herself away from the beggar on the bridge. The fact that Alina, like Bruno in "El perseguidor," or like the man obsessed with the axolotl, walks away after a magical moment of contact, reasserts realism, and simultaneously preserves the status quo. In these stories, the romancesque transformation, that narrative sleight of hand when the monster becomes a prince, is restricted to an abrupt exchange at the level of consciousness. Perhaps all this points to the idealistic conditioning of Cortázar's worlds, in which the "fantastic" ultimately occludes the social lens and ends up identifying class separation with loss of psychic object. The former is shortchanged while the latter, unnamed, provides the obsessive intensity. Beyond the intriguing literary fireworks of the change of consciousness (between free observer and trapped axolotl, or between "queen" and "beggar"), the true magic pass may be the story's perplexed suppression of a realistic confrontation.

History and civilization regularize both the pastoral lands of Sarmiento's Argentina and the world of dreams, self-deceits, and desires of Cortázar's bourgeoisie. In the first case, the discourse celebrates the dissolution of difference as the beginning of utopia; in the second, the (frequently momentary) elimination of difference is a tragic destruction. This destruction is the inverted image—i.e., it is the replica of—the providential "civilization": it is the same because it is absolute, but it is the inverted image because it is now understood as a repression that cancels the future. We could summarize this contrast by suggesting that the limitless pampa as the site of adventure has been replaced by a "mean" aquarium (in "Axolotl"). Or that, in Cortázar's "Final de juego," the railroad desired by Sarmiento erases a last remnant of the romance in a pampa turned suburb. In the structural place of the earlier happy ending, we find the repeated punishment that the characters suffer for their desire, which is their crime: that of aspiring to a land of otherness, a secret space, denounced as fraudulent (whether it is so or not, and it is in many cases) by an inflexible social symbolism. The obsessive repetition of so many "finales de juego," so many "no se culpe a nadie," suggests that these stories are a disillusioned, or desperate, transformation of the foundational romance.

In the case of Juan Rulfo's *Pedro Páramo*, the similarities with the *Facundo* are obvious and are not only structural: both are narratives of a trip to the past; in both, the archaic American father is called to account for his crimes; both are Oedipal texts, and even the episode of Severa Villafañe, the young woman whom Quiroga unsuccessfully pursues, contains the seed of what will become the impossible love of Páramo for Susana San Juan. The oneiric vision of destructive omnipotence is similar and is linked in both cases to an imago of the archaic father: just as Facundo stretched his arms and destroyed La Rioja, Páramo crossed his so that Comala would starve and, with that gesture, annihilated his town.[40]

With regard to the exclusively romancesque elements which, at this point in the analysis, can easily be anticipated, we find that, indeed, halfway through the novel (and not at the very end) occurs the change of sign of the protagonists: those who appeared to be alive turn out to be dead. Once again, the element that determines the symbolic function of the u-topia, the no-place, ir-reality, is the name-of-the-father. In the world of Comala, without future, without an ideal father, without even a fantastic element to disguise an implacable reality principle, fragmentation is inevitable and the consequent dissemination of signification makes impossible any totalizing reading.[41] The absence of the name-of-the-father, nevertheless, is incorporated in Rulfo's discourse in the form of a pervasive lack, as intense as Sarmiento's dogmatism of hope, as devastating as Cortázar's fantasies of destruction. The nostalgia for a principle of intelligibility, that which Juan Preciado searched for in vain, is silenced without concessions. Such a destabilizing silence pushes to its coherent and rigorous limit the contemporary problematization of the ideal father of the foundational romance. What is interesting to point out, within the frame of the present essay, is that a nostalgia for that ideal remains and serves as an empty center, an absent icon around which Rulfo's narrative is organized. To put it differently, the erosion of the plenitude envisioned in *Facundo* did not lead to a realist literature—i.e., to a literature that abandoned its idealizing tendency—but rather produced another romance in which "el ideal brilla, literalmente, por su ausencia."

To speak of genre in literature is to speak of the long duration, as Josefina Ludmer pointed out, or as Bakhtin stated in dramatic terms: "They [the historians of literature] do not see beneath the superficial hustle and bustle of literary process the major and crucial fates of literature and language, whose great heroes turn out to be first and foremost genres, and whose 'trends' and 'schools' are but second- or third-rank protagonists."[42] Beyond, or underneath, the differences between "fantastic" literature, "magic realism," and other forms of contemporary nonrealist literature, some representative examples share both a structural and a semantic continuity with Sarmiento's text. Those shared traits are what I have called a genre: specifically, the romance. In some cases, generic characteristics and primal scene appear in pristine form, as in a story I have not yet mentioned, Gabriel García Márquez's "El ahogado más hermoso del mundo." In it, the beautiful drowned man is the pharmakos whose appearance in the world of the living brings about a magical regeneration of society. The story has been analyzed along similar lines by Lida Aronne-Amestoy, so there is no need here to elaborate it further.[43] In other cases, the genre is in internal conflict with a different, opposite one, as in Borges's "El Evangelio," or in Sarmiento's own "book." In all the texts studied in this essay, the romance constitutes an interpretive viewpoint from which to represent history as either providential or demonic. In his own prologue to *Facundo*, Borges significantly refers to the Joycean recognition that "history is a nightmare from which I want to wake up."[44] That nightmare, dramatized by the violent death of the protagonist, and its opposite, the vision, are the two poles around which these romances are organized. Wavering between one and the other, these narratives transform history into utopia "all at once" (this is the vision) or condemn history by estranging it to the radical alterity of the unintelligible, the devastating, or the absurd.

Notes

I am grateful to the editors who invited me to participate in this collection and who organized the excellent conference for which many of these papers were prepared. My essay is a substantially revised and expanded version of an earlier study, which did not include the sections on Borges and Ribeyro: "El *romance* latinoamericano: El género del *Facundo* y algunas de sus proyecciones recientes," *Dispositio* 15, no. 39 (1990): 67–84. Diana Sorensen Goodrich offered intelligent suggestions for that initial study. I also wish to thank the following colleagues for probing questions or helpful comments: Jaime Concha, Martine Gantrel, William Katra, Erna Berndt Kelley, Reyes Lázaro, and Sylvia Molloy. Julie Jones originally shared with me her interest in Ribeyro's wonderful stories, and Alberto Julián Pérez directed me to his own excellent study of genre in Borges's fiction. Thomas Montgomery read this essay with extreme thoroughness and kindness and, as always, Daniel Balderston encouraged my research and shared his own with me.

1. Umberto Eco, *The Role of the Reader: Explorations in the Semiotics of Texts* (Bloomington: Indiana University Press, 1979). In general, I am relying for these definitions on pp. 27–31 and the last chapter of Eco's study, titled "Lector in Fabula" (pp. 200–260). Here is further elaboration by Eco of what a fabula is and of its level of generalization, intermediate between plot and theme: "In order to recognize a given *fabula* the reader has to identify a narrative topic or a main theme. A narrative topic is nothing but a higher-level *fabula* or an ultimate macroproposition" (p. 209).

2. Domingo Faustino Sarmiento, *Facundo, Civilización y barbarie* (henceforth *Facundo*), 9th ed. (Buenos Aires: Espasa-Calpe, 1972), p. 154. Unless otherwise noted, all translations of this and the other Spanish-language texts discussed are my own.

3. The reader can "blow up or narcotize" given semantic properties of texts (Eco, *Role of the Reader*, p. 27). For Noël Salomon's reading, see his "Los valores románticos y novelescos en el 'Facundo,' " in *Realidad, ideología y literatura en el "Facundo" de D. F. Sarmiento* (Amsterdam: Rodopi, 1984), p. 154.

4. The genre, a contract between author and reader and not a preceptive, is the formal configuration that gives coherence to the narrative material and that, in the process of so doing, controls the reception of the text. Consequently, it is not an ideologically inert construct but rather a signifying strategy which, as such, resolves, contests, or sidesteps social contradictions. To posit a generic filiation for *Facundo*, therefore, is not an attempt to neutralize its polemic nature as a political tract, but an effort to reorient its analysis toward other parameters, also producers of intelligibility.

5. William Katra, "Reading *Facundo* as Historical Novel," *The Historical Novel in Latin America: A Symposium*, ed. Daniel Balderston (Gaithersburg,

Md.: Hispamérica and the Roger Thayer Stone Center for Latin American Studies, Tulane University, 1986), p. 39.

6. In Spanish, a "romance" is either a type of poem (whose English equivalent might be the ballad) or a sentimental love story. The absence of an explanation of the term is troublesome in Djelal Kadir's recent study of the topic: *Questing Fictions: Latin America's Family Romance,* foreword by Terry Cochran (Minneapolis: University of Minnesota Press, 1986). His Latin American or, in general, Hispanic readers may not grasp the implications of a genre that Kadir simply defines as a quest, a form of errantry. As such, the term seems vaguely applicable to all literature. For an excellent bibliographic review essay of deconstructive readings of the North American romance, see R. C. de Prospo's "Deconstructive Poe(tics)," *Diacritics* 18, no. 3 (1988): 43–64.

7. The now classic definition of the genre is Northrop Frye's in *The Anatomy of Criticism* (1957). I have used the Spanish translation, in which the pertinent section is "El *mythos* del verano: El Romance," *Anatomía de la crítica* (Caracas: Monte Avila, 1977), pp. 245–271. Essential is Fredric Jameson's very lucid study, "Magical Narratives: Romance as Genre," *New Literary History* 7 (1975): 135–164. I have also profited from Gillian Beer's *The Romance* (London: Methuen, 1970); John Stevens's *Medieval Romance: Themes and Approaches* (London: Hutchinson, 1973); and Frye's more recent *The Secular Scripture: A Study of the Structure of Romance* (Cambridge: Harvard University Press, 1976).

It is interesting that we do not have in Spanish the category of "romance" in the sense in which I am using it here. A. D. Deyermond addresses this issue in "The Lost Genre of Medieval Spanish Literature," *Hispanic Review* 43 (1975): 231–259. Hispanists have ignored this genre, proposes Deyermond, because of an axiomatic adherence to Ramón Menéndez Pidal's equation of the Spanish ethos with realism. Works that are not realistic have either been ignored as not representative or have been reduced to a few examples of a subgenre: the novels of chivalry.

Deyermond, a medievalist, apparently is not aware of the nineteenth-century familiarity with the concept, at least among the Argentine Generation of 1837, nor does he explain the presumed absence of theoretical formulations anywhere in the Hispanic world prior to Menéndez Pidal's writings. After all, if the category exists in English, it is as a result of extensive elaborations throughout the eighteenth century, which led to the establishment of a clear distinction between "old" and "new" romances. The wavering and initially uncertain usage of these terms is amply illustrated in Geoffrey Day, *From Fiction to the Novel* (London: Routledge & Kegan Paul, 1987). Edith Kern supplies abundant documentation on the earlier origin and usage mutations, in Romance languages and in English, of the terms "romance," "novel," and "novella." See her "The Romance of Novel/Novella," in *The Disciplines of Criticism: Essays in Literary Theory, Interpretation and History Honoring*

Renée Wellek, ed. Peter Demetz et al. (New Haven and London: Yale University Press, 1968), pp. 511–530.

In *Facundo*, Sarmiento uses the term "romance" several times: when he refers to the literary elaboration of what is peculiarly American, which he understands in terms of a majestic nature (p. 24), original human types (p. 29), and, above all, as the struggle between "European civilization and indigenous barbarism, between intelligence and matter" (p. 24); or when he explains that the "romancesque fame" (p. 132) of Juan Lavalle is derived from the admiration elicited by his cavalry charges, which are a gaucho, Argentine way of fighting in war. Thus understood, then, the term "romance" connotes the exotic, vast, intense, or original. Valentín Alsina uses "romance" as synonymous with fiction. Both Sarmiento and Alsina oppose, tacitly or explicitly, "romance" (i.e., fiction) to history (i.e., truth, facts). (Alsina's letter to Sarmiento is included in Alberto Palcos's edition of *Facundo* [La Plata: Universidad Nacional de La Plata, 1938], p. 364. Hereafter: *Facundo*, Palcos ed.)

Elizabeth Garrels has studied Sarmiento's use of the term in the *Facundo* and infers that he considered it the appropriate genre for descriptions of past times of war and anarchy. From this, Garrels draws the inevitable corollary that no more "romances" about heroic figures will be written once Argentina becomes civilized. The new genre for the new country, she concludes, will be the novel, with its mediocre protagonists. See her "La historia como romance en el *Facundo*," in Balderston, ed., *The Historical Novel in Latin America*, pp. 75–84. Doris Sommer, for her part, proposes that the nineteenth-century Latin American novel is all a romance. Her definition of the genre, however, differs from mine in that she is concerned with the sentimental romance, the love story. On this basis, Sommer establishes a metaphoric equivalence between the conjugal union of the protagonists of the novels and national reconciliation. See Sommer, "Not Just Any Narrative: How Romance Can Love Us to Death," in Balderston, ed., *The Historical Novel in Latin America*, pp. 45–74.

8. Pound, *The Spirit of Romance* (London: Dent & Sons, [1910]), p. 77.

9. That this resulted in the absence of a true romantic movement is Octavio Paz's thesis in *Los hijos del limo: Del romanticismo a la vanguardia* (Barcelona: Seix Barral, 1974). According to Paz, the essence of romanticism—the revolt against systematic reason—was delayed in Latin America, where it did not appear until the advent of the fin de siècle modernist movement.

10. Mitre's remark is quoted in Ana María Barrenechea, "Función estética y significación histórica de las campañas pastoras en el *Facundo*," *Nueva Revista de Filología Hispánica* 15 (1961): 319.

11. This is Peter Brooks's thesis in his very suggestive study of nineteenth-century melodrama, *The Melodramatic Imagination: Balzac, Henry James, Melodrama and the Mode of Excess* (New Haven and London: Yale University Press, 1976). The romance has many points of contact with the melodrama.

12. Since I am more familiar with modern Latin American literature than with medieval romances, I am offering here Latin American examples. The reader is referred to the studies cited in note 7, above, for numerous illustrations taken from medieval literature as well as for discussions of other characteristics of the genre.

13. The name-of-the-father is, in Lacan's psychoanalytic terminology, the equivalent of the cultural (patriarchal, obviously) order. It breaks the symbiotic, imaginary relationship between mother and child, and forces the latter to enter the shifting grounds of language and society, where her/his place is no longer one of absolute, interchangeable positions, of I–thou, of mirror images, of pure love or hatred. It is important to add that both stages of development, the imaginary and the symbolic, are forms of alienation: there is no original, authentic, or essential ground. Elaborations and definitions of this and other Lacanian terms are found, for example, in his *Ecrits: A Selection*, trans. Alan Sheridan (New York: Norton, 1977) or in *The Language of the Self: The Function of Language in Psychoanalysis*, preliminary study, ed. and trans. Anthony Wilden (Baltimore: Johns Hopkins University Press, 1968). I have studied the function of the father and have analyzed *Facundo* as an Oedipal text in "Sarmiento y el (anti)-padre americano," *Revista Occidental* 6–7 (1985): 153–166.

14. Respectively: Juan Bautista Alberdi, *La barbarie histórica de Sarmiento* (Buenos Aires: Pampa y Cielo, 1964), p. 19; Julio Caillet-Bois, "Naturaleza e historia, providencia y libertad en "Facundo" de Sarmiento," *Bulletin Hispanique* 75, nos. 3–4 (1973): 350; and Garrels, "La historia como romance," p. 79.

15. Kant, *On History*, ed. Lewis White Beck; trans. Lewis White Beck et al. (Indianapolis: Bobbs-Merrill, 1963), pp. 24–25 (emphasis added).

16. Lionel Gossman, *Augustin Thierry and Liberal Historiography*, introduction by Hayden White (Middletown, Conn.: Wesleyan University Press, 1976), p. 39.

17. Starting with the gothic novel, these characters can be internal, conflicting parts of a single personality which tend to double each other. Examples are Mary Shelley's *Frankenstein* and Robert Louis Stevenson's *Dr. Jekyll and Mr. Hyde.*

18. These were Sarmiento's words in 1885, when he visited Facundo's grave in the Recoleta (*Facundo*, Palcos ed., p. 464).

19. This is in an article published in *El Nacional*, September 22, 1881, upon publication of the Italian translation of *Facundo* (see Palcos ed., pp. 459–460).

20. René Girard, *Violence and the Sacred*, trans. Patrick Gregory (Baltimore and London: Johns Hopkins University Press, 1977), p. 107. The *pharmakos* (scapegoat), both despised and elevated, guilty and redeemer, is prerationalistic, mythic—i.e., outside the domain of the identity principle—and thus, in modern terms, a contradictory cultural function which will later, in

modern societies, be replaced by the law. Sarmiento's "book" is precisely the identification of a pharmakos, who is condemned, eventually exalted in contradictory fashion, and ultimately transcended as society accedes to the domain of the law. The latter transition is the happy ending of his romance and, in Lacanian terms, constitutes the shift from the imaginary to the symbolic realm. My emphasis thus departs from Caillet-Bois's binary summary concerning Quiroga: "Facundo is the symbol of nature redeemed by society and reconciled to it; he is the martyr for the generous cause of future unity" ("Naturaleza e historia," p. 350). "Martyr," furthermore, seems to imply that the Tiger of the Llanos willingly renounced his life for the sake of unity.

21. "And thus humanity goes along erecting laws, principles, immense monuments, on these obscure foundations whose origins, whose hollow recesses enclose an error, a mystery, a crime." Joaquín V. González, *La tradición nacional*, excerpted in Armando Zárate, *Facundo Quiroga, Barranca Yaco: Juicios y testimonios* (Buenos Aires: Plus Ultra, 1985), p. 214.

22. Julia Kristeva refers to "the sacrificial logic of separation and syntactical sequence at the foundation of language and the social code" (*The Kristeva Reader*, ed. Toril Moi [New York: Columbia University Press, 1986], p. 199). Similarly, Jacques Derrida has pushed to a rigorous extreme the nonessentialist, purely differential system of culture and language, whose originary violence consists of "inscribing within a difference, . . . classifying, . . . suspending the vocative absolute" (*Of Grammatology*, trans. Gayatri Chakravorty Spivak [Baltimore and London: Johns Hopkins University Press, 1976], p. 112). "To think the unique *within* the system," he elaborates, "to inscribe it there, such is the gesture of the arche-writing: arche-violence, loss of the proper, of absolute proximity, of self-presence."

23. In *El informe de Brodie* (Buenos Aires: Emecé, 1970). The other Borges texts mentioned in the present essay are all found in his *Obras completas, 1923–1972*, ed. Carlos V. Frías (Buenos Aires: Emecé, 1974). In the case of "El Evangelio," for reasons that will become apparent in my analysis, I will refer variously to the original 1970 edition, to the subsequent English translation (*Doctor Brodie's Report*, trans. Norman Thomas di Giovanni in collaboration with the author [New York: Dutton, 1972]), and to the final version (in *Obras completas*).

24. And an antithesis of what may have been the historical source for this story. The protagonist, Espinosa, had studied at the Ramos Mejía School. The story thus alludes, en passant, to the historical figure after whom the school was named: a progressive landowner in the south of the province of Buenos Aires shortly after independence. On his farm on the frontier, Ramos Mexía had pioneered good relations with the Indians, had paid them for the land he needed, and had hired many of them to work for him for wages. He had also taught them religion, his own version of Christianity. The government used him as guarantor when it signed a treaty with the Indians. The sad end of this affair, in 1820, was not brought about by the "barbarians," as in Borges's

story, but on the contrary by the arbitrary violence of the Buenos Aires government. For a historical narrative of this little-known episode, see, for example, Roberto H. Marfany, "La guerra con los indios nómadas," in Academia Nacional de la Historia, *Historia de la Nación Argentina (desde los orígenes hasta la organización definitiva en 1862)*, director general Ricardo Levene (Buenos Aires: Imprenta de la Universidad, 1944), 6:1050–1056.

25. Alberto Julián Pérez, *Poética de la prosa de J. L. Borges. Hacia una crítica bakhtiniana de la literatura* (Madrid: Gredos, 1986), p. 283.

26. Here are the two impoverished and modified versions, first in the English translation and then the correspondingly altered paragraph in Spanish. In both cases, the parataxis of the girl weeping and the vision is annulled by an interpolated explanation (here italicized). The indexical quality of opening a door is equally lost when the noun is replaced with a pronoun.

> Then they mocked at him, spat on him, and shoved him toward the back part of the house. The girl wept. *Espinosa understood what awaited him on the other side of the door.* When they opened *it*, he saw *a patch of sky.* A bird sang out. A goldfinch, he thought. [*Doctor Brodie's Report*, p. 22; emphasis added]

> Después lo maldijeron, lo [*sic*] escupieron y lo empujaron hasta el fondo. La muchacha lloraba. *Espinosa entendió lo que le esperaba del otro lado de la puerta.* Cuando *la* abrieron, vio el firmamento. Un pájaro gritó; pensó: Es un jilguero. [*Obras completas*, p. 1072; emphasis added]

27. Structurally homologous to Borges's "Tlön," Sir Thomas Browne's "Urn Burial" discusses the vain attempts of the pagan world to achieve immortality, and contrasts them, at the end of his meditation, with the mystery of the only true transcendence, Christian salvation. I have studied the significance of these similarities between Borges's and Browne's texts in " 'Tlön, Uqbar, Orbis Tertius' and 'Urn Burial,' " *Comparative Literature* 36 (1984): 328–342.

28. Julio Ramón Ribeyro, *La juventud en la otra ribera* (Barcelona: Argos Vergara, 1983).

29. These words from his first book, *Rhapsodies*, are repeated by Borel in the preface to his following collection of stories, where he attributes them to the fictive Champavert—the protagonist who commits suicide in the last story (*Champavert, contes immoraux*, ed. Jean-Luc Steinmetz [Paris: Chemin Vert, 1985], p. 12). To complicate matters even more, Borel explains in his "Notice" that the true author of the whole collection is the dead Champavert, who used as his pseudonym . . . the "fictive" name Petrus Borel!

30. Terry Eagleton, *Against the Grain. Essays: 1975–1985* (London: Verso, 1986), p. 134.

31. Perhaps it is not a coincidence that mention is made in "La juventud" of a certain Dumesnil, who is the father of the supposedly innocent young girl at Borel's party and a Sorbonne professor whom the criminals fear. This

may be an allusion to René Dumesnil, the author of scholarly studies on Flaubert—who, in turn, so feared (his own) romanticism.

32. To speak of class conflict in this story might seem less excessive when one remembers that the pattern is similar and clearer in other stories by Ribeyro, as well as in his novel *Los geniecillos dominicales*, all set in Peru. The object of desire is repeatedly a member of a different social class, as if class and not gender defined otherness (indeed, two of those stories deal with homosexual desire). In the novel, as in "La juventud," the perceived dangers of this situation end in murder.

33. Flaubert, *Trois Contes*, chronology and foreword by Jacques Suffel (Paris: Garnier-Flammarion, 1965), p. 83. The English translation reads: "and when she drew her last breath, she fancied that she saw, in the opening heavens, a gigantic parrot soaring above her head" (*Three Tales by Gustave Flaubert*, introduction by Guy de Maupassant, n.t. [New York: Limited Editions Club, 1978], p. 48).

34. Sylvia Molloy, *Las letras de Borges* (Buenos Aires: Sudamericana, 1979), p. 11.

35. Linda Hutcheon, *A Theory of Parody* (New York and London: Methuen, 1985), pp. 5–6. Unlike satire, which is always moral and social in its focus and ameliorative in its intention, the art of our time, essentially parodic in Hutcheon's definition of the term, has as its "target . . . another work of art or, more generally, another form of coded discourse" (p. 16).

36. Borges and Bioy Casares, *Los orilleros. El paraíso de los creyentes*, 2nd ed. (Buenos Aires: Losada, 1975), p. 8.

37. Eagleton's thesis is that, in modernist art, the "self-regulating agent of humanism" still exists, uncomfortably side by side with the postmodern, dispersed, and fetishized fragments of the self. In other words, the unified subject is not dead, but is in conflict with what postmodernity has proposed as its substitute: a "decentered network of libidinal attachments, emptied of ethical substance and psychical interiority" (*Against the Grain*, p. 145 et pass.). His conclusions apply both to Borges's and Ribeyro's stories—which are, in Eagleton's sense, modernist texts: "Postmodernism persuades us to relinquish our epistemological paranoia and embrace the brute objectivity of random subjectivity; modernism, more productively, is torn by the contradictions between a still ineluctable bourgeois humanism and the pressures of a quite different rationality, which, still newly emergent, is not even able to name itself" (p. 144).

38. All but one of the stories I will mention appear in Cortázar's *Ceremonias* (Barcelona: Seix Barral, 1968). "Lejana," which I refer to in some detail, is included in *Bestiario*, 9th ed. (Buenos Aires: Sudamericana, 1969).

39. The mythic background presupposed by Cortázar's story is clarified in Roberto Moreno, "El axolotl," *Estudios de Cultura Nahuatl* 8 (1969): 157–174.

40. Juan Rulfo, *Pedro Páramo* (Mexico: Fondo de Cultura Económica, 1964), p. 121.

41. Steven Boldy has contributed several excellent studies on the function of the name-of-the-father in Rulfo's novel. See, for example, his "The Death of the Father, Language and Others in Juan Rulfo's *Pedro Páramo*," *Romance Quarterly* 33 (1986): 463–476.

42. M. M. Bakhtin, *The Dialogic Imagination,* ed. Michael Holquist; trans. Caryl Emerson and Michael Holquist (Austin: University of Texas Press, 1981), pp. 7–8. For Josefina Ludmer's summary, see her "La lengua como arma. Fundamentos del género gauchesco," *Homenaje a Ana María Barrenechea,* ed. Lía Schwartz Lerner and Isaías Lerner (Madrid: Castalia, 1984), pp. 471–472, n. 2.

43. The story appears in the collection *La increíble y triste historia de la cándida Eréndira y de su abuela desalmada* (Barcelona: Bruguera, 1978). Lida Aronne-Amestoy's interpretation is found in her *Utopía, paraíso e historia: Inscripciones del mito en García Márquez, Rulfo y Cortázar,* Purdue University Monographs in Romance Languages no. 19 (Amsterdam and Philadelphia: Benjamins, 1986), pp. 13–38.

44. Jorge Luis Borges, "Prólogo" to Domingo F. Sarmiento, *Facundo* (Buenos Aires: Ateneo, 1974), p. vii.

18   The Opulent *Facundo*: Sarmiento and Modern Argentine Fiction

MARTA MORELLO-FROSCH

The adventure is recorded in a notable book whose subject matter
may be all things to all men (I Corinthians 9:22); indeed, it has
the capacity for almost infinite repetitions, versions, and
perversions.
> —Jorge Luis Borges, "Biografía de Tadeo Isidoro Cruz
> (1829–1874)"

Borges's epigraph refers to *Martín Fierro*, but it could well be applied to
Facundo, perhaps the other most paradigmatic work in Argentine literary
history. Inspired by these classic texts, a number of contemporary writers—much like Borges himself—have undertaken a revision of the literary past in order to structure their fictions. They have invoked canonical
authors and texts from this century and the last in an effort to bring these
consecrated books into the modern tradition. With reverential imitation
or irrepressibly parodic inflections, modern Argentine writers unfold a
two-tiered project with which they merge national literary traditions while
simultaneously imposing a distance between the author and his literary
past and prompting a radically original reading of the dialectics of a national culture. This confrontation and rapprochement of seemingly es-
tranged literary programs form the basis of a recent literary consciousness
in Argentina. Through these strategies of reappraisal, the continuity of
national heritage is assured especially at a time when cultural process is
threatened by state intervention or historical stagnation.

Sarmiento and Borges are perhaps the two exemplary figures whose
presence is most often echoed in the work of recent authors, particularly
in those who believe in the dominant role of a lettered elite in national
culture.[1] In the case of Sarmiento, modern authors see an insistent preoccupation with the process of national development as it relates to an analysis
of more recent historical circumstance. The historical view projected in
the pages of *Facundo* and *Recuerdos de provincia*[2] often provides a basis
for comparison, argument, and difference which sustains the disquisitions

347

of contemporary authors. In the work of recent authors, it is not a matter of adopting a canonical text of more-or-less fixed meaning. On the contrary, one seeks—and finds—in Sarmiento a common ground for dialogue among Argentines and among many other Latin Americans, allowing the proliferation of new and specific interpretations about present and past. We are thus confronted with multiple readings of the original text. In this condition, Sarmiento's writing is maintained as an open artifact, a vivid reminder of the past: it is alive and in a state of constant production, read and understood through recent social and historical experiences[3] and through an acutely critical perspective made obvious by current dilemmas.

Nineteenth-century texts offer three challenges to modern writers: to rethink Argentine history, to reconceive the semantics of certain events which mark that history, and to reconstitute national culture. Ironically, all these projects informed Sarmiento's own experience with writing. Thus, current authors not only carry considerable cultural baggage—what Foucault calls the historical a priori[4]—but they also discover in their ancestor a series of discursive practices, a kind of literary archive they assume to be known to a number of readers. As a result of the manipulation and use of familiar texts, they even suggest transformations in the reading of Sarmiento. By rereading Sarmiento through the lens of contemporary fiction, the nineteenth-century model is often subjected to a strange exegetical process, displacing signifiers, exploding commonplace centers of meaning, and interrupting the discursive logic that organized Sarmiento's texts. Although the echoes of Sarmiento's writing prompt certain expectations in the reader, they often conclude in a challenge to one's conventional understanding of the canonical book and its history. The new text positions itself against the space of Sarmiento's original, marking precisely the differences and deviations from the original work. In effect, the modern historical focus is articulated through a current state of knowledge in constant dialogue with a tradition that it accepts as its own, but whose boundaries it expands and fragments as the basis for new analyses and understanding.

The words of Sarmiento are taken neither as reliable documentation nor as the grounds for a faithful representation of history. For this reason, it is important here to analyze the mechanisms by which the texts are appropriated, the differences between the current and earlier uses of language, and the presence of new objects of meaning that destabilize icons of the past. We must also look at the recuperation of national memory belonging to those sectors of society which profess cultural amnesia or which have been excluded from access to the language of a historical past. In other words, from the surface of contemporary novels, we must measure the intrusion of previously silenced voices or the mutations of ideas and images that had enjoyed a certain privilege before. As modern writers emphasize what is *different* in the context of what is *analogous,* here I will attempt to analyze such differences as a *relational* concept (as suggested by Jameson[5]) rather than make an inventory of disparate images and symbols.

One of the central topics that modern writers share with Sarmiento is a reevaluation of the role of the intellectual in the reconstitution and development of culture. This analysis has been volunteered intermittently throughout Argentina's national history, especially in the wake of social upheavals that profoundly altered the social fabric. Civil war, the end of Peronism, and the fall of the recent military dictatorship have been especially rich stimuli, prompting a dramatic self-criticism about the intellectual's function in modern society. In recent texts, Sarmiento is often invoked as a model for these concerns; and in the particular examples of Ricardo Piglia's *Respiración artificial*[6] and Andrés Rivera's *En esta dulce tierra,*[7] the legacy of the nineteenth-century statesman becomes a topic of prolonged meditation. In the works of both novelists, but especially in Piglia's *Respiración artificial,* errors are revealed in the conduct of cultural and ideological mediators with respect to social change and the kinds of alliances made possible within the context of historical events. In addition, in their modern novels, Piglia and Rivera also identify surrogate figures—new mediators of the intellectual's task—who can carry out of the mission of cultural change in dramatically unexpected ways. Thus, these tasks are no longer relegated (as they were in Sarmiento's time) to the responsibility of a small lettered elite, but extend to broader social sectors who voice an opinion about national destiny.

In these recent texts, intellectual discourse emerges from the margins of society: poorly employed professionals, frustrated writers, and well-trained immigrants whose education rarely leads to employment. This discourse is focused on a study of the possibilities of inserting culture within a political praxis whose definition nonetheless remains vague. The intellectual described in modern texts concerns himself with ways to produce new forms of mediation,[8] facilitating symbolic constructions that link the masses with national culture. Thus, writers like Piglia and Rivera attempt to extend cultural participation to include a greater number of voices, and they convert this impulse stylistically into texts of multiple narrators and abundant points of view. These authors are not guided by a goal of vindicating relativism; rather, the presence and value of *otherness* orients these writing practices.

At first glance, these are texts that reveal a composition of disorderly fragments. They are made up of quotations or mixtures of readings, composed of elements drawn from diverse stylistic conventions and distinct political and scriptural origins. In this respect, they are very distant from the *totalizing* vision of Sarmiento, who incorporated dissident voices into the heterogeneous texture of *Facundo* and dealt with the multiple forces that had shaped the life he described in *Recuerdos de provincia*, but who tried to coalesce these elements into a single meaning—all under the self-proclaimed role as *truthbearer* of the nation. From this position Sarmiento assigned discursive spaces to "the others"—to the pathfinder, the bad gaucho, the tracker, the *caudillos*—but he also circumscribed them historically and textually to predefined roles without possibility of change. Thus, even if he gave them access to print (and Facundo Quiroga serves as a central example) he did not let them articulate alternative visions of society; rather, they were held as deviations from bourgeois culture and provided deleterious examples for the nation. Sarmiento gave them voice, recognized their presence, but did not formulate any program in which they played a role as legitimate actors. While he recognized the failure of the lettered elite belonging to the ingenuous city of Buenos Aires—an elite that failed to perceive approaching dangers—he would not suggest a third position whereby old antagonists could settle scores with new forms of mediation.

In contrast to Sarmiento's fixed articulation of warring camps (only remember the most notable antagonism: civilization *or* barbarism), the modern authors under discussion here conceive a third position. Like Sarmiento they discover new relational possibilities, traverse considerable territory, and contemplate extraneous models. But beyond the nineteenth-century model, recent authors are fully conscious of the *relative* viability of these propositions in view of the national situation before them; they problematize events in seemingly interminable discussions and letters, and in moments of intense reflection. If Sarmiento's favorite recourse was to re-create scenes and settings—even battles figure in his inclusive and unique gaze—recent writers are obsessed with dialogue, both oral and written, and with the dialectic of their characters, who are sometimes represented in reflexive dialogue with themselves. In Piglia's novel, for example, apparently composed of a patchwork of texts, what interests him most is accounting for *otherness*, the marginal figures who are also seen as historical agents. Situating his characters in small political groups (no large associations were possible in the late 1970s under the shadow of military rule), where personal relationships are of utmost importance, he shows the complementary or shared interests that link individuals in unusual alliance. To the extent that all the actors are marginal, the ex-politician is exemplary, paralyzed, tied to his wheelchair and to his memories of a triumphant past. But his mind transforms these memories under the light of personal failure and the historical failing of his landowning class in one of the most lucid analytical moments of the national present.

Apart from the symbolic value of this ex-actor in history, paralyzed by the present and condemned to reflect upon the past, it is clear that in Piglia's novel, as opposed to the autobiographical enterprise of Sarmiento in *Recuerdos de provincia*, historical future and personal destiny are not linked in common projects of a fundamental providentialism. On the contrary, Piglia shows us the nonrealization of personal lives as viewed in historical terms. Thus, lives are interrupted, they go off course, careers are aborted in crime, vocations are frustrated, and destinies destroyed only to begin again on tracks totally opposite to those for which they had been prepared. This suggests that history is either an alien space with no room for such themes or a fiction told more often by others.

In Piglia's novel, however, it is precisely those who are excluded who will assume their own discourse and history. These are the degraded figures of the national scene: crippled politicians, Polish philosophers who retreat to endless games of chess, European nobles who no longer have an audience to receive ceremonious lessons about an irreversibly decadent world. They tell a personal history from the edges of the Argentine landscape and from the margins of the social corpus (in Concordia, on the national frontier, in the quiet shelter of abandoned houses); in this way, they enlarge the semantics of narrating national events. We are no longer presented with archetypal figures of the grandeur of those in *Facundo*; the immigrants are neither rural nor urban proletariat, neither respectable intellectuals nor famous teachers who provoke analysis of national reality. Thus, as displaced persons from European wars and internal conflicts, they emerge as moderately impassioned figures enlivened by commentary on philosophy and culture. Absent, too, are picturesque anecdotes, singular events of distinction. All of these new characters are subject matter for fiction, known but seldom articulated until now by sponsors of a national project.

Respiración artificial tells the story of a relationship—through epistolary exchange—of Renzi with his uncle, Marcelo Maggi. Both are interested in the genre of biography; the nephew wants to uncover the real life of his uncle, but he ends up getting interested in the nature of the fictions plotted by the family itself, including those promoted by the subject in question. This is a biography in which the deformations, perversions, and often apocryphal *readings* of specific deeds take on more importance than the deeds themselves. It is by what is said, rejected, or accepted that the actions are validated or annulled, for they acquire meaning only in the text. Here Piglia echoes the importance of the *reception* of facts, of the legend itself, in the constitution of a public personality as it was used by Sarmiento in *Facundo*. But while Sarmiento used these anecdotes to register the organic nature of his subject, including his ambiguities and contradictions, Piglia resorts to different versions of the life of the uncle, the fabulous and distant Maggi, in order to accentuate the personality of speaking subjects. Meanwhile Maggi, the object of their declarations, remains a distant character, geographically and psychologically, except in his letters, his texts.

The relationship between uncle and nephew provides an opportunity to make observations about national history, literature, and the immediate past—all as a function of discussions about a mysterious personage who is the object of a biographical project of Maggi. This important person, Enrique Ossorio, intellectual disciple of Pedro de Angelis, was a collaborator with Juan Manuel de Rosas and Juan Lavalle during the reign of terror of 1837–1838. His betrayal discovered, he hides in the basement of a relative's home where he survives for a couple of months, procreates, and finally is able to flee the country. This figure of the conscious traitor, who later leaves his memoirs to Juan Bautista Alberdi, whom he considers his intellectual soul mate, is the figure of the failed mediator. He occupies the third position, the one who conceives a state in which federalists and unitarians would not be the only historical agents called into action. The irony of his position is undeniable, for it concerns an exiled person who lives from and within utopia, a nonexistent, unreal place conceivable only in the mind of a convicted traitor. Thus the nineteenth-century Ossorio struggles from *outside* his country to elucidate a better future and writes utopian letters in exile dated 1979—the year in which Piglia's novel is set—developing a possible program which corresponds to the deliriums of one displaced. The crippled ex-politician is his nephew, heir to his patrimony in terms of land but not in terms of vision. In Piglia's terms, then, the efforts of the human species have neither produced nor prepared an exemplary life. If Sarmiento, in his own text and in his admiration for Benjamin Franklin, could be seen as a self-made man, then Ossorio is a self-*unmade* man,[9] a ruined patrician. His descendants have done well thanks to a fortune amassed in exile, but they lack historical imagination at the moment of the ascent to power.

The second part of *Respiración artificial* takes place in Concordia, where Renzi turns up in search of his uncle. The nephew thinks they will finally see one another and be able to talk about their biographical projects, about Argentine history which is a passion of both, and about the remote and heterodox Ossorio of the nineteenth century. So it will be the figure of this utopian traitor/hero, contemporary of Sarmiento and Alberdi, who will dominate both parts of the novel and spark the epistolary and verbal interchange of the central characters. This portion of the novel consists of a *payada*, or poetic duel, between marginal intellectuals reunited on the eastern frontier of the country. There, in a provincial coterie, these individuals (who are openly out of touch with the cultural and social events of the urban centers) produce their personal history, their version of the national and foreign past, creating an odd interrelationship and mutual dependence. Likewise, this heterogeneous group is aware of the asynchronic rhythms produced on the periphery of metropolitan culture, and they comment on the advantages and dangers. So even if news arrives late from the capital (the center continues to disseminate new ideas as in Sarmiento's time), on the periphery there is more space for the dissidents—the strange ones, as some members of this group would be seen—for they read and apply cultural signs in an unexpected way.

This discussion among marginal characters breaks with the assumed cultural unity represented by Buenos Aires as absolute and unique producer of national signs of culture. In Concordia—a real and ironic name which designates what is absent in national discourse—literature is also composed; people think and read; and the social and cultural spectrum of the country (often restricted to the most visible groups in the capital) is expanded. In addition, the vision from a distance cultivated by these observers and resembling that of the exile, provides a new perspective by denaturalizing and distancing known events through the time and space traversed. It is a singular group: the Russian nobleman whose coat of arms has no basis in truth and who shrewdly designates himself as a living museum; the Polish philosopher-linguist, disciple of Wittgenstein, who observes the survival of gaucho life in the language of Entre Ríos; the teacher of Argentine history exiled from the capital, *magister ludi in absentia* of the intellectual marginal group. Together, they fashion a new mode of speech. Neither voices in the desert nor central characters, they propose a representational style designed to narrate history and culture. Piglia here offers a response to Sarmiento's early proposal: the interior is seen as an agent not of historic barbarism, but of cultivated options not previously recorded within official texts; too, he displaces the traditional northwest with the historically less valid northeast. This, then, is a modernized version of the proposal of *Facundo*. It benefits from a concept of the past as open, available, and transformable; it is the product of a textual reception that is never considered static.

In the work by Andrés Rivera, *En esta dulce tierra*, the action occurs during the tyranny of Rosas, a paradigmatic space in Argentine literature, starting with Sarmiento. The narrative centers on the persecution and concealment of Doctor Cufré as a result of the assassination of Maza in 1839 and the subsequent crimes and massacres of the Mazorca. Apart from this obvious historical and temporal relationship, Rivera provides a coordinate for analyzing the problem of the intellectual in moments of repression and civil crisis. What value does European education and a civilized perspective have at the peak moments of barbarism? How can Cufré resist and oppose it without going mad from it all? This character is the voice of reason: he is a doctor educated in France who has returned to Argentina despite his lack of faith in the historical destiny of his country. His ambivalence is explicit in the commentary he makes to his professor in France: "I struggle against all hope. This is what it means to be Argentine today." The narrative mainly focuses on the moment when Cufré learns of the assassination from a small and thin man who will later disappear at the hands of the Mazorca. The story is composed, like Piglia's, of incriminating letters that should be burned, of conversations that spread culpability and suspicion, of false reports disseminated by newspapers and small groups of readers. It is a patchwork of reliable and false information which circulates around the destroyed city, "that land which subjected its children to rites and suffering so horrifying that even the most debased slaves of the czar would resist them."

Cufré must take refuge in the house of Isabel Starkey, his ex-lover. Hidden in the cellar, he tries to reestablish relations with his damaged body, with his ex-lover, and with the outside world whose echoes Isabel brings him only reluctantly. In this way, she reads him the texts of the enemy. In almost total darkness, Isabel is transformed into the obsessive voice of official history that has hounded him and holds him captive. Cufré feels like the inmates he saw when he studied medicine in distant Paris. Delirious, he is converted into a messenger of God; from one accused, he becomes supreme accuser. We witness his physical and mental deterioration until his final fortuitous escape.

The end of the novel consists of two possible versions, both conjectural. Rivera refers to the survival of federalism in national territory after Rosas's defeat at Caseros and suggests the presence of Cufré at the side of Felipe Varela, a lieutenant of "El Chacho" Peñaloza, the federalist caudillo from La Rioja. Cufré could, then, end up identified with dissident sides of the federalist ranks and not with the unitarians, who are promoting national organization. In either of the possible epilogues, Cufré represents the role of the other, the alternative with his scientific knowledge put to the service of the agonizing Varela in his final retreat to the northwest.

Both the narrative and Cufré's presence come to an end at the moment Sarmiento assumes the presidency in 1868, a historic crossroads in which the protagonist decides, significantly, to descend once again of his own volition into the "cellar, hole, or cubicle" where he had hidden before. Does he escape the hour of triumph of the anti-Rosas forces? This possible ending reopens the problem of the function of the intellectual in relation to history. Neither pro-Rosas nor pro-Sarmiento, Cufré "directed his eyes toward the future, that abstraction which incites men like him to conspiracy and combat, and which survives defeat . . . with the inevitable signs of utopia."

Both epilogues are narrated with fragments of alien discourse, of opposing eyewitnesses and writers, none of whom holds rights to the truth. A plurality of contradictory signs converges in the figure of the strange and exceptional being who distances himself from the capital, abandoning the center of political power in order to join the resistance struggle in the provinces. Not only does the text by Rivera produce a history of defeat in the face of infamy, but it chronicles continued resistance against the excesses of power. It takes up again the function not just of the intellectual but of the civilized person who returns from Europe and joins the tenacious defenders of the federation—the consistently defeated Peñaloza and Varela—rather than the victorious enemies of Rosas. Rivera's historical view settles, as does Piglia's, on those figures marginalized from history, on those who proposed modifications to dominant choices. For these writers, it is not a matter of satisfying an eccentric taste for the devalued or the obscure, but one of reformulating the validity of alternative positions in the past.

In the preceding pages, I have discussed novels that show textual markings and a rather obvious indebtedness to *Facundo*, works that reveal a desire to ally a historical-cultural dilemma with the function of the intellectual as critical conscience of the national project. But *Facundo* also provides the historical model for a novel by José Pablo Feinman, *El ejército de ceniza*.[10] Providing the background for two wrongs caused by an imputation of cowardice and military dishonor, Feinman reverses the tale of the presumed civilizing action of the national army on the frontier. Lieutenant Quesada, veteran of Ituzaingó, marches to a small fort where Colonel Andrade, hero of San Martín's campaigns and the Army of the North, considers that destiny now reserves for him alone the possibility of destroying the enemies of civilization: the attacking irregulars from the desert. Andrade, formerly a soldier with a perfect record, feels physically and geographically confined in the small fort he commands. His campaign in search of an enemy is visible only in the destruction and the decimated victims he abandons; his is a war of total extermination, personal and alien, inasmuch as his zeal moves him to harass and massacre the weakest. Andrade, an implacable persecutor, carries the enemy within, and impels him to embark upon fatal marches that destroy horses as well as troops. Andrade wants to impose order and authority on an almost empty prairie exposed to the violence of both sides. In this sense, Feinman concentrates on the mental and moral alienation of Andrade. Andrade is the voice of reason and justice who loses the former and abuses the latter, who disregards, suspects, and executes his pathfinders but who protects a small frightened victim.

Here the desert is transformed into the scene of barbaric tragedy, although it does not necessarily become the creator and source of barbarians. The wars have served to harden everyone: some stay in the regular army, others desert to join the opposition. It is impossible to detect any reason for the positions of the different sides. Former heroes and deserters alike have changed the desert into a field of cadavers fit only for the birds of prey. Absent from this field are the native singers of *Facundo*, the vigilant eye of the pathfinder, the knowledge of the land of the tracker, and the symbolic patrimony of the illiterate. In a story that parallels recent national history, the exercise of war has devastated, but not won over, the enemies. Analogous in ferocity, equal in obsessions, they destroy each other under a "rain of ash." The lettered tradition, after its martial apprenticeship, has elected a new battleground.

Feinman's novel does not mention public projects at the national level; it mentions only obscure or secret orders that emanate from Buenos Aires. Local participation is represented only by marauding deserters who attack the ranchers. Weapons are the only form of mediation: the dueling pistol in the city, the saber and lance in the desert, and finally madness and ignominy. Feinman has chosen to place his novel in the period of warfare that ends with the campaign against Brazil, when doubt began to grow about the efficacy of bellicose ventures. As in the desert, what is at issue here is quitting or securing the territory of others, never the emancipation of people. The model of *Facundo* has multiplied until its contradictions have been obliterated. Everyone is Facundo in Feinman's desert of ash.

Sarmiento, the illustrious predecessor, is converted in these works into a cultural-historical object of greatest importance for younger writers, who in turn become new recording subjects of their experience with the past. The relationships between modern writers and their precursor are not dictated exclusively by styles of subjectivity. Rather, their rapport develops as if present and past represented two distinct forms of cultural production, two forms of socialization of the intellectual, and two possible modes of praxis—all of which confront and question one another in modern fiction. Thus, recent narrative becomes a kind of allegory about these modes of confrontation.

The past and its representation are not, therefore, inert objects that demand interpretation. Instead, literature transforms them into an open system, dynamic and accessible, and allows the reader to question the experience of modern cultural practice. A dialectic is established between modern fiction and the earlier text, allowing us to see what remains to be done in a contemporary social context. Thanks to this enriching dialectic, a hermeneutic contact between past and present is established. This contact can provide the impulse toward a transformational utopia, that place where the intellectual will finally be able to enunciate a voice of protest and the hope of social reform.

Notes

1. I refer to the specific use of the term "letrados" as it is applied to a nineteenth-century group of educator-politicians.

2. Domingo Faustino Sarmiento, *Facundo* (Caracas: Biblioteca Ayacucho, 1977) and *Recuerdos de provincia* (Buenos Aires: Centro Editor de América Latina, 1979).

3. For extensive studies of Sarmiento, see the introduction by Tulio Halperín Donghi to Domingo Faustino Sarmiento, *Campaña en el Ejército Grande Aliado de Sud América* (Mexico: Fondo de Cultura Económica, 1958); the introduction by Noé Jitrik to Sarmiento, *Facundo* (Caracas: Biblioteca Ayacucho, 1977); and Carlos Altamirano and Beatriz Sarlo, *Ensayos argentinos: De Sarmiento a la vanguardia* (Buenos Aires: Centro Editor, 1983).

For studies that treat these issues in part, see *Revista Iberoamericana* 143 (April–June 1988); Ana María Barrenechea, "Estudios sobre el *Facundo*," in *Textos Hispanoamericanos* (Caracas: Monte Avila, 1978); and Noé Jitrik, *Muerte y resurrección de Facundo* (Buenos Aires: Centro Editor de América Latina, 1968).

4. Michel Foucault, "The Historical *a Priori* and the Archive," in *The Archeology of Knowledge* (New York: Pantheon, 1972), p. 126.

5. Fredric Jameson, *The Political Unconscious* (Ithaca: Cornell University Press, 1981).

6. Ricardo Piglia, *Respiración artificial* (Buenos Aires: Editorial Pomaire, 1980).

7. Andrés Rivera, *En esta dulce tierra* (Buenos Aires: Folio Editores, 1984).

8. See Oscar Oszlak, "Privatización autoritaria y recreación de la escena pública," and Oscar Landi, "Cultura y política en la transición democrática," in *"Proceso": Crisis y transición democrática. I*, ed. Oscar Oszlak (Buenos Aires: Centro Editor de América Latina, 1984).

9. This term appears in Altamirano and Sarlo, *Ensayos argentinos*, p. 13.

10. José Pablo Feinman, *El ejército de ceniza* (Buenos Aires: Legasa, 1986).

19   Domingo Faustino Sarmiento: The Unnamed Presence in *El hombre que está solo y espera* of Raúl Scalabrini Ortiz

NICOLAS SHUMWAY

Hispanists have the unfortunate habit of discussing Spanish American writers and thinkers as though they had never lived in Spanish America. We devote so much time to discussing European roots, theoretical minutia, textual details, and the like that we all but ignore the national and historical contexts with which Latin American writers are in constant dialogue. Perhaps this aspect of Spanish American criticism derives from a colonial complex that in some sense sees value in Spanish American culture only to the degree that it can first claim European roots. Here I will follow a different path by discussing two Argentine essayists specifically within their national context and exploring the degree to which the latter is in dialogue with the former. The first one, Domingo Faustino Sarmiento, we know as one of the great ideologues and political actors of Argentine liberalism, which in the nineteenth century transformed an underpopulated, isolated, and divided land into a modern nation that once held promise to become the most influential country of the Hispanic world. The second essayist, the one I claim descends from Sarmiento, is Raúl Scalabrini Ortiz, a writer of the present century best known for the revisions of Argentine history he wrote in the 1930s and 1940s and, later, for his articulate support of Peronism. As a revisionist historian, Scalabrini Ortiz zealously criticized Argentine liberalism and, by extension, Sarmiento, one of liberalism's chief mentors. My plan is to demonstrate that, however much Scalabrini rebels against Sarmiento, he can discuss Argentina only by using the rhetorical categories, symbols, and images that Sarmiento left him.

Chief among these images for both writers is the Argentine soil. Sarmiento inveighed against chaos, against those vast expanses of land which, as he says in the *Facundo*, "are yet awaiting the command to produce

358

plants and seeds of every kind."[1] In another section of *Facundo*, Sarmiento maintains that "the evil that afflicts the Argentine republic is its vastness" (p. 50), and in yet another place he argues that Buenos Aires would already have attained greatness "if the spirit of the pampa had not blown on her" (pp. 52–53). Similarly, Sarmiento attributes the barbarism of the gauchos to the land, holding that Argentines are not by nature more savage than other people; rather, he argues, the land, the limitless pampas, had transformed them into a primitive society—a society that seduces the romantic Sarmiento while repelling Sarmiento the reformer. Invoking a kind of environmental determinism, he claims that plains dwellers throughout the world, whether North American Plains Indians or North African Bedouins, all exhibit characteristics similar to those of Argentina's gauchos.

In his first important book, and the only one I will refer to here, *El hombre que está solo y espera* (The Man Who Is Alone and Waiting),[2] Scalabrini Ortiz also uses the land as one of the defining symbols of Argentina, but his intentions could not be more different from Sarmiento's. For Scalabrini, the spirit of the land is "like a gigantic man [who] because of his immense size is as invisible to us as we are to microbes. The spirit of the land is an enormous archetype that fed itself and grew with the arrival of immigrants, devouring and assimilating millions of Spaniards, but without ever losing its special character. . . . This gigantic man knows where he is going and what he wants. Destiny shrinks before his grandeur" (p. 19). In other words, the pampean spirit that for Sarmiento is the source of barbarism becomes in Scalabrini Ortiz the authentic and ultimately unavoidable destiny of all Argentines. Moreover, Scalabrini argues that only those Argentines who attune themselves to the spirit of the land can sense its motions. To explain the nature of the Argentine who submits to the land, Scalabrini invents a representative Argentine. Sometimes he calls him "The Man of Corrientes and Esmeralda," alluding to the intersection of two famous Buenos Aires streets. On other occasions he calls him simply the "porteño," but for Scalabrini that term suggests more than a mere resident of Buenos Aires; rather, the real porteño, like the Man of Corrientes and Esmeralda, is sensitive to the spirit of the land and submits to its influence.

Indeed, as we see in the following passage, Scalabrini's "porteño" would appear to exclude a sizable portion of the city's population: "The porteño is restrained in the flow of time by a sense of his accountability to the destinies of the spirit of the land, to which his destiny is affectively and unchangingly tied. To free himself from this responsibility, of which he is both author and agent, he must give up a portion of himself and turn

over to the collectivity some of the rights and duties that are his" (p. 64).
The porteño, then, in Scalabrini's lexicon, is a being whose qualities are
negative rather than positive; that is to say, Scalabrini describes his ideal
porteño in terms of what he is *not*. His virtue lies in his subservience to
the spirit of the land and his submission to the collectivity of people who
likewise yield themselves to that spirit's motion. Liberal individualism is
subsumed in this collective man who responds only to the autonomous
impulses of the spirit of the land. Thus, we see, both Sarmiento and Scalabrini use the land as a point of departure. But what in Sarmiento is a
power to be resisted, in Scalabrini becomes a power to which one must
submit in the name of authenticity.

Having established the importance of the land as a source of Argentine
culture, Sarmiento and Scalabrini attempt to describe significant details of
that culture—but, predictably, come to quite different conclusions. Although Sarmiento never deserved the accusation of blind enthrallment to
European ways that his detractors frequently hurl at him, he nonetheless
felt that civilization was born of reason, specifically from reason elaborated first in the cities of Europe and later in those of North America.
Using such reason as his ground, Sarmiento sought to impose a rational
order on the chaos of his country, complete with modern transportation
systems and political institutions. The efforts of Argentine liberalism in
this regard reflected the organizational schemes of all Western societies
and therefore do not strike most of us as either surprising or inappropriate. Scalabrini Ortiz, however, felt that such schemes betrayed the spirit
of the land, as we see in the following passage:

> [The liberals] had ideals, or at least outlines of ideals, that seemed eas-
> ily in reach. Like eager schoolchildren, they believed in science. Biolo-
> gists, physiologists, chemists, astronomers, and mechanics were the
> secular priests of their religion. . . . In only a few years they upset the
> dynamic of the country. They allied themselves to foreign capital,
> with which they founded towns, laid railroads, constructed ports, dug
> canals, built dikes, imported machinery, and distributed and settled the
> land. With these ventures, they kept busy, but they also ignored the
> spirit of the land. [p. 55]

Here Scalabrini indicates that liberal aspirations were frustrated by the
spirit of the land and that spirit's representative: the Man of Corrientes
and Esmeralda who "is immune to all that is not born of him" (p. 40).
The authentic Argentine, according to Scalabrini, distrusts "all the conventional lies of European culture" (p. 92). In short, he argues that liberalism could never have triumphed in Argentina, because the land itself

rejected the liberal dream. Interestingly, on this point, Sarmiento and Scalabrini are in intimate agreement: for both of them, the Argentine land militates against European culture. However, what Sarmiento deplores, Scalabrini considers a mystical encounter with destiny. Yet there is something even more destructive in Scalabrini's thought, for his argument ends up being a subversion of all rational and empirical paths to knowledge. He renders invalid all science and reasoned discourse, the very forms we use to comprehend the world. For him, the only path to understanding is to sensitize oneself to the spirit of the land and to enhance the capacity of "authentic" Argentines to understand it.

Another way Sarmiento sought to impose a reasoned order on Argentina was through public education, one of the great passions of his life. But Sarmiento's efforts and those of his intellectual descendants hold little worth for Scalabrini. Scalabrini argues that authentic Argentines don't think; indeed, he even suggests that, in the final analysis, they don't need to think. Rather, the authentic Argentine intuits; he trusts his feelings (pálpitos). "The porteño," writes Scalabrini, "does not think, he feels. 'I feel, therefore I am' is a more appropriate aphorism than the Cartesian one. . . . The porteño doesn't read, he is not a man of prior planning, but rather of sudden intuitions" (p. 75). And, of course, it is understood that in these pálpitos one hears the spirit of the land. Moreover, since intellectuals educated in the ways of Europe don't understand that spirit, they are not only mistaken but are in some sense traitorous. "The Man of Corrientes and Esmeralda," Scalabrini argues, "does not challenge, nor does he aspire to challenge, either Europeans or their cultural fortress. The authentic Argentine understands that Argentina's most educated men, compared to a European . . . are vulgar apprentices" (pp. 77–78). The best means to truth, for Scalabrini, is listening to the land, and that means improvising rather than planning. "The Man of Corrientes and Esmeralda," he tells us, "honors our Europeanized intellectuals with disdain as they improvise nonsense against improvisation. And this is one of the causes for the unbridgeable divorce that separates intellectual life in Argentina from the true Argentine spirit" (pp. 77–78). For Scalabrini, feeling rather than knowing is one's patriotic duty. Education betrays the patria since the porteño "senses (palpita) rightly that in no book will he find solutions for his uncertainties" (p. 77). Again we see that while Scalabrini defines himself against Sarmiento, he can do so only in Sarmiento's terms.

Another part of Sarmiento's program was the creation of democratic institutions to replace caudillos and personalist leaders like Juan Manuel de Rosas, leaders who in Sarmiento's memorable phrase were "the mirror that reflects in colossal proportions the beliefs, the necessities, the concerns and customs of a nation at a given moment in history" (*Facundo*, p. 6), leaders whose rise to power is "destined, inevitable, natural and logical" (p. 4). But Sarmiento's seeing the caudillo as natural and inevitable hardly meant approval; indeed, Sarmiento argues at length that nature must be pushed back, the land developed, and the populace transformed so that the caudillos will lose their natural base and rise no more.

Scalabrini's view of the caudillo could not be more different. Since Scalabrini has already shown himself several times to be a kind of anti-Sarmiento, it should not surprise us that Scalabrini's sense of authentic Argentine government, of government in tune with the land, should build on, rather than reject, the tradition of the caudillos. Indeed, Scalabrini insists that the Man of Corrientes and Esmeralda cannot be governed by traditional democratic processes as established in Europe and North America; he insists that only a government based on *caudillismo* can survive in Argentina. To govern the Man of Corrientes and Esmeralda, Scalabrini argues that one must understand him. And to understand him, Scalabrini tells us,

> it is necessary to be identical to him. The divination of his will is the desperation of politicians, supervisors, newspaper chiefs, and of all others who somehow depend on him. Men who are only intelligent fail in their public duties. The Man of Corrientes and Esmeralda, before all else, demands that public leaders have, not knowledge nor bookish ideas, but powerful instincts, rapid comprehension: in sum that they be men of *pálpitos*. For that reason, the Man of Corrientes and Esmeralda is not interested in programs, platforms or the windy proclamations of political parties. Faced with the complex nature of Argentina, such programs defraud men and proper behavior. . . . The *pálpito* is the only effective guide in the chaos of Argentine life and the only virtue that the porteño admires. [pp. 79–80]

In sum, the legal apparatus—with its institutions, laws, procedures, and methods—amount to little for Scalabrini. In his scheme of things, the only possible government in Argentina must include someone at the top who hears and understands the unarticulated, inchoate voice of the authentic people. In a word, Scalabrini wants a caudillo on whom the spirit of the land has conferred its mystical priesthood, the universal priesthood of the voiceless believers who feel the spirit of the land and respond with recognition to the leadership of its ordained spokesman. Sarmiento also believed in this voice, but for him it was the voice of barbarism, of unreason, of chaos. And again we see how Scalabrini is the mirror image of Sarmiento.

In addition to education and the creation of democratic institutions, Sarmiento vigorously supported immigration as a means of taming Argentina's barbarous land and developing a modern country. His goal was to bring supposedly more civilized people from Europe so that their blood and their culture could take root in Argentine soil and transform the pampas into an exemplar of Western civilization. Sarmiento was particularly interested in attracting immigrants from Germany, England, and Northern Europe, immigrant stock he viewed as the best of Europe. His plans went awry, however, since the majority of immigrants who arrived on Argentina's shores came from Italy and Spain, countries whose societies Sarmiento had roundly condemned in the travel journals he wrote during his European tour of 1849–1851: he describes the Spanish as "a ferocious people, ragged and hardened in ignorance and laziness," and the Italians as "the lowest degree below zero to which human dignity can descend."[3] Nonetheless, Argentina's immigrants did come primarily from Spain and Italy, a fact that, as Sarmiento saw it, contributed to Argentina's ills. Thus, in one of his most controversial books, *Conflictos y armonías de razas en América,* written more than thirty years after the *Facundo,* Sarmiento describes Argentina's failure to create democratic institutions as a partial result of the low quality of immigrant stock that Argentina attracted.

Scalabrini Ortiz, as a rebellious child of Sarmiento, also speaks of immigration as a solution to Argentina's problems; but, as we have seen elsewhere, he inverts Sarmiento's schema. For example, his description of the immigrants:

> The intruders consisted of hordes of the worst sort, of the lowest class. They were refugees of races driven by unbridled envy, mobs unleashed by dreams of fortune who brought with them, in an exaggerated way, all the defects of their societies, and none of their virtues. They were wretched in their interests, hardened by unsatisfied gluttony. They were sensual, tempestuous beings, without continence, who liked the bedlam of their music, dance, and revelry. [p. 45]

With ironic celebration, Scalabrini repeats in this passage the prejudices Sarmiento revealed in his *Viajes* as well as those of the conservative oligarchy which also deplored the low culture of the immigrants. Unlike Sarmiento, though, Scalabrini goes on to insist that these benighted people were destined to become the salvation of Argentina because they were sensitive and submissive to the spirit of the land. Scalabrini argues that before the arrival of the immigrants "Buenos Aires was in danger of remaining segregated from the land, of forming a corporate structure with no resemblance to the pampa that nourished her and of which she was a symbol. . . . The city was in critical danger of becoming European" (p. 45). This danger, however, was averted because the spirit of the land imposed itself on the city, claiming her for its own purposes and converting the immigrant children into adoptive children similar to those inhabitants of the countryside who had never abandoned the spirit of the land. Because of the immigrants, their nonelitist ways, and their affinity for the spirit of the land, Scalabrini rejoices that "Buenos Aires is again the capital of the countryside" (p. 51). The result of these lines is the denationalization of the cultured classes. Scalabrini finds true Argentineness in the working classes of both the city and the countryside: the children of immigrants in the city and the descendants of provincial *criollos* in the pampas beyond. All others (except for intellectuals like Scalabrini who claim sensibility to the spirit of the land) are antinational and in some sense traitors.

Scalabrini's ideas would run a long course in Argentina, informing the thought of people as varied as Arturo Jauretche, Juan José Hernández Arregui, and numerous leftist thinkers over the past few decades. My goal here, though, is not to speak of Scalabrini as an important founder of Peronist ideology. Rather, I have tried to direct our attention to an often ignored ancestor of Scalabrini Ortiz, an ancestor that Scalabrini never confessed and whose role in Argentine history he surely abominated. I recognize that we can link Scalabrini to a number of European thinkers, from Johann Herder to Charles Maurras, who also postulated the importance of the national soil, the mythical destiny of peoples, and the failure of liberal universality. I would argue, however, that ultimately the most remarkable progenitor of *El hombre que está solo y espera* is Domingo Faustino Sarmiento, and that Raúl Scalabrini Ortiz is the rebellious son of a father he never wanted to recognize. (In fact, he may have been acting out another Oedipal drama, since his literal father was also one of the Europeanizers he so deplored.) Scalabrini's book thus has the flavor of patricide, for Scalabrini's categories are also those of Sarmiento. In the final analysis, then, Scalabrini Ortiz demonstrates the extraordinary fecundity of the grand patriarch of Argentine letters; for Scalabrini could argue against Sarmiento's Argentina, but he could do so only by using the rhetorical categories Sarmiento bequeathed to him.

Notes

1. Domingo Faustino Sarmiento, *Civilización y barbarie: Vida de Juan Facundo Quiroga* (henceforth *Facundo*) (Mexico: Editorial Porrúa, 1977 [1845]), p. 51.

2. Raúl Scalabrini Ortiz, *El hombre que está solo y espera* (Buenos Aires: Editorial Plus Ultra, 1976 [1931]).

3. Domingo Faustino Sarmiento, *Viajes por Europa, Africa y Estados Unidos*, ed. Julio Noé, 3 vols. (Buenos Aires: La Cultura Argentina, 1922 [1849–1851]), 1:220.

Selected Bibliography

Included here are some of the best and most widely available books on Domingo Faustino Sarmiento. A few items listed here concern the history and politics of Argentina. In addition, a rich bibliography of periodical literature is available in English and Spanish. Representative collections are included in special journal issues devoted to Sarmiento on the occasion of the centennial of his death. These include *Cuadernos Americanos* 3, no. 13 (1989); *Revista Iberoamericana* 54, no. 143 (April–June 1988); *Filología* 23, no. 2 (1988); and *Río de la Plata: Culturas*, nos. 8 and 9 (1989).

Alberdi, Juan Bautista. *La barbarie histórica de Sarmiento.* Buenos Aires: Ediciones Pampa y Cielo, 1964.

———. *Cartas quillotanas.* Preceded by an explanatory letter by D. F. Sarmiento. Buenos Aires: Editorial La Cultura Argentina, 1916.

———. "Facundo y su biógrafo." In *¿Los escritos póstumos de Alberdi fueron publicados en oposición con sus últimos deseos?* Edited by Alberto Córdoba. Buenos Aires: Ediciones Theoria, 1966.

———. *Grandes y pequeños hombres del Plata.* Buenos Aires: Fernández Blanco, 1962.

———. *Proceso a Sarmiento.* Prologue by Leon Pomer. Buenos Aires: Editorial Calden, 1967.

Altamirano, Carlos, and Beatriz Sarlo. *Ensayos argentinos: De Sarmiento a la vanguardia.* Buenos Aires: Centro Editor, 1983.

Anderson Imbert, Enrique. *Genio y figura de Sarmiento.* Buenos Aires: Editorial Universitaria de Buenos Aires, 1967.

Avila Màrtel, Alamiro de. *Sarmiento en la Universidad de Chile.* Santiago: Ediciones de la Universidad de Chile, 1988.

Barrenechea, Ana María, and Beatriz R. Lavandera. *Domingo Faustino Sarmiento.* Buenos Aires: Centro Editorial América Latina, 1967.

Belín Sarmiento, Augusto. *Sarmiento anecdótico (Ensayo biográfico).* Saint-Cloud: Imprenta P. Belin, 1929.

Botana, Natalio R. *La tradición republicana.* Buenos Aires: Sudamericana, 1984.

Bunkley, Allison Williams. *The Life of Sarmiento.* Princeton: Princeton University Press, 1952.

Campobassi, José. *Sarmiento y su época.* 2 vols. Buenos Aires: Losada, 1975.

Castro, Antonio P. Introduction to *Rasgos de la vida de Domingo F. Sarmiento por su hermana Bienvenida.* Buenos Aires: Museo Histórico Sarmiento, 1946.

Cortés Conde, Roberto, and Ezequiel Gallo. *La formación de la Argentina moderna.* Buenos Aires: Paidós, 1967.

Criscenti, Joseph, ed. *Sarmiento and His Argentina.* Boulder: Lynne Rienner Publishers, 1992.

Del Pino de Carbone, María Luisa. *Correspondencia entre Sarmiento y Lastarria, 1844–1888.* Buenos Aires: Bartolomé U. Chiesino, 1954.

Donoso, Armando, ed. *Sarmiento en el destierro.* Buenos Aires: M. Gleizer, 1927.

Foster, David William, ed. *Argentine Literature: A Research Guide.* 2nd ed., revised and expanded. New York: Garland Publications, 1982.

———. "A Bibliography of Critical Monographs and Articles on Domingo Faustino Sarmiento." *Bulletin of Bibliographies* 39, no. 1 (March 1982).

Gálvez, Manuel. *Vida de Sarmiento.* Buenos Aires: Editorial Tor, 1952.

Guerra, J. Guillermo. *Sarmiento: Su vida i sus obras.* Santiago: Imprenta Elzeviriana, 1901.

Guerrero, César. *Mujeres de Sarmiento.* Buenos Aires: n.p., 1960.

Guerrero, Luis Juan. *Tres temas de filosofía argentina en las entrañas del Facundo.* Buenos Aires: Editorial Docencia, 1945.

Halperín Donghi, Tulio. Edición, prólogo y notas a *Campaña en el Ejército Grande Aliado de Sud América* by Domingo F. Sarmiento. Mexico: Fondo de Cultura Económica, 1958.

———. *Politics, Economics, and Society in Argentina in the Revolutionary Period.* Cambridge: Cambridge University Press, 1975.

Jitrik, Noé. *Muerte y resurrección de "Facundo."* Buenos Aires: Centro Editor de América Latina, 1968.

———. Prologue to *Facundo, o, Civilización y barbarie* (Edición crítica y documentada) by Domingo F. Sarmiento. Caracas: Biblioteca Ayacucho, 1977.

Jones, C. A. *Facundo.* London: Tamesis Books, 1974.

Katra, William H. *Domingo F. Sarmiento: Public Writer (between 1839 and 1852).* Tempe: Center for Latin American Studies, Arizona State University, 1985.

Lugones, Leopoldo. *Historia de Sarmiento.* 2nd ed. Buenos Aires: Publicaciones de la Comisión Argentina de Fomento Interamericano, 1945.

Mann, Mrs. Horace (Mary). Preface to *Life in the Argentine Republic in the Days of the Tyrants; or, Civilization and Barbarism* by Domingo F. Sarmiento. 1st American from the 3rd Spanish edition. 1868. Reprint, New York: Hafner Press, 1960.

Martínez Estrada, Ezequiel. *Meditaciones sarmientinas.* Santiago: Editorial Universitaria, 1968.

———. *Sarmiento.* 1946. Reprint, Buenos Aires: Sudamericana, 1966.

———. *X-Ray of the Pampa.* Translated by Alain Swietlicki. Introduction by Thomas F. McGann. Austin and London: University of Texas Press, 1971.

Martínez Villergas, Juan. *Sarmenticidio, o a mal Sarmiento buena podadera.* Paris: Agencia General de la Librería Española y Extranjera, 1853.

Operé, Fernando. *Civilización y barbarie en la literatura argentina del siglo XIX: El tirano Rosas.* Madrid: Conorg, 1987.

Orgáz, Raúl. *Sarmiento y el naturalismo histórico.* Córdoba: Imprenta Rossi, 1940.

Oszlak, Oscar. *La formación del estado argentino.* Buenos Aires: Belgrano, 1982.

Ottolenghi, Julia. *Sarmiento a través de un epistolario.* Buenos Aires: Jesús Méndez, 1939.

Palcos, Alberto. Prologue to *Facundo.* (Edición crítica y documentada) by Domingo F. Sarmiento. La Plata: Universidad Nacional de La Plata, 1938.

———. *Vida de Sarmiento. El hombre de autoridad.* Buenos Aires: Emecé, 1945.

Patton, Elda Clayton. *Sarmiento in the United States.* Evansville, Ind.: University of Evansville Press, 1976.

Peña, Milciades. *Alberdi, Sarmiento, el 90: Límites del nacionalismo argentino en el siglo XIX.* Buenos Aires: Ediciones Fichas, 1970.

Pinilla, Norberto. *La polémica del romanticismo en 1842.* Buenos Aires: Americalee, 1943.

Prieto, Adolfo. *La literatura autobiográfica argentina.* Rosario: Editorial Biblioteca, 1968.

Rock, David. *Argentina, 1516–1987: From Spanish Colonization to Alfonsín.* Berkeley and Los Angeles: University of California Press, 1987.

Rockland, Michael. Translation and Introduction to *Sarmiento's Travels in the United States in 1847* by Domingo F. Sarmiento. Princeton: Princeton University Press, 1970.

Romero, José Luis. *A History of Argentine Political Thought.* Translated by Thomas H. McGann. Stanford: Stanford University Press, 1968.

Sáenz Hayes, Ricardo. *La polémica de Alberdi con Sarmiento y otras páginas.* Buenos Aires: Gleizer, 1926.

Salomon, Noël. *Realidad, ideología y literatura en el "Facundo" de D. F. Sarmiento.* Biblioteca Hispanoamericana y Española de Amsterdam. Amsterdam: Rodopi, 1984.

Scobie, James R. *Argentina: A City and a Nation.* 2nd ed. New York: Oxford University Press, 1971.

Shumway, Nicolas. *The Invention of Argentina.* Berkeley and Los Angeles: University of California Press, 1991.

Verdevoye, Paul. *Domingo Faustino Sarmiento: Educar y escribir opinando, 1839–1852.* Buenos Aires: Editorial Plus Ultra, 1988.

———. *Domingo Faustino Sarmiento, éducateur et publiciste (entre 1839 et 1852).* Paris: Centre de Recherches de l'Institut d'Etudes Hispaniques, Institut des Hautes Etudes de l'Amérique Latine, 1963.

Index

Popular sovereignty, 109, 115
Populism, 187
Portales, Diego, 37, 108
Posse, José, 69
Post office, 120, 122
Potosí, 115
Pound, Ezra, 316–17
Poverty: association with urbanization, 89; mitigation by talent, 165;
relationship to richness in writing,
188–89; Sarmiento's depiction of,
21, 70
Power: equation with knowledge,
228; exercise of, under republicanism, 110; literature as road to, 9–
10, 142, 216; texts as battleground
for, 295–96, 303, 304, 305; of
written word, 127, 128–29, 132,
174
Preciado, Juan, 337
Press: attempts to control émigré activity in, 47–48, 180; censorship
of (Chile), 33, 37–38; and Chilean
elections of 1851, 48–49; circulation of (Chile), 40–41; conduct of
public debate in, 44–47, 266–68;
conflict between the state and, 31–
32; confrontational stance of, 38–
40, 43–44; effects on battle, 154 n.
14; encouragement of activists by,
146; excessive freedom of, 43–44;
government subsidies to, 40, 41 &
table, 58 n. 28, 266, 270 n. 15;
identification of readership of,
259–62; laws regulating (Chile),
35–38, 39, 40, 48, 57 nn. 24,25;
list of newspapers and periodicals
(Chile), 49–54; literary polemics
in, 295; partisanship of, 35; political authority of journalism questioned, 302–5; proliferation of, in
Chile, 34–35, 36 (table), 55 n. 8;
proper role of, 43; public support
for, 43, 44; as record for autobiographical writing, 196; recruitment of readers by, 262–68; trials
of, 38–40, 48; as vehicle of emancipation, 148, 149, 150; as weapon,
150, 155 n. 20

Prieto, Adolfo, 75–76, 172, 175, 302
Prieto Vial, Gen. Joaquín, 32, 35, 38
El Progreso, 15, 38, 47, 150, 164, 173,
194, 278; conduct of public debate
in, 266–68; and elections of 1851,
48; literary polemics in, 295;
readership of, 44, 262–68; Sarmiento's career with, 42; subsidies
to, 270 n. 15; writings of women
in, 291 n. 49
Progress: in achievements of Sarmiento administration, 120–21,
122; as antidote to Argentine crisis, 114; as development of province, 61–63, 68, 118–19; as doctrine of Argentina's founders, 114;
and expansionism, 78; foreordina-
tion of, 321–22; infrastructure of,
121–22; liberal idea of, 4; and
market system, 119, 122; and political consolidation, 118; and scientific travelers, 228; and status of
women, 279, 282; and urban misery, 89; village as center of, 89–
90
Property, defense of, by social order,
22–23
Prospecto de un establecimiento de
educación para señoritas, 272–73
Provinces: despoiling by cities, 172,
189; development of, as progress,
61–63, 68; distribution of national
resources among, 117, 118; eradi-
cation of oral tradition of, 95;
good and bad in, 68; identification
of civilization with, 309–10, 353;
influence over Sarmiento's
thought, 92–93; intellectual life
of, 353; and national economic crisis, 145; nobility of, 21; as obstacle to self-education, 157–58; political repression in, 95; renewal
of, 66, 67–68, 118–19; social interaction in, 116; status of women
in, 287–88; struggle against cities,
104–5; war costs of, 117–18, 123
n. 8. See also Pampa
Prussia, 89, 107
"Le public" (de Jouy), 259

Public debate, conduct of, in press, 44–47, 266–68
Public education: and citizenship, 102–3, 111, 112; enrollment in, 120; exclusion of Indians and mestizos from, 76; expansion of, 122; liberal faith in, 361; and market system, 119; and political modernization, 27; protection of social order by, 81–83; and provincial renewal, 67, 68; Sarmiento as champion of, 3–4, 5, 95; and spirit of the land, 361; in training of readers, 262, 269 n. 9; for women, 272–74, 276, 277–78, 285–86
Public opinion, pressure toward conformity from, 85
El Pueblo, 39
Pulperías (taverns), 116, 240–41
Puritanism, and republicanism, 102

Questions, as device in polemical refutation, 308–9
Quinet, Edgar, 195, 310
Quiroga, Facundo. See Facundo Quiroga, Juan (caudillo)
Quiroga, Horacio, 223
Quiroga Rosas, Manuel J., 42–43, 147, 161, 172, 260, 274, 288 n. 1
Quiroga Sarmiento, Bishop José Manuel, 157
El Quiteño Libre, 40
Quotations, in polemical refutation, 306–9
Le Quotidien, 263

Race: and Catholic superstition, 66–67; and prejudice, 6, 75–77, 215–16, 363. See also American Indians; Blacks
Rachowiecki, Rob, 254 n. 20
Radicalism, opposition with Peronism, 145
Radiografía de la pampa (Martínez Estrada), 93
Railroad: destructiveness of, 337; expansion of, 121; and provincial renewal, 119
Ramírez, Francisco, 225

Ramos Mexía, Francisco, 343 n. 24
Reader(s): identification of, by press, 259–62; interpretation of polemic by, 296–300; social class of, 260, 264, 269 n. 9; support of press by, 40–41, 43, 44, 262–68; textual points of reference for, 318; training of, 262, 269 n. 9
Reading(s): and the "chain of books," 159–61; mastery of foreign language through, 162–63; as means of intellectual emancipation, 156–57, 158; plurality of, for given text, 294–95; as social activity, 188
Realism, rational causality in, 318
Reality: conflict between orders of, 317–20; confusion of texts with, 327; creation of, by fiction, 135
Recuerdos de provincia (Sarmiento), 2, 3, 7, 9–10, 13, 33, 110, 140, 141, 147, 153 n. 10, 215, 216, 217; account of author's origins in, 20, 21–22; attitudes toward blacks in, 75; audience for, 210 n. 20; bourgeois morality of, 218–19; on bridging of social distance through merit, 166, 167–68 n. 20; classification as biography, 193, 194, 195, 196; creation of documentation for, 195–96; demands of self-image on, 199, 200, 201–6, 207; description of cultural climate, 161; on desperation of failure, 164; on displacement of fiction, 130; displacement of women in, 205–6; exemplary nature of, 196, 198; fabulation in, 199, 209 n. 16; family lineage in, 156–57, 165, 166–67; on formation of ideas, 101; on function of biography, 183; historical responsibility of personal memory in, 197–98; incorporation into modern literary tradition, 347–48, 350, 351; on mastery of foreign language, 162; maternal portrait in, 287; as political propaganda, 74; portrait of nobility in, 24–27, 29, 30; presen-

Library of Congress Cataloging-in-Publication Data

Sarmiento, author of a nation / Tulio Halperin Donghi . . . [et al.].
    p.   cm.
    Includes bibliographical references and index.
    ISBN 0-520-07531-5 (alk. paper).—ISBN 0-520-07532-3 (pbk. : alk.
paper)
    1. Sarmiento, Domingo Faustino, 1811–1888.   I. Halperin Donghi,
Tulio.   II. Title: Sarmiento.   III. Title: Author of a nation.
F2846.S26S28   1994
982'.04'092—dc20   93-16613

Compositor: Maple-Vail
Text: 10/13 Aldus
Display: Aldus
Printer: Maple-Vail
Binder: Maple-Vail

.